THE PUBLIC INTERNATIONAL LAW THEORY OF HANS KELSEN

This analysis of Hans Kelsen's international law theory takes into account the context of the German international legal discourse in the first half of the twentieth century, including the reactions of Carl Schmitt and other Weimar opponents of Kelsen. The relationship between his Pure Theory of Law and his international law writings is examined, enabling the reader to understand how Kelsen tried to square his own liberal cosmopolitan project with his methodological convictions as laid out in his Pure Theory of Law. Finally, Jochen von Bernstorff discusses the limits and continuing relevance of Kelsenian formalism for international law under the term of "reflexive formalism," and offers a reflection on Kelsen's theory of international law against the background of current debates over constitutionalization, institutionalization, and fragmentation of international law. The book also includes biographical sketches of Hans Kelsen and his main students Alfred Verdross and Joseph L. Kunz.

JOCHEN VON BERNSTORFF is a senior fellow of the Max Planck Institute for Comparative Public Law and International Law in Heidelberg and a lecturer at the University of Frankfurt. As a legal adviser in the UN Department of the German Federal Foreign Office, he was a member of the German delegation at the Commission on Human Rights in Geneva in 2004 and 2005 and the UN Human Rights Council in 2006, as well as a member of the German delegation at the UN General Assembly in 2003, 2004 and 2005 in New York.

CAMBRIDGE STUDIES IN INTERNATIONAL AND COMPARATIVE LAW

Established in 1946, this series produces high quality scholarship in the fields of public and private international law and comparative law. Although these are distinct legal sub-disciplines, developments since 1946 confirm their interrelation.

Comparative law is increasingly used as a tool in the making of law at national, regional and international levels. Private international law is now often affected by international conventions, and the issues faced by classical conflicts rules are frequently dealt with by substantive harmonisation of law under international auspices. Mixed international arbitrations, especially those involving state economic activity, raise mixed questions of public and private international law, while in many fields (such as the protection of human rights and democratic standards, investment guarantees and international criminal law) international and national systems interact. National constitutional arrangements relating to 'foreign affairs', and to the implementation of international norms, are a focus of attention.

The Board welcomes works of a theoretical or interdisciplinary character, and those focusing on the new approaches to international or comparative law or conflicts of law. Studies of particular institutions or problems are equally welcome, as are translations of the best work published in other languages.

A list of books in the series can be found at the end of this volume.

THE PUBLIC INTERNATIONAL LAW THEORY OF HANS KELSEN

Believing in Universal Law

JOCHEN VON BERNSTORFF
and
THOMAS DUNLAP

CAMBRIDGE
UNIVERSITY PRESS

CAMBRIDGE UNIVERSITY PRESS
Cambridge, New York, Melbourne, Madrid, Cape Town, Singapore,
São Paulo, Delhi, Dubai, Tokyo, Mexico City

Cambridge University Press
The Edinburgh Building, Cambridge CB2 8RU, UK

Published in the United States of America by Cambridge University Press, New York

This book was originally published as *Der Glaube an das universale Recht: Zur Völkerrechtstheorie Hans Kelsens und seiner Schüler* (Baden-Baden: Nomos, 2001).

www.cambridge.org
Information on this title: www.cambridge.org/9780521516181

Translated by Thomas Dunlap

English translation first published 2010

Printed in the United Kingdom at the University Press, Cambridge

A catalogue record for this publication is available from the British Library

Library of Congress Cataloging-in-Publication Data
Bernstorff, Jochen von.
[Der Glaube an das universale Recht. English]
The public international law theory of Hans Kelsen : believing in universal law / Jochen von Bernstorff, Thomas Dunlap.
p. cm. – (Cambridge studies in international and comparative law)
Originally published as Der Glaube an das universale Recht : zur Völkerrechtstheorie Hans Kelsens und seiner Schüler. Baden-Baden: Nomos, 2001.
Includes bibliographical references.
ISBN 978-0-521-51618-1
1. Kelsen, Hans, 1881–1973. 2. International law–History. I. Dunlap, Thomas, 1959– II. Title. III. Series.
KZ3375.K45B47 2010
341–dc22
2010000336

ISBN 978-0-521-51618-1 Hardback

CONTENTS

PREFACE

This book first appeared in 2001 in Germany. It is based on my doctoral thesis written at the Max-Planck-Institute for European Legal History in Frankfurt between 1997 and 2000 in the context of a broader research project of the German Research Foundation on the history of international law and international legal scholarship in Germany in the first half of the twentieth century. As gratefully acknowledged in the German edition, many people helped me along the way, but my greatest debt is to Prof. Dr. Dr. h.c. Michael Stolleis, the director of the Max-Planck-Institute in Frankfurt and initiator of the research project, and to Prof. Dr. Eibe Riedel, who inspired, encouraged, and actively supported my work on Kelsen's international law theory.

I can now take great pleasure in the appearance of the expanded English version of the book. I have resisted the temptation to rewrite parts of the book. Instead, I have added a postscript that reflects on the potential and limitations of Kelsenian formalism in the context of recent general debates in international law. I am indebted, first and foremost, to the director of the Max-Planck-Institute for Comparative Public Law and International Law in Heidelberg, Prof. Dr. Armin von Bogdandy, for his enthusiasm, intellectual inspiration, and active support regarding the idea and execution not only of this project. My gratitude extends to Prof. Dr. Dr. h.c. Rüdiger Wolfrum, the co-director of the Institute, and to the Max-Planck-Society for very generously supporting the translation of the book.

I would like to thank the careful and patient translator, Thomas Dunlap, for his extremely skillful translation of the text. His understanding of the German legal-historical background was crucial for this project. Prof. Martti Koskenniemi made suggestions on how to improve the book and make it more accessible to an English-speaking audience, for which I am very grateful. I would also like to thank the director of the Lauterpacht Centre for International Law at the University of Cambridge, Prof. James Crawford, and his colleagues, who kindly provided me with the opportunity to write and present the new postscript during my stay as a visiting fellow at the Centre. Back at the Institute in Heidelberg, my colleagues from the *Dienstagsrunde* also gave me very important feedback on an earlier version of the new postscript.

The manuscript benefitted greatly from careful proofreading by Daniel Oberhofer and the help and encouraging support of Finola O'Sullivan, Brenda Burke, Carolyn Fox, and Richard Woodham at Cambridge University Press.

Introduction

This book deals with the history of the theory of international law in the twentieth century. At its center stands the historical reconstruction of the ideas on international law advanced by Hans Kelsen and his most important students. Those ideas arose for the most part in the period between 1916 and 1950. My goal is to develop an overarching approach that explains the specific orientation and inner structure of Kelsen's works on international law against the background of the debates over the theory of international law and legal policy carried on in his day. To that extent, the reconstruction I have undertaken is grounded in a historical perspective on the evolution of the discipline of international law.[1] At the forefront is an examination of the discourses about the method and construction of international law that influenced Kelsen and his students and which were at the same time substantially shaped by them. In the process, however, attention will also be given to nineteenth- and early twentieth-century theoretical approaches to international law that Kelsen encountered before and during the First World War. I will use these theoretical debates to develop a historical approach to explaining the particular orientation and inner structure of the theory of international law articulated by the Austrian jurist Kelsen. The "key" to Kelsen's writings on international law that I offer here can also provide an answer to the question why they were, on the one hand, among the most vehemently criticized approaches to the theory of international law of the twentieth century, and, on the other hand, do not seem to have lost their fascination for scholars even at the beginning of the twenty-first century.[2]

[1] For a methodoligically reflected approach to legal history see M. Stolleis, *Rechtsgeschichte als Kunstprodukt: Zur Entbehrlichkeit von 'Begriff' und 'Tatsache'* (Baden-Baden: Nomos, 1997).

[2] The continuing interest in Kelsen's theory of international law is evident from the special issue of the *European Journal of International Law* on Hans Kelsen that was published in 1998 (*EJIL*, 9 [1998]), and in which various essays by well-known scholars of international law staked out critical positions on Kelsen's theory of international law.

To anticipate the findings of my interpretation, let me say at this point that the reconstructed doctrine of international law can be adequately grasped only if we place it within the tension-filled relationship between the two crucial goals of the international law theorist Kelsen: (1) establishing a non-political method for the field of international law, and (2) promoting the political project – which originated in the interwar period – of a thoroughly legalized and institutionalized world order. Kelsen's approach to international law was characterized by the constant effort to advance these two prima facie conflicting goals through his writings on international law.

Kelsen saw himself as the founder of a method of jurisprudence that was critical of ideology, the so-called "pure theory of law." This new jurisprudential methodology was to allow jurists to engage with law as a subject of study in a non-political and thus purely "scientific" way. In addition, as a political person, Kelsen developed during the interwar period – probably influenced by his experiences in the First World War – into a committed internationalist, who saw in the creation of an institutionalized legal community of states the only path toward a more peaceful world order. Subsequently, Kelsen, as a legal scholar, found himself confronted with the problem that he was not able to openly pursue his own political preferences for the "cosmopolitan project" of an institutionalized rule of law in international relations, but was compelled to make the non-political method he postulated the yardstick also of his own legal-theoretical works when dealing with the normative material. Kelsen's solution, this much can be anticipated here, was a methodologically guided critique of those theoretical and doctrinal constructs that stood in the way of his own political program, which he developed at the end of the First World War.

The explanatory approach laid out here thus reconstructs the inner connection between Kelsen's legal methodology and his own cosmopolitan project underlying his fundamental critique of the *fin-de-siècle* mainstream German international legal scholarship. Kelsen's way of working, which seems largely "destructive" toward the traditional doctrine of international law, can therefore be understood and explained as a strategy for uniting two goals whose impetus seems at first glance contradictory. This interpretation of his works, derived from a historical study of the primary and relevant secondary literature, allows me to explain the inner structure of Kelsen's theory of international law by setting it against the inherent tension between the postulate of a non-political science of international law, and his own "highly political" project developed during the interwar period. Thus, behind the interpretation presented here stands the question about the self-understanding and role of the international lawyer as both a scholar and a political individual, a question that has by no means been resolved even at the beginning of the twenty-first century.

Since the time of his *Habilitation* in 1911, Hans Kelsen had been searching for a more "scientific" method of jurisprudence. By applying contemporary insights from the theory of science to jurisprudence, Kelsen became, with his project of the "Pure Theory of Law," which found its scholarly culmination in 1934 in the monograph of the same name, the "*Alleszermalmer*" ["universal destroyer"][3] of the traditional methodology in German-language jurisprudence.[4] This modern revolt arose before and during the First World War in the collapse of the old Viennese world, which was marked by the rise of the masses, nationalism, and anti-Semitism.[5] Moreover, the "kakanian" multi-ethnic state, whose unity had been secured not least through an efficient, thoroughly juridical administrative structure, was beginning to break apart. During the increasing ideological usurpation of the societal discourse, Kelsen called for a scientifically correct, non-political approach to the law. The project of the Pure Theory of Law, which was initially directed against the scientific premises of the preceding German voluntaristic positivism [*Staatswillenspositivismus*], can thus be understood simultaneously as a legal-scientific reaction to the centrifugal forces of the ideologized zeitgeist.

The foundation of Kelsen's theory of international law was the 1920 monograph *Das Problem der Souveränität und die Theorie des Völkerrechts* [The Problem of Sovereignty and the Theory of International Law]. This book, which, according to Kelsen himself, was largely already completed during the war, was the second important

[3] As Adorno and Horkheimer said of Kant in *Dialektik der Aufklärung: Philosophische Fragmente* (reprint of the 1947 original edition, Frankfurt am Main: Suhrkamp, 1998), 100.

[4] The most compact and lucid recent account of the methodological orientation of the Vienna School from the perspective of the history of public law, along with extensive references, can be found in M. Stolleis, *A History of Public Law in Germany 1914–1945* (Oxford University Press, 2004, trans. Thomas Dunlap), 151–160. For a comprehensive analysis and interpretation of Kelsen's doctrine of international law see H. Dreier, *Rechtslehre. Staatssoziologie und Demokratietheorie bei Hans Kelsen* (Baden-Baden: Nomos, 1986).

[5] On this see C. E. Schorske, *Fin-de-Siècle Vienna: Politics and Culture* (New York: Knopf, 1980), 116–180.

monographic publication after Kelsen's *Habilitation* thesis of 1911, "Hauptprobleme der Staatsrechtslehre" [Main Problems in the Theory of Public Law]. Its critical thrust was directed against the main traditional approaches to international law theory by German-speaking theorists, from Adolf Lasson to Georg Jellinek, from Heinrich Triepel to Erich Kaufmann. In its constructive aspect, this monograph, with its emphasis on the primacy of international law, connected with the theory of international law developed by C. Kaltenborn in the mid nineteenth century. As an important contribution to the development of the Pure Theory of Law, Kelsen's monograph had a lasting impact on the conception of international law by the two Viennese students and companions, Alfred Verdross and Joseph L. Kunz.

Verdross, who had endeavored already during the war to transfer to international law the foundations of the Kelsenian notion of law and the state as laid out in "Hauptprobleme," published *Einheit des rechtlichen Weltbildes* [The Unity of the Legal Conception of the World] in 1923 and *Verfassung der Völkergemeinschaft* [Constitution of the Community of Nations] in 1926, two monographs on international law that were shaped by the understanding of international law shared by the school. Also three years after the appearance of Kelsen's *Das Problem der Souveränität und die Theorie des Völkerrechts*, Joseph L. Kunz published *Völkerrechtswissenschaft und Reine Rechtslehre* [The Science of International Law and Pure Theory of Law], a work with an epistemological focus. His subsequent books, *Die Anerkennung von Staaten und Regierungen im Völkerrecht* [The Recognition of States and Governments in International Law] and *Die Staatenverbindungen* [Confederacies of States], provide explicit evidence of the school's shared foundation of legal theory. The trained concert pianist Joseph L. Kunz, who – like Kelsen – had been shaped by the basic liberal convictions of the Austrian bourgeoisie,[6] became Kelsen's closest student with respect to international law.

6 Schorske, *Fin-de-Siècle Vienna*, 116–120 on Austrian liberalism and its decline at the *fin de siècle*; on liberalism, the Enlightenment, and the Austrian Jews see S. Beller, *Vienna and the Jews, 1867-1938* (Cambridge, MA: Harvard University Press, 1989), 122–137; on Jewish emancipation and the German theory of state law since the *Vormärz* by way of individual biographies see M. Stolleis, *"Junges Deutschland," jüdische Emanzipation und liberale Staatsrechtslehre in Deutschland.* Sitzungsberichte der Wissenschaftlichen Gesellschaft an der Johann Wolfgang Goethe-Universität (Stuttgart: F. Steiner, 1994); on the political and cultural environment in Vienna see also K. Günther, "Hans Kelsen (1881–1973). Das nüchterne Pathos der Demokratie," in Th Blanke et al. (eds.), *Streitbare Juristen: Eine andere Tradition* (Baden-Baden: Nomos, 1988), 368–371.

The monographs on international law published by these two authors in the 1920s, along with a large number of essays on the topic by other scholars belonging to Kelsen's academic circle,[7] grappled intensively with Kelsen's theoretical grounding of international law. In the process, Verdross and Kunz, especially, but also Métall and Pitamic, sought to advance the critical development of the international-law foundations of the Pure Theory of Law and to apply them to special problems in international law.[8] At the end of the 1920s, the critical distance of the Catholic-conservative Verdross toward the methodological basis of the Pure Theory of Law had grown so large that one could no longer speak of a shared school in relation to Verdross, in spite of the efforts by Kunz to bridge the deepening theoretical divide.

However, a reading of the international law doctrines of the Vienna School that is limited to Pure Theory of Law would fail to take into account the influence that authors outside the School exerted on the legal theorists within the School. If we shift our view to the broader environment of international law theory, it is apparent that the authors of the interwar period saw themselves as part of a modernization movement in international law. This international movement for a new law of nations had already begun during the First World War and reached its climax in the 1920s. The shared enthusiasm for a changed, more peaceful world order prompted legal scholars in various countries, coming from different methodological backgrounds, to try and prepare, in a scholarly fashion, the road to what they called "a new international law." As part of this movement one could mention, in addition to the authors of the Vienna School, Lammasch, Nippold, Krabbe, and Duguit from the prewar generation, and from the younger generation Scelle, Politis, Brierly, and Lauterpacht, for example.[9] During the First World War, Kelsen had

[7] On his students in general see R. A. Métall, *Hans Kelsen. Leben und Werk* (Vienna: Deutike, 1969), 28–47; M. Stolleis, "A critique from the '*Wiener Kreis*.' Margit Kraft-Fuchs (1902–1994) on Carl Schmidt," in D. Diner and M. Stolleis (eds.), *Hans Kelsen and Carl Schmitt: A Juxtaposition*. Schriftenreihe des Instituts für Deutsche Geschichte, Universität Tel-Aviv, 20 (Gerlingen: Bleicher, 1999), 123 *et seq*. On the 'School' specifically in international law see J. L. Kunz, "The 'Vienna School' and International Law" [1934], in J. L. Kunz, *The Changing Law of Nations: Essays on International Law* (Ohio State University Press, 1968), 59–124, with a compilation of the most important publications on international law from the circle around Kelsen.

[8] On Kunz's self-understanding see J. L. Kunz, "The 'Vienna School' and International Law" [1934], 59–124, and J. L. Kunz, *Völkerrechtswissenschaft und Reine Rechtslehre* (Leipzig: F. Deuticke, 1923), 83 *et seq*.

[9] J. W. Garner, in the Hague lectures in 1931, sought to provide an overview of the reform movement in the 1920s: "Le développement et les tendances récentes du droit international," in: *RCADI* 35/I (1931), 605 *et seq*.

been an active office-holder of the declining Habsburg monarchy, and unlike the Austrian pacifist, politician, and legal scholar Lammasch, he had refrained from publishing pacifist works or works promoting international understanding.[10] But the publication of his monograph *Das Problem der Souveränität und die Theorie des Völkerrechts* in 1920 made him into a pacesetter in international law theory within the renewal movement during the interwar period.

Driven by a spirit of enlightenment, these thinkers set out to destroy what they felt were the detrimental tenets of classic international law theory. At the center of the critical analyses stood the concept of state sovereignty and its place within the international legal order.[11] Although methods and results diverged strongly, what characterized the representatives of this movement was a shared claim to modernization.[12] The dynamic of this movement sprang from the reaction against classic international law, which was regarded as the product of European prewar nationalism. For example, Brierly, in his inaugural lecture in 1924, emphasized that "the world regards international law today as in need of rehabilitation."[13] In the light of this criticism, the theoretical landscape of

[10] This probably had something to do with his involvement at the ministerial level of the Austrian war department during the First World War, a position that was beneficial to his career; on this see G. Oberkofler and E. Rabofsky, *Hans Kelsen im Kriegseinsatz der k.u.k. Wehrmacht. Eine kritische Würdigung seiner militärtheoretischen Angebote* (Frankfurt am Main and New York: P. Lang, 1988), 13.

[11] With a good survey of the literature on the concept of sovereignty, see Garner, "Le développement et les tendances récentes du droit international," 698.

[12] The term "modernization" describes the self-understanding of this movement and in that sense departs from other uses of the notion of "modern" international law theory. For Quincy Wright, the "modern" jurisprudence of international law was characterized by the renaissance of natural law in the interwar period in conjunction with the emerging conception of the international organization: *The Study of International Relations* (New York: Appleton-Century-Crofts, 1955), 228–334. By contrast, Richard Falk sees the defining characteristic of "modern" international jurisprudence in the incorporation of the political context into the analysis of norms: *The Status of Law in International Society* (Princeton University Press, 1970), 41–47. Nathaniel Berman understands "international legal modernism" in terms of cultural history as a "primitivist/experimentalist alliance" in the international law literature of the interwar period: "But the Alternative is Despair: European Nationalism and the Modernist Renewal of International Law," *Harvard Law Review*, 106 (1993), 1800–1808.

[13] J. L. Brierly, *The Basis of Obligation and Other Papers* (Oxford: Clarendon, 1958), 68; on Brierly see C. Landauer, "J. L. Brierly and the Modernization of Transnational Law," *Vanderbilt Journal of Transnational Law*, 25 (1993), 881–917; on the cultural-historical rupture of 1914 see M. Stolleis, *Der lange Abschied vom 19. Jahrhundert. Vortrag gehalten vor der Juristischen Gesellschaft zu Berlin am 22. Januar 1997* (Berlin and New York: W. de Gruyter, 1997).

international law in the nineteenth century seemed dominated by mystically transfigured notions of sovereignty. From this perspective, the traditional doctrines of international law, with their "subjective" orientation focused on the "will" of the individual state, had contributed to the rupture of civilization represented by the First World War.[14] For the reformers, it was not only international politics, but also international legal scholarship infected by the dogma of sovereignty, that bore responsibility for the inadequate elaboration of the Hague order.[15]

This somewhat distorted picture of the nineteenth century as a "dark" era of international law theory (which is still handed on today) was to boost the readiness for a fundamental reform of the doctrines of international law.[16] From the perspective of the modernization movement, there was a need for an updated theory of international law in order to invest the international legal order, shattered by the war, with new authority. The reformist spirit of this movement was a reaction to the corpse-strewn battlefields of the war to a peaceful world legal order. The developments in the international conduct of states offered contemporaries plenty of reasons to believe that a new era in international law had begun. And here the newly founded League of Nations served initially as a screen onto which the hopes for a more peaceful world order were projected. A description of the situation at the beginning of the 1920s by Kunz illustrates the hopeful, cosmopolitan mood of this movement:

> At the end of World War I, fought under the leadership of Woodrow Wilson "to end the war," boundless optimism prevailed. There was everywhere, in victors, neutrals, and vanquished, not only the will to achieve a better world through international law, but also the firm conviction that it could be done. Hence, the ambitious experiment of the League of Nations. Away with power politics! No more secret diplomacy, no more entangling alliances, no longer the forever discredited balance of

14 The criticism focused above all on Jellinek's doctrine of self-obligation: J. L. Brierly, "Le fondement du caractère obligatoire du droit international public," *RCADI* 23/III (1928), 482–484; H. Lauterpacht, *The Function of Law in the International Community* (reprint of the 1933 edn., New York: Garland, 1973), 409–412, with extensive references on the critique of the doctrine of self-obligation; A. Verdross, *Die Verfassung der Völkerrechtsgemeinschaft* (Vienna: J. Springer, 1926), 12–20; J. Spiropolous, *Théorie generale du droit international* (Paris: Librairie générale de droit & de jurisprudence, 1930), 46–50.

15 N. Politis, "Le problème des limitations de la souveraineté et la théorie de l'abus des droits dans les rapports internationaux," *RCADI*, 6 (1925), 5–27.

16 On this distorted image see D. Kennedy, "International Law and the Nineteenth Century: History of an Illusion," *Nordic Journal of International Law*, 65 (1996), 403–420.

> power, no more war! Democracy and the rule of international law will change the world. . . . In all the dealings of the League, international law was at the heart of the discussion. Idealistic approach, optimism, emphasis on international law created the Geneva atmosphere.[17]

Against the lamentations of the doubters and naysayers,[18] international law was to emerge from the war not only unscathed, but stronger. In this process, an objective theoretical construction of international law was to back and push the creation of a peaceful international order based on the rule of law.

Among German international lawyers, the cosmopolitan spirit of the times was carried above all by the Vienna School and the pacifist movement around Schücking and Wehberg as well as Strupp. As for the rest, the "modern" approaches in international legal theory were received with greater reserve than in France and England, for example, by the rather conservative mainstream around Triepel, Kaufmann, Hold-Ferneck, and the rising Walz. The weaker resonance of this "modern" current in German writings compared to other countries can be attributed largely to the political situation following the defeat in the war. In Germany, the new world order created by the Treaty of Versailles and guaranteed by the League of Nations was regarded as unjust and rejected.[19] This often went hand in hand with a politically motivated reserve on the part of German international lawyers toward the "new" international law. In spite of a growing acceptance of the Geneva institutions among the

[17] J. L. Kunz, "The Swing of the Pendulum: From Overestimation to Underestimation of International Law," *AJIL*, 44 (1950), 136.

[18] Under the hegemony of the Jellinek–Triepelian construct, the legal character of international law had no longer been fundamentally questioned at the beginning of the century. That changed profoundly only in the course of the First World War. The international legal debate was characterized by a more existential tone. For example, the question by John Austin, whether law between sovereigns was law properly so called, which had been the topic of frequent philosophical speculations in the nineteenth century, though without shaking the belief of international lawyers in the legal nature of their field of study, had caused cracks in the foundation of international legal theory after 1914. A number of publications cast doubt on the legal character of international law: F. Somló, *Juristische Grundlehre* (Leipzig: F. Meiner, 1917; 2nd edn. 1927), 167 *et seq.*; and in the interwar period, A. von Hold-Ferneck, "Anerkennung und Selbstbindung. Ein Beitrag zur Lehre vom Wesen des Völkerrechts," *Zeitschrift für Rechtsphilosophie*, 4 (1929), 179; W. Burckhardt, *Über die Unvollkommenheit des Völkerrechts* (Bern: P. Haupt, 1923); A. V. Lundstedt, *Superstition or Rationality in Action for Peace? Arguments against Founding a World Peace on the Common Sense of Justice. A Criticism of Jurisprudence* (London: Longmans, Green, 1925).

[19] M. Stolleis, *A History of Public Law in Germany 1914–1945*, 60–64. (See also Chapter 5 D 1 in the present book.)

German population at the time of Germany's entry into the League of Nations in 1926, the "Versailles trauma" had a palpable and lasting after-effect in the field of international law.[20]

Kelsen and Kunz emigrated in the 1930s. Both men eventually ended up in the United States, where they continued to publish on international law during and after the Second World War. Verdross, having been suspended for a semester in 1938 as the new Nazi rulers vetted him carefully, remained a full professor at Vienna University during the 1930s and 1940s.

Kelsen's work on international law, which he expanded upon during his exile in Geneva at the Institut de hautes études internationales and later at Berkeley, culminated in his commentary on the UN Charter and his *Principles of International Law*. Joseph L. Kunz worked in the United States as an editor of the *American Journal of International Law* and taught at the University of Toledo. With the predominance of Anglo-American pragmatism in the field of international law, the audience for Kelsen's writings shrank increasingly after the Second World War. The renewed renaissance of natural law[21] and the "realistic" current that began in international legal jurisprudence in the 1950s also did little to boost the acceptance of Kelsen's theory of international law. At the beginning of the 1960s, the optimism of the 1920s had given way to a deep skepticism about the potential and value of law in international relations.

In addition, Kelsen's own draft for a new world organization institutionalizing the international rule of law in the post-war era, published in 1944, was not considered during the negotiations in San Francisco. Kelsen's two central projects thus proved impossible to implement. Both the attempt to introduce a "scientific" method of international law on the basis of the Pure Theory of Law, and the political project of a thoroughly legalized global order had to be regarded by Kelsen and Kunz as failures for the time being during the crisis of the United Nations in the Cold War era. The goal of the historical reconstruction undertaken here is to make it easier to assess the real contribution that Kelsen's work made to the development of the field of international law.

20 Ibid.

21 The term "natural law" is used with a variety of meanings: first, as ontological natural law of the scholastic tradition; second, in the sense of the "rational" natural law of the Enlightenment; and third, by way of negative demarcation against legal positivism to describe an extra-judicial justification of norms. Unless specified, the term is used here with the first meaning.

The structure of the book is guided by the two central goals of Kelsen's theory of international law. Part I, "The Quest for Objectivity: The Method and Construction of Universal Law," reconstructs the attempt by Kelsen and his students to introduce a "pure" – i.e. non-political – method in international law. Part II, "The Outlines of the Cosmopolitan Project – the Actors, sources, and courts of universal law," takes a closer look at Kelsen's own, highly political project of a world order that was thoroughly pervaded by law and largely institutionalized. The concluding reflections examine the prevailing destructive thrust of the Kelsenian doctrine of international law as the result of the inherent tension between the claim to a non-political method of international legal scholarship and his own cosmopolitan project. Moreover, with respect to the analyzed texts, the reconstruction undertaken here follows largely the actual historical chronology. Chapters 1–4 are devoted largely to texts from the nineteenth century, the 1920s, and early 1930s, while Chapters 5 and 6 tend to focus on texts from the 1930s to early 1950s.

In Part I, the discussion emphasizes Kelsen's application of his own fundamental methodological beliefs to the traditional theoretical construct of international law of the nineteenth and early twentieth centuries. Kelsen claimed to have developed a new, more objective method of legal scholarship. Following the lead of the natural sciences, jurisprudence was to be reshaped into a post-metaphysical "science" of the law that was logically verifiable and purified of political value judgments. In the critical methodological analyses reconstructed in Part I, Kelsen subjected the traditional notion of sovereignty, the voluntaristic foundation of international law, and Heinrich Triepel's dualistic doctrine to a fundamental critique. With the help of his critical tools, Kelsen ruthlessly unmasked the inherent limitations and contradictions of the traditional constructs of international law.

In their stead, Kelsen and his students, building on the primacy thesis borrowed from Kaltenborn, constructed international law as a law above the state. As the highest and thus sovereign strata of norms within the hierarchically structured legal cosmos, international law was to delegate the respective state legal orders and delimit them from one another in their sovereign spheres. The traditional, voluntaristic theories of international law were to be replaced by an "objective" construction of international law that was independent of the subjective "will" of individual states.

Part II of the book seeks to outline more sharply the contours of the political project of a universal order that was largely institutionalized through the medium of the law. The analyzed texts can be divided into epistemological, doctrinal, sociological, and openly political (*de lege ferenda*) writings. The less numerous political and sociological works by Kelsen aimed at realizing the cosmopolitan project of a thorough institutionalization of international relations. But even the "purely" legal-dogmatic works analyzed in Part II make a contribution – not always openly acknowledged by Kelsen – to the political project. The goal here is to clarify how the revision of the traditional central concepts of international law described in Part I affected the areas of international law theory that were particularly relevant to the cosmopolitan project. The issues here were the emerging law of international organizations, the individual as a subject of international law, the law-creating instruments of international law, and international adjudication. My intent is to show the reader step by step how Kelsen sought to advance his political project not only through writings clearly labeled as political, but also through his doctrinal contributions. In the process, Kelsen's doctrinal contribution to his own political project consisted almost entirely of an attempt to repress a substantial notion of sovereignty in international law, which he regarded as an obstacle to his cosmopolitan project. Time and again in Part II, I will outline the models of political order that arose behind the destroyed dogmatic constructs. As I intend to show, however, the destructive strategy chosen by Kelsen to resolve the tension between "purity of method" and "cosmopolitan project" led simultaneously to a self-limitation that was hardly bearable for the theorist of international law in his role as a legal scholar, and it brought Kelsen's theory of international law to the brink of giving up international legal doctrine in the narrower sense. This circumstance may also explain the sharp rejection that Kelsen's ideas on international law frequently encountered, and still do. To that extent, the belief in universal law went hand in hand with a fundamental mistrust of legal scholarship.

The concluding section summarizes once more the role that remains for the international legal scholar after Kelsen, and looks at Kelsen's understanding of himself as an international lawyer by looking at his commentary on the Charter of the United Nations.

PART I

The quest for objectivity: the method and construction of universal law

"Subjective and objective notions of law are locked in a struggle over contemporary jurisprudence. The theory of international law, in particular, vacillates back and forth uncertainly between the antipodes of a state-individualistic and a human-universalistic perspective, between the subjectivism of the primacy of the legal order of the state and the objectivism of the primacy of international law... And yet, it is on a sure path toward an objectivistic conception of law."[1] This programmatic statement by Hans Kelsen from 1920 leads directly to the core of the Vienna School's theory of international law: creating a scientific foundation for an "objective" international law. From Kelsen's perspective, the primary task of legal scholarship was the theoretical construction of an international law whose validity was disconnected from the sovereign will of the state. To that end, the medium of the law was to be newly conceived as universal law with the help of the "objectivistic" conception of law, that is, one that proceeded from the primacy of international law.

In their striving for a "more objective" and simultaneously methodologically superior construct of international law, Kelsen and his students harked back on important points to intellectual precursors from the nineteenth and early twentieth centuries – though they developed them further or set themselves emphatically apart from them. The approach I have taken here will place their struggle for an objectivized universal law into the context of the historical discourse. The specific orientation and significance of the Kelsenian doctrines of international law can be adequately grasped only by setting them off against theoretical constructs of international law in German-speaking scholarship in the nineteenth and early twentieth centuries.

[1] H. Kelsen, *Das Problem der Souveränität und die Theorie des Völkerrechts. Beitrag zu einer Reinen Rechtslehre* [1920], 2nd edn. (Tübingen: J. C. B. Mohr, 1928).

in 1847, G. Kaltenborn, in his *Kritik des Völkerrechts* [A Critique of the

1

Method and construction of international law in nineteenth-century German scholarship

Those German-speaking writers who thought of themselves as positivists used different methodological conceptions in their search for an "objective" principle of international law. This principle was to contribute to a theoretical harmonization of the presumed binding nature of international law on the one hand, with the assumption that the sovereign will of the state formed the basis of the validity of international law on the other. Such a construct posed considerable problems for those who wrote about international law, because in contrast to state law, there was no central authority that stood above the states and was charged with enacting norms and enforcing the law. Those who created the law and those to whom it was addressed were one and the same. Moreover, starting from various definitions of law, nineteenth-century authors sought to provide what they considered a methodologically superior answer to the challenge of John Austin's question of whether law was possible at all between sovereign entities, and if so, how. This question assumed central importance in the second half of the nineteenth century also because a simple identification of international legal norms with rules of morality and reason seemed increasingly untenable under the rule of positivism in general jurisprudence.

A Kaltenborn and the "objective principle" of international law

In 1847, C. Kaltenborn, in his *Kritik des Völkerrechts* [A Critique of the Law of Nations], had undertaken a comprehensive analysis of the textbooks on international law that had appeared in Germany in the first half of the century.[1] On the basis of this critical examination he went on to

[1] C. Kaltenborn von Stachau, *Kritik des Völkerechts* (Leipzig: G. Mayer, 1847), 266 on the "common international existence" [*internationale Gemeinexistenz*] as the first principle of the law of nations.

develop his own positivistic approach to international law, which would substantially shape Kelsen's theory of international law that emerged sixty years later. Kaltenborn had published his *Kritik des Völkerrechts* at a time that was particularly fruitful for the German field of international jurisprudence. The work of the same title published by Heinrich v. Gagern as early as 1840 had ended what Kaltenborn called a time of "lazy stagnation," and it had sparked a series of fundamental monographs on international law over the next seven years.[2] As Kaltenborn noted in his introduction: "Added to this is the fact that precisely the abundant recent literature has laid an important groundwork for criticism, and because of the strictly scientific character of the post-Gagern achievements, especially for learned criticism. The splendid studies of the likes of Heffter, Pütter, Oppenheim, Wheaton, Cussy, and Stein have made a scientific critique of international law easier, though, they have inevitably also raised the bar for such a critique."[3] His critique of the literature on international law, which took Grotius as its starting point, was based on a concept of modernization. For Kaltenborn, a modern "science" of international law had to proceed first of all from the positive law of nations of the European states. To that extent, G. F. Martens had laid a foundation stone for a "further elevation of the positive science of international law" through his "*primae lineae juris gentium Europaearum practici*" of 1785. His grasp of the genuinely positive material had made him the father of the nineteenth-century science of international law.[4]

Since that time, however, the field, in the view of Kaltenborn, had not moved beyond the collection and arbitrary systematization of the positive material.[5] Still missing was a philosophical permeation of the positive material, in the sense of an identification of the highest objective principles.[6] Although various attempts at a philosophical interpretation of positive international law had been undertaken in recent times, these had not led to the establishment of an objective principle of international law: "Fully in the spirit of this general subjective direction of philosophy, the more recent conception and account of the philosophy of law, and especially of the philosophy of international law, is encumbered with a subjective type. All the numerous treatments of the law from a philosophical point of view,

[2] H. von Gagern, *Critik des Völkerrechts. Mit praktischer Anwendung auf unsere Zeit* (Leipzig: F. A. Brockhaus, 1840).

[3] Kaltenborn von Stachau, *Kritik des Völkerrechts*, 9–10. [4] Ibid., 101.

[5] Ibid., 103. [6] Ibid., 128.

especially those of Kant, Fichte, and Hegel, more or less carry the stamp of subjectivity within themselves."[7] Kaltenborn was referring to the reception of Kantian or Hegelian philosophy in the science of international law, which had supposedly led to international law being given a state-focused, subjectivist foundation.

A closer look at Kaltenborn's critique of the "subjective principle" in international jurisprudence in the first half of the century must be preceded by an explanation of how this term was used in Kant and Hegel.

I The "subjective principle" in Kant and Hegel

For Kant, "a state, as a moral person, is considered as living in relation to another state in the condition of natural freedom and therefore in a condition of constant war."[8] This tenet, which goes back to Hobbes, and which Kant took from Pufendorf,[9] applied the state of nature between humans to relations between states. For Kant, however, the goal of international law in the sense of an a priori postulate of reason was the gradual overcoming of the subjective will of the states by creating universal peace as a legal state of affairs [*Rechtszustand*]. Although "perpetual peace" remained for Kant an "unachievable idea," the constant approximation to this condition through a permanent league or congress of states was a task for humans and states.[10]

Hegel, by contrast, described international law as "external state law" [*äußeres Staatsrecht*]. The foundation of this law was the "autonomy" of nations, which, and here he agreed with Kant, were in a state of nature in their relationships to one another.[11] The law between states rested merely on its recognition, interpretation, and application by the

7 Ibid., 129–130.

8 I. Kant, *The Metaphysics of Morals*, trans. and ed. Mary Gregor (Cambridge University Press, 1996), §53, 114.

9 Th. Hobbes, *Leviathan* [1651], (Harmondsworth: Penguin, 1968) ch. 13; on the history of the reception of Hobbes see H. Steiger, "Völkerrecht" in O. Brunner, W. Kunze, and R. Koselleck (eds.), *Geschichtliche Grundbegriffe. Historisches Lexikon zur politisch-sozialen Sprache in Deutschland* (Stuttgart: E. Klett, 1992), vol. 7, 97 *et seq*.

10 Kant, *The Metaphysics of Morals*, §61, 119; this was not a world republic or world state, which Kant regarded as impossible because of the fear of despotism by a supreme ruler; see H. Steiger, "Völkerrecht und Naturrecht zwischen Christian Wolff und Adolf Lasson" in D. Klippel (ed.), *Naturrecht im 19. Jahrhundert* (Goldbach: Keip, 1997), 45 *et seq*.

11 G. W. F. Hegel, *Die Philosophie des Rechts, die Mitschriften Wannemann (Heidelberg 1817/18) und Homeyer (Berlin, 1818/19)*, edited and annotated by K.-H. Ilting (Stuttgart: Klett-Cotta, 1983), §159.

individual states.[12] Because of the principle of autonomy, the rights of states toward each other had their reality only in a special, and not in a constitutionalized, general will.[13] Given that treaties of international law in the Hegelian system had no reality within the "general will," their observance should, in the final analysis, also be left to the discretion of the states: "A mere ought-to-hold [*Haltensollen*] of the tractates takes effect. This ought is a coincidence."[14]

Thus in Hegel, in contrast to Kant, a continuous approximation to a "perpetual peace" through the gradual overcoming of the subjective principle in the sense of an a priori postulate of reason is not possible. Rather, in Hegel the place of the Kantian league of peace is taken by the historical-philosophical assumption of "world history as world judgment," in which competing "national spirits" struggle for hegemony.[15] According to the Hegelian approach of "external state law," later adopted by Karl Theodor Pütter,[16] international law thus has its reality only in the sovereign will of individual states. For Pütter, the "peculiar nature of international law lies in the fact that the will of the state, in its conduct toward other nations, is self-determined with absolute freedom."[17]

*II Humanity as a "community of law" [*Rechtsgemeinwesen*] in Kaltenborn*

In his quest for an objective philosophical principle of international law, Kaltenborn subjected especially the Hegelian construct of international law to a sharp critique. He described the sole recourse to the "subjective principle" of the sovereign will of the state in Pütter as too one-sided a construct. Such an idolization of the state excluded a priori the notion of a higher order – in the sense of an international community – above the states.[18]

This critique of the Hegelian doctrines of international law already adumbrated Kaltenborn's own conception. To him, the state is not the

[12] Hegel, *Die Philosophie des Rechts*, §161, and Ilting's commentary on page 348.
[13] Ibid., §162. [14] Ibid.
[15] G. W. F. Hegel, *Grundlinien der Philosophie des Rechts oder Naturrechts und Staatswissenschaft im Grundrisse.* Auf Grundlage der Werke von 1832–1845. Mit Hegels eigenhändigen Notizen und den mündlichen Zusätzen. 4th edn. (Frankfurt am Main: Suhrkamp, 1995), §341 *et seq.*
[16] K. Th. Pütter, "Die Staatslehre oder – Souveränität als Prinzip des praktischen europäischen Völkerrechts" in *ZStW*, 6 (1850), § 14, 304 *et seq.*; on p. 307, Pütter himself points to Hegel's philosophy of law as the theoretical foundation of his own scientific elaborations.
[17] Quoted in Kaltenborn von Stachau, *Kritik des Völkerrechts*, 163. [18] Ibid.

highest and absolute institution of the law. There is a still higher community, one that makes the state appear as a subordinate branch of a higher legal entity: "In this way, the legal life of the state, which is inherently only national, is elevated into a general human community of law that goes beyond the nation, into an international order of law."[19] For Kaltenborn, we are dealing here with the "objective principle" of international law, which did not, however, rule out the recognition of states as subjects of the international community. Rather, it was not possible for the international community to rise to a height that would completely undermine the "subjective principle" in the sense of a legitimate autonomy of the individual state.[20]

In Kaltenborn, international law over and above the state thus results from the assumption of an international community that emerges organically from the coexistence of the nations.[21] However, this supreme principle of international law cannot be deduced from the tenets of natural law or reason, but follows from the profound realization of the historically evolved culture of the European-Christian community of nations.[22] Here we see Kaltenborn's methodological closeness – demonstrated by A. Carty through Kaltenborn's doctrine of sources – to the historical school of law.[23] This methodological orientation also

[19] Here is the full quote:

> But just as the nation is thus merely a part, a branch of humanity, and as a branch of a whole has its wholeness in humanity, the state, as the expression of the legal community of a nation, must recognize in the legal community of states as the political unity of humanity a higher power than itself, and to act as a branch of this higher legal community [. . .] In this way, the legal life of the state, which is inherently only national, is elevated into a general human community of law that goes beyond the nation, into an international order of law. If, then, the law is the norm and order for the human community in all its dimensions and gradations, that community of state must be described as the highest and final community of the law. The law here is what one usually calls the law of nations.
>
> Ibid., 260–261.

[20] Ibid., 262. [21] Ibid., 260.

[22] In this way, the international law that arose in Europe is identified with the international law of all of humanity and in this sense seems indissolubly linked with Christian culture; on this see H. Steiger, "Völkerrecht," 133.

[23] A. Carty, *The Decay of International Law*? (Manchester University Press, 1986), 30–35; on the legal source doctrine in Kaltenborn see L. Ehrlich, "The Development of International Law as a Science" in *RCADI*, 105/I (1962), 246–247; on the methodological orientation of his work on state law see M. Stolleis, *Public Law in Germany, 1800–1914* (New York: Berghahn Books, 2001), 313.

prompted Kaltenborn's critique of Christian Wolff's conception of international law, formulated a hundred years earlier. Wolff's work on international law, which Kelsen himself tells us was the inspiration, along with Kaltenborn, for his own theory of international law developed in *Problem der Souveränität*, had declared that the community of international law, as an abstract system, was situated above the state as a *civitas maxima*.[24] The idea of the *civitas maxima*, which originated in Stoicism, was understood by Wolff as a politically organized entity that stood above the state and had a comprehensive legislative authority.[25]

Kaltenborn's critique of Wolff maintained that his construction had been developed purely deductively as an analogy to the natural law conception of international law, and not out of the specific nature of the conditions of the law of nations:[26] "This deduction seems to us to be completely inadequate, and were it truly possible, it would destroy international law and turn it into state law."[27] For Kaltenborn, the "universal state" is an exaggeration of the objective principle of international law. By positing it, Wolff failed to recognize that a certain autonomy of the individual states was justified.[28] Wolff's "*civitas maxima*" was, as Heinhard Steiger has pointed out, the object of criticism early on.[29] Wolff's contemporaries and students already feared that the individual states could be entirely stripped of their sovereignty in a despotic super-state.[30]

Despite this criticism, the proximity of Kaltenborn's conception to Wolff's approach on the question of the objectification of international law remains striking. Kaltenborn also rejected the doubts – put forth by the so-called deniers of international law – that international law had the quality of law because it lacked enforceability by referring back to Wolff's notion.[31] The enforcement of international law takes place either through voluntary behavior on the part of states, through mediation,

[24] Ch. Freiherr von Wolff, *Jus gentium* (reprint of the 1749 edition, New York: Olms, 1972), §§7 *et seq*., 5 *et seq*.; on this see Steiger, "Völkerrecht," 114–115; on the reception of Wolff's *civitas maxima* in Emer de Vattel, see Steiger, "Völkerrecht und Naturrecht zwischen Chr. Wolff und A. Lasson," 46–53.

[25] Von Wolff, *Jus gentium*, §11, 9.

[26] Kaltenborn von Stachau, *Kritik des Völkerrechts*, 72. [27] Ibid. [28] Ibid., 73.

[29] Steiger, "Völkerrecht," 115.

[30] D. H. L. von Ompteda, *Literatur des gesamten natürlichen und positiven Völkerrechts* (Regensburg, 1785; reprint Aalen: Scientia, 1963), vol. 1, §94, 324; however, what was preserved was, for example, the "société universelle" in Emer de Vattel: E. de Vattel, *Le droit des gens ou principes de la loi naturelle* [1758], edited by W. von Euler, P. Guggenheim, and W. Schätzel (Tübingen: Mohr, 1959), §11, 21; instructive: Steiger, "Völkerrecht," 115.

[31] Kaltenborn von Stachau, *Kritik des Völkerrechts*, 75.

or – as a final resort – through physical force. The latter option leads to war, which should thus be seen as the implementation of the legal claims of the community: "War differs only in degree from the other means of enforcing the law. A criminal judge, in the worst case, has an individual beheaded and broken on the wheel. War, in the worst case, destroys the existence of this or that criminal state. The fact that at times innocent people are beheaded and that innocent states are defeated or even subjugated in war in spite of their good law negates neither state law nor the international legal order."[32] That the international community of states possessed a monopoly of force that was implemented in a decentralized fashion by way of lawful wars was something that Wolff had already spelled out a hundred years earlier to defend the coercive character of international law.[33]

Both Wolff and later Kaltenborn thus saw international law as an objective law above the state with coercive character. Moreover, in Kaltenborn this universalistic view of the law of nations, which originated in the natural law concept of the Spanish late scholastics, had found in the nineteenth century a proponent who regarded himself as a positivist. The scientific contradiction between the grounding of international law on a voluntaristic basis of individual states and a view of that law as standing above the state and thus universalistic remained alive also in the second half of the nineteenth century. Under changing methodological premises, the discourse on the theory of international law continued to oscillate between the "subjective" and the "objective" principle. Within the German-language theory of international law in the second half of the nineteenth century, which was moving increasingly away from the basic assumptions of the historical school of law, the question as to the relationship between the subjective and the objective principle now arose against the backdrop of a specifically juridical construct of international law.

B Bergbohm and Fricker: "The problem of international law revisited"

This debate found new nourishment immediately after the founding of the Reich. In 1871, Adolf Lasson had picked up again on the Hegelian

32 Ibid., 312.

33 "Paradoxum, hoc videbitur iis, qui nexum veritatum non prospiciunt et ex factis jura aestimant [. . .] Et in genere notandum est, nobis jam quaestionem esse de jure, cujus capaces sunt homines pro conditione praesenti, minime vero de factis, quibus jus vel contemnitur, vel violatur." Von Wolff, *Jus gentium*, §13; this passage is invoked by Kaltenborn von Stachau, *Kritik des Völkerrechts*, 75.

approach centered on the individual state. But in his conclusions he went far beyond Pütter: "The state can therefore never submit to a legal order, nor, in fact, to any will outside of itself. The state that prevails between states is therefore a completely lawless one."[34] But this assumption did not prevent Lasson from drawing up a system of prudent rules to which states should voluntarily adhere. However, given the lack of a supra-state authority endowed with coercive power, for him it was not possible to speak in this context of law.[35]

In a work published six years later, *Staatsverträge und Gesetze als Quellen des Völkerrechts* [State Treaties and Laws as Sources of International Law],[36] Carl Bergbohm, a professor from Dorpat, affirmed, on the basis of similar theoretical premises, the legal character of the law of nations. Bergbohm had likewise set international law on the sole foundation of the will of the sovereign state. For Bergbohm, however, international law was not merely "external state law" in the Hegelian sense, but objective law resting on the will of the state. That was expressed most clearly in the positive treaties of international law.[37] Over the course of history, Bergbohm argued, international law had freed itself increasingly from being intermingled with related matters, such as politics and morality, and was slowly evolving from mere custom and habit to written law:[38] "The legal norm, which destroys the rule of feeling, wrests itself away from the mere feeling of right [*Rechtsgefühl*], which is subject to every change in sentiment; the subjective-internal conviction becomes the objective-external norm."[39] Custom appears in Bergbohm as an obsolete, pre-positive source of law, which had to gradually yield to written law as a higher stage of legal development.

Bergbohm criticized the repeated theoretical attempts to devise closed systems or codifications of international law.[40] It was unavoidable in such attempts that gaps would be filled with recourse to the law of reason or politics, which had nothing to do with the positive law of nations.[41]

[34] A. Lasson, *Princip und Zukunft des Völkerrechts* (Berlin: W. Hertz, 1871), 22.
[35] On Lasson see K. Lüderssen, "Anerkennungsprobleme im Völkerrecht" in his *Genesis und Geltung in der Jurisprudenz* (Frankfurt: Suhrkamp, 1996), 223 *et seq.*
[36] C. Bergbohm, *Staatsverträge und Gesetze als Quellen des Völkerrechts* (Dorpat: C. Mattiesen, 1877).
[37] Ibid., 81 *et seq.* [38] Ibid., 3. [39] Ibid., 3–4.
[40] The best-known attempt was that of Bluntschli, who had drawn up a law book built on individual paragraphs, in the sense of a comprehensive codification of the law of nations: J. C. Bluntschli, *Das moderne Völkerrecht der civilisierten Staaten, als Rechtsbuch dargestellt*, 3rd edn. (Nördlingen: C. H. Beck'sche Buchhandlung, 1878).
[41] Bergbohm, *Staatsverträge und Gesetze*, 8.

Bergbohm's was a reductionist approach to international law, which sought to explain the existence of objective international law solely from positive "general state treaties," as for example the Act of the Congress of Vienna (1815), the Paris Declaration of Maritime Law of 1856, and the Geneva Convention of 1864. For Bergbohm, law was not, as it still was with Kaltenborn, a historical product of the Christian-European community of states, but a secularized, universally valid expression of the positive will of all "civilized states" [*Culturstaaten*].[42]

For Bergbohm, the validity of this objective law depended always on the consent of all recognized "civilized states" as the law-creating "total authority": "For this final authority is never a single one, is not a legal unity, but remains always merely an aggregate of sovereign, individual wills, each of which, independent of all others, maintains his territory subject to his law."[43] Bergbohm's objective law thus consisted of what was in the 1870s still a very fragmentary body of general multilateral treaties, which, moreover, would cease to belong to this body of objective law if merely a single state withdrew from a treaty.[44] As a result of the disregard of a historically evolved body of customary legal norms that was relatively immune to expressions of individual will, the "subjective principle" had a particularly strong effect in Bergbohm's theory. Because both the genesis as well as the validity of international law was consistently linked to the will of the state as manifested in written law, his objective law remained utterly dependent on the individual expressions of will by the states.

From the perspective of the objective principle, this conception of international law left itself vulnerable by invoking the subjective will of the state as the formal basis of the law. The most pointed critique is found in Karl Viktor Fricker's 1878 essay "Noch einmal das Problem des Völkerrechts" [The Problem of International Law Revisited].[45] This was the reincarnation of the quarrel between an "objective" and a "subjective" grounding of international law against the backdrop of a changed

42 On the dissolution of the distinction between the law of nations of Europe and of other legal communities outside of Europe into a universal international law, David Kennedy has remarked: "By the end of the nineteenth century, there was but one sovereignty and one international law." D. Kennedy, "International Law and the Nineteenth Century: History of an Illusion," *Nordic Journal of International Law*, 65 (1996), 411.

43 Bergbohm, *Staatsverträge und Gesetze als Quellen des Völkerrechts*, 89.

44 Ibid., 90.

45 K. V. Fricker, "Noch einmal das Problem des Völkerrechts" in *Zeitschrift für die gesamte Staatswissenschaft* 34 (1878), 368–405.

methodological orientation in public law and an increasingly universalized practice of international law in the last decades of the century. Fricker analyzed Bergbohm's voluntaristic foundation from the perspective of the question of whether it was indeed possible to construct an objective law of nations in this way. Forty years later, Kelsen made Fricker's argument the basis of his critical analysis of the voluntaristic theory that he developed in *Das Problem der Souveränität und die Theorie des Völkerrechts*.[46]

As Fricker saw it, Bergbohm's attempt – using the sovereign will of the state as his basis and simultaneously rejecting a law of nations that stood above the states – to arrive at an "objective international law" between states in the form of general treaties was doomed to failure from the outset:[47]

> I believe that this attempt has not succeeded and cannot succeed. I do not think it possible to escape the following dilemma: either the wills of the individual states stand above the common will, that is, the latter is in no way detached as a special, objective will from the individual wills – in which case an objective law of nations is unattainable; or the common will, once it has taken shape, stands above the wills of the individual states with its own objective authority – in which case one does arrive at an international law, but the latter is a special will that is distinct from the will of the state.[48]

Nowhere, either before or after Fricker, was the dilemma of the voluntaristic model in the theory of international law spelled out more incisively than in this brief passage. To Fricker, the "power of the objective law," regardless of whether one described it as between or above the states, lay in the fact that the individual state, once the law has been created with its participation, can no longer unilaterally escape its authority.[49] But it was precisely this construct of a united legal authority in the form of the Kaltenbornian community of states that Bergbohm had replaced with an "aggregate of sovereign wills of individual states." By allowing the state to withhold its consent at its own discretion, Bergbohm had relinquished the common objective law of nations he was seeking.[50]

By contrast, Fricker regarded the prerequisite of a higher authority as indispensable for positing an objective law that could claim to have

[46] Kelsen, *Problem der Souveränität*, 183.
[47] Fricker, "Noch einmal das Problem des Völkerrechts," 368.
[48] Ibid., 377. [49] Ibid., 382. [50] Ibid.

binding force. The lack of a power organized above the states had to be recognized – in agreement with those who denied international law – as a weakness of the international legal order. To that extent, international law was still an incomplete law.[51] A certain degree of organization had already been achieved in that the state was acting as the organ of international law and thereby endowing the legal order with power.[52] In Fricker's own conception, which he merely adumbrated, the state, following Kaltenborn, became an organ of a community of law that stood above the state. Fricker thus followed the Wolffian-Kaltenbornian notion of a higher community of states and conceived of international law as the legal order of that community. For him, this legal order was fundamentally capable of developing a stronger, centralized overall authority, even if it should still be seen as incomplete in this regard.[53]

In spite of his fundamental critique of placing international law on a voluntaristic foundation, Fricker sought to end his article, if not on a harmonizing, then at least on a conciliatory note:

> Bergbohm's notion and the notion of international law as an incomplete law are much closer than Bergbohm believes. They both spring from a critical stance, they both still want to conceive of international law as law, and they both recognize that it cannot be conceived of as a formally structured law above the states. Because B. regards as law only the law in its most developed form, as the will of the state, he has to dissolve the law into a multitude of laws belonging to the individual states and valid for each only as its own will, while the other view, invoking the concept of development, regards the same thing as an attempt to place the actions of states under the rule of law . . . Bergbohm cannot forego the notion of communality for his law of nations, without, however, being able to conceive of it as something legal; but he does recognize it as a necessary effect of a cultural development. The other view understands this notion itself already as a manifestation of a legal development.[54]

Fricker's view of international law as "incomplete law" is a conception open to development, one that contains an evolutionary-dynamic component in the direction of a progressive degree of organization of the community of states, reminiscent of the Kantian telos of progressive legal institutionalization. To that end – and this was going beyond Kant's continuous commitment to state sovereignty – the sovereign will of the state must be transcended in favor of an international community of states pervaded by law. Kelsen would consistently advance this view of

[51] Ibid., 395. [52] Ibid., 398. [53] Ibid., 399. [54] Ibid., 399–400.

international law with the help of his own new theoretical approach. He received the crucial methodological impulses from his critical engagement with Georg Jellinek's notion of international law.

C Jellinek as synthesis

In 1880, the Viennese docent Georg Jellinek inserted himself into the "Bergbohm–Fricker controversy" about the foundation of international law. With the goal of continuing to develop Bergbohm's doctrines methodologically, and as an answer, as it were, to Fricker's contribution, Jellinek articulated his own theoretical approach, one that sought to take into account both the objective and the subjective principle of international law. The impact of Jellinek's doctrine of international law was considerable. All large theoretical constructs of international law before the First World War and during the Weimar period entered into an extensive dialogue with Jellinek's conception. In part they did so by adopting his theoretical approach or developing it further, in part, as with the Vienna School, by turning ostentatiously away from it. The methodological orientation of the Kelsenian theory of the law of nations can therefore be fully understood only against the backdrop of Jellinek's work.

Both in his first monograph on international law, *Die rechtliche Natur der Staatenverträge* [The Legal Nature of State Treaties], and in his *Lehre von den Staatenverbindungen* [Theory of International Federations], Jellinek considered it advisable to "cast a searching look at the foundations and the method of state and international law."[55] Jellinek claimed to be introducing a new, "more secure method"[56] for the study of the basic concepts of international law. The law of nations, he argued, should catch up with the "formal development" of the general notion of law that had been achieved in the previous decades through systematic works.[57] Evidently Jellinek was referring here to the accomplishments of positivism in German legal scholarship. His intent was to apply a strict, positivist methodology also in the field of international law.[58] In spite of the triumph of state law positivism in Germany, natural law

[55] G. Jellinek, *Die Lehre von den Staatenverbindungen* (Vienna: A. Hölder, 1882), 4.

[56] Ibid., 10. [57] Ibid., 2.

[58] On the early Jellinek, who was close to Laband, see C. Schönberger, "Ein Liberaler zwischen Staatswille und Volkswille. Georg Jellinek und die Krise des staatsrechtlichen Positivismus um die Jahrhundertwende" in S. L. Paulson and M. Schulte (eds.), *Georg Jellinek. Beiträge zu Leben und Werk* (Tübingen: Mohr Siebeck, 2000), 4–9; on the crisis of state law positivism in the 1890s, see the important study by C. Schönberger, *Das*

approaches and principles – which Kaltenborn had already criticized – still played a considerable role in the leading textbooks on international law in the middle of the nineteenth century. To be sure, the complete identification of natural law, divine law, and international morality was hardly found any longer in the continental discipline of international law in the second half of the century. Still, frequent recourses to "philosophical" or "natural" international law can still be found in the important monographs in the nineteenth century.[59]

The high phase of international law positivism in Germany thus coincided with the time of Bergbohm and Jellinek.[60] All subsequent important German textbooks on international law[61] dispensed entirely with a philosophical-natural law basis until the mid 1920s. Jellinek argued that only a positivistic method that did without material ideas of law and was in line with the rest of public law could, once and for all, allay the frequent doubts that international law was genuine law and lead the discipline of international law toward the "scientific" level of a modern public law. What Jellinek was after was a theoretical construct of international law that was to be erected without recourse to the principles of natural law.[62] Jellinek sought to arrive at an objective

Parlament im Anstaltstaat. Zur Theorie parlamentarischer Repräsentation in der Staatsrechtslehre des Kaiserreichs (1871–1918) (Frankfurt am Main: Suhrkamp, 1997).

59 For example in A. G. Heffter, *Le droit international de l'Europe* (Berlin and Paris: E. H. Schröder, 1873) (French translation), 5; H. B. Oppenheim, *System des Völkerrechts*, 2nd edn. (Stuttgart: A. Kröner, 1866), 2–4; J. L. Klüber, *Droit des gens moderne de l'Europe* (Stuttgart: J. G. Cotta, 1819), 15–16; on philosophical natural law in the discipline of international law in the nineteenth century see Steiger, "Völkerrecht und Naturrecht zwischen Chr. Wolff und A. Lasson," 64–74.

60 For an assessment by a contemporary see A. M. von Bulmerincq, "Book review of: G. Jellink, *Die rechtliche Natur der Staatenverträge*" in *Jahrbuch für Gesetzgebung, Verwaltung und Volkswirthschaft*, 4 (1880), 183.

61 F. von Liszt, *Völkerrecht*, 11th edn. (Berlin: Springer, 1918); E. R. von Ullmann, *Völkerrecht* (Tübingen: Mohr, 1908) (revised ed. of 1st edn., 1898); P. Heilborn, "Grundbegriffe des Völkerrechts" in F. Stier-Somlò (ed.), *Handbuch des Völkerrechts*, vol. 1, part 1 (Stuttgart: Kohlhammer, 1912); J. Hatschek, *Völkerrecht als System rechtlich bedeutsamer Staatsakte* (Leipzig and Erlangen: Deichert, 1923).

62 On this, Jellinek unambiguously remarked, in line with the positivistic tradition of Kaltenborn and Bergbohm: "While all other areas of the law have long since recognized the untenability of a doctrine that creates both legal subjects and rights and duties on the basis of a legal order that precedes positive law and commands it, the old natural law is still celebrating its well-known orgies in the systems of international law, which are only now and then rudely interrupted by a 'denier of international law' and then soon begin again." G. Jellinek, *System der subjektiven öffentlichen Rechte*, 2nd edn., anastatic reprint of the 1905 edn. (first edn., 1892) (Tübingen: Mohr, 1919), 311.

principle by proceeding in a strictly positivistic manner and thus positing a sovereign will of the state as the basis from which the law of nations drew its validity. The middle way taken by Jellinek was an attempt to synthesize the two opposing constructs of international law, that is, the individualistic one based on the state, and the universalistic one. And Jellinek did not wish to dispense with either the free will of the state as the basis of the validity of all law, or with the assumption of an objective law of nations. The formal stringency of the Hegelian notion of will was to be reconciled with the liberal notion of a binding obligatory international law of a universal community of states, which was close to Jellinek's own liberal worldview. What Jellinek believed to be merely an apparent contradiction between the freedom of the sovereign state and a legally ordered community of states became the crucial theoretical question of his theory of international law.

I *The free will of the state as the formal ground of all law*

Jellinek's intent was to show that "the same notion of law that underlies the unquestioned parts of the law also forms the essence of the provisions that are valid for international relations."[63] With this, Jellinek was turning away from the assumption of a special substantive source for the law of nations, as for example the legal consciousness of the nations (Savigny, Hälschner),[64] or the idea of a reasonable order of the international community (Kaltenborn, von Mohl).[65] Instead, Jellinek, following Bergbohm, insisted that the same formal foundation had to be demonstrated for international law as for the other sub-fields of law.[66]

[63] G. Jellinek, *Die rechtliche Natur der Staatenverträge* (Vienna: A. Hölder, 1880), 1.

[64] P. E. Hälschner, "Zur wissenschaftlichen Begründung des Völkerrechts" in *Zeitschrift für volkstümliches Recht und nationale Gesetzgebung*, 1 (1844), 26 *et seq.*, adopted Savigny's conception.

[65] R. von Mohl, "Die Pflege der internationalen Gemeinschaft als Aufgabe des Völkerrechts" in his *Staatsrecht, Völkerrecht und Politik*, vol. 1: "Staatsrecht und Völkerrecht" (Tübingen: Mohr, 1860; reprint Graz, 1962), 584; for another, later example see F. von Martens, *Das internationale Recht der civilisierten Nationen*, German edn. by C. Bergbohm (Berlin: Weidmann, 1883), vol. 1, 200.

[66] Jellinek, *Die rechtliche Natur der Staatenverträge,* 2; the critical review of this work by Bulmerincq opposed this approach: "Every legal discipline is sovereign as a science and will not tolerate mediatization by other legal disciplines [...] The law of nations, however, remains a legal discipline also with a different legal principle and a different legal systematics." Quoted from: "Book review of: G. Jellinek, *Die rechtliche Natur der Staatenverträge,*" 254–257 (here 257); for Bulmerincq, the international belief in the law was the source of the law of nations (256).

It was this quest for a monistic conception of law that led Jellinek to the nation [*Volk*] as an organized entity and thus to the state as a basis of his conception. For from a strictly positivist perspective, one could recognize the legal character only of those propositions that could be traced back to a verifiable act of establishment. However, only the state – which established law as the "sovereign will of all"[67] – was a candidate for a law-creating organ.

Here Jellinek also explicitly invoked Hegel, who had demonstrated that as long as there was no power that was superimposed upon the states, the rights and duties of the states could find their origins only in their particular will.[68] Consequently, only propositions that were demonstrable as the will of the state could be regarded as law. In this way, the legal quality of international law was directly linked to the empirically verifiable process of creation. The attempt at a theoretical separation of the question of legal character [*Rechtsqualität*] from the norm-creating entity (states) by invoking the notion of the "idea of law" [*Rechtsidee*] was dismissed, in classic positivist fashion, as "speculation" from the realm of formal jurisprudence. Although Jellinek did not go so far as to describe the free will of the state as the final philosophical basis of the law, which he, too, believed could be found only in an "objective-metajuridical" principle, the jurist could not and should not recognize any formal ground of the law other than the free will of the community of nations and states.[69] Otherwise he would relinquish the boundaries he had so laboriously drawn around his subject, and that could very likely cast the legal scholar "into the confusion and lack of clarity that is to him the real chaos."[70]

Therefore, the legal character of international law – and for Jellinek there was no getting around this if one took a strict positivist approach – had to be grounded in the sovereign will of the state:

> The sharp formal development that the concept of law has undergone through the systematic work of the last decades, causes all demands that flow solely from the idea of law, for all the other value they may possess, to appear no longer as a law that can assert its existence alongside, above, or even against positive law . . . With this, the only possible path for a legal grounding of international law is indicated. It must be shown to be grounded in the free will of states or nations.[71]

[67] Jellinek, *Die rechtliche Natur der Staatenverträge*, 2.
[68] Ibid.; Hegel, *Grundlinien der Philosophie des Rechts oder Naturrechts und Staatswissenschaft im Grundrisse*, §333.
[69] Jellinek, *Die rechtliche Natur der Staatenverträge*, 3, note 3. [70] Ibid. [71] Ibid., 2.

The criticism that Kaltenborn and Fricker, as well as Bluntschli and von Mohl directed against Pütter's incorporation of the Hegelian concept of will into international law[72] was rejected by Jellinek, who argued that it negated the applicability of the general concept of law to the law of nations and in so doing prevented that area of the law from becoming more deeply pervaded by legal scholarship.[73]

In grounding international law theoretically in the sovereign will of the state, Jellinek was drawing directly on Carl Bergbohm's monograph mentioned previously, which had appeared three years earlier and which he described as an "excellent work."[74] But Jellinek wanted to go beyond Bergbohm and construct a truly binding law of nations on the shared voluntaristic premise. With this endeavour, Jellinek was turning against the theory of the "external state law," which had denied that international law possessed its own quality as objective law.

How, then, did Jellinek attempt to escape the dilemma of the voluntaristic foundation of international law that Fricker had spelled out? Jellinek's answer was two-tiered. First, by way of an abstract, preliminary examination, Jellinek discussed the question of how the free will of the state can be thought of as law in the first place. Here he introduced the figure of the self-obligating will. It was only in the second step that Jellinek raised the question whether the law created by the free will of the state could be objectified.

II The concept of "self-obligation" [Selbstverpflichtung] *and the obligatory nature of public law*

It is the idea of law's binding nature that Jellinek linked with the free will of the state when he wrote: "It does not exhaust the nature of law that it is the will of the state, for it is not the will of the state as such that is law, but the binding will of the state."[75] Because Jellinek sought to construct international law on the basis of the autonomy of the individual state, proof of the juridical existence of international law depended in his view

[72] R. von Mohl, *Die Geschichte und Literatur der Staatswissenschaften* (Erlangen: Enke, 1855), vol. 1, 382; Bluntschli, *Das moderne Völkerrecht der civilisierten Staaten*, 60.

[73] Jellinek, *Die rechtliche Natur der Staatenverträge*, 3, note 3. Bluntschli, in his review of this work, criticized precisely this starting point of the destructive Hegelian "juristic construct" and pointed instead to the "originary natural law" as the foundation of every legal statute; see Bluntschli, "Book review of G. Jellink, *Die rechtliche Natur der Staatenverträge*," 581.

[74] Jellinek, *Die rechtliche Natur der Staatenverträge*, 5. [75] Ibid., 6.

on the question of whether the state could bind itself through its own norms. For without a supraordinated, law-creating power, a relationship of obligation could be conceived of only as the identity between the party imposing the obligation and the party being obligated.[76]

The theoretical justification of the concept of self-obligation or "auto-limitation" provides a deeper insight into Jellinek's methodological approach. In a first step, the goal was to furnish the abstract proof of the possibility and necessity of creating law through self-obligation. In a second step, Jellinek then examined the deduced category of self-obligation against the practice of state law.[77]

This methodological approach proves to be characteristic of Jellinek's theory of international law. Deductively derived, clearly delimited concepts are inductively established – as simultaneous proof of their high potential for systematization – through the praxis of the state. First, the logical possibility of self-obligating one's own will is demonstrated through the insights of modern ethics and with examples from everyday life.[78] The plane of comparison here is the human will as the object of psychological understanding.[79] The verifiable act of will was merely the formal legal basis of the obligation. The final, psychological basis of every legal obligation, however, lay in the fact that the will regarded itself as bound by its expression.[80] Jellinek thus ascribed the idea of the binding nature of the law not to a normative-theoretical manifestation, but to the psychological manifestation of "the feeling to have obliged oneself."

Jellinek carried out the subsequent, inductive demonstration of the concept of self-obligation by way of state or constitutional law [*Staatsrecht*]: "It must be shown that a reflexive element exists within internal state law, that there are legal propositions – whose juristic quality is evident – that emanate from the state and bind the state. Should this demonstration succeed, the legal basis of international law will have been found."[81] In order to prove that the power of the state can be limited, he pursued a dialogue with the classic (Bodin, Hobbes, Rousseau) and contemporary (Stahl and Ihering) proponents of a theory

[76] Ibid., 7.
[77] "Deduction shall be followed by induction, to confirm as real, through the analysis of the concrete manifestations, what presented itself to us as necessary a priori." Ibid., 18.
[78] Ibid., 15.
[79] "Once the logical thinkability of self-obligation has been derived in this way, it is, on the other hand, ethically and legally necessary, legally in the sense of the idea of law, because it is the indispensable precondition of an ordered life within a community." Ibid., 16.
[80] Ibid., 17. [81] Ibid., 6–7.

of unlimitable state power, ultimately by using the practice of state law itself. In the realm of state law, he concluded, we are dealing with norms by which the state limited itself. Every law was, in the final analysis, a self-limitation of the will of the state.[82]

III The theory of the guaranteed norm

For Jellinek, the law was a psychological phenomenon inherent in human beings:[83] "This is the necessary consequence of the realization that the law is within us, that it is a function of the human community and must therefore rest on purely psychological elements."[84] Because Jellinek thus saw the law as merely a part of human intellectual constructs, the question of validity could also be disconnected from the prerequisite of an authority endowed with coercive power. Instead, the validity of the law rested on the belief in its validity among those to whom a legal norm was addressed.[85] Still, Jellinek, too, proceeded from the assumption that this psychological validity had to be "guaranteed." Such a guarantee existed if "socio-psychological forces" reinforced the motivating power of the prescriptions, thereby endowing them with a general ability to assert themselves against countervailing, individual motivations of the addressees of the norms.[86]

Jellinek thus gave preference to the broader notion of "guarantee" over that of "coercion." As guarantees of state law Jellinek pointed to the organization of the state, and for international law to the conditions of international relations and other shared interests of the community of states.[87] On the basis of this psychological approach, international law was placed on an equal footing with state law, and via the "theory of the guaranteed norm" it acquired, for Jellinek, the quality of law in spite of the absence of a supraordinated coercive power.

IV Jellinek's "objective international law"

1 The "nature of the thing" [*Natur der Sache*] as a principle of objectification

Jellinek conceptualized the sovereign will of the state as the final formal ground and the "feeling of self-obligation" as the final psychological

[82] Ibid., 27.

[83] G. Jellinek, *Allgemeine Staatslehre*, 2nd revised and expanded edn. (Berlin: O. Häring, 1905), 324.

[84] Ibid., 326. [85] Ibid. [86] Ibid. [87] Ibid., 328.

ground of the law. But how was it possible, on this basis, for norms to emerge that could bind the state to the self-obligation it had entered into, independent of individual changes in will? In answering this question, Jellinek's interest was directed above all at those legal rules that dealt with the creation, duration, and termination of treaties in international law: "Treaties between states can have the character of law only when there exist norms that stand above the treaties, and from which the treaties receive their legal validity."[88] These norms created a standard against which individual treaties between states had to measure themselves, and they were to that extent "objective in nature."[89] With this, Jellinek had arrived at the central question, namely, how such general norms that are the equivalent of law can be conceived between sovereign actors on the level of international law. To answer that question, Jellinek searched for a principle of objectification that could hold up to the arguments that the idea of self-obligation always implied simultaneously the possibility that the state could also free itself again from any possible content of will. Fricker articulated this critique of the voluntaristic theoretical approach this way: "What is valid only for me because I will it cannot create law between me and someone else who is my equal."[90]

The possibility, inherent in free will, of self-liberation through a change of will had to be limited in Jellinek's construct through an objective principle. And here the recourse to natural law principles was ruled out by Jellinek from the outset. Nor, according to Jellinek, was it possible to see the more frequently advocated analogies to private law as a sustainable construct on such a vital question.[91] Jellinek was clearly searching for a meta-juristic principle, since he also did not embark on the conceivable path of a positivistic derivation of a system of norms of customary international law with a relatively inherent stability vis-à-vis the changing will of the individual state.

Instead, Jellinek at this point revealed to his curious readers the – long withheld – final *philosophical* ground of law, which could be found only in an "objective principle": "This principle, which we must now name, is the nature of the conditions of life that require legal normativization.

[88] Jellinek, *Die rechtliche Natur der Staatenverträge*, 5. [89] Ibid., 4.

[90] Fricker, "Noch einmal das Problem des Völkerrechts," 394.

[91] "There must first be an objective international law, before analogy can begin its supplementary function." Jellinek, *Die rechtliche Natur der Staatenverträge*, 51.

This nature is as untouchable by the will of the state as nature is by the will as such . . . Here, then, we have an objective barrier to the will that is beyond any question."[92]

According to Jellinek, the objective nature of the state and of relations between states thus entailed a logically inherent limitation on the individual will of the state. It was among the elementary purposes of a state to engage in relations with other states, and to that extent it was also a demand of the nature of the state to create norms by which the relations to other states were regulated.[93]

Jellinek further attempted to identify a connecting link between the self-obligating will of the state and the "objective" law of nations that arose from the nature of the relations between states. To that end, Jellinek turned to the concept of "recognition." The moment a treaty was entered into, the contracting states, according to Jellinek, recognized the "objective elements" of the treaty. Through this "recognition,"[94] the subjective will admitted into itself the "objective elements," that is to say, the binding rules underlying the conclusion of the treaty and its termination.[95] Recognition is thus drawn from the subjective will and is regarded as confirmation on the part of the individual state of the objective nature of international relations. Objective law arises by way of this objective-legal enrichment of the element of the subjective will through the vehicle of recognition.

The circularity of this argument becomes especially obvious in Jellinek's answer to Fricker's question what would happen should the state refuse recognition. According to Jellinek, that should not be possible in the sense that recognition itself was, in turn, not within the discretion of the states, but followed inevitably from the objective nature of the relations between

[92] Ibid., 43; on the "nature of the thing" as an instrument for objectifying legal argumentation and for an overview of the relevant legal-theoretical literature see Th. Mayer-Maly, "Die Natur der Sache und die österreichische Rechtspraxis" in W. Krawietz, Th. Mayer-Maly, and O. Weinberger (eds.), *Objektivierung des Rechtsdenkens. Gedächtnisschrift für Ilmar Tammelo* (Berlin: Duncker & Humblot, 1984), 273 *et seq.*

[93] Jellinek, *Die rechtliche Natur der Staatenverträge*, 45; here the connection to Jellinek's doctrine of the purposes of the state becomes apparent, though it is striking that Jellinek rejected the existence of objective state purposes in the general theory of the state. For Jellinek this must therefore be a subjective purpose of the state, though one that is inherent in all states because of its objective nature. On the doctrine of the purpose of the state see Jellinek, *Allgemeine Staatslehre*, 223–258.

[94] "Recognition" [*Anerkennung*] thus means for Jellinek not merely recognizing another state as a legal subject; it has the additional function of the "acceptance" [*Übernahme*] of the objective law of the community of states into their own will. On recognition see Jellinek, *System der subjektiven öffentlichen Rechte*, 320.

[95] Jellinek, *Die rechtliche Natur der Staatenverträge*, 51.

states.[96] It is at this methodological point of fracture between a legal construction of international law based on the formally verifiable will of the state, and the sociological assumption of the state's communal constraint [*Gemeinschaftsgebundenheit*] as a necessity that precedes the will of the state that Jellinek's conception of himself as a jurist becomes clear: beyond formal positivism, legal scholars should or must incorporate psychological and sociological perspectives into the understanding of the law. Kelsen would later criticize this approach as "methodological syncretism" and contrast it with his own "pure" method of legal scholarship.

2 "Shared interests" and "purpose of the state" as the final sociological foundation of objective international law

Behind the objective nature of international relations as a barrier to the sovereign will of the state stood Jellinek's own conception of an international "community of states." For him, however, this community of states was not an idea of natural law, but the sociological product of the growing international intertwinement of state interests, of the kind that had become especially apparent in the nineteenth century.[97] To that extent, the cooperation of the individual state with other states was in accord with the purpose of the state.[98] From Jellinek's perspective, the state could no longer be described abstractly as an entity that was autarkic and could not be placed under obligation, since the assumptions derived from such a premise utterly failed to reflect the real conditions.[99] Instead, the state was contingent on the totality of the states in all aspects of its existence and actions. The "community of states" was a fact, and ignoring it made any deeper comprehension of the problems related to the state impossible.[100] This was especially true in the realm of the "civilized" European nations, which was, in Jellinek's words, wrapped in a "web of international legal norms."[101]

Ten years after his monograph on international treaty law, Jellinek continued to develop the relationship between "state community" and the "objective law of nations" in his work *System der subjectiven öffentlichen Rechte* [The System of Individual Rights]. Through membership[102] in the

[96] Ibid., 48.
[97] Jellinek, *System der subjektiven öffentlichen Rechte*, 320.
[98] Jellinek, *Die rechtliche Natur der Staatenverträge*, 41.
[99] Jellinek, *Die Lehre von den Staatenverbindungen*, 92.
[100] Ibid., 92–93. [101] Ibid., 96.
[102] A state acquired membership in turn through the instrument of recognition under international law: Jellinek, *System der subjektiven öffentlichen Rechte*, 320.

"community of states," the state was bound to "objective international law." From the perspective of the individual state, this resulted in demands upon the various members that they respect the state's personhood, extend the right of legation, and fulfill their obligations arising from treaties.[103] However, because of the specific architecture of his theory of international law, Jellinek could count not only the rule *pacta sunt servanda*, but also the *clausula rebus sic stantibus* as part of the objective law of nations.[104] The coexistence of the *clausula rebus sic stantibus* as a doctrinal emanation of state sovereignty and *pacta sunt servanda* as the basic precondition of a binding international law reflects Jellinek's attempt to bring together contrary constructs of international law.

For Jellinek, the derived "objective" norms of international law give rise to claims with a public-law character, which were admitted as rights of states [*Staatenrechte*] into his system of public law. However, this objective international law, which arises from the nature of the relations between states, constituted only about one-tenth of the tenets of international law.[105] The other nine-tenths were subjective treaties involving legal transactions, in which the states behaved like parties to a contract.[106] In that sense, the objectification of international law comprised for Jellinek only the sphere of an elementary constitution, which was in the final analysis deduced from an "objective nature" of the community of states that was presupposed a priori. However, in contrast to the principles of natural law, it was more like a procedural order of relations between states than a substantive constitution.[107]

[103] Ibid., 321.

[104]

> The state's self-obligation cannot be an absolute one either in duration or in terms of the sphere to which it applies. Since every state obligation, with respect to its substantive side, is a fulfillment of the purpose of state, it exists only as long as it satisfies that purpose. That is why every act of will by the state carries within itself the clause: *rebus sic stantibus*. The self-obligation of the state has absolute binding force only for the time during which the objective conditions, for the normativization of which the law is intended, have remained the same unchanged.
>
> Jellinek, *Die rechtliche Natur der Staatenverträge*, 40–41.

[105] Jellinek, *System der subjektiven öffentlichen Rechte*, 321. [106] Ibid.

[107] It is also in this context that one should place Jellinek's critique of the construction of so-called "basic rights" of states. These were nothing other than a description of the "*status libertatis*" under international law, though it could never be unequivocally laid down in legal terms. However, claims were being arbitrarily deduced from the basic rights derived from natural law. Instead of describing what was permitted to the state, the point was to examine the limitations on the state's freedom through the objective

The international law derived in this way carried the dual aspect of a universalistic construction of international law, on the one hand, and a construct based on the individual state, on the other: it was objective and thus binding law, but because of the absence of a superimposed authority, it remained for Jellinek an "anarchic law."[108] In Jellinek, the sought-after synthesis between the perspective of international law based on the individual state and the universalistic perspective was accomplished through a sociological approach that reckoned relations with other states among the most elementary or inherently necessary purposes of the state. For him, the legal community of states was not, as in Kaltenborn or Wolff, the starting point for the construction of international law; instead, the "objective law of nations" of this community of states[109] was the sociologically necessary, final limitation on the state's presupposed freedom of will. In that sense, the emphasis on the sociological dimension of international law was certainly congruent with Jellinek's two-sided theory of the state, according to which the state should be seen and analyzed on the one side as a sociological, and on the other side as a legal phenomenon.[110] In addition, he sought to defend the legal character of international law against those who denied its very existence with the help of the concepts of "self-obligation" and "guarantee," which he introduced via a psychological perspective on the law.

With this, Jellinek had methodically expanded Bergbohm's strictly voluntaristic international law positivism through his own multi-dimensional approach. As he saw it, this allowed him to dissolve the

law of nations. On the basic rights see Jellinek, *System der subjektiven öffentlichen Rechte*, 316–320.

108 Jellinek, *Allgemeine Staatslehre*, 368.

109 Jellinek had already tried in his *Habilitation* thesis on criminal law to reconcile the premise of the free individual with the conception of a community of individuals. In his construct, the community took precedence, "because we stand from the first to the last breath under the rule of large, social laws, in accordance with which we must all complete the cycles of existence." Quoted from G. Jellinek, *Ausgewählte Schriften und Reden von Georg Jellinek* (Berlin: O. Häring, 1911), vol. 1, 69. The construct state/community of states from *Die rechtliche Natur der Staatenverträge*, published a year later, followed the same structural principle. The freedom of the state encounters its limits only in its reasonable nature as a state, which is shaped by the necessary coexistence with other states. The objective law of nations thus appears as the "ethical minimum" in the coexistence of the states. In connection with criminal law, Reinhard Moos spoke of an "objective social ethics" in Jellinek: R. Moos, *Der Verbrechensbegriff in Österreich im 18. und 19. Jahrhundert. Sinn und Strukturwandel* (Bonn: L. Röhrscheid, 1968), 489–493 (here 493).

110 Jellinek, *Allgemeine Staatslehre*, 9 *et seq.*

antagonism between the view of international law as based on the concrete will of individual states, and the universalistic view of international law as a legal order binding upon states. In fact, however, Jellinek had not dissolved the oscillating movement between the subjective and the objective principle, but had instead integrated it into his own theory as an inherent tension.

D Heinrich Triepel and the "common will" [*Gemeinwille*] as a principle of objectivization

The positivist explanatory model for a binding law of nations à la Jellinek initially found numerous adherents in Germany, but also in other European countries. The main German-language textbooks on international law at the time,[111] by Ullmann,[112] Heilborn,[113] and Liszt,[114] referred directly to Jellinek when explaining the basis of obligation of international law. Although French international lawyers mostly drew upon the doctrine of the basic rights of states [*droits fondamentaux des états*], criticized by Jellinek as a kind of clandestine natural law, Carré de Malberg,[115] under the influence of Jellinek, also traced international law back to the self-obligating will of the state.[116]

The foundation that Jellinek had offered, by bridging the premise of the free will of the state and the idea of a binding order of international law, had an unusual ability to connect with other theories. Precisely because this approach did not rely exclusively on the idea of the sovereign will of the state, it set itself apart from the conservative "Bonn School" and its revival of the Hegelian theory of "external state

[111] Karl Strupp prefaces his own principles of international law with an overview of the most important textbooks: K. Strupp, *Grundzüge des positiven Völkerrechts*, 5th edn. (Bonn and Cologne: L. Röhrscheid,1932), VII.

[112] Von Ullmann, *Völkerrecht*, 250.

[113] Heilborn, "Grundbegriffe des Völkerrechts," 29–31.

[114] Von Liszt, *Völkerrecht*, 2.

[115] R. Carré de Malberg, *Contribution à la théorie générale de l'état, spécialement d'après les donnés fournis par le droit constitutionnel français* (Paris: L. Tenin, 1920), 234.

[116] On the French development at the *fin de siècle* and the prevailing doctrine of the basic rights of states see L. Duguit, *Souveraineté et Liberté. Leçons faites à l'Université Columbia (New York) 1920–1921* (Paris: Alcan, 1922), 105–110. In his lectures, Duguit compared the German doctrine, influenced by Jellinek, to the French doctrine of the basic rights of states: "La doctrine allemande était plus brutale. J'en trouve surtout l'expression dans les ouvrages d'un juriste allemand éminent, dont on ne saurait méconnaître le role et l'influence, le professeur d'Heidelberg, aujourd'hui décédé, Jellinek" (107–108).

law."[117] It could even be used by progressive international lawyers with a pacifist background like the Swiss Nippold, who, within the milieu of the Hague Movement, was one of the most ardent champions of the idea of international arbitration and a general juridification of international relations.[118]

Heinrich Triepel's doctrine of agreement [*Vereinbahrungslehre*] can also be seen as a critique and simultaneously as the further development of Jellinek's ideas. Triepel, among Germany's most renowned scholars of international law until the 1930s, likewise sought to construct the law of nations as an objective legal order without having to give up the subjective principle. However, he rejected the recourse solely to the self-obligating individual state as inadequate: "That the will is capable of subordinating itself to its own commandments is certainly correct for the realm of ethics. But that a legal obligation for a subject toward other subjects can come only from its own commandment to itself, is something I regard as a logical absurdity."[119]

According to Triepel, state law and international law must be traceable to different sources because of their invariably different objects of regulation.[120] Triepel further maintained that only a will that was superior to those to whom the law was addressed was capable of creating objective law. This consideration led him to posit the existence of a "common will" [*Gemeinwille*] of the states that was independent of the will of the individual state.[121] This common will did not arise from treaties of a

[117] The so-called Bonn School revived the subjective principle of international law in strict adherence to Hegel. On the members of the Bonn School see Strupp, *Grundzüge des positiven Völkerrechts*, 9–10. Rejecting the attempts at objectivization undertaken by Jellinek and Triepel, this School drew again directly on the Hegelian construct of international law. The sovereign state was the center of law, and international law was merely "external state law." According to Philipp Zorn – the founder of the School and advisor on international law to Emperor Wilhelm II – and his son, Albert Zorn, an agreement among states should "occur only by way of self-obligation after a preceding agreement about the shared interests to be regulated, and the legal nature of international law thus rests on this obligation of the individual state through its will and thus on its right vis-à-vis the other states." Quoted from Ph. Zorn, *Das Staatsrecht des Deutschen Reiches* (Berlin: J. Guttentag, 1883), 422.

[118] O. Nippold, *Die Fortbildung des Verfahrens in völkerrechtlichen Streitigkeiten* (Leipzig: Duncker & Humblot, 1907), 46; however, Nippold described "international solidarity" as the source of objective international law.

[119] H. Triepel, *Völkerrecht und Landesrecht* (Leipzig: C. L. Hirschfeld, 1899), 77.

[120] Ibid., 18 *et seq.*

[121] The same argument was put forth by Anzilotti with the "volontà collettiva": D. Anzilotti, *Corso di diritto internazionale*, 2nd edn. (Rome: Athenaeum, 1912), 26;

contractual nature, which represented only the respective wills of the individual states, but only from "agreements" [*Vereinbarungen*] that carried objective obligations.[122] According to Triepel, such agreements arose when states, through an agreement of wills, not only established subjective rights and obligations through a legal transaction, but also sought to create objective, lasting law.[123] In this way, Jellinek's "objective international law," which was tied back to state recognition and derived from the objective nature of the community of states, was thus replaced with the concept of "agreement" adopted from Binding.[124] For Triepel, the question from where the agreement acquired its binding force was a meta-legal one: "I believe one can be content with the assurance that the state feels obligated by it."[125]

The tremendous impact of *Völkerrecht und Landesrecht* in legal scholarship was based less on the doctrine of agreement, however, and more on the conclusion that Triepel drew from these reflections for the relationship between international law and national law: "International law and national law are not only different segments of the law, but different legal orders. They are two orders that at most touch, never intersect."[126]

The train of thought that led to the dualist separation of international law and national law proceeded by two steps: starting from the premise that the object of regulation in international law was invariably separate from state law, Triepel first construed the "common will" arising from the "agreement" as a specific source of international law. From the existence of different sources, Triepel's circular argument in turn concluded that international law and state law were separate legal orders.

This line of argument stands and falls with the assumption that the objects of regulation in international law and state law are necessarily separate and distinct. Against the backdrop of state practice at the *fin de siècle*, such a premise apparently seemed convincing. International law regulated relations among states, state law regulated the life of individuals on the territory of the state. From the objects of regulations that

later, Anzilotti would resort to Kelsen's concept of the basic norm; see D. Anzillotti, *Lehrbuch des Völkerrechts* (Berlin and Leipzig: W. de Gruyter, 1929), 33.

122 Triepel, *Völkerrecht und Landesrecht*, 63 *et seq.*

123 "The states can create objective law if they agree on a rule by which their future behavior shall be permanently determined." Triepel, *Völkerrecht und Landesrecht*, 70.

124 K. Binding, "Die Gründung des norddeutschen Bundes" in *Festgabe der Leipziger Juristenfakultät für Windscheid* (Leipzig: Veit, 1889), 69 *et seq.*

125 Triepel, *Völkerrecht und Landesrecht*, 82.

126 Ibid., 156, 256.

were supposedly ineluctably distinct, Triepel inferred a separate source for international law; the different sources in turn gave rise to the inherent logical division into two legal orders that should be completely separated from each other. With this circular reasoning, the notion of "dualism" had made its way into international legal scholarship.

Triepel did not stop there, however, but placed the legal order of international law above that of state law. As evidenced by the relationship of the state law of the German empire to the legal orders of the member states, supraordinated legal sources could to a certain extent grant subordinated legal entities the power to create their own law, or take away that power.[127] Thanks to the construction of international law out of the "common will," it could rightly be described as a "higher legal order."[128] Triepel thus arrived in the end at the assumption of the primacy of international law. Whereas many public lawyers had declared the sovereign state in the nineteenth century the alpha and omega of any legal order, the young Berlin lecturer at the end of the century subordinated national law to international law through a new positivist explanatory model. One year after the first Hague Conference, Triepel, building on fragments of voluntaristic theoretical constructs, had conceived a model to explain the binding effect of interstate regulations that were spreading in various sectorial areas, without having to engage in an open conflict with the prevailing notion of sovereignty. Separating the spheres of state law and international law and introducing the notion of agreement or common will as the source of international law had allowed Triepel to cloak the dilemma of the voluntaristic basis through the concept of agreement. For while the agreement arose from the sovereign will of the state, it simultaneously transformed the sum of individual wills into the "common will" as a source of international law that was different and autonomous from state law.

Völkerrecht und Landesrecht became the most successful German-language monograph on international law at the dawn of the twentieth century. The influence of Triepel, who still upheld the fundamentals of his theory in the 1920s,[129] on the international legal literature, especially in Germany and Italy, was multifarious. Hold-Ferneck declared the "agreeing will" of the states[130] to be the foundation of the law of nations,

[127] Ibid., 166. [128] Ibid., 266–277.

[129] H. Triepel, "Les rapports entre le droit interne et le droit internationale," *RCADI*, 1 (1923), 77 *et seq.*

[130] A. von Hold-Ferneck, *Lehrbuch des Völkerrechts* (Leipzig: Meiner,1930), 110.

Niemeyer said it was the "consensus of states,"[131] and Hatschek adopted the separation between agreements and contractual treaties in his textbook on international law.[132] The common will appeared as "common consent" also in Oppenheim.[133] Moreover, this dualistic approach was widely adopted not only in Germany,[134] but also in Italy.[135]

Conclusion

German international law theory in the nineteenth century follows, beyond its close link to the theory and method of general public law, a particular discursive logic. The explanation for this lies in the central question underlying every quest for a theoretical foundation of international law: namely, the relationship of the state to the norms of international law. It is the problem of whether – and if so, how – international law can be theoretically construed as an objective law of an international community of states that confronts the individual states with a claim to be binding upon them. Such a construal posed specific difficulties for scholars, because in contrast to state law, international law lacked a central institutionalized authority that stood above the states and was charged with enacting norms and implementing the law. Those who created the law and those to whom the law was addressed were identical.

As a result, two contrary constructs of international law emerged in the debate over a positivistic foundation within German-language international legal scholarship: according to the "objective principle" that Kaltenborn introduced into the positivist discourse, the "community of states" represented a higher legal community in which the states functioned as organs of this legal order. By contrast, the move to place international law on a voluntaristic foundation, which went back to Hegel, regarded the sovereign will of the state – in the sense of a subjective-individualistic understanding – as the fundamental principle

[131] Th. Niemeyer, *Völkerrecht* (Berlin: W. de Gruyter, 1923), 12.

[132] Hatschek, *Völkerrecht als System rechtlich bedeutsamer Staatsakte*, 8 *et seq.*

[133] L. F. Oppenheim, *International Law. A Treatise* (London: Longmans, Green, 1905), vol. 1, 15.

[134] Explicitly in G. A. Walz, *Völkerrecht und Staatliches Recht. Untersuchungen über die Einwirkungen des Völkerrechts auf das innerstaatliche Recht* (Stuttgart: W. Kohlhammer, 1933), 11 *et seq.*, though he regards the term "dualism" as linguistically incorrect and speaks instead of a "pluralistic" theory. After the Nazis came to power, Walz readily placed his creative academic energy in the service of Nazi ideology; see Stolleis, *A History of Public Law in Germany, 1914–1945*, 412–413.

[135] For example, Anzilotti, *Lehrbuch des Völkerrechts*, 36–47.

of the law of nations.[136] Throughout the nineteenth century, these two positions were repeatedly revived – under the influence of methodological revisions – in German and Austrian jurisprudence. I have tried to show that the objective and the subjective approaches in German legal discourse, by each neglecting the other principle, opened themselves up – or became invariably vulnerable – to attack. Thus, the objective grounding of international law, which dispensed with the concretely demonstrable will of the individual state, was criticized as mere deduction or blatant natural law. Conversely, critics of the construct that based itself on the vacillating will of individual states charged that it was unable to establish the objectively binding nature of international law.[137]

At the end of the nineteenth century, Jellinek and Triepel (building on Jellinek) sought to synthesize the subjective and the objective principle in their theories. The "common will" (Triepel) and the sociologically grounded "objective nature" of relations between states (Jellinek) were set up as objectifying principles that constrained the subjective will of the state. However, the two antagonistic positions were not really synthesized in this way; rather, they were incorporated into the theoretical approaches as an unresolved tension.

[136] J. von Bernstorff, "Georg Jellinek – Völkerrecht als modernes öffentliches Recht im fin de siècle" in S. L. Paulson and M. Schulte (eds.), *Georg Jellinek. Beiträge zur Leben und Werk* (Tübingen: Mohr Siebeck, 2000), 185–186.

[137] For a comprehensive postmodern account of the inner movement ("ascending" and "descending" arguments) of current international legal doctrine, see M. Koskenniemi, *From Apology to Utopia. The Structure of International Legal Argument* (Helsinki: Finnish Lawyers' Pub. Co., 1989).

2

Kelsenian formalism as critical methodology in international law

On the basis of a new, critical methodology of public law, Kelsen and his students sought to come up with an "objective" architecture of international law. One factor that was particularly influential for Kelsen's theory of international law was his critical engagement with that of Georg Jellinek and the German *Staatswillenspositivismus* [state-centered positivism]. Kelsen had outlined his fundamental critique of Jellinek's theory of the state already in his *Hauptprobleme der Staatsrechtslehre* [Main Problems in the Theory of Public Law], and he carried it further in his first monograph on international law, written during the First World War, *Das Problem der Souveränität und die Theorie des Völkerrechts* [The Problem of Sovereignty and the Theory of International Law]. It is remarkable how deeply Kelsen, in this fundamental work, was influenced by the Wolffian–Kaltenbornian construction of an "objective" international law, combining it with his new methodological approach to public law. In that sense, this monograph, a foundational work for the Vienna School's theory of international law, can be seen as picking up on Kaltenborn's work while turning away emphatically from the international law theories of Georg Jellinek.

A A new methodological tool kit

Kelsen's *Main Problems in the Theory of Public Law* and *The Problem of Sovereignty* sought to place the traditional doctrine of state and international law on a new methodological foundation. In the final analysis, Kelsen was concerned with nothing less than establishing legal scholarship as an autonomous "scientific" field. To that end, he developed a separate juristic methodology, one that was increasingly epistemologically underpinned in the 1920s. The application of what was a novel methodological tool kit in legal scholarship led Kelsen to a fundamental critique of the central, doctrinal conceptions of the German public-law tradition.

I Methodological dualism as the starting point

The main point of attack for Kelsen was what he regarded as the inadequate methodological distinction between *Sein* [Is] and *Sollen* [Ought], which made a scientific construction of public law impossible.[1] The concept of methodological dualism, the beginnings of which were already evident in Jellinek,[2] was radicalized by Kelsen, who was drawing on Georg Simmel, Wilhelm Windelband, and Heinrich Rickert.[3] Kelsen regarded the multi-dimensional analysis of law, which was characteristic of Jellinek, as epistemologically inadmissible. Especially the use of insights from sociology and psychology in interpreting legal norms was for Kelsen an unacceptable jumble of different methods. According to Kelsen's strict methodological dualism, one could not derive from the "Is-statements" of sociology any conclusions that were relevant for jurisprudence as a doctrine of normative "Ought." The principle difference in the explanatory *Denkform* [form of thinking] of the "Is" and the normative *Denkform* of the "Ought" revealed, in Kelsen's words, two "separate worlds" that were irreconcilable.[4]

And yet, while insisting on the separation between these divergent methodologies, there was no question for Kelsen that there could be a mutual enrichment of "Is-sciences" [*Seinswissenschaften*] like sociology, for instance, and legal scholarship:[5] "Nor let it be said that the jurist may not also undertake sociological, psychological, or historical studies. On the contrary! These are necessary; except that the jurist must always remain aware that as a sociologist, psychologist, or historian he is pursuing a very different path from the one that leads him to his

[1] On the methodological dualism in his early work see S. L. Paulson, "Kelsen's Earliest Legal Theory: Critical Constructivism" in S. L. Paulson and B. Litschewski Paulson (eds.), *Normativity and Norms. Critical Perspectives on Kelsenian Themes* (Oxford University Press, 1998), 23 *et seq.*; C. Heidemann, *Die Norm als Tatsache. Zur Normentheorie Hans Kelsens* (Baden-Baden: Nomos, 1997), 24–28.

[2] On Jellinek's rejection of methodological syncretism see Jellinek, *System der subjektiven öffentlichen Rechte*, 17.

[3] Paulson, "Kelsen's Earliest Legal Theory: Critical Constructivism," 29 *et seq.*

[4] H. Kelsen, *Hauptprobleme der Staatsrechtslehre, entwickelt aus der Lehre vom Rechtssatz*, 2nd edn. with an added preface (Tübingen: J. B. Mohr, 1923), 8; on this see G. H. von Wright, "Is and Ought" in Paulson and Paulson (eds.), *Normativity and Norms*, 365–367.

[5] H. Kelsen, "Zur Soziologie des Rechts. Kritische Betrachtungen," *Archiv für Sozialwissenschaft und Sozialpolitik*, 34 (1912), 602; on this see M. Kraft-Fuchs, "Kelsens Staatstheorie und die Soziologie des Staates," *ZöR*, 11 (1931), 413, and from the perspective of the history of the discipline, Stolleis, *A History of Public Law in Germany*, 157–158.

specifically juridical insights. He must never incorporate the results of his explanatory examination into his construction of normative concepts."[6]

Legal "science" was to be established as an autonomous, purely normative discipline. To that end, Kelsen developed in his *Main Problems in the Theory of Public Law* a separate doctrine of the legal proposition [*Rechtssatz*] that was supposed to encompass the special Ought-structure of the law. The legal proposition represented a normative interpretative pattern for the existing, enacted legal norms that were available to the legal scholar. In its further developed form of 1925, the legal proposition, made up of a primary and a secondary norm, stated the following: under certain circumstances, a person ought to behave in a certain way; if he does not act this way, another person should coerce him through a specific legal procedure.[7] The legal proposition thus asserts that a specific coercive act "*ought*" to take place if certain preconditions are being fulfilled (behavior by a person that deviates from the norm). The legal proposition is not a substantive moral command, but a "hypothetical judgment" that constitutes the reciprocal interconnection of factual preconditions referred to by the norm [*Rechtsbedingung*] and the prescribed legal consequences [*Rechtsfolge*].[8] Kelsen described the "*ought*" linkage between the factual incident referred to by the norm and the prescribed legal consequences as "imputation."[9]

The "normative imputation" concept [*normative Zurechnung*] was introduced by Kelsen as the specific inherent principle [*Eigengesetzlichkeit*] of the law.[10] Comparable to causality in the natural sciences, it functions as an a priori category of legal knowledge. In this way, Is and Ought as the two forms of scientific thinking introduced in his *Main Problems in the Theory of Public Law* assumed, in the "classical phase" of the Pure Theory of Law after 1921 (in Paulson's periodization), the status of "pure" epistemological devices in the sense of the Kantian categories.[11] The Is was now to correspond to the a priori category of causality as a form of knowledge in natural sciences. By contrast, Ought, as the form

[6] Kelsen, *Hauptprobleme*, 42; H. Kelsen, "Law, State, and Justice in the Pure Theory of Law," *Yale Law Journal*, 57 (1958), 383; for a more comprehensive discussion of this problem see Dreier, *Rechtslehre*, 136–140.

[7] H. Kelsen, *Allgemeine Staatslehre* (Berlin: J. Springer, 1925), 51.

[8] H. Kelsen, *Reine Rechtslehre. Einleitung in die rechtswissenschaftliche Problematic* (Leipzig and Vienna: F. Deuticke, 1934) 22; *Introduction to the Problems of Legal Theory*. A translation of the First Edition of the *Reine Rechtslehre* or Pure Theory of Law. Translated by B. Litschewski Paulson and S. L. Paulson. With an introduction by S. L. Paulson (Oxford University Press, 1992), 23.

[9] Ibid. [10] Ibid. [11] Heidemann, *Die Norm als Tatsache*, 56–57.

of normative imputation, was to function as the specific form of knowledge in jurisprudence.[12] As Kelsen saw it, the legal norms were generated by the jurist through the intellectual process of applying this form of knowledge to the legal material.[13] In this way, the neo-Kantian doctrine of the object-creating power of methodology gained entry into legal scholarship through Kelsen.[14] In spite of the change in meaning that the Is-Ought juxtaposition experienced, morphing from merely different forms of thinking in the early work into transcendental categories of scientific and legal knowledge in the classical phase, the critical thrust remained the same. The autonomy of legal science as a purely normative science[15] was to be secured by identifying a specifically jurisprudential concept of Ought (normative imputation). With this, Kelsen had developed a theoretical approach to the field of law that allowed him to banish sociological Is-statements from legal scholarship as methodologically erroneous.[16]

By introducing the concept of normative imputation, however, Kelsen sought to free the science of the law not only from sociological "Is-statements," but also from non-legal "Ought-statements." The issue here was especially the rejection of natural law.[17] For Kelsen, the Pure Theory of Law was a "theory of positive law" in that its aim was to eliminate from the subject matter theories of substantive justice, morality and ethical considerations.[18] By distancing itself from natural law thinking as well as from the methodologically "syncretistic" blending of Is and Ought, the Pure Theory of

12 Kelsen, *Hauptprobleme*, Preface, 7. 13 Ibid.

14 On Kelsen and neo-Kantianism see S. L. Paulson, "Läßt sich die Reine Rechtslehre transzendental begründen?," *Rechtstheorie*, 21 (1990), 155–179; S. Hammer, "Kelsens Grundnormkonzeption als neukantianische Erkenntnistheorie des Rechts?" in S. L. Paulson and R. Walter (eds.), *Untersuchungen zur Reinen Rechtslehre* (Vienna: Manz, 1986), 210–213; H. Holzhey, "Kelsens Rechts- und Staatslehre in ihrem Verhältnis zum Neukantianismus" in S. L. Paulson and R. Walter (eds.), *Untersuchungen zur Reinen Rechtslehre*, 167–192; Dreier, *Rechtslehre*, 56–90.

15 W. Ebenstein, *Die rechtsphilosophische Schule der Reinen Rechtslehre* (Prague: Taussig & Taussig, 1938, reprint Frankfurt am Main: Sauer & Auvermann, 1969), 71; W. Schluchter, *Rationalismus der Weltbeherrschung. Studien zu Max Weber* (Frankfurt am Main: Suhrkamp, 1983).

16 On this see the critical reflections by S. L. Paulson, "Kelsen's Earliest Legal Theory: Critical Constructivism" in Paulson and Paulson (eds.), *Normativity and Norms*, 33 *et seq.*; on the impossibility of a "pure" perception of the law in the Kelsenian sense see O. Weinberger, "Reine oder funktionalistische Rechtsbetrachtung?" in O. Weinberger et al. (eds.), *Reine Rechtslehre im Spiegel ihrer Fortsetzer und Kritiker* (Vienna and New York: Springer, 1988), 226–234.

17 On this see J. Raz, "The Purity of Pure Theory" in Paulson and Paulson (eds.), *Normativity and Norms*, 239–241.

18 H. Kelsen, *Reine Rechtslehre* (1934), 1; *Problems of Legal Theory*, 7.

Law created the cognitive preconditions for the autonomous existence of a legal medium whose content was not scientifically predetermined but fully contingent.[19] According to Kelsen, legal positivism in this sense secured the autonomy of the law, since "only the positivistic understanding of the law creates the prerequisite for the existence of an autonomous legal order and legal 'science,' while the natural law perspective allows the law, finally and ultimately, to be absorbed into reason, morality, and nature, and legal scholarship into ethics, politics, or even natural sciences."[20] In Kelsen's view, then, there was a reciprocal connection between the autonomy of the sphere of law and a purified "science" of the law.[21] According to Kelsen, only strict positivism, understood as the most neutral possible description of the law, allowed for emergence of an autonomous legal order. At the same time, jurisprudence, as well, could historically only emerge as a truly autonomous "science" once the law had uncoupled itself from religion and from the sole basis of customary law.[22] The Pure Theory of Law reflected the process by which the law itself had attained autonomy in that it sought to shield legal scholarship from limits imposed from outside the law.[23]

In international law, this process of autonomization proved especially difficult in that, contrary to the modern constitutional state, most of its norms were of a customary-law nature. In addition, compared to state law, its link to philosophical natural law continued to be very close. As a reaction to the renewed, fundamental challenge to the legal character of international law during the First World War, the 1920s had witnessed a renaissance of natural-law theories in international legal scholarship.[24] Following the First World War, which contemporaries experienced as a civilizational rupture on a world-historical scale,[25] a growing longing for eternal values, metaphysics, and a substantive foundation of the law had

[19] On the "idea of the autonomy of jurisprudence" see A. Baratta, "Rechtspositivismus und Gesetzespositivismus: Gedanken zu einer 'naturrechtlichen' Apologie des Rechtspositivismus," *ARSP*, 54 (1968), 337.

[20] Kelsen, *Problem der Souveränität*, 87. [21] Dreier, *Rechtslehre*, 104.

[22] Kelsen, *Hauptprobleme*, 40.

[23] See the characterization of the Pure Theory of Law by Dreier: "With its thesis of the inherent arbitrariness [*Beliebigkeit*] and boundlessness it reflects – virtually – modern society's total power of disposition over itself" in *Rechtslehre*, 104.

[24] Josef Kohler, for example, saw the reason for the incompleteness of international law in the fact that it still lacked the shared basis of a natural law, from which every law had to proceed: J. Kohler, *Grundlagen des Völkerrechts* (Stuttgart: Enke, 1918).

[25] On this see M. Stolleis: "The world 'after,' after the 'storms of steel,' was hardly recognizable as an offshoot of the world 'before.' In that sense, 1914 remains an enormous rupture. It marked the first great explosion of aggression in the era of nationalism." Stolleis, *Der lange Abschied*, 22.

made itself felt. The old positivist law of nations had been unable to prevent either the outbreak of the war nor the large-scale violations of the laws of war.[26] Once again, the objective principle was sought out in the Christian doctrine of natural law, which was believed to have been overcome by the "juristic method." Under the impact of the gas-poisoned trenches, Catholic natural law had been rediscovered in Germany first by Cathrein, Mausbach, and Schilling,[27] and in France by Louis le Fur.[28] Kelsen and Kunz also rejected these newer natural law approaches with the goal of ensuring the "purity of the science of international law."[29]

The introduced dichotomy of Is/Ought, and the specifically jurisprudential Ought-category they worked out allowed Kelsen and his students henceforth to castigate both sociological and ethical and moral considerations in the analysis of norms as methodologically inappropriate. As they saw it, this was the only way for the law to become a medium of contingent norm-creation also on the international level. But without noticing it, the Vienna School of legal theory – driven by its rigorous, dualistic-methodological impulse – had thus stepped onto the fine line that separated a "purified" jurisprudence of international law from the discipline's complete loss of meaning as one approach to explaining the multi-layered phenomenon of the law in international relations. For that reason, Kelsen and Kunz tried, especially from the beginning of the 1930s, to recover a multi-dimensional perspective of the function of law in international relations by shoring up their theory with publications that were clearly displayed as falling within the categories of

[26] On this from the French perspective, the speech of A. Weiss in 1924 before the French Académie des sciences morales et politiques: "Les populations civiles ont étés décimés, ranconnées, déportés, martyrisées de toute manière de l'envahisseur. En un mot, toutes les règles jusqu'ici considérées comme assurant, en temps de guerre, la commune sauvegarde de l'humanité, ont étés foulées aux pieds." Quoted in B. Miliouch, *Le Fondement du Droit International* (Paris: A. Pedone, 1928), 90.

[27] In 1918, immediately following the end of the war, the Jesuit Viktor Cathrein tried to revive the Christian roots of international law. The theologians Josef Mausbach and Otto Schilling, in their own monographs, drawing on the Spanish late scholastics, endorsed this view. See V. Cathrein, *Die Grundlage des Völkerrechts* (Freiburg i. Br.: Herder, 1918); J. Mausbach, *Naturrecht und Völkerrecht* (Freiburg i. Br.: Herder, 1918); O. Schilling, *Das Völkerrecht nach Thomas von Aquin* (Freiburg i. Br.: Herder, 1918).

[28] In France, Louis le Fur established a natural law theory of international law; see L. Le Fur, "La théorie du droit naturel depuis le XVIIème siècle et la doctrine moderne," *RCADI*, 18/III (1927), 259 *et seq*.

[29] On natural law in the doctrine of international law see J. L. Kunz, *Völkerrechtswissenschaft und Reine Rechtslehre* (Leipzig: F. Deuticke, 1923), 72–74.

legal sociology and legal policy, though without having to renounce their strict methodological dualism. However, building on the premise of a methodological dualism, Kelsen, in his 1920 book *The Problem of Sovereignty and the Theory of International Law*, initially developed a new kit of critical tools that allowed him to fundamentally question the traditional conceptual apparatus of public international law.

II Methodological critique through the "identity thesis"

Starting from his strict separation of Is and Ought, Kelsen had already – in his "constructivist" phase – criticized the "dogma of the will" in jurisprudence as the result of a blending of psychological and sociological Is-considerations and normative Ought-considerations.[30] In fact, from a strict normative perspective, the "will" of the assumed personified state [*willensfähige Staatspersönlichkeit*] was nothing other than the central point of imputation for all acts of the organs of the particular state.[31] In this way, Kelsen had tried, in his *Habilitation* thesis, to replace the "state as a legal person of will" with the concept of formal imputation.[32] Kelsen developed this approach further in *The Problem of Sovereignty and the Theory of International Law* and arrived at the assumption of the complete identity of state and law. The "identity thesis" became the pivotal point in the sought-after revision of the conceptual apparatus of international law.

The provocative assumption that the state and the law were congruent terms for the legal scholar was based on two different strands of justification, though Kelsen often intertwined them in *The Problem of Sovereignty and the Theory of International Law*. The first strand is the demand for methodological dualism described above, according to which the state can be represented in jurisprudence not as an Is- or causal construct, but exclusively as a normative order.[33] The second strand is Kelsen's theory or critique of "juristic fictions" [*Juristische Fiktionen*]. It was part of Kelsen's critical methodology already in his

[30] Kelsen, *Hauptprobleme*, 162 *et seq.*; see Heidemann, *Die Norm als Tatsache*, 35.

[31] Kelsen, *Hauptprobleme*, 189; on the notion of imputation and its origins in nineteenth-century German legal thought see S. L. Paulson, "Kelsen's Earliest Legal Theory," 33 *et seq.*, and generally N. MacCormick, "Persons as Institutional Facts" in: Weinberger et al. (eds.), *Reine Rechtslehre*, 371–393.

[32] Paulson, "Kelsen's Earliest Legal Theory," 33; Paulson calls this early phase of Kelsen's legal theory the constructivist phase; on this phase see also Heidemann, *Die Norm als Tatsache*, 23–33.

[33] Kelsen, *Hauptprobleme*, XVI.

work *The Problem of Sovereignty and the Theory of International Law*. According to this theory, the notion of the state as a "person" and "bearer" of the law was a "personifying fiction" [*personifikative Fiktion*] used by the prevailing doctrine.[34] With reference to Vaihinger's *Die Philosophie als Ob*, Kelsen recognized in the jurisprudential use of the concept of the "*willensfähige Staatsperson*" a doubling or "hypostatization."[35] The real function of the legal person as a unifying point of imputation of norms became in traditional legal scholarship a living, human-like figure, a state organism. The latter was mythically transfigured and endowed with primal omnipotence: "Legal thinking is a thoroughly personifying one and – to the extent that it hypostatizes the persons it creates – can be compared to mythological thinking, which, anthropomorphically, suspects a dryad behind every tree, a spring god behind every spring, Apollo behind the sun, thus doubling nature as an object of cognition."[36]

The construction of the legal person, an achievement of nineteenth-century legal thought, was reduced by Kelsen down to its normative core. In Kelsen's eyes, this was merely a metaphor for the unity of a system of legal norms.[37] The notion of a dualism of state and law, according to which the "unbounded Leviathan" had to be tamed by the law, was to be abolished by the identity thesis.[38] Kelsen saw the identity thesis as a fundamental break with the existing science of the state and international law, as represented above all by Jellinek's *Allgemeine Staatslehre*.[39] Interestingly enough, however, for Jellinek, as well, the essential characteristic of the state from a purely jurisprudential perspective was a binding normative order established by its own law.[40] In fact, Kelsen stood more firmly in the tradition of Jellinek than his vehement critique of the latter's methodological approach would suggest.[41] Jellinek, for his part, had already elevated the methodological separation between causal and

34 Kelsen, *Problem der Souveränität*, 18; H. Kelsen, "Zur Theorie der Juristischen Fiktionen. Mit besonderer Berücksichtigung von Vaihingers Philosophie des Als-ob," [1919] *WRS* I, 1215 *et seq*.

35 Kelsen, *Problem der Souveränität*, 18. 36 Ibid.

37 M. Baldus, *Die Einheit der Rechtsordnung* (Berlin: Duncker & Humblot, 1995), 158.

38 Horst Dreier speaks of a "profanization" of the state in Kelsen, *Rechtslehre*, 208–213.

39 On this see the discussion in Chapter 1 C.

40 Jellinek, *Die Lehre von den Staatenverbindungen*, 40.

41 On the relationship between Jellinek and Kelsen see O. Lepsius, *Die gegensatzaufhebende Begriffsbildung. Methodenentwicklungen der Weimarer Zeit und ihr Verhältnis zur Ideologisierung der Rechtswissenschaft im Nationalsozialismus* (Munich: C. H. Beck, 1994), 156–158.

normative sciences into the structural principle of his general doctrine of the state.[42] He, too, demarcated the "juristic method" of state law theory from ethical-political considerations, on the one hand,[43] and the empirical social doctrine of the state, on the other. However, he continued to believe that a methodologically multidimensional perspective on the same object of knowledge and – in contrast to Kelsen – a unification of the insights that were gained were possible.[44] This was thus already a strongly juridified notion of the state, though still under the premise of a more moderate conception of methodological dualism in the field.

Kelsen, by contrast, applied the Neo-Kantian notion of the object-creating power of methodology directly to legal scholarship.[45] For him, the use of different methods of understanding invariably created different objects of understanding.[46] It followed from this for Kelsen that Jellinek's attempt at a multi-dimensional perspective on the *singular* "phenomenon of the state" was doomed to failure from the outset. In fact, in Kelsen's view, different methodological perspectives necessarily generated different objects of cognition. A scientific grasp of the epistemological object of the state through intertwined sociological and legal analyses was for Kelsen ruled out already by this epistemological premise. Instead, the jurist could conceive of and analyze the state – from a "purely" normative perspective – exclusively as a legal order. Thus, the attempt to more strongly juridify the concept of the state, which was certainly familiar from the nineteenth-century science of state law,[47] was conceptually further radicalized by Kelsen through his identity thesis based on Neo-Kantianism.[48] Kelsen was very critical of a scholarly view of the state derived merely from current positive law, in

[42] Jellinek, *Allgemeine Staatslehre*, 19 *et seq.*; on this see O. Lepsius, "Georg Jellineks Methodenlehre im Spiegel der zeitgenössischen Erkenntnistheorie" in S. L. Paulson and M. Schulte (eds.), *Georg Jellinek. Beiträge zu Leben und Werk* (Tübingen: Mohr, 2000), 309–343.

[43] Jellinek, *Allgemeine Staatslehre*, 13; on Jellinek's influence on Kelsen see S. L. Paulson, "Zur Neukantianischen Dimension der Reinen Rechtslehre. Vorwort zur Kelsen-Sander-Auseinandersetzung" in S. L. Paulson (ed.), *Die Rolle des Neukantianismus in der Reinen Rechtslehre. Eine Debatte zwischen Sander und Kelsen* (Aalen: Scientia Verlag, 1988), 13.

[44] Stolleis, *Public Law in Germany*, 441–443.

[45] Lepsius, *Die gegensatzaufhebende Begriffsbildung*, 158.

[46] H. Kelsen, *Über den juristischen und den soziologischen Staatsbegriff. Kritische Untersuchung des Verhältnisses von Staat und Recht* [1922] (reprint of the second edition of 1928, Aalen: Scientia, 1962), 106.

[47] H. Krabbe, *Die Lehre der Rechtssouveränität* (Groningen: J. B. Wolters, 1906).

[48] For a thorough contemporary critique of the identity thesis see W. Jöckel, *Hans Kelsens rechtstheoretische Methode. Darstellung und Kritik ihrer Grundlagen und hauptsächlichsten Ergebnisse* (Reprint of the 1930 Tübingen edition, Aalen: Scientia, 1977), 130–141.

the sense that the state was a concrete association of persons on a specific territory with a government as the three elements of statehood, a notion that held central importance for the prevailing international law doctrine at the beginning of the twentieth century.[49] To be sure, the study of the content of specific legal concepts of statehood was a legitimate task of the *special* doctrine of the state and international law [*Besondere Staats- und Völkerrechtslehre*]. However, the use of a concept of the state derived from the respective legal content posed the danger that this concept could be confused with an abstract concept of the state from the *general* doctrine of the state [*Allgemeine Staatslehre*], which would give rise to "a virtually inexhaustible source of misunderstandings and contradictions." Although Kelsen agreed that both the special and the general doctrine of the state and international law referred to positive law, the methodological approaches of the two sub-disciplines were different.[50] The special doctrine of the state studied positive law as concrete law in its manifestations. The general doctrine of the state examined positive law for its logical preconditions and the conditions of its existence and thus preceded any empirical experience. Within this abstract intellectual framework, Kelsen reduced the concept of the state to the legal order.

With the identity thesis – developed out of the strict Is/Ought dualism, the principle of the object-creating power of methodology, and the doctrine of legal fictions – Kelsen had found the central methodological starting point for his "purification" of the "science" of state and international law. Every concept of the state from within the traditional doctrine of the state that was derived from the substantive content of concrete legal norms (as for example the state concept expressed by the Three-Elements Doctrine), for Kelsen had no explanatory function beyond mirroring the exact image of a certain legal order. It was of no scientific value for a *general* doctrine of the state, in which the state had been reduced to an abstract symbol for a normative order. The intended critique of the conventional inductive method of forming legal concepts in international law served the higher goal of the "Pure Theory of Law" of introducing into legal scholarship a methodology that was non-political or critical of ideology. What follows is a closer illustration of the anti-ideological thrust of the claim to pure method.

[49] Kelsen, *Allgemeine Staatslehre*, 275. [50] Kelsen, *Hauptprobleme*, V.

III *The anti-ideological thrust of the new methodology*

In his 1923 epistemological "confessional tract" *Völkerrechtswissenschaft und Reine Rechtslehre* [The Science of International Law and the Pure Theory of Law], Kunz described the methodologically "pure" approach to the law as follows: "The name pure theory of law is initially misleading, especially if one comes to it by way of Kant. 'Pure' is here not intended to mean, as it has from Plato via Kant to Cohen, 'To which nothing empirical has been added'; rather, it is supposed to be a pure theory of law, freed from sociological, ethical, political, and psychological dross. The law, and only the law, is the object of legal scholarship."[51] The epistemological foundation of the Pure Theory of Law offered the School the possibility to develop its own, theoretically underpinned program of modernization of international legal scholarship. With methodologically sharpened weapons, the fight was joined for the "new international law" and against alleged nationalistic tendencies in the law of nations. International law, in particular, because of its highly political nature and the paucity of codified norms, offered many points of attack for ideological distortions by international legal scholarship. Trends toward the nationalistic instrumentalization of this field of law had occurred not only in Germany before and during the First World War.[52] Kunz wrote: "The dependence of the science of international law on politics took on great importance; the science of international law often taught less what was 'lawful among nations' [*Völker-Rechtens*] and instead how the politics of one's own country could be justified in terms of international law. The motto of many international law jurists was not the legal question: Quid juris?, but the purely ethical or political maxim: Right or wrong – my country."[53]

A view of his field that was critical of ideology, which Kunz had already adopted as a young scholar in Kelsen's seminar, also encouraged him to vigorously champion judgments of international law that were politically unpopular. For example, as a candidate for *Habilitation* in 1926, Kunz argued to Hold-Ferneck, a full professor in Vienna, that the German entry into Belgium in 1914 had violated international law.[54]

51 Kunz, *Völkerrechtswissenschaft und Reine Rechtslehre*, 60.

52 Leonard Nelson described and criticized this trend in his 1917 monograph *Rechtswissenschaft ohne Recht* (1st edn., 1917; 2nd edn., Göttingen: Verlag Öffentliches Leben, 1949).

53 Kunz, *Völkerrechtswissenschaft und Reine Rechtslehre*, 70.

54 With reference to Kunz's personal file: P. Goller, *Naturrecht, Rechtsphilosophie oder Rechtstheorie. Zur Geschichte der Rechtstheorie an Österreichs Universitäten (1848–1945)* (Frankfurt am Main: P. Lang, 1997), 254.

Although Hold-Ferneck rebuked him by saying that he was not entitled to make such a critical statement, Kunz published an article in Strupp's *Wörterbuch des Völkerrechts* in which he upheld his assessment.[55] In spite of this, the faculty in Vienna approved Kunz's *Habilitation* in 1927, with Hold-Ferneck voting against it.[56] Just how politically important publications and positions on international law were felt to be in the interwar period is also evident with the publication of Kunz's monograph on the right of option in the Treaty of Versailles.[57] In his essay, Kunz subjected the precise functioning and application of the option right in the peace treaties, a right that Germany frowned upon, to a careful analysis. He concluded that the institution of the option was by no means an outdated and therefore theoretically obsolete element of international law.[58] Publication of the book, which Kunz had already finished in 1922, was delayed until 1925 in response to the intervention of the Reich minister of the interior with the Prussian ministry of the interior, for fear that the book could weaken Germany's position in negotiations with Poland.[59]

The engagement with the international problems of the interwar period from a position critical of ideology was an essential element of how Kelsen and his students conceived of their discipline. Especially the biased move to place international law scholarship in the service of the "national interest" went against their own professional ethos. A non-political method of international legal scholarship was supposed to help make international law usable as a border-less medium for creating and guiding society. In the view of both Kunz and Kelsen, a solution to the complex problems of international politics through new international legal experiments presupposed a perspective on the law of nations that was critical of ideology.

[55] Ibid. [56] Ibid.

[57] J. L. Kunz, *Die völkerrechtliche Option*. Handbücher des Ausschusses für Minderheitenrecht (Breslau: F. Hirt, 1925) vol. 1.

[58] Ibid., XI.

[59] R. Schattkowsky, *Deutschland und Polen von 1918/19 bis 1925: deutsch-polnische Beziehungen zwischen Versailles und Locarno* (Berlin and Vienna: Lang, 1994), 241, with reference to GStA, Rep. 77, Tit. 856, No. 217, fols. 12 *et seq*. Kunz's comment about this on the first page: "Note! The publication of this, the first volume, which the author completed a long time ago, was delayed until now by unforeseen, largely technical difficulties."

B. The function of the critical methodology: law as a universal medium for shaping society

However, freeing jurisprudence from meta-legal "dross" was not an end in itself for Kelsen and Kunz, but arose from their nearly unconditional confidence in society's ability to change through the medium of law. As Kelsen put it, the law was a "social technique"[60] to shape and thus change social reality.[61] But what that social reality should look like was, according to the Pure Theory of Law, beyond the subject matter of legal scholarship. Instead, the purpose of the purification of legal doctrine was to expel hidden political or sociological conceptions of society from scholarly analysis. An a priori picture of society as a whole on the part of legal science constrained the possibility of modern societies or the community of states to freely employ the law as a medium of social change.[62]

I. Volk, *nation, and state in international law*

Especially at the beginning of the 1920s, Kelsen grappled intensively with psychological and sociological studies on the nature of society, which were not without influence on the modern doctrine of state law.[63] In a contribution to Freud's theory of the masses, Kelsen subjected the contemporary attempt at a socio-psychological approach to the phenomena of "nation" and "*Volk*" to a methodological critique.[64] Kelsen saw in Simmel, Durkheim, Le Bon, and also Freud what he believed to be a disastrous "syncretism of methods" that was contributing to an "organic theory of society."[65] What these newer approaches of sociology shared was that they started from studies on the psyche of the individual and

[60] H. Kelsen, *Reine Rechtslehre* (1934), 28; *Problems of Legal Theory*, 28. On Kelsen's conception of the law as a social technique see C. Roehrsen, "Die Kelsensche Auffassung vom Recht als ein Ausdruck der modernen sozio-politischen Kultur," *Der Staat*, 21 (1982), 236.

[61] Kelsen, *Hauptprobleme*, 14; on this see Dreier, *Rechtslehre*, 141–145.

[62] H. Kelsen, "Eine Grundlegung der Rechtssoziologie," *Archiv für Sozialwissenschaft und Sozialpolitik* (1915), 871.

[63] H. Kelsen, "Der Begriff des Staates und der Sozialpsychologie. Mit besonderer Berücksichtigung von Freuds Theorie der Masse" in Sigmund Freud (ed.), *Imago*, VIII/2 (1922).

[64] For a perspective on this from the vantage point of the sociology of culture, see A. Carty, "Interwar German Theories of International Law: The Psychoanalytical and Phenomenological Perspectives of Hans Kelsen and Carl Schmitt," *Cardozo Law Review*, 16 (1995), 1235 *et seq.*

[65] Kelsen, "Der Begriff des Staates und der Sozialpsychologie," 125.

drew conclusions from them about a "collective soul" or a "mass or national soul," and thus about an objective entity above the individual.[66] It was erroneously assumed that "social constructs," as for example that of the "mass" in Le Bon, "consolidated" themselves or "crystallized" out of the interplay of psychological elements.[67] These formulations, Kelsen maintained, were a leap from psychology into sociology that was typical of psychological sociology.[68] From there, it was then only a small step to housing the constructed collective psyche in an "organic casing" that was called "nation" or "state."[69] As with Gerber's or Jellinek's concept of the state in relation to state law,[70] the organically understood notions of the "collective," the "mass," the "nation," or the "*Volk*" were for Kelsen fictions of a methodologically misguided theory of society.

The jurist Kelsen was thus trying, as a member of the German Society for Sociology and the Vienna Psychoanalytic Society around Sigmund Freud, to relegate the young discipline of sociology to the bounds of his theory of fictions, which built on the work of Vaihinger.[71] In the construction of "social facts" in Durkheim or the "psychology of the mass" in Le Bon he detected the "syncretism of methods" he was fighting against in jurisprudence. For example, Durkheim's assumption of supra-individual, objective "social facts" was a veiled political value proposition and thus an Ought, which Durkheim was seeking to present as an unchangeable reality.[72] However, a judgmental Ought-statement that claimed empirical "reality" in the sociological "Is guise" went against Kelsen's dualistic understanding of scientific methodology.

Kelsen's methodological critique of these sociological conceptions was, however, not an innocent excursion into sociology; rather, it was supposed to help prevent a misguided theory of society from feeding back into public law scholarship. From Kelsen's perspective, a "social reality" that was derived from the subjective value judgments of a social scientist amounted to a limitation on the changeability of society. As soon as one posited objective "social facts" or a "homogeneous society" the use of the law as a technique of social change was also fundamentally called into question. The assumption of an unchanging social *substratum* contradicted Kelsen's basic assumption of law as the result of a

66 Ibid., 125–126. 67 Ibid., 125. 68 Ibid. 69 Ibid., 126.

70 On Jellinek see Chapter I, C.

71 On Kelsen's relationship to Freud see C. Jabloner, "Kelsen and his Circle: The Viennese Years," *EJIL*, 9 (1998), 368 *et seq.*; Carty, "Interwar German Theories of International Law," 1258 *et seq.*

72 Kelsen, "Der Begriff des Staates und der Sozialpsychologie," 130.

contingent process of norm-creation aimed at altering the behavior of individuals subject to these norms.[73]

Kelsen's battle against an organic conception of society thus prompted him to reject all conceptions that assumed homogeneous collective entities, such as those of the "nation state" or the "*Volk*." In so doing, he was striving to eliminate concepts that could become politically charged in the scholarly discourse. This led to the reduction of the concept of the state to the legal order, and to the reduction of the concept of the *Volk* to the groups and individuals authorized and obligated by the medium of the law:

> For as a concordance of thought, feeling, and will, as a solidarity of interests, the unity of the *Volk* is merely an ethical-political postulate that equates the national or state ideology with a fiction, though one that is used quite generally and for that very reason, alone, it is no longer verifiable. In essence there is only one legal concept, which can be precisely described as national unity: the unity of the state's legal order which governs the individuals subject to the norms.[74]

By this definition, the term "*Volk*" was for Kelsen nothing more than the sum of the individuals of a specific legal order who were subject to the norms belonging to that order. This reductionist understanding of legal terminology, laid out through the example of the term *Volk*, was intended to free the science of the law from meta-legal ballast.

For Kunz, the "fiction" of the nation state was a "bitter enemy" of modern procedures in international law from the interwar period aimed at protecting minorities.[75] As a consequence of national chauvinism, "the fundamental evil of our time," the nation state becomes for Kunz the dogma precisely of those states in which it corresponds the least to reality because of the existing cultural and ethnic diversity: "For precisely the

[73] On Kelsen's understanding of democracy see his *Vom Wesen und Wert der Demokratie*, 2nd revised edn. (Tübingen: Mohr, 1929; 1st edn., Tübingen: Mohr, 1920; reprint of the 2nd edn., Aalen: Scientia Verlag, 1981); of the secondary literature especially Dreier, *Rechtslehre*, 271–281, with extensive references.

[74] Kelsen, *Wesen und Wert der Demokratie*, 15.

[75] "It is the one tragic contradiction of our problem that the nation state becomes the biggest enemy of national minorities, even though both are rooted in the same idea, namely the appreciation of ethnicity [*Volkstum*] as a value ... But every nation counts only its own nation. In this way, the fictive nation state is led to placing the entire state merely in the service of the majority nation and thus to take an unfriendly stance toward national minorities from the outside." J. L. Kunz, "Prolegomena zu einer allgemeinen Theorie des internationalen Rechtes nationaler Minderheiten," *Zeitschrift für öffentliches Recht* 12 (1932), 237.

fictive nation states adopt the idea of the nation state in exaggerated form. The national minorities therefore appear to them, quite logically, as defects, as 'blemishes,' which are best surgically removed, be it through open de-nationalization, be it through more or less disguised assimilation."[76] It comes as little surprise that Kelsen and Kunz, who had grown up in an efficiently administrated, multi-ethnic state, composed of individuals from the most diverse religions, language, culture, and background, could muster no understanding for the notion of the psychological or biological unity of the nation.[77] Before the First World War, the unity of this heterogeneous polity had been created substantially by the law and through an efficient administrative apparatus that pervaded it. In Kelsen's eyes, the Habsburg monarchy in 1917 possessed "a basic stock of legal norms capable of development, which, given a good will, can be shaped into the best possible system of legal protection for nationalities." Kelsen believed that on the nationality question, Austrian public law could "step confidently before the bar of history." And yet in spite of this, the concept of the "nation" had become an explosive political charge that threatened the unity of the Habsburg state, with which Kelsen, Kunz and Verdross had identified themselves so strongly before and during the First World War.[78]

By contrast, a critical distance to the concepts of "nation" and "*Volk*" was no longer apparent from the mid 1930s in Kelsen's original companion and student Verdross. In the chapter "*Volk* and State" in his 1937 textbook on international law, Verdross transfigured the value of the "pure nation state":

> But if *Volkstum* [ethnic nationhood] constitutes the highest natural form of humanity, every person can attain the development of his natural talents only within the *Volksgemeinschaft* [national community]. With this, the *Volkstum* becomes the natural foundation of all culture. The political unity of the state, too, must do justice to this fact, since the state, by its very conception, forms the perfect community of life (*civitas*

[76] Ibid., 237.

[77] As Kelsen stated himself in an autobiographical piece, in Métall, *Hans Kelsen. Leben und Werk*, 42; on this see M. Baldus, "Habsburgian Multiethnicity and the 'Unity of the state' – On the Structural Setting of Kelsen's Legal Thought" in Diner and Stolleis (eds.), *Hans Kelsen and Carl Schmitt: A Juxtaposition*, 13–15.

[78] In a book review in 1917, Kelsen defended what he believed was the progressive Austrian law on nationalities and languages, and opposed the "fairy tale" of the "oppressed nationalities [*Völker*] of Austria": "Book review of: Rudolf Laun. *Zur Nationalitätenfrage Haag 1916*," *ZÖR*, 3 (1917), 585–586; Oberkofler and Rabofsky, *Kelsen im Kriegseinsatz der k.u.k. Wehrmacht*, 26–27.

> *perfecta*) for its members, but can fulfill this task only if it makes it possible for them to bring their natural talents and abilities to fruition. However, as a result of the natural [*artmäßige*] diversity of humanity, such a formation is possible only in the *Volksgemeinschaft*. The most perfect realization of this idea is possible in pure nation states.[79]

Even if Verdross wanted to see the "principle of respect for ethnicities [*Volkstümer*]" applied to ethnically mixed states, his textbook provides evidence that the central concepts of international law were geared toward the increasingly "volkish" zeitgeist of German legal scholarship.[80]

II *Law as a universal medium of societal change*

Kelsen believed that for the law to fulfill its function as a tool of societal change that was unrestricted in terms of content, what was needed was a jurisprudential method that took a critical stance toward preconceived conceptions of society. According to the Pure Theory of Law, the law was thus a medium to realize political and social goals.[81] These extra-legal goals and motives, however, were in principle removed from the analytical purview of jurisprudence.[82] Rather, jurisprudence should describe the law as a variable medium, that is, as a form of societal change that could be put to use for any purpose. With the help of a radical methodological dualism, Kelsen thus reduced the subject of the law to its "pure" form, which could be filled with any conceivable content. Kelsen firmly believed that through this gain in formal rationality, legal scholarship respected the political spheres in which the authorized creators of norms acted.[83] For the use of the medium of law did not subject the authorized organs to any material restrictions dictated by ideologized doctrinal

79 A. Verdross, *Völkerrecht* (Berlin: Springer, 1937), 40.

80 Ibid., 43: "The state of international law is thus not merely the state apparatus (state in the narrower sense), but the *Volk* organized as a state (state in the broader sense)." On the relationship between Verdross and Spann and on his ambivalent stance toward National Socialism see A. Carty, "Alfred Verdross and Othman Spann: German Romantic Nationalism, National Socialism and International Law," *EJIL*, 6 (1995), 78 *et seq.*; on the 1937 textbook see Stolleis, *A History of Public Law in Germany*, 429–430.

81 H. Kelsen, "The Law as a specific Social Technique," *University of Chicago Law Review*, 9 (1941), 80; H. Kelsen, *General Theory of Law and State* (Cambridge, MA: Harvard University Press, 1949), 19.

82 H. Kelsen: "Die Idee des Naturrechts," *WRS*, I, 251; "Allgemeine Rechtslehre im Lichte materialistischer Geschichtsauffassung" in N. Leser (ed.), *Demokratie und Sozialismus* (Vienna: Wissenschaftliche Buchgesellschaft, 1967), 81. On this see Dreier, *Rechtslehre*, 145.

83 On the law as the object of political decision see H. Kelsen, *Reine Rechtslehre* (1953), 620.

concepts. The function of the critical method I have described was thus to scientifically reflect "the – virtually – total power of disposal that modern society had over itself."[84]

For the science of international law, this formal orientation of the Pure Theory of Law meant that the law was also not subject to any preconceived substantive restrictions in international relations. If one included the perspective of international law, the medium of law could thus be described as "universal" in a double meaning: Kelsen had constructed it as a "universal" medium with respect to both its purposes and content, as well as with regard to the territorial sphere in which it was valid.

C The fundamental critique of the conceptual apparatus of international law

As I will lay out in what follows, the new methodological tools allowed Kelsen to undertake a fundamental revision of the conceptual apparatus of public law. In the process, he used the destructive potential of his radical methodological dualism to "free" international law from the ideological structures of the contemporary discourse. To that end, he repeatedly invoked the identity thesis described above and his theory of legal fictions. Through his critique, Kelsen was trying to overturn the pillars of the prevailing theoretical models of international law in Germany and Austria. That included the doctrine of the sovereign will of the state, Jellinek's doctrine of self-obligation, and the dualistic separation of international law and state law that went back to Triepel. The goal that Kelsen pursued for international law with this broad-based critique was to make the "universal" medium of the law available for novel political experiments on the international level.

I. The conceptual uncoupling of the notion of sovereignty from the "state as a legal person of will" [willensfähige Staatsperson]

Kelsen had begun with a comprehensive analysis of the basic concepts of international law as early as the First World War. The monograph *The Problem of Sovereignty and the Theory of International Law*, largely completed in 1916 but not published until 1920, was the product of this critical examination. Kelsen's starting point was the central concept

[84] Dreier, *Rechtslehre*, 104.

of sovereignty: "Like no other concept, that of sovereignty, in particular, has provided the theoretical garb for highly practical postulates. As a result, its history, especially, can provide a classic example for the methodological anarchism that threatens the theoretical character of jurisprudence, specifically for the disastrous blending of moral-political and juristic, but also of juristic and sociological-psychological perspectives."[85] Triepel, in his important monograph *Völkerrecht und Landesrecht* [International Law and State Law], had only carefully hinted at the need for a revision of the concept of sovereignty: "Let no one object that a law of nations above the states stands in contradiction to their sovereignty. If the law of nations were not a power above the states, it would not be a law of nations at all. If that were the case, it would be high time to undertake an even more thorough revision of this notorious concept."[86] Under the impact of the escalating World War, direct attacks on the doctrine of absolute state sovereignty had increased: Kelsen's *The Problem of Sovereignty* was penned in 1916 around the same time as Lammasch's *Das Völkerrecht nach dem Kriege* [International Law after the War],[87] Nelson's *Rechtswissenschaft ohne Recht* [Jurisprudence without Law],[88] and the new Catholic-natural law critiques of the sovereignty doctrine.[89] In the 1920s, the engagement with the concept of sovereignty became one of the central topics of the "modern" theory of international law. In particular, the engagement with the League of Nations gave rise, especially in England and France, to the notion that the concept of individual state sovereignty in the sense of an unconstrainable fullness of power was in need of revision.[90] In Strupp's 1924 *Wörterbuch des Völkerrechts* [Encyclopedia of International Law], Kelsen gave his view

[85] Kelsen, *Probleme der Souveränität*, 2–3.

[86] Triepel, *Völkerrecht und Landesrecht*, 76–77, note 2.

[87] See H. Lammasch's critique of the dogma of absolute sovereignty in his *Das Völkerrecht nach dem Kriege* (Kristiana: H. Ashehoug, 1917), 82–83, and *Der Friedensverband der Staaten* (Leipzig: Der Neue Geist Verlag, 1918), 169–173.

[88] Nelson, *Rechtswissenschaft ohne Recht*, 169–173.

[89] Cathrein, *Die Grundlage des Völkerrechts*; Mausbach, *Naturrecht und Völkerrecht*; Schilling, *Das Völkerrecht nach Thomas von Aquin*.

[90] See K. Strupp, *Élements du droit international public, européen et américain* (Paris: Rousseau & Co., 1924), 24: "Il faut éliminer du droit international public la notion de la souveraineté, notion erroné et donnant lieu à des dangereux malentendus. On ne la trouve nulle part dans le present ouvrage." See also V. Dupuis, *Le droit des gens et les rapports des grandes puissances avec les autres états* (Paris: Plon-Nourrit et cie, 1924), 484 *et seq.*; H. Lauterpacht, *Private Law Sources and Analogies of International Law* (London: Longmans, Green, 1927), 44–48; V. Zanten, "Le problème de la souveraineté des états et le droit international," *RDILC*, XI (1930), 494 *et seq.*; G. Butler, "Sovereignty and the

on the traditional conceptions of sovereignty within international law.[91] His critique was aimed especially at a material understanding of sovereignty in the sense of a core stock of unconstrainable competencies of the state or a minimum degree of de facto power.

1 Critique of the conception of sovereignty as a core stock of state competencies

For Kelsen, the "nature of sovereignty" could not be derived jurisprudentially from the content of existing positive law. In that sense, he turned against sovereignty as a "*Rechtsinhaltsbegriff*," a concept determined from within the law.[92] In this false understanding of sovereignty, state sovereignty represented a bundle of substantive competencies. A loss of sovereignty was then deduced from a curtailment of this core stock of state competencies. In this scheme, the ideal state possessed certain "subjective rights" or "basic rights" whose impairment was incompatible with its "nature" as a sovereign state.[93] Kelsen regarded this view as a "symptom of the anarchy of jurisprudential terminology . . . which loves to present as subjective 'right' all content that had any legal relevance or content that was desired as legally relevant from the perspective of the presenter."[94]

In the end, however, for him any list of core competencies or de facto power was arbitrary and theoretically unjustifiable. If one described sovereignty – as was done in parts of the doctrine – as the totality of state competencies, sovereignty was transformed from an attribute of the state into a symbol of the state itself. After all, in the final analysis the

League of Nations," *British Yearbook of International Law*, 1 (1920), 38; J. L. Brierly, "The Shortcomings of International Law," *BYIL*, III (1924), 4 *et seq.* (12–14); J. L. Brierly, *Law of Nations* (Oxford: Clarendon Press, 1928), 62; J. Barthélemy, "Le problème des la Souveraineté des États et la coopération européenne," *RDI*, 5 (1930), 420 *et seq.*; J. W. Garner, "Des limitations à la souveraineté nationale dans les relations extérieures," *RDILC*, 52 (1925), 36 *et seq.*

91 H. Kelsen, "Souveränität" in K. Strupp (ed.), *Wörterbuch des Völkerrechts und der Diplomatie* (Berlin and Leipzig: W. de Gruyter, 1925), vol. 2, 554 *et seq.* On Kelsen's critique of Umberto Campagnolo's conception of the sovereign state and order of international law see N. Bobbio, "Campagnolo alievo e critico di Hans Kelsen" in M. G. Losano (ed.), *Hans Kelsen – Umberto Campagnolo. Diritto internazionale e Stato sovrano* (Milan: A. Giuffrè, 1999), 81–98.

92 The distinction between concepts that precede positive law (*Rechtsvoraussetzungsbegriffe*) and those derived from the content of existing law (*Rechtsinhaltsbegriffe*) goes back to the Hungarian legal philosopher Felix Somló and his 1917 work *Juristische Grundlehre* (Leipzig: F. Meiner, 1917; 2nd edn., Leipzig: F. Meiner, 1927); on this see Chapter 2 D.

93 Kelsen, "Souveränität," 555. 94 Ibid.

latter was, from a legal perspective, nothing other than a legal order.[95] Kelsen described the "logic displacement" he had identified as follows: "The place of unity of content is taken by the content as such."[96] This critique by Kelsen stands and falls with his premise that the state, from the perspective of a scientific jurisprudence, is merely a legal order. After all, the listing of substantive core competencies to describe the sovereign state – which he criticized – had served to grasp more clearly the nature of the person of the state. From the vantage point of the identity theory, which denied that the state existed outside of the law, this approach had to seem utterly nonsensical. For that reason, listing the material core competencies or the state's rights of liberty as a way of describing state sovereignty was for Kelsen "scientifically" useless:

> It is obvious that such a concept of sovereignty is much too broad to have any kind of concrete value. Above all, however, the ideal case of a state in unrestricted possession of the full range of all legal possibilities to act does not exist within the sphere of the community of international law. "Law" means at the same time the possibility of restrictions on legal action. Through the order of international law, every state is restricted not only with regard to individual actions, but also in a general way. Every right of one party is necessarily a duty, that is, an obligation and restriction on the other party.[97]

2 Sovereignty as a hierarchy-creating, ordering element of the legal system

For Kelsen, the normative-logical essence of all great theories of sovereignty since Bartolus was the view of the bearer of sovereignty as an entity occupying the highest place in a given order. Through this attribute, the subject to which sovereignty is accorded is characterized as the "highest" or "uppermost."[98] This was initially merely a "visual image" to illustrate a relationship of supraordination or subordination. However, this relationship could not be inductively determined by way of a causal examination of political power relations. In this way, Kelsen, just like Jellinek, was opposing the definition of sovereignty as a minimum of *de facto* power.[99] A view of sovereignty directed only at social reality, he argued, was not only methodologically unacceptable, but also not very useful. For in a factual sense, every state was politically dependent on other states and therefore not conceivable as the highest, completely

[95] Ibid., 556. [96] Ibid. [97] Ibid.
[98] Kelsen, *Problem der Souveränität*, 5. [99] Ibid., 41.

unconstrained entity.[100] Instead, sovereignty should be seen as merely a logical attribute; in normative-logical terms, the notion of "being the highest" was to be understood as the order of norms that could "not be derived any further."[101] Here we get an indication of to which entity Kelsen wishes to assign the normative-logical and hierarchy-establishing attribute of sovereignty. In his eyes, only a system of norms or a legal order can be described as sovereign. With this, the concept of sovereignty was completely disconnected from the personified state or another factual entity of will.[102] If one wanted to speak of the sovereignty of the state, from a purely jurisprudential point of view this could refer only to the state's legal order as a system of norms that could not be further derived from anything else. As it was, in a juridical study, the concept of the state was coterminous with that of the state's legal order.[103] From a normative perspective, the state was to that extent identical with its legal order. According to Kelsen, then, the state as a legal order could be regarded as sovereign only if that order was to be seen in fact as a normative system that was not further derivable.[104] This normative-logical conception of sovereignty had advanced Jellinek's sovereignty concept of "obligation exclusively through its [the state's] own will" in one crucial point.[105] Both definitions referred to the normative-logical "originality" of a legal order, but they differed in that Jellinek had continued to link the concept of sovereignty to the will of the state and

100 Ibid., 7. 101 Ibid., 8.

102 S. L. Paulson, "Methodological Dualism in Kelsen's *Das Problem der Souveränität*" in A. Carrino (ed.), *Kelsen e il problema della sovranità* (Naples: Edizione scientifiche italiane, 1990), 89–94.

103 Kelsen, *Problem der Souveränität*, 10.

104 The "purely" formal articulation of the concept of sovereignty reveals a close kinship to Hugo Krabbe's doctrine of the "sovereignty of law" [*Rechtssouveränität*]. As early as 1906, Krabbe had tried to replace the concept of state sovereignty with that of the *Rechtssouveränität*: Krabbe, *Die Lehre der Rechtssouveränität*, 254. Because the power of the state in the modern constitutional state (*Rechtsstaat*) was for Krabbe in the final analysis entirely "the power of the law," one could no longer speak of state sovereignty (245). To that extent, the identity of state and law was for Krabbe a historically evolved achievement, and not, as for Kelsen, a methodological premise. Even though Kelsen criticized in Krabbe's approach precisely this missing assumption of a complete identity of state and law (Kelsen, *Problem der Souveränität*, 22–25), his own notion did bring back Krabbe's idea of a concept of sovereignty that was thoroughly normativized. In conjunction with the quality of logical originality, which also appears in Jellinek, Kelsen's understanding of sovereignty emerges as a juridical perspective through which the legal order is defined as the "highest, not further derivable" [*höchste, nicht weiter ableitbare*] order. On this formulation see Kelsen, *Problem der Souveränität*, 14.

105 On Jellinek see Chapter 1 C.

thus to the de facto process that created law.[106] The crucial difference to Jellinek's conception of sovereignty thus lay in the fact that Jellinek could and would assign the quality of sovereignty – understood as obligation exclusively through one's own will – only to the personified state as the de facto bearer of will. By contrast, Kelsen was able to pose the question of sovereignty (i.e. the question about the highest, not further derivable legal order), now disconnected from the assumption of a state person with the "capacity of will" [*willensfähig*], in a new way.

In answering this question, Kelsen, as was to be expected, turned critically against the notion of the state as the highest legal order. To that end he invoked the fundamental norm of the equality of states that was enshrined in positive international law. Kelsen argued that one could imagine a multitude of equal states only if a higher order normatively guaranteed that equality. Legal equality therefore demanded an equality norm. That norm, however, presupposed a legal order that stood above the states and placed them under obligation. We are dealing here with the notion that two legal subjects can be described as equal only in relation to a higher normative order that subordinated them both. Kelsen made clear that as soon as one spoke at all of the existence of a binding order of international law, it was necessary to carry out the establishment of a hierarchy via the formal concept of sovereignty in favor of the order of international law.[107]

German public lawyers for the most part regarded this "purely" formal conception of the problem of sovereignty as a provocation.[108] For Heller, one of the most ardent critics of the formalized understanding of sovereignty, the notion of sovereignty was inextricably linked to the "factual will-entity" of the sovereign state:

> It may sound paradoxical, but it is the plain truth: the existence or positivity of a legal order is conditioned by the existence of the factuality of a decision-making entity that can also violate that legal order, if necessary. Once the existence of an entity of will that individualizes the law and preserves its validity is recognized as an absolute precondition for the positivity of the law, it is tantamount to the very recognition that this decision-making entity, if threatened in its existence, must, for the sake of

[106] Kelsen indirectly admitted his closeness to Jellinek in his critique of the latter's doctrine of sovereignty: H. Kelsen, *Problem der Souveränität*, 40–43.

[107] Kelsen, "Souveränität," 554.

[108] H. Heller, *Die Souveränität. Ein Beitrag zur Theorie des Staats- und Völkerrechts* (Berlin and Leipzig: W. de Gruyter, 1927), 120; E. Kaufmann, "Kritik der neukantischen Rechtsphilosophie" [first published 1921] in E. Kaufmann, *Gesammelte Schriften, III, Rechtsidee und Recht* (Göttingen: O. Schwartz, 1960), 198.

> the law, violate the law, that is, at some point it must be *legibus soluta potestas*.[109]

According to Heller, as long as one did not engage in a "rationalistic metaphysics" as Kelsen did, one could not dissolve the state into law.[110] By virtue of its de facto power, the state remained sovereign also vis-à-vis positive law.[111] The strict separation that Kelsen introduced between the factual creation of the law and the question of sovereignty was rejected by Heller as an expulsion of sociological reality from jurisprudence. With its abstract approach to the central concepts of public law scholarship, the methodological premises of the Pure Theory of Law opened a deep, virtually unbridgeable chasm between supporters and opponents.

II The critique of the doctrine of self-obligation

Jellinek's doctrine of the self-obligating, sovereign will of the state was also subjected to a fundamental critique by Kelsen. From the vantage point of the identity thesis and the theory of fictions, Kelsen already rejected the assumption of a "state will" that was relevant to the foundation of international law. With respect to the thrust of his argument, he stood in the tradition of Fricker.[112] In Kelsen's view, as well, the fact that states created international law through custom and treaties "by an act of will" [*willentlich*] did not yet permit any inferences about a voluntaristic basis for the validity of international law. According to Kelsen, the factual process of creation could not provide any information about the question of the normative validity-basis of international law. Kelsen maintained that the inadequate differentiation between the basis on which international law was created and the basis on which it was valid was the cause of the logically inconsistent constructs of "self-obligation."[113] The validity-basis of international law could be found only outside of the fictions of the will.[114] Given the possibility for the state to change its expressed will at any time, something Fricker had

[109] Heller, *Die Souveränität*, 120; on the concept of sovereignty in Heller, M. Hebeisen, *Souveränität in Frage gestellt* (Baden-Baden: Nomos, 1995), 399–440.

[110] Heller, *Die Souveränität*, 120.

[111] For Heller, the validity of international law was grounded, first, in the "ideality of legal principles," and, second, in the will-entity of the state, which was, in the final analysis, decisive: *Die Souveränität*, 120.

[112] On Fricker see Chapter 1 B.

[113] Kelsen, *Problem der Souveränität*, 228, 142, 263.

[114] For a refutation by way of the problem of the validity of international law for the newly created state, ibid., 224–241.

already demonstrated, it was not possible, according to Kelsen, to erect a binding international law on the basis of the will of the state.[115]

In addition, however, Kelsen had his own methodological approach for attacking the notion of self-obligation on the level of conceptualization. The creation of the law through the meta-legal state and its subsequent subordination to the law was no longer tenable following the dissolution of the meta-legal entity of the state.[116] Even if the state possessed an "Is"-quality outside the law, this factual dimension could not be invoked to construct international law because of the epistemologically necessary distinction between Is and Ought.[117] The "state person" as a fiction was identical with the legal order and could not be constructed as standing behind the law. To that extent, Kelsen regarded the doctrine of self-obligation as the typical product of the fictive doubling of the state – an erroneous thought that had to be overturned.[118] In the voluntaristic theories, the state appeared as a self-fettering, originally "untamed Leviathan," who could, for political reasons, cast those fetters off again if need be.[119] For Kelsen, this ideological notion always entailed the possibility of self-liberation from the legal fetters on the grounds of "higher" political interests of the state organism.[120] In fact, Jellinek had based the necessity for the *clausula rebus sic stantibus* as the reason for terminating the obligations under international law on the existential interests of the state organism that stood outside the law, in this way opening for the state a back door through which its political interests could, at any time, recover the primacy over legal obligations.[121] This conception was irreconcilable with Kelsen's notions of a binding order of international law.

Moreover, in his *Problem of Sovereignty and the Theory of International Law*, Kelsen tried to demonstrate to the proponents of the theories of recognition and self-obligation that there were inconsistencies in their arguments. To that end, he zeroed in on a question that was crucial to the project of modernizing international law: was it

[115] Ibid., 182; with an attempt at a refutation by reference to state practice: A. Verdross, "Völkerrecht und einheitliches Rechtssystem," *ZfV*, XII (1923), reprinted in *WRS*, II, 2023 *et seq.*

[116] Kelsen, *Problem der Souveränität*, 201; Kelsen, *Hauptprobleme*, 188 *et seq.*; on this see Dreier, *Rechtslehre*, 212–213.

[117] Kelsen, *Probleme der Souveränität*, 169; Kelsen, *Hauptprobleme*, XVIII–XIX.

[118] Kelsen, *Hauptprobleme*, XIX. [119] Dreier, *Rechtslehre*, 213.

[120] Kelsen, *Über den juristischen und den soziologischen Staatsbegriff*, 138.

[121] On Jellinek see Chapter 1 C.

possible, by starting from a subjective will of the state, to construct an objective law of nations that was, at least to a degree, autonomous from the will of individual states? The champions of the theory of self-obligation were aware that in order to posit a binding international law, they had to rely on a theoretical component that was disconnected from the individual will of the state and objectified in some form or another.[122] If one carried the concept of the self-obligation of the free will of the state further, it demanded a limitation on the possibility of unilaterally dissolving this self-obligation. This objective component had to contain substantive norms of international law (e.g. the maxim *pacta sunt servanda*) that were not subject to the power of the will of the individual state. In addition, jurists had been searching for a solution to the theoretical problem of how a newly created state could be bound to this legal order that had arisen completely independently of its will. Kelsen criticized the various attempts to arrive at a binding international law that started from the sovereign will of the state and proceeded via "self-obligation" (Jellinek) or the concept of "agreement" (Triepel). Because an objective binding force was brought to the subjective will of the state from the outside via the concepts of agreement and self-obligation, these views in the end did posit a validity of international law beyond the will of the state, which was inconsistent with their initial premise. The applied strategies of objectification, according to Kelsen, were irreconcilable with the idea of the free will of the state as the basis of international law.[123] To Kelsen's mind, the limitation on the will of the state that Jellinek derived from the objective nature of relations between states was nothing other than the assumption that there was an international law that could compel states and stood above them. This amounted to an impermissible shift in the epistemological perspective. According to Kelsen, Jellinek and Triepel left the ground of the doctrine of the will and did assume, in their subsequent argumentation, the existence of an international law above the states.[124]

In the 1920s, the theory of self-obligation became the primary target of critique from the reform movement in international law that had already begun to emerge during the First World War.[125] This movement in the

[122] On this see the discussion in Chapter 1 C IV 1.
[123] Kelsen, *Problem der Souveränität*, 186–187. [124] Ibid., 184.
[125] For a critique of the theory of self-obligation: Duguit, *Souveraineté et liberté*, 107–108; J. L. Brierly, "Le fondement du caractère obligatoire du droit international public," *RCADI*, 23/III (1928), 482–484; Lauterpacht, *The Function of Law in the International Community*, 409–412, with extensive references to the critique of the

1920s, which saw itself as progressive, even criticized Jellinek's theoretical model as a nationalistic, anachronistic construct that had fallen prey to the Hegelian dogma of the sovereign will of the state. In the final analysis, Lauterpacht argued in 1933, taking Jellinek seriously was tantamount to denying the existence of international law.[126] Along with Leonard Nelson, Léon Duguit, and Hugo Krabbe, Kelsen was among the early pioneers of the critical turn away from the voluntaristic basis of international law after the First World War.[127]

III The critique of a dualism of state law and international law

The attack that Kelsen, in his *The Problem of Sovereignty and the Theory of International Law*, directed against the dogma of the sovereign will of the state and the theory of self-obligation derived from it, was joined by a critique of Triepel's strict dualist separation of international law and state law. Kelsen sought to present the dualistic theory as internally contradictory. Here, too, he used the destructive potential of the identity thesis to attack the separation of international law and state law into two completely distinct systems of norms as a construct that was logically untenable. In the process, Kelsen aimed his criticism at the two central theses of Triepel's argument: the proposition that the two systems had different sources, and the proposition that the objects of regulation were different in international law and state law.

1 A critique of the duality of sources

Kelsen began by subjecting Triepel's theoretical approach to an internal critique. In order to construct an international law that was autonomous at least to a degree, Triepel had introduced the concept of the "common will" [*Gemeinwille*] as a separate source of international law. According to Triepel, the "common will" would arise from the law-creating "agreements" between the states. By way of the "agreement," the will of the

doctrine of self-obligation; Verdross, *Die Verfassung der Völkerrechtsgemeinschaft*, 12–20; A. Verdross, "Le fondement du droit international," *RCADI*, 16 (1927) 262–274; W. Sukiennicki, *Essai sur la souveraineté des états en droit international moderne* (Paris: A. Pedone, 1926), 174–222; Spiropolous, *Théorie generale du droit international*, 46–50.

126 Lauterpacht, *The Function of Law in the International Community*, 412; Lauterpacht described Jellinek as the founder of the approach of "legal coordination" [*koordinationsrechtlicher Ansatz*] in contrast to that of "legal subordination" [*subordinationsrechtlicher Ansatz*], which assumed the existence of a higher order of international law.

127 Nelson, *Rechtswissenschaft ohne Recht*, 51–59.

individual state could then be transported into the "common will" as a separate source for international law.[128]

Kelsen maintained that the introduction of the concept of "agreement" could not conceal the fact that the will of the individual state on which the agreement was based was and remained, in Triepel, the final source of international law.[129] Even if one followed Triepel there was thus no dualism of sources. Moreover, normative conflicts between international law and state law, a typical sign of two different law-creating sources, was not conceivable in Triepel's construct in that the will of the individual state remained part of the common will. Hence, in the final analysis, Triepel's model, notwithstanding the conceptual blurring, did presume a shared source for international law and state law: "In spite of the fact that Triepel's theory of a source of international law different from the source of state law in the end amounts to the Bergbohmean-Jellinekian theory of the self-obligation of the state, which means that international law must become a component of the state's legal order, in spite of this obvious identical nature of the source for state law and international law, Triepel clings to the possibility of an irresolvable conflict between the two legal systems."[130] Apart from the general inadequacy of the psychological concept of will, Kelsen argued that the notion of agreement did not sustain Triepel's postulated split into two different systems of norms.

2 A critique of the duality of regulatory objects

From the postulated existence of different sources for international law and state law, Triepel had deduced a difference in the objects of regulation.[131] International law normativized the relationship between states as equal subjects, whereas state law regulated the relationships between the supraordinated state and its citizens.[132] Triepel believed that such a demarcation of the regulatory objects of international law and state law flowed conclusively from the assumption of different sources. In his *The Problem of Sovereignty and the Theory of International Law*, Kelsen used two arguments in a radical attack on this standard view in the literature on state and international law.

First, the relationship of international law to the state or of the state to the citizen was one between legal subjects within a legal order: in a legal sense, legal subjects were merely theoretically personified sub-orders of

[128] On Triepel's construct see Chapter 1 D.

[129] Kelsen, *Probleme der Souveränität*, 136. [130] Ibid., 138.

[131] Triepel, *Völkerrecht und Landesrecht*, 22. [132] Ibid., 11 *et seq.*

the legal system. Kelsen argued that as a complex of obligations and rights, they possessed no quality outside of the legal system, but were partial sub-orders derivable from an overarching legal order.[133] According to Kelsen, the notion of the legal person of the citizen subordinated to the state was to be translated into the relationship of the legal order of the state to a delegated sub-order.[134] In this view, the relationship of both the state to the citizen and of the order of international law to the state were merely normative linkages between legal subjects that were themselves nothing more than the personified entity of a derived complex of rights and obligations. Once again, Kelsen had used the identity thesis to arrive at a novel, critical look at a traditional theoretical distinction.

Second, Kelsen postulated that the object of legal norms was, in the final analysis, always the conduct of individuals, thereby challenging Triepel's assertion that international law regulated only the conduct of states. When all was said and done, international law, as well, independent of the question of the attribution of legally desired or non-desired human behavior toward a legal subject in the sense described above, always had as its ultimate object the conduct of human beings. From a purely juridical perspective, the statement that international law regulated the relationships among states merely meant that individual human behavior regulated by norms of international law could be attributed to the state as the personified unity of a complex of norms.[135] For Kelsen, both the international law norm and the state law norm thus regulated human behavior. The fact that this behavior could, in turn, be attributed through legal norms to different, personified legal sub-orders had no bearing on their shared regulatory object.

In addition, Kelsen criticized what he regarded as the lack of logical consistency in Triepel's construct. The strict separation of regulatory spheres was to Kelsen inherently self-contradictory for the simple reason that the associated assumption, namely that international law regulated merely the conduct of states, already presupposed a norm-logical nexus between the relevant norm of international law and the state organs as legal sub-orders of the state.[136] Because the norm of international law regulated human behavior and could be attributed to the individual state

[133] Kelsen, *Probleme der Souveränität*, 126. [134] Ibid., 126–127. [135] Ibid., 128.

[136] For a critical view of this see H. L. A. Hart, "Kelsen's Doctrine of the Unity of Law" in H. L. A. Hart (ed.), *Essays in Jurisprudence and Philosophy* (Oxford University Press, 1983), 316.

(state legal system) via its organs (sub-orders of the state legal system), Kelsen saw a normative nexus between the international legal order and the state legal order. For Kelsen, the statement that international law regulated the conduct of states described, from a strictly legal perspective, a norm-logical "incorporation" of domestic norms of attribution by the norm of international law, thus contradicting Triepel's thesis of the duality of the two legal orders.[137]

By bringing out the normative ties between state law and international law, Kelsen sought to depict Triepel's position as inherently contradictory. He was able to do so by consistently transforming the relationship of the citizen to the state and to the international legal order into legal connections between personified legal orders. The dualism thesis would not hold up in the face of the Kelsenian ideal of a logically coherent, interwoven structure of the legal system.

D The opponents of the critical method: Kelsen's abstract conceptual world as a "radical-logicistic metaphysics"

With the help of his strict methodological dualism, Kelsen had subjected the pillars of traditional German international law architecture to a fundamental critique. Especially the identity thesis and Kelsen's demand for logical consistency allowed for provocative attacks on the conventional understanding of the sovereign will of the state, the doctrine of self-obligation, and the dualistic separation of international law and state law. Kelsen's reductionist method met with little approval within mainstream German public law.[138] Kelsen's opponents criticized especially the "de-materialized" approach to the law and his faith in logical conclusions in dealing with legal constructions. In particular, the reduction of central concepts such as that of sovereignty, to their logical meaning for a description of legal orders was felt to be unacceptable. The chief argument against Kelsen's novel method of conceptualization was aimed at the high degree of abstraction of his theoretical conclusions, which were regarded as unrealistic and "empty." Erich Kaufmann emerged as one of Kelsen's most vehement critics through his essay "A Critique of

137 Kelsen, *Problem der Souveränität*, 137.

138 H. Heller, *Staatslehre* (Leiden: A. W. Sijthoff, 1934), 31: "If the German doctrine of the state rejects Kelsen's own methodology and its results nearly unanimously, it is undoubtedly right in doing so." On the reaction of the jurisprudence of state law see Stolleis, *A History of Public Law in Germany*, 159–160.

Neo-Kantian Legal Philosophy," which was very influential in Germany.[139] Writing in a biting tone, Kaufmann rejected the "logicism" of the "rationalistic superhuman" [*Übermensch*] in Kelsen:

> Positivist jurisprudence begins precisely where Kelsen ends. It can therefore be justified only through a radical-logicistic metaphysics, if Kelsen is convinced that the purification of the concepts according to the monistic ideal of world law has anything to contribute. Not a single "atom" would change in the "sociological-historical reality" if a "purely" "norm-logical" legal theory denies the concept of sovereignty for methodological reasons.[140]

Kaufmann described Kelsen's approach to state and international law as grotesque "rationalistic logicism."[141]

This Kaufmann quote from 1921 represents a widespread reaction against the radical methodology of the Pure Theory of Law. The desubstantialization of legal theory undertaken by Kelsen was supposed to free jurisprudence from predetermined contents, values, and myths, and as such it was also a specifically modern response to the decay of homogeneous religious or social values at the beginning of the century.[142] In striking parallelism to contemporary developments in modern art, the pure form of the law emerges in Kelsen's texts as an abstract empty form without identifiable content. It was also this aesthetic dimension of the Pure Theory of Law, the product of Kelsen's lucid language, which had a polarizing effect on his contemporaries.

The high level of abstraction was to make possible an "objective" grasp of law as the object of "scientific" analysis, comparable to what was done in the natural sciences.[143] The effort to establish legal scholarship as a real and objective "science" on a par with the natural sciences, which were seen as the leading academic disciplines, is a phenomenon that is already apparent in German scholarship of the late nineteenth century.[144] The attempt to derive from enacted positive laws a generalizing, rational "deep grammar"[145] of the

[139] E. Kaufmann, "Kritik der neukantischen Rechtsphilosophie" [first published 1921] in his *Gesammelte Schriften*, III. *Rechtsidee und Recht* (Göttingen: O. Schwartz, 1960), 176 *et seq.* On Kaufmann see M. Friedrich, "Erich Kaufmann (1880–1972). Jurist in der Zeit und jenseits der Zeiten" in H. Heinrichs et al. (eds.), *Deutsche Juristen jüdischer Herkunft* (Munich: C. H. Beck, 1993), 693 *et seq.*

[140] Kaufmann, "Kritik der neukantischen Rechtsphilosophie," 198.

[141] Ibid.

[142] N. Berman, "A Perilous Ambivalence: Nationalist Desire, Legal Autonomy, and the Limits of the Interwar Framework," *Harv. IJL* 33 (1992), 367.

[143] Dreier, *Rechtslehre*, 104–112, with additional references.

[144] G. Dilcher, "Der rechtswissenschaftliche Positivismus," *ARSP*, 61 (1975), 509.

[145] Dreier, *Rechtslehre*, 109.

law, already found in Bergbohm, Merkel, Stammler, and Somló,[146] was carried on by Kelsen.[147] "A system of the most precise and objective concepts possible"[148] was to replace the old legal philosophy as a general doctrine or theory of law. To that end, the conceptual apparatus had to demonstrate a certain independence from the content of the historically contingent normative material. The authors of this school therefore differentiated between abstract *Rechtsvoraussetzungsbegriffe*, concepts preceding the law, and *Rechtsinhaltsbegriffe*, concrete concepts derived from the normative material.[149] For example, the description of sovereignty as the characteristic of a "highest order that cannot be further derived" was for Kelsen a *Rechtsvoraussetzungsbegriff*, that is, a theoretical, auxiliary concept of jurisprudence that was not deduced from the concrete content of existing law. The discrepancies that sometimes emerged between the concrete normative content and the abstract conceptualization were the main point of attack for critics of the theories of Kelsen and his students. Verdross repeatedly tried to immunize himself to such criticism, and to portray his theories as being in line with the "international law of experience."[150]

The methodological incorporation of the *Rechtsvoraussetzungsbegriffe* and their relationship to the *Rechtsinhaltsbegriffe* require a more detailed explanation.[151] For the "classic phase" of the Pure Theory of Law that we are looking at here, it must be assumed that the *Rechtsvoraussetzungsbegriffe* as central concepts of legal scholarship were derived from the so-called "normative imputation," that is, the specifically legal Ought as a pure, transcendental category.[152] They share in the transcendental status of the legal proposition [*Rechtssatz*]

[146] K. Bergbohm, *Jurisprudenz und Rechtsphilosophie* (Leipzig: Duncker & Humblot, 1892); A. Merkl, "Ueber das Verhältnis der Rechtsphilosophie zur 'positiven' Rechtswissenschaft und zum allgemeinen Teil derselben," *Grünhuts Zeitschrift für das Privat- und Öffentliche Recht der Gegenwart*, 1 (1874), 1–10, 402 *et seq*.; R. Stammler, *Die Lehre vom richtigen Rechte* (Berlin: J. Guttentag, 1902); Somló, *Juristische Grundlehre*.

[147] Stolleis, *A History of Public Law in Germany*, 153.

[148] H. Kelsen, "Juristischer Formalismus und Reine Rechtslehre," *Sonderdruck aus der Juristischen Wochenschrift*, 23 (1929), 9.

[149] For an example see J. L. Kunz, *Die Staatenverbindungen* (Stuttgart: W. Kohlhammer, 1929), 33–37.

[150] Verdross, *Die Verfassung der Völkerrechtsgemeinschaft*, Introduction, V–VI.

[151] Kunz, *Die Staatenverbindungen*, 58, sought to specify the relationship using the sovereignty prolem.

[152] Thus Kelsen explicitly with regard to the new, "transcendental" concept of the state that he wanted to put in place of the "metaphysical" idea of the state: Kelsen, *Hauptprobleme*, V.

and are thus regarded as the conditions for a correct understanding of the law that precede any experience. In this way they must be seen as a conceptual world that is completely separate from the concrete content of the legal norms.[153] For example, the concept of sovereignty, as a *Rechtsvoraussetzungsbegriff*, becomes in Kelsen a precondition for understanding a legal order as a uniform, hierarchically-structured normative system that proceeds from the highest and thus sovereign level of norms. By introducing transcendental "legal categories," Kelsen provided retroactive support for his own doctrine of the preconditions of legal cognition. The created concepts, with an unprecedented level of abstraction, were shifted into a realm that preceded experience and were now no longer subject to being measured against existing law. The laws of this conceptual world are the principle of the unity of cognition, of hierarchy, rigorous rationality, and logic. These basic structures of Kelsen's thinking, already evident in his doctoral dissertation on Dante Alighieri from 1905,[154] had been given a retroactive methodological backing through the transcendental argument.

The constructive uncoupling of the abstract conceptualizations from the prevailing norm content offered critics a double point of attack under the slogan of a "logicistic metaphysics."[155] Because of their distance from prevailing law, the created concepts, on the one hand, seemed to have little usefulness for the jurist, and, on the other hand, were not – as Erich Kaufmann and Wilhelm Jöckel noted early on – truly "pure" in the sense

[153] H. Kelsen, *Reine Rechtslehre* (1934), 3–5; Kelsen, *Über den juristischen und den soziologischen Staatsbegriff*, 200.

[154] In this regard, Kelsen's admiration for the Medieval world view, which he believed had found in Dante's works the "most splendid and consistent implementation," is especially instructive. The virtues of the system erected by Dante, according to Kelsen, were the depth of its thinking and its "strictly logical unity." This created a conceptual edifice of "grandiose architecture," in which the entire universe is intellectually reconstructed: H. Kelsen, *Die Staatslehre des Dante Alighieri*, Wiener Staatswissenschaftliche Studien, ed. E. Bernatzik and E. von Phillippovich (Vienna and Leipzig: F. Deuticke, 1905), 38.

[155] Examples: F. Sander, *Rechtsdogmatik oder Theorie der Rechtserfahrung. Kritische Studie zur Rechtslehre Hans Kelsens* (Vienna and Leipzig: Deuticke, 1921), 30, and Kelsen's reply in "Rechtswissenschaft und Recht. Erledigung eines Versuches zur Überwindung der 'Rechtsdogmatik'," *ZöR*, 3 (1922), 98 *et seq.*; E. Schwind, *Grundlagen und Grundfragen des Rechts* (Munich: M. Hueber, 1928), 26, 29, and Kelsen's reply, *Rechtsgeschichte gegen Rechtsphilosophie. Eine Erwiderung* (Vienna: Springer, 1928), 11; Kelsen distanced himself from norm-logic in his later work, see M. Pawlik, *Die Reine Rechtslehre und die Rechtstheorie H. L. A. Harts. Ein kritischer Vergleich* (Berlin: Duncker & Humblot, 1993), 146; O. Weinberger, *Normentheorie als Grundlage der Jurisprudenz und Ethik* (Berlin: Duncker & Humblot, 1981), 94; R. Walter, "Das Problem des Verhältnisses von Recht und Logik in der Reinen Rechtslehre," *Rechtstheorie*, 11 (1980), 299 *et seq.*

of the Kantian categories. Both Kaufmann and Jöckel had pointed out that Kelsen's *Rechtsvoraussetzungsbegriffe* were not transcendental legal concepts in the sense of pure legal categories, but merely highly abstract "general empirical concepts" of jurisprudence, which were by no means prior to any experience.[156] However, because Kelsen's conceptual world had abstracted itself more thoroughly from the underlying, concrete legal material than conventional conceptualizations of a general theory of state and international law, it could be integrated into a logically coherent system aimed at unity, hierarchy, and logic.

Kelsen devoted a large part of his scholarly attention to the attempt to reduce the general doctrine of state and international law to an abstract conceptual apparatus that could meet the highest demands of rationality and logic, independent of the content of specific legal norms. This enabled him to attack not only conceptualizations that carried a visible charge of psychology, sociology, or legal policy, but also those that had been derived, from a generalizing approach, out of the existing law. For the content of the prevailing law (the state concept in a constitution or the concept of sovereignty in a specific treaty of international law), which jurisprudential concepts sought to incorporate in a generalizing fashion, usually failed to meet Kelsen's standards of rationality simply because of the political process that had created the legal text. The desired destruction of the major traditional concepts created for Kelsen and his students the necessary space for their own objective construct of international law.

156 Kaufmann, *Gesammelte Schriften, III, Rechtsidee und Recht*, 193; Jöckel, *Hans Kelsens rechtstheoretische Methode*, 162.

3

An "objective" architecture of international law: Kelsen, Kunz, and Verdross

On the basis of a critical challenge to the traditional theoretical edifice, Kelsen, Kunz, and Verdross developed their own construct of international law at the beginning of the 1920s. In contrast to Triepel and other dualists, their own "objective" theory proceeded from a unitary view of the law. From the monistic perspective, international law and national law were parts of a single, unitary legal system. Moreover, this foundation was to be used to demonstrate that international law – despite the complaints of deniers and doubters – could be conceived as a law fortified with the power of coercion. To that extent it could be subsumed under a uniform legal concept along with domestic law. International law and national law were thus part of a unitary system of norms endowed with the power of coercion. Within this overarching system, the thesis of the primacy of the law of nations was then used to place international law above national law. This objective edifice of international law reflected the confidence of Kelsen and his students in the effectiveness of the medium of international law. In the wake of the First World War, the "new" international law in the era of the League of Nations was to be available to international politics as an effective instrument for securing the peace.

A Constructing a unitary system

The roots of the systems idea, which exerted a substantial influence on Kelsen's articulation of international law, are more difficult to pin down than the clearly neo-Kantian works following his *Main Problems of State Law* would suggest.[1] In fact, already in his 1905 doctoral dissertation on the theory of the state in Dante Alighieri, Kelsen expressed his

[1] For example, Weinberger, "Reine oder funktionalistische Rechtsbetrachtung?" 225, speaks in addition of logicistic and neo-Positivist roots of the systems idea.

admiration for the system-oriented idea of unity in the medieval world view: "The system of the medieval world view experienced its most splendid and consistent realization in Dante's works. All the advantages of this system, the profundity of its thinking, its strictly logical consistency, emerge clearly in the bright light of a great person. The entire universe is here mentally reconstructed into a conceptual edifice of magnificent architectural design."[2] Kelsen's desire for a logically coherent conceptualization and for a systems architecture free of contradiction, which was put on an increasingly sure footing of transcendental logic only after his *Habilitation* thesis during the First World War, is already clearly evident in his doctoral thesis of 1905.

I Systemic unity as an epistemological postulate

Kelsen formulated his own position on the relationship between international law and national law concisely: "The unity of the epistemological standpoint demands imperiously a monistic view."[3] The uncompromising monistic premise was argumentatively secured from a neo-Kantian perspective. For Kelsen, the task of the jurist was to conceive of the law as a system of Ought-propositions free of contradictions.[4] Later, he presented this postulate as the product of the basic, epistemological assumption of the object-creating power of methodology.[5] In this view, it is only the application – carried out in the mind of the jurist – of the a priori legal Ought-categories to empirically verifiable norms that creates the law as an Ought-order. It was then no longer possible to deny that the object cognitively created in this way had a connection to epistemological unity. In that sense, the epistemological unity of all law was for Kelsen the *conditio sine qua non* for the establishment of jurisprudence as an independent, self-contained scientific discipline: "Here it suffices to note that legal scholarship becomes a science to the extent that it fulfills the postulate of the unity of its knowledge, that it succeeds in conceiving of the law as a unitary system."[6]

As Kelsen saw it, the systemic unity could be denied only if one excluded either international law or national law entirely from the

[2] Kelsen, *Die Staatslehre des Dante Alighieri*, 38.
[3] Kelsen, *Problem der Souveränität*, 123.
[4] For a detailed discussion of this see Baldus, *Die Einheit der Rechtsordnung*, 134–143.
[5] Dreier, *Rechtslehre*, 33; however, the systems idea also has logicistic and neo-Positivist roots: Weinberger, "Reine oder funktionalistische Rechtsbetrachtung?" 225.
[6] Kelsen, *Problem der Souveränität*, 152.

normative system of law. Only then would the two orders be on two entirely different levels of cognition, a circumstance in which the unitary connection would disappear.[7] As long as one referred to both international law and national law as "law," one could conceive of both only as norms of a unitary system.[8] For Kelsen it was therefore an epistemological premise to place all normative material into a logical interpretative context. This methodological argument, alone, argued against a division into two normative systems derived from different sources. How deeply this epistemological notion of systemic unity had shaped Verdross[9] is clear from the introductory lines in his 1923 monograph, which was dedicated to Kelsen, *Die Einheit des rechtlichen Weltbildes* [The Unity of the Legal World View]:

> "If we take a closer look," writes Planck, "the old system of physics did not at all resemble a single picture, but rather a collection of paintings, as there was a separate picture for every class of natural phenomena. And these various paintings were not hanging together; one could remove one without detracting from the others. This will not be possible in the future physical picture of the world. Not a single one of its features will be able to be left out as unessential; rather, each is an indispensable element of the whole and possesses as such a definite meaning for observed nature; conversely, every observed physical manifestation will have to find its precise place within the picture." These words apply also to positive legal scholarship, both historically and programmatically.[10]

In the mind of Kelsen, Kunz, and Verdross, a "scientific" construction of international law had to do justice to the postulate of a unitary understanding.

II "Delegation" as a unity-creating structural principle

To construct a logically verifiable structure of the legal system, Kelsen had recourse to the concept of "delegation."[11] According to the norm-logical

[7] Ibid., 124.

[8] Ibid., 123; on this see A. Rub, *Hans Kelsens Völkerrechtslehre. Versuch einer Würdigung* (Zurich: Schulthess, 1995), 419 *et seq.*

[9] B. Simma, "The Contribution of Alfred Verdross to the Theory of International Law," *EJIL*, 5 (1995), 41.

[10] A. Verdross, *Die Einheit des rechtlichen Weltbildes auf Grundlage der Völkerrechtsverfassung* (Tübingen: J. C. B. Mohr, 1923), Preface. The quote comes from Max Planck's 1909 monograph *Die Einheit des physikalischen Weltbildes* (Leipzig: Hirzel, 1909).

[11] Hart refers to the unity of norms established via delegation as a "structural" reference to unity and depicts it as the "weaker version" of Kelsen's unity thesis. The "stronger

delegation scheme, introduced in *The Problem of Sovereignty and the Theory of International Law* to criticize the dualism of international law, every norm could be traced back to a supraordinated norm that created it. This supraordinated norm constituted the basis of validity for the delegated norm and regulated at least the formal prerequisites for the creation of the subordinated norm.[12] In this way, legal norms could be arranged in a graduated, hierarchical relationship. By incorporating the so-called "*Stufenbau der Rechtsordnung*" [hierarchical ordering of the legal system], which went back to Adolf Merkl,[13] Kelsen was able to describe the legal system as a unitary system for the creation and meaning of norms.[14]

In the process, Kelsen did not fail to consider that the western jurist trained in rationality, when applying this hierarchical interpretive schema, would have to arrive intellectually at a point when no further empirically verifiable norms could be found. He thus asked himself the question about the source of the supreme delegating norm and thus of the entire legal system, or – to extend the thought further – about the origin of this source and so on. At this point, Kelsen cut off the emerging *regressus ad infinitum* by hypothetically positing the so-called 'basic norm' [*Grundnorm*].[15] As the last, hypothetically presupposed well-spring, the basic norm was the final capstone on a legal system that was dynamically structured by delegation. The basic norm thus embodied the formal unity of the legal system. For Kelsen, international law and national law were therefore the law of a monistic system that could be traced back to a single basic norm.[16]

version" is the concept of unity as an epistemological premise: see Hart, "Kelsen's Doctrine of the Unity of Law," 309 *et seq.*

12 H. Kelsen, *Reine Rechtslehre* (1960), 228; A. Merkl, "Prolegomena einer Theorie des rechtlichen Stufenbaus," *WRS*, II, 1339.

13 As Kelsen explicitly noted in *Hauptprobleme*, XV *et seq.*

14 On the *Stufenbau* see J. Behrend, *Untersuchungen zur Stufenbaulehre Adolf Merkls und Hans Kelsens* (Berlin: Duncker & Humblot, 1977); Baldus, *Die Einheit der Rechtsordnung*, 105–116; G. Winkler, *Glanz und Elend der Reinen Rechtslehre* (Saarbrücken: Europa-Institut, 1988), 27–29.

15 Kelsen, *Problem der Souveränität*, 137. Kelsen later thanked Verdross for deepening his understanding of the basic norm, but he claims the idea of the basic norm as his own: Kelsen, *Hauptprobleme*, XV *et seq.*

16 I am referring to the function of the basic norm as the supreme authority to make law or delegate other norms; on the various formulations and functions of the basic norm in Kelsen's work, and with extensive bibliographic references to the issue of the basic norm, see S. L. Paulson, "Die unterschiedlichen Formulierungen der Grundnorm" in A. Aarnio et al. (eds.), *Rechtsnorm und Rechtswirklichkeit. Festschrift für Werner Krawietz zum 60. Geburtstag* (Berlin: Duncker & Humblot, 1993), 53–74.

III The idea of unity in the discourse on international law

Verdross was the first to try to demonstrate the concept of unity by way of positive international law, the "international law of experience." In his 1923 work *Die Einheit des rechtlichen Weltbildes auf Grundlage der Völkerrechtsverfassung* [The Unity of the Legal World View on the Basis of the Constitution of International Law], he subjected the link between international law and domestic law to a more detailed analysis. In the process, he examined both positive law norms of international law as well as stipulations in the Weimar and Austrian constitutions about the validity of international law. Verdross turned his attention to the question of how states created and applied international legal norms.[17] In this way, the epistemological premise of unity as a "theory about the law" became a "theory within the law."[18] Subsequently, supporters of the monistic position,[19] as well as opponents,[20] sought to substantiate their positions by way of positive law.[21] The discourse took on a dynamic of its own and homed in on the question of the positive law preconditions for the applicability of international law norms within the state legal order[22] and the question whether individuals could be deemed legal subjects

[17] Verdross, *Die Einheit des rechtlichen Weltbildes*, 111–118.

[18] Ilma Tammelo maintains that both approaches are simultaneously present in the general debate; see I. Tammelo, "Beziehungen zwischen der Völkerrechtsordnung und den staatlichen Rechtsordnungen in 'perspektivischer' Sicht" in *Rechtslogik und materiale Gerechtigkeit. Beiträge zur Rechtsphilosophie und zur Theorie des Völkerrechts von Ilmar Tammelo* (Frankfurt am Main: Athenaeum, 1971), 86; on this aspect see also Rub, *Hans Kelsens Völkerrechtslehre*, 446–453.

[19] Kunz, "The 'Vienna School' and International Law," 397; differentiating: P. Guggenheim, "Zum Verhältnis von Völkerrecht und Landesrecht," *IZTR*, 9 (1935), 91.

[20] For one among many see H. Wagner, "Monismus und Dualismus: eine methodenkritische Betrachtung zum Theorienstreit," *AöR*, 89 (1964), 214.

[21] Rub, *Hans Kelsens Völkerrechtslehre*, 447.

[22] On the transformation problem within positive constitutional law see A. Verdross, "Das Verhältnis der verfassungsmäßigen Staatsverträge zum österreichischen Gesetzesrecht, insbesondere zum Strafrecht. Ein Beitrag zur Anwendung der Haager Konvention von 1899 bzw. 1907 durch die Gerichte," *Juristische Blätter*, 46 (1917); A. Verdross, "Staatliches Recht und Völkerrecht. Die Stellung der neuen deutschen und österreichischen Verfassung zum Völkerrecht," *Schweizerische Juristenzeitung*, 17 (1920), 246 *et seq*. Likewise, with a justification on the basis of positive law, H. Kelsen, "Les rapports de système entre le droit interne et le droit international public," *RCADI*, 14/IV (1926), 231 *et seq*., and "La transformation du droit international public en droit interne," *RGDIP*, 43 (1936), 5 *et seq*.; Guggenheim, "Zum Verhältnis von Völkerrecht und Landesrecht," 91. See also the references in Rub, *Hans Kelsens Völkerrechtslehre*, 447 *et seq*., with a general survey of the literature on the problem; K. Ipsen, *Völkerrecht*, 3rd edn. (Munich: C. H. Beck, 1990), 1072 *et seq*.

under international law.[23] In the process, the moderate versions of the positions increasingly converged. In Germany, the dualistic theory continued to be defended before the Second World War chiefly by Gustaf Adolf Walz,[24] and after the war by Walter Rudolf.[25]

Independent of the question of the verifiability of the two theoretical approaches, the monistic approach to the theory of international law made possible a new way of looking at international law during the interwar period. This approach recognized no theoretical boundary between international law and domestic law when it came to either the object of regulation or the entities to whom it was addressed; both normative entities were part of a unitary system. All of a sudden, questions about international organs, about people and minorities as the subjects of international law, about international law-making, and about an international administrative law appeared in a new light. No objects of regulation were by definition exempt from the system of international law, as the traditional doctrine had hitherto posited.[26] The monistic idea now allowed the authors to pursue and analyze new experiments in the realm of international law. As a result, the postulate of unity, epistemologically presupposed, triggered a wave of research within and outside of the Vienna School; led by Verdross, it sought to overturn the old dogmas of international law on the basis of new state practice.[27]

As the members of the School saw it, the voluntaristic foundation of international law and the strict dualism of international law and national law as the primary pillars of the theoretical edifice of international law had blocked the view of the overall legal architecture. The monistic perception of the legal system now raised the question of primacy in a more urgent way; state sovereignty broke free of its doctrinally cemented anchor. The enthusiasm for a universalistic-unitary view of the law took hold also of other writers in the movement for a "new international law." In Duguit[28] and Scelle,[29] universalism drew on the notion of

[23] On this issue see M. Grassi, *Die Rechtsstellung des Individuums im Völkerrecht* (Winterthur: P. G. Keller, 1955), 38.

[24] G. A. Walz, "Zum Problem der 'monistischen' oder 'dualistischen' Konstruktion des Völkerrechts," *ZöR*, 10 (1930), 538 *et seq.*

[25] W. Rudolf, *Völkerrecht und deutsches Recht* (Tübingen: Mohr, 1967).

[26] On the discussion about the so-called "domaine reservé" see Chapter 3 C IV.

[27] Verdross, for example, had already tried in his 1923 work *Die Einheit des rechtlichen Weltbildes* to demonstrate the postulate of unity by neo-Kantian legal philosophy by way of state practice; on this see his comments in ibid., XV.

[28] L. Duguit, *Traité du droit constitutionnel*, 2nd edn. (Paris: E. de Boccard, 1921–25), 551.

[29] G. Scelle, "Règles générales du droit de la paix," *RCADI*, 46/IV (1933), 350–356.

international solidarity; in the natural law jurist Le Fur and later also in Verdross it drew on the teachings of the Spanish late scholastics.[30] What they all shared was the conviction, reinforced by the First World War, that a view of the law that emphasized its global unity was indispensable. International law was to be rethought in a new way, the top was now the bottom and the center became the periphery. As part of the scientific and scholarly world, these authors of the modernization movement believed that this would allow them to open up new spheres of action for international politics and create new theoretical foundations for a stronger juridification of international relations.[31] For Kelsen, Kunz, and Verdross, uniting international law and national law into a monistic legal cosmos was a central precondition for a new, objective edifice of international law.

B International law as law endowed with the power of coercion

Another central element of the objective construction, especially for Kelsen, was the demonstration that international law was, like domestic law, made up of legal norms endowed with the power of coercion. Kelsen wanted to conceptualize international law as a binding law with the ability of enforcement. Defying the complaints of the new doubters and deniers,[32] international law was to emerge from the war not only intact, but strengthened. The construction of an international law with enforcement powers was intended to support and accelerate the building of an international order of peace.

*I Central compulsion and the "world state trap" [*Weltstaatsfalle*]*

The construction of international law as binding law had caused nineteenth- and twentieth-century writers on international law such great difficulties because in contrast to national law, the order of international

[30] On the concepts of unity, universalism, and community, and their roots in natural law in Verdross, see Simma, "The Contribution of Alfred Verdross to the Theory of International Law," 38 *et seq.*

[31] J. L. Kunz, "The Swing of the Pendulum: From Overestimation to Underestimation of International Law," *AJIL*, 44 (1950), 135 *et seq.*

[32] Somló, *Juristische Gundlehre*, 167 *et seq.*, and during the interwar period, von Hold-Ferneck, "Anerkennung und Selbstbindung," 161 *et seq.*; Burckhardt, *Über die Unvollkommenheit des Völkerrechts* A. V. Lundstedt, *Superstition or Rationality in Action for Peace? Arguments against Founding a World Peace on the Common Sense of Justice. A Criticism of Jurisprudence* (London: Longmans, Green, 1925).

law lacked a central authority that was superimposed upon the states and charged with enacting norms and enforcing the law. The creators of the law and the objects bound by it were identical. In the nineteenth century, the lack of a centralized coercive power was the chief argument of the so-called "international law deniers." At the same time, however, theorists of international law could not demand or presuppose a centralized coercive power, for this would have opened them up to the accusation that they supported a tyrannical "world state."

As Adolf Lasson wrote in 1871: "A legal order with coercive power to which the states are subordinated would itself be a state, and the states subjected to it would now no longer be states, but subjects [*Unterthanen*]. Instead of many states, we would thus have a universal state, and such a thing cannot and must not be."[33] For Lasson, international law did not possess a compulsory character comparable to domestic law, and for that reason it was not "objective law." And international law could not be made coercive, since this was conceivable only in a world state with a monopoly of force. While such a world state could eliminate the "martial anarchy," in so doing it would lead to a static state of common "rot and decay."[34] In dealing with this seemingly unresolvable dilemma, international lawyers who wished to question neither the binding nature of international law as an objective law nor the existence of individual states had no choice but to give up the element of coercion. To avoid this "world state trap" [*Weltstaatsfalle*], German writers generally decided against the construction of an element of coercion superimposed upon the states. Instead, they sought to separate the question of the effectiveness or binding nature of international law from the issue of coercion. The binding nature of international law was traced back to an emerging "legal consciousness among the nations,"[35] or, as in Jellinek, to the new concept of the "guarantee."[36]

Another possible solution, later adopted by Kelsen, had been developed by Kaltenborn as early as 1847.[37] Drawing on Christian Wolff's theory of international law, Kaltenborn had searched for a conclusive construction of international law, one that defined it as higher-ranking law endowed with coercive power without having to posit a world state in

[33] Lasson, *Princip und Zukunft des Völkerrechts*, 23. [34] Ibid.

[35] For Bulmerincq, "Book review of: G. Jellinek, *Die rechtliche Natur der Staatenverträge*," 256, the "international belief in the law" [*internationale Rechtsüberzeugung*] was the source of international law.

[36] On Jellinek's concept of guarantee see Chapter 1 C III.

[37] On Kaltenborn see Chapter 1 A II.

the political sense. Kaltenborn was able to do this by resorting to coercion that was exercised in a decentralized fashion. In his model, international law acquired the status of a legal order with coercive power on the basis of the possibility of a decentralized enforcement of the law through individual states by way of reprisals and war. International law was thus an objective law endowed with coercive power, and it did not require that one abandon the "subjective principle" of state sovereignty to a tyrannical world state.

The response by the Vienna School to the critique – which had regained currency after the First World War – that international law lacked a coercive character drew on Kaltenborn's theory of a decentralized coercion exercised by individual states. Since for Kelsen it was specifically the element of coercion that set the law apart from other Ought-orders, that is, morality and religion, the idea of the decentralized sanctioning of violations of the law took on an important function in his conception of international law. The assumption of the coercive character of international law was to Kelsen a prerequisite for designating international law as law in the sense of the Pure Theory of Law: "This is presupposed here as a coercive order in the sense of an order that can decree coercion; namely that the legal proposition [*Rechtssatz*], that is, the schema in which the entire positive legal material must be presented, expresses, as a condition, the link between the legal preconditions of a particular norm [*Tatbestand*] and a specific coercive act resulting from it."[38] The legal proposition "if A (sanction-triggering behavior), then B (sanction)" encompassed, according to Kelsen, the two elements of the legal proposition that were mutually dependent: the legal preconditions of a particular norm and the coercive act. In the linkage between the two elements lay the specific inner logic of the law, which Kelsen referred to as "imputation."[39] The peculiarity of the law as a social technique lay in the fact that it sought to achieve the socially desired state by linking the socially undesirable state with a coercive act, which the person in question experienced as something negative.[40] Thus the consequences of unlawfulness in national law were state-imposed punishment and

[38] H. Kelsen, *Unrecht und Unrechtsfolge im Völkerrecht* (Vienna and Berlin: J. Springer, 1932), 483.

[39] Ibid., 482; on the term 'imputation' see his *Allgemeine Staatslehre*, 47 *et seq.*

[40] Kelsen, *Unrecht und Unrechtsfolge im Völkerrecht*, 482. Because of the strict separation of Is and Ought, Kelsen argued, the actual observance of norms as Is-categories should be of no concern to the jurist. Instead, Kelsen sought to take account of the relationships between actual observance and validity by restricting the definition of the law a priori to

execution (coercive enforcement). What made this coercive act a legal sanction was the fact that it did not, in this exceptional instance, constitute a breach of law in the form of state interference in interests that were otherwise protected by the legal order.

According to Kelsen, one could thus speak of law only if the respective norms could be interpreted as a coercive order.[41] Kelsen viewed international law from this legal-theoretical premise: "If the so-called international law is to be a legal order, this system of norms, too, must be a coercive order."[42] Subsequently, Kelsen scoured international law for legally enacted coercive acts that were connected, in the sense of the legal proposition, to a breach of legal rules. He sought to prove that reprisals and war as legal acts of coercion constituted the specific consequences of unlawfulness in international law.[43] This proof was of central importance to Kelsen. Had it failed, Kelsen would have had to question either the legal character of international law or his doctrine of the legal proposition.

II Reprisals and war as decentralized means of coercion

The traditional theory of international law saw reprisals as the response by one state to a breach of international law committed by another state. As such it was regarded as a violation of international law that was permitted under this special circumstance.[44] The reprisals therefore took on the

actual coercive orders. Kelsen already made this restriction to actual, usually effective legal orders in *Problem der Souveränität* (96 *et seq.*) and linked it to the hypothesis of the Basic Norm. Kelsen justified this theoretical restriction, which he himself described as arbitrary, with Mach's *Erkenntnisökonomie;* on this see Dreier, *Rechtslehre*, 121 *et seq.* Later, the Basic Norm was directly given the function of an a priori definition of the law as a coercive order: Kelsen, Reine Rechtslehre, 211 *et seq.* For the place of this formulation of the basic norm within a multi-dimensional reading of the basic norm see Paulson, "Die unterschiedlichen Formulierungen der Grundnorm," 53–74, 60.

41 Kelsen, *Unrecht und Unrechtsfolge im Völkerrecht*, 483; for a fundamental legal-theoretical critique see H. L. A. Hart, *The Concept of Law* (Oxford: Clarendon Press, 1961), 32 *et seq.*; O. Weinberger, "Der Begriff der Sanktion und seine Rolle in der Normenlogik und Rechtstheorie" in H. Lenk (ed.), *Normenlogik* (Pullach: Verlag Dokumentation, 1974), 107 *et seq.*; on Kelsen's later work see W. Krawietz, "Sind Zwang und Anerkennung Strukturelemente der Rechtsnorm?" in O. Weinberger et al. (eds.), *Reine Rechtslehre im Spiegel ihrer Fortsetzer und Kritiker* (New York: Springer, 1988), 327; for a comparison of Kelsen and Hart on this question see Pawlik, *Die Reine Rechtslehre*, 79–85.

42 Kelsen, *Unrecht und Unrechtsfolge im Völkerrecht*, 483. 43 Ibid.

44 This notion has remained the dominant one to this day: Ipsen, *Völkerrecht*, § 57, marginal note 44.

character of a legal instrument employed by the state whose legally protected interests had been violated. Kelsen picked up this notion and tried to harmonize it with his own schema of the legal proposition. The reprisal was not only a legal instrument, it was theoretically above all an instrument of enforcement of international legal rules. It was thus a legally stipulated consequence of a breach of law. Following the schema of the legal proposition, reprisals flowed as a sanction from illegal behavior.[45] Kelsen could thus draw on the customary law of reprisals to prove that international law constituted law properly so called.

Far more difficult was the demonstration that in addition to reprisals, war, within the positive international law at the time, also had the function of a legally prescribed enforcement action in the sense of the schema of the legal proposition. War constituted the most comprehensive act of violent or coercive intervention in the legal sphere of another state. If international law was to be described as a legal community, from Kelsen's perspective this legal order had to exhaustively regulate especially this most serious form of violence. To that end, it had to establish legal preconditions for the application not only of reprisals, but also, and especially, of war: "We can call a community constituted by an order a legal community only if the application of coercion in it, while not ruled out, is tied to very specific preconditions, if the application of coercion is restricted such that it is permitted only as a response to a breach of the order."[46] The prerequisite for this argumentative proof was that the positive international law at the time permitted war only to enforce legal claims. Kelsen tried to derive from customary law the distinction between lawful and unlawful wars. In the process he relied on the theory (which had still been central to Grotius) of the *bellum iustum*, which, in the nineteenth-century literature on international law, had given way to the proposition that states had the unlimited right to wage war.[47] Only after 1910 can one point to a revived interest in the theory of the *bellum iustum* in the literature.[48] In the wake of the world war, the question of a juridification of the concept of war became more urgent. Towards the end of the 1920s, such a juridification

45 Kelsen, *Unrecht und Unrechtsfolge im Völkerrecht*, 580.

46 Ibid., 583.

47 J. L. Kunz, "Bellum Justum and Bellum Legale," [1951] in his *The Changing Law of Nations. Essays on International Law* (Ohio State University Press, 1968), 583.

48 J. von Elbe, "The Evolution of the Concept of Just War in International Law," *AJIL*, 33 (1939), 665–688. Louis Le Fur used the theory of the *bellum iustum* to establish the lawfulness of the Treaty of Versailles: "Guerre juste et juste paix," *RGDIP*, 26 (1919), 9–75, 268–309, 349–405.

had already advanced quite far through the charter of the League of Nations and the Briand–Kellogg Pact. Kelsen regarded this trend as an indication of a legal conviction with respect to the theory of the *bellum iustum*. In his interpretation, both the charter of the League of Nations and the Briand–Kellogg Pact did not establish a general prohibition against war, but merely sought to internationalize the decision as to whether war as a legal sanction could be waged.[49]

It is difficult to demonstrate whether, within the framework of customary international law, the nineteenth-century right to freely wage war was in fact compelled to yield to a general differentiation between lawful and unlawful wars during the interwar years.[50] There is no doubt, however, that especially the mediation procedure as laid down in Articles 12–15 of the charter of the League of Nations had established at least for its member states what was for now a regimentation of war through procedural law. The restriction on the law to freely wage war had been among the dominant reform themes of the pacifist movement ever since the Hague Conferences. In the interwar years, the movement to reform international law devoted much of its scholarly attention to the attempt to tame war legally through the experiment of the League of Nations and the Briand–Kellogg Pact.

Within this framework, Kelsen attempted to accomplish two things with the *bellum iustum* theory: first, to provide a general demonstration also by means of customary international law that the possibility of waging war was already legally restricted through treaties;[51] second, to prove the

[49] H. Kelsen, "Zur rechtstechnischen Revision des Völkerbundstatuts," *ZöR*, 17 (1937), 549; on this see Rub, *Hans Kelsens Völkerrechtslehre*, 233 *et seq*.

[50] One can also regard the prohibitions against war agreed upon by treaties and the non-aggression pacts of the interwar period as an indication that there was in fact no legal conviction on the part of the states concerning a limitation through customary law on the earlier right to freely wage wars.

[51] Kelsen, *Unrecht und Unrechtsfolge im Völkerrecht*, 581–582:

> Nor can one argue, in opposition to the doctrine that positive international law limits war to being a response to unlawfulness, that a restriction on the freedom of the state to wage war is incompatible with the sovereignty of the state or contradicts the purpose of international law, whose sole purpose is preservation, and that the state's basic right of self-preservation in international law necessarily includes the possibility to wage war also under conditions other than those asserted by the thesis of the *bellum justum*. For the state sovereignty that is invoked here has no place at all within the framework of an international legal order that stands above the states, and the alleged basic right of self-preservation cannot be demonstrated in terms of positive law.

legal character of international law through this demonstration. With this, war as a sanction-mechanism of international law took on a prominent function in the School's construct of international law. This fact had to produce tensions between the School and the pacifist movement, which sought to place war completely outside the bounds of the law ("outlawry of war").[52] However, from their conception of the law as a coercive order, Kelsen and Kunz clung to the function of war as a sanction: "For only if one sees war, just like the reprisal, as the reaction of the law against unlawfulness, can one discern in it the beginnings of a development that slowly transforms it from an instrument of self-help into a coercive act by central organs of legal protection that operate with a division of labor; a legal-technical development whose first, though of course still very modest, structures can be seen in the charter of the League of Nations."[53]

The decline of the League of Nations in the 1930s disappointed the high hopes that had been placed in the juridification of war as a legal sanction. The system of sanctions that had been set up by Article 16 of the League's charter in conjunction with the Briand–Kellogg Pact had been unable to withstand the dynamic forces of European nationalism and fascism. The realistic-skeptical view of international law gained considerable ground during this time. Kelsen and Kunz saw in the failure of the League of Nations a confirmation of their own theoretical premises. The prohibition of war in the Briand–Kellogg Pact had tried to abolish war as a decentralized, juridified sanction-mechanism, but without replacing it with an effective, centralized sanction-mechanism on the universal level.[54] Through the *bellum iustum* doctrine, Kelsen secured the claim that international law was a coercive system of legal rules.

III The coercive character as an evolutionary achievement

For Kelsen, however, international law was "primitive" law compared to modern domestic law.[55] It was comparable to archaic forms of society,

[52] For a critical and more recent view of war as a sanction see D. Zolo, "Hans Kelsen: International Peace through International Law," *EJIL*, 9 (1998), 316 with additional references.

[53] Kelsen, *Unrecht und Unrechtsfolge im Völkerrecht*, 586.

[54] H. Kelsen, *Peace through Law* (Chapel Hill: University of North Carolina Press, 1944), 18; on the notion of sanction within international law see M. Reckhard, *Die rechtlichen Rahmenbedingungen der Sanktionierung von Beitragsverweigerung im System der Vereinten Nationen* (Frankfurt am Main: P. Lang, 1999), 9–13, with additional references.

[55] Kelsen, *Unrecht und Unrechtsfolge im Völkerrecht*, 572, and *Reine Rechtslehre* (1934), 131–132; *Problems of Legal Theory*, 108–109. Kelsen and Kunz repeatedly emphasized

which, though they possessed a concept of unlawfulness, were still based on the principle of self-help when it came to sanctions. Still, for Kelsen, and this is what he was trying to prove with the *bellum iustum* theory, international law had already reached the developmental stage where the exercise of violence was prohibited outside of legally permitted sanctions. It was only from this stage on that one could even speak of a legal order.[56] This was the point where the program of modernization in the sense of a further development of international law could connect. The School could thus counter the challenge to the legal character of international law by invoking the evolutionary achievement of a regulated exercise of coercion in the law of nations. Even though international law did not provide for a central coercive power, it possessed the decentralized possibilities of sanction in reprisal and war. With the theory of the *bellum iustum*, the exercise of coercion and force could be seen as comprehensively regulated by international law. As such, the latter thus constituted a still-primitive coercive order of norms. Because Kelsen analyzed international law and national law through the lens of a uniform theoretical concept, international law, with its decentralized sanction structure, appeared as "primitive" law. At the same time, drawing the analogy to domestic law opened up a developmental perspective in the direction of a stronger centralization of the sanction function.

Kelsen compared not only the degree of centralization of international law to highly developed domestic law, but also the inherent stability of the legal norms vis-à-vis political power. In the Kelsenian construct of international law, the validity of international law had been disconnected from the facticity of the vacillating will of the state. Although the individual states factually created international law, from Kelsen's perspective the validity of the created norm of international law was derived from the assumption of

the "primitive nature" of international law. The reference to the underdeveloped state of international law was part of the standard canon of international lawyers in the 1920s. The assessment derived from the comparison with national law reflects the great hopes and expectations that were projected onto international law at that time. The standard of comparison for international law was the modern state under the rule of law. In contrast to domestic law, they argued, the decision about the imposition of sanctions was not transferred to a court as an objective body, but had to be made by the affected state itself. It was this absence of centralized organs operating with a functional division of labor that supposedly demonstrated the lower stage of development of international law as compared to national law.

56 On the evolutionary-theoretical thinking in Kelsen see Dreier, *Rechtslehre*, 100.

an abstract basic norm. In this "pure" interrelationship of validity, "every irruption of facticity is excluded."[57] Even if a norm made the triggering of the legal consequence it established dependent on a particular constellation of power, this was for Kelsen no real irruption of facticity.[58]

In this context, Kelsen examined the principle of effectiveness in international law, according to which a state existed as such in the sense of international law only if an effective public authority had asserted itself vis-à-vis the population within a circumscribed territory.[59] He maintained that the principle of effectiveness *qua* international legal norm was, in spite of its direct reference to factual conditions, already a legal "metamorphosis"[60] of power: "Through its incorporation into the content of a norm, the element of facticity is denatured, as it were."[61] Even though international law was reaching the "outermost limits of the realm of normative understanding" when it came to the principle of effectiveness, one could not identify it with power. Compared to national law, many international legal norms were, with respect to their transformational achievements from the factual to the normative, "barely still law" in Kelsen's eyes: "And in this weakness of international law vis-à-vis factual power, in this proclivity of international law to capitulate before the facts, we see its true weakness as law, we see the problem of its legal nature more clearly than in the supposed lack of an element of coercion."[62] In spite of this weakness, international law, to Kelsen, was still part of the immanent normative logic [*Eigengesetzlichkeit*] of the legal system conceived as unitary. With this, Kelsen set himself apart from Kaufmann, who had conceived of the boundary between power and law in international law as rather fluid: "Thus, the victorious war emerges as the test of the idea of law, as the norm that decides which state is right."[63] For Kelsen, by contrast, international law was still "weak" and "primitive," to be sure, but through a stronger institutionalization it could be brought closer, in terms of its capacities, to the level of the more highly evolved legal orders of the state. The rather negative finding of the "primitive" nature of international law opened up far-reaching prospects of development for the future institutional consolidation of the international legal order.

[57] Kelsen, *Über den juristischen und den soziologischen Staatsbegriff*, 101.
[58] Ibid., 104–105. [59] Kelsen, *Problem der Souveränität*, 240–241.
[60] Ibid., 241. [61] Kelsen, *Staatsbegriff*, 105. [62] Ibid.
[63] E. Kaufmann, *Das Wesen des Völkerrechts und die Clausula rebus sic stantibus* (reprint of the 1911 Tübingen edition, Aalen: Scientia, 1964), 153.

C The primacy thesis: the construction of an international law above the state

Although international law in the construct of the Vienna School was still a "primitive" law, it was accorded the character of law via the coercive instruments of reprisal and war. Moreover, in the Kelsenian understanding of legal theory, the norms of both international law and national law were parts of a legal system conceived as unitary. This raised the question of how the two legal orders related to each other. According to Kelsen, international law and national law had to be placed into a logically consistent, hierarchical context of delegation. That was done by the primacy thesis, which placed international law above national law in the monistic legal cosmos. The thrust of the primacy thesis was aimed against the dogma of the sovereignty of individual states. It was the most important element in the "objective" construction of international law, and it was emphatically propagated also by Verdross and Kunz, especially at the beginning of the 1920s. If one can speak at all of a Kelsenian "school" of international law, the primacy thesis can be regarded as its shared, central project.

I The delimitation of the state's spheres of competence through international law

Kelsen, Kunz, and Verdross saw the central function of international law in coordinating and delimiting the various national legal orders.[64] This function presupposed an international legal order standing above the individual states. It was only under the premise of a hierarchical structure of delegation that customary international law could be interpreted to fulfill this task. In the view of the School, the customary rules governing the creation and demise of states, as well as those on state borders and jurisdiction, fulfilled these tasks of coordination and delimitation of public authority.

Kelsen made this clear in the first edition of the *Pure Theory of the Law* (1934) by means of the principle of effectiveness in international law.[65] According to this rule of customary law, even a government that came to power through revolution or a coup was to be regarded as legitimate in terms of international law if it effectively exercised public authority in its

[64] H. H. G. Post, "Classification of the rules of International Law according to spheres of validity," *Netherlands Yearbook of International Law*, 7 (1976), 161–174.

[65] H. Kelsen, *Reine Rechtslehre* (1934), 147–149; *Problems of Legal Theory*, 120–121.

territory. In this case, international law protected the territorial sphere of validity of the state's legal order by legally prohibiting certain interventions in this sphere of power. But if the order collapsed, one could no longer speak of a state in terms of international law because of the legal principle of effectiveness. With this, Kelsen argued, a norm of international law determined the spatial and temporal sphere of validity of state legal orders. But also the material validity of state legal orders was delimited by international law.[66] Since international law could potentially regulate any human conduct through the instrument of the treaty, this was also true of real-life contexts that had previously been governed solely by the state's legal order. With this, the state's claim to totality was, for Kelsen, subject to a limitation through the order of international law also with respect to its material regulatory competencies.[67] From this perspective, international law determined not only the creation and demise of the state legal order, but also its territorial and material spheres of validity. With regard to the temporal, territorial, and material validity of its norms, a given national law was thus merely a "sub-order" that was subordinated to international law.

With this move, Jellinek's three-elements doctrine of the state was replaced by the doctrine of the validity spheres of the state's legal order delegated by international law. Working from the premise of the identity of state and law combined with the primacy thesis, this was a consistent reinterpretation of the doctrine of the three elements of the state.[68] The doctrine of the primacy of international law regarded the state legal order as a sub-order delegated by international law. Within the hierarchically structured generative edifice of the overall legal system, international law was thus at a level above national law. But how could such a construct be reconciled with the fact that in the final analysis, it was the states, after all, that created international law by state practice or entering into treaties? This fact had led Jellinek and Bergbohm to categorically reject a construct that elevated international law above the states.[69]

To counter this, Kelsen introduced the following argument: the only reason why several states can establish a treaty under international law is because international law empowers them to do so through the

[66] Kelsen, *Reine Rechtslehre* (1934), 149; *Problems of Legal Theory*, 121.

[67] Kelsen, *Reine Rechtslehre* (1934), 150.

[68] H. Kelsen, *Centralization and Decentralization. A Paper delivered at the Harvard Tercentenary Conference of Arts and Sciences* (Cambridge, MA: Harvard University Press, 1936), 7.

[69] See the earlier discussion, Chapter 1 B and C.

customary legal rules governing the process by which treaties are entered into. When the treaty is signed and ratified, the representatives of the states are primarily organs of the community of international law created by customary international law, and only secondarily organs of their states.[70] "Thus, it is not really individual states that create international law by way of treaty, as those writers influenced by the dogma of sovereignty usually stress; rather, it is the community of states or, more correctly, the international legal community – just as it is the state that creates domestic law by way of state organs."[71] In this way, Kelsen regarded the specific process that created new international law as a process that was already regulated by international law and one in which the states acted as organs of the universal legal order. The higher degree of abstraction in his norm-logical examination thus allowed Kelsen to refute the main argument that the voluntaristic theoretical models advanced against an international law that stood above the states.

At the beginning of the century, Hugo Krabbe had been the first author to resort again to the idea of regarding the state, when legislating, as an organ of the international legal order.[72] Given the lack of a supraordinated organizational power of the community of states, Georges Scelle would later also declare the state to be an organ of the order of international law. He spoke in this respect of the "dédoublement fonctionnel." According to this principle, the same representative of the state could become active, from a legal point of view, in both a national and an international function.[73] The construction of international law as an objective law that stood above the states and limited their competencies, and in which the states operated as organs of the community of states, came originally from Wolff, and, as outlined above, had been reintroduced into the positivist discourse on international law in the nineteenth century by Kaltenborn. Kelsen laid bare this origin of his conception in *The Problem of Sovereignty and the Theory of International Law*, though he did not hold back in his criticism of Kaltenborn, who, in spite of the presumed superordinated nature [*überstaatliche Natur*] of international law, had not been willing to deny outright the notion of the sovereignty of the state.[74]

70 H. Kelsen, *Reine Rechtslehre* (1934), 152; *Problems of Legal Theory*, 123.
71 Kelsen, *Reine Rechtslehre* (1934).
72 Krabbe, *Die Lehre der Rechtssouveränität*, 230.
73 G. Scelle, *Précis de droit des gens. Principes et systématique*, 2 vols. (Paris: Librairie du Recueil Sirey, 1932–1934), 10, 21; on Scelle see W. Schiffer, *The Legal Community of Mankind* (New York: Columbia University Press, 1954), 260 *et seq.*
74 Kelsen, *Problem der Souveränität*, 241–257.

II The primacy thesis and the problem of norm conflicts

Placing international law above national law in a monistic legal system raised the question of how the problem of normative conflicts could be theoretically resolved. At first glance, at least, the emergence of normative conflicts within a hierarchically structured legal universe under the primacy of international law challenged the assumption of a legal system that was unitary and in principle free of contradictions. While Kelsen initially ruled out the existence of conflicts between norms of various levels on principle,[75] he later acknowledged that possibility.[76] However, he maintained that such a normative conflict would not threaten the unity of the logically structured legal system.[77] It was possible "that the legal organs did in fact establish norms that were in conflict with each other."[78] But that fact could not puncture the theoretical connection between international law and national law.[79] The validity of the conflicting norm had to be assumed initially and it remained dependent on whether the supraordinated norm had at its disposal a procedure for destroying the unlawful but valid legal act: "The norm created by the legal order of the individual state in violation of international law remains valid, also from the standpoint of international law."[80] "For the latter envisages no process by which the illegal domestic norm can be annulled."[81] Still, the enactment of national law that was contrary to international law could be sanctioned, as a violation of international law, by other states through reprisals.[82] According to Kelsen, the order of international law, as a supraordinated legal system, thus used state

[75] Kelsen, *Problem der Souveränität*, 113: "The unity of the supraordinated and the subordinated system, however, proves itself in the impossibility of a contradiction between the content of the norms of the two systems." On the problem of normative conflicts in Kelsen from a legal-theoretical point of view see S. L. Paulson, "Stellt die 'Allgemeine Theorie der Normen' einen Bruch in Kelsens Lehre dar?" in *Die Reine Rechtslehre in wissenschafttlicher Diskussion. Referate und Diskussionen auf dem zu Ehren des 100. Geburtstages von Hans Kelsen vom 22. bis 27. September 1981 abgehaltenen Symposium* (Vienna: Manz, 1982).

[76] H. Kelsen, *Reine Rechtslehre* (1934), 84–89.

[77] Ibid., 84; *Problems of Legal Theory*, 71.

[78] H. Kelsen, *Reine Rechtslehre* (1960), 209. [79] Ibid., 331.

[80] Kelsen, "Les Rapports de Système," 315; at this point Wagner sees the transition from the radical to the moderate monism: Wagner, "Monismus und Dualismus," 212, note 1; on this see also Rub, *Hans Kelsens Völkerrechtslehre*, 426.

[81] H. Kelsen, *Reine Rechtslehre* (1960), 331; for the doctrine of the alternative authorization [*Alternativermächtigung*] see Pawlik, *Die Reine Rechtslehre und die Rechtstheorie H. L. A. Harts*, 140.

[82] H. Kelsen, *Reine Rechtslehre* (1960), 331.

organs to sanction the creation of national law that violated international legal rules. As Kelsen saw it, the appearance of normative conflicts between international law and national law did not challenge either the unity thesis or the primacy thesis.

III The defense and further development of the primacy thesis

Verdross and Kunz vigorously defended the doctrine of the primacy of international law in the 1920s. To that end, they both resorted to studies of the history of jurisprudence, which were intended to prove that this approach had a long tradition. [83] They argued that the universalistic conception, according to which the state owed its legal existence to the law of nations, originated with the natural-law doctrines of the Spanish late scholastics Suarez and Vitoria, and had been advocated subsequently by Grotius, Pufendorf, Leibniz, Bynkershoek, Thomasius, and Wolff as well as by Moser, who was considered the founder of the positivist school of international law.[84] Even Bodin had recognized that sovereignty was bound by divine law, of which international law was seen in his day to be a part.[85] Verdross and Kunz saw the fundamental break with that tradition in de Vattel's *Droit des gens* from the year 1758. He was the first to understand sovereignty as the ability of the state to decide freely about its rights and obligations in international relations.[86] In that sense, de Vattel had been the first proponent of the doctrine of the primacy of national law.[87] However, both authors believed that Hegel's doctrine of international law had had a far greater and more harmful influence on international law theory. They maintained that his glorification of the state and his doctrine of absolute sovereignty had – via Pütter, Lasson, and all the way to Jellinek – turned the centuries-old, universalistic tradition of the theory of international law on its head in favor of the primacy of national law.[88] The doctrine of the "external state law" and of "self-obligation," but also the doctrine of

[83] J. L. Kunz, "La primauté de droit des gens," *RDILC*, VI (1925); Verdross, *Die Einheit des rechtlichen Weltbildes.*

[84] Verdross, *Die Einheit des rechtlichen Weltbildes*, 25–31, 39–45; Kunz, "La Primauté de droit des gens," 572.

[85] Verdross, *Die Einheit des rechtlichen Weltbildes*, 13–18; Kunz, "La Primauté de droit des gens," 570. This interpretation of Bodin comes originally from Lammasch, *Das Völkerrecht nach dem Kriege*, 87. On the general history of the notion of sovereignty see M. Stolleis, "Die Idee des souveränen Staates," *Entstehung und Wandel verfassungsrechtlichen Denkens.* Der Staat. Beiheft 11 (Berlin: Duncker & Humblot, 1996), 63 *et seq.*

[86] Kunz, "La Primauté de droit des gens," 574. [87] Ibid. [88] Ibid., 575–576.

dualism, was thus the result of a nineteenth-century international legal theory that had been misdirected by Hegel.[89]

The attempts by Jellinek and Triepel to construct a binding, objective international law received but scant consideration in the critique from Verdross and Kunz, a fact that makes it difficult to avoid the general impression of a certain simplifying "ruthlessness" in how they dealt with the voluntaristic constructs of international law.[90] After all, Triepel as well as Jellinek had attempted precisely to distance themselves from central aspects of the Hegelian doctrines of international law. In its critique, the Vienna School picked up on the ideas of Fricker, but also on the critique of the concept of will by Krabbe, Nelson, and Duguit. What receded completely into the background of this critique (which was oversimplified also for strategic reasons) was the recognition of Triepel as the most recent proponent of a construction of international law that endowed it with primacy.[91] For wherever the notion of will appeared "there is a Hegel in it" – the core was rotten and thus the construct in its entirety was bad.

Verdross, for his part, modified Kelsen's primacy thesis from his work *The Problem of Sovereignty and the Theory of International Law.* As Verdross saw it, it was not international law as a whole that was to "rise above" state constitutions, but only certain legal norms, to which he had accorded a constitutional status as early as 1923. Only those constitution-like norms of international law had primacy over national law.[92] These norms should be only those rules of international law that demarcated the substantive, spatial, and temporal spheres of validity of the state's legal orders from one another. Because international law was otherwise dependent on the state organs to enact law, normal international treaty law ranked below the state constitutions.[93] In Verdross's view, the construction of Krabbe and Kelsen, according to which the treaty-concluding state functioned as an organ of the international legal order, failed to take into account that international law left it to the state's legal order to appoint the organs authorized to conclude treaties. For that reason it truncated the issue by leaving out the crucial function of the state constitution in the process that created the norms of international law.[94]

Kunz, by contrast, following Kelsen, placed international law with its entire stock of norms within the hierarchical structure on a level above the state.[95] In his view, international legal scholarship was able to do full

[89] Ibid., 577. [90] On this see Chapter 1 C, D. [91] Chapter 1 D.
[92] Verdross, *Die Einheit des rechtlichen Weltbildes*, 134.
[93] Ibid., 127. [94] Ibid., 134. [95] Kunz, "La Primauté de droit des gens."

justice to the progressive development of the international legal order only if one posited the thesis of the primacy of international law. As he put it in his 1925 essay "La primauté du droit des gens":

> We are living in an era that is preoccupied with the law of nations, and which takes an interest in international law like no other era before us. There is no doubt that the law of nations is striving toward a progressive development such as the world has never seen. At the same time, it is true that the theory of international law has been overtaken by historical events, by the evolution of international law. It is the great task of the learned to open up in theory the path by destroying all the false conceptions which, like serious obstacles, have been barring to this day the road to this development, such as the doctrine, assumed but not proven, of the absolute sovereignty of states.[96]

Here Kunz was revealing the thrust of the primacy thesis. It was less about establishing a theoretical rule of primacy in order to dissolve potential normative conflict, and more about fighting against the dogma of sovereignty as an impediment to a new international law. The move to establish an international legal order, which was autonomous vis-à-vis the sovereign will of the state, had reached a new high point in the history of legal scholarship through the notion of supraordinated international law that delegated competencies to the state legal order. The competencies of the state were now derived rights that remained dependent on the given stock of international legal norms.

The notion of a delegation-link between international and national law and the degree of theoretical abstraction it achieved found little resonance especially among German international lawyers. Triepel and later Walz, as well, described the objective construction of the school as "unhistorical." For Triepel, normative delegation presupposed the historical precedence of the order doing the delegating. In fact, however, from a historical point of view states existed first, and then the rules of international law; a delegation connection that flowed from international law to national law was therefore ruled out.[97] To which Verdross responded in his Hague lectures: "Mr. Triepel is thus confounding a historical category with a logical and juristic category."[98] This dispute over the delegation question can be seen as representative of the reaction

[96] Ibid., 598.

[97] Triepel, "Les rapports entre le droit interne et le droit internationale," 87; Walz, *Völkerrecht und Staatliches Recht*, 94.

[98] Verdross, "Le fondement du droit international," 291.

of German legal scholarship to the Vienna School's theory of international law in the sense that it vividly demonstrates the mutual "refusal to understand." With its abstract understanding of the primacy issue, the School, as is very clear here, did not introduce a new doctrinal differentiation that could be readily embraced, but carried out a break with the traditional doctrine.

Notwithstanding this, Kelsen and Kunz believed that their approach to the structure of international law was a more "scientific" one.[99] In their eyes, the primacy thesis was a theoretical "conceptual hypothesis" [*Denkhypothese*] of legal scholarship that was suited to placing international law and national law into a logical interpretive relationship. Not only did it meet the requirement of logical coherence, it was also able to describe international law and national law as part of a universal legal system and relate them to each other. Although Kunz conceded that this jurisprudential hypothesis had to be solidified further through additional studies on the content of positive law, it was already available as an effective theoretical tool for further research in international law.[100]

IV The primacy thesis, domestic jurisdiction, and the decisions of the Permanent Court of International Justice (PCIJ)

Kelsen, Verdross, and Kunz were in agreement that according to the primacy thesis, the order of international law determined the way in which jurisdiction was allocated between the international legal order and the state's legal orders.[101] This applied not only to the spatial and temporal dimension, but also to the material allocation of jurisdictional spheres. In the process, it was not possible to draw from the "nature" of a substantive sphere to be regulated inferences about whether international law or national law would be the competent level of norms. Rather, Verdross argued that in the "constitution of the community of international law," the allocation of jurisdiction had to be derived from

[99] J. L. Kunz, "On the theoretical basis of the Law of Nations," *Transactions of the Grotius Society*, 10 (1925), 141.

[100] Ibid., 141: "With this reservation we may say: To treat International Law scientifically (which has not yet really been done), to justify the hypothesis of the primacy of International Law juridically, theoretically, by the positive rules of the Law of Nations, and then to use this hypothesis as a useful means of further research, seems to me the programme of the science of International Law, in so far as it is a theoretical science."

[101] Verdross, *Die Verfassung der Völkerrechtsgemeinschaft*, 168–170.

the positive content of the order of international law: "There are thus no characteristics inherent in the subject matter that would be decisive for its allocation into one sphere of jurisdiction or another. And the circumstance that a matter concerns the 'internal' of a state is also not such a characteristic, since matters of this kind can also lie within the sphere of international jurisdiction."[102]

The relationship between state competencies and the international legal order had been formulated in terms of positive law in Art. 15 para. 8 of the Covenant of the League of Nations with respect to the question of the League's role in a dispute between members. This norm was among the most widely discussed provisions of the Covenant and had also been interpreted and applied by the PCIJ.[103] According to the wording of Art. 15 para. 8, the Council of the League of Nations was precluded from taking action if the dispute concerned an issue that was "by international law solely within the domestic jurisdiction" of one of the states involved. This was the so-called clause of "domestic jurisdiction" or "*domaine réservé*."[104]

The quarrel in the literature over the interpretation of this norm[105] makes sense only if one considers that Art. 15 para. 8 could be taken in two theoretical directions. The article could be read as a positive-law proof of both the individualist-state doctrine of the primacy of national law and the universalistic primacy thesis. The conceded exception of "domestic jurisdiction" could be understood, on the one hand, as a positive confirmation of a theory of international law that proceeded from the original freedom of the states and assigned to the state exclusive jurisdiction for specific areas. According to this view, Art. 15 para. 8 links up with the nineteenth-century conception of the basic rights of states, which was based on the assumption that states enjoyed by their nature a range of sovereign spheres of freedom.[106]

[102] Ibid., 169–170.

[103] For a classification of Art. 15 para. 8 of the Covenant and a comparison with Art. 2 para. 7 of the statutes of the United Nations, along with an extensive analysis of legal decisions and the underlying interpretative tensions, see Koskenniemi, *From Apology to Utopia*.

[104] On this problem see C. H. M. Waldock, "The Plea of Domestic Jurisdiction before International Law," *BYIL*, XXXI (1954), 143–186.

[105] Verdross, *Die Verfassung der Völkerrechtsgemeinschaft*, 172–177, with extensive references to the literature of the interwar period.

[106] On the doctrine of the basic rights of international law see G. Gidel, "Droits et devoirs des nations. Théorie classique des droits fondamentaux des États," *RCADI*, 10/V (1925), and after 1955, A. Verdross, *Völkerrecht*, 3rd edn. (Vienna: Springer, 1955), 164 *et seq.*

According to a universalistic reading of the statute, on the other hand, international law determined whether a question fell exclusively within a state's jurisdiction. In agreement with the primacy thesis, the international legal order delegated material regulatory jurisdiction to the states, which states could then invoke in cases of dispute according to Art. 15 para. 8. From this perspective, the *domaine réservé* could not be deduced from the nature of the state, but experienced a legal relativization. The existence of national regulatory spheres depended on the respective content of the international legal order and was in that sense externally predetermined. This universalistic view of international law as initially affirmed by the PCIJ in an *avis consultatif* on the occasion of the Franco-British dispute over nationality decrees issued in Tunis and Morocco. According to the wording of the opinion, the so-called "exclusive" jurisdiction was relative in nature and dependent on the development of international relations.[107] On the other hand, in the same opinion the judges switched to an individualist-state perspective when they elaborated as follows on the notion of "exclusive" jurisdiction:

> From one point of view, it might well be said that the jurisdiction of a State is *exclusive* within the limits fixed by international law – using this expression in its wider sense, that is to say, embracing both customary law and general as well as particular treaty law. But a careful scrutiny of paragraph 8 of Article 15 shows that it is not in this sense that exclusive jurisdiction is referred to in that paragraph. The words "solely within the domestic jurisdiction" seem rather to contemplate certain matters which, though they may very closely concern the interests of more than one State, are not, in principle, regulated by international law. As regards such matters, each State is its sole judge.[108]

At this point of the opinion, the court thus seemed to proceed once again from original spheres of state jurisdiction that follow almost naturally from the character of the state. International law merely retraced the boundaries of this a priori regulatory sphere of the state. The judges argued that it was in the "essential interest of the individual State to maintain intact its independence in matters which international law recognizes to be solely within its jurisdiction."[109] This position was also reiterated in the famous *Lotus* judgment in 1927, where the court, in the absence of a relevant prohibitive norm of international law, concluded that "Restrictions upon the independence of States cannot therefore be

[107] PCIJ (*Nationality Decrees* case), Avis consultatif of 7 February, Ser. B 4, 24.
[108] Ibid., 23–24. [109] Ibid., 25.

presumed."[110] Subsequently, Strupp, in his Hague lectures, referred to the "*Lotus* principle" as the modernized version of the doctrine of the basic rights of states.[111]

In the *Wimbledon* case (1923) and the *Free Zones* case (1932), as well, the PCIJ did not conceive of the notion of sovereignty in the sense of jurisdictions allocated by international law, but as an a priori freedom of the state.[112] The discussions in the scholarly literature regarding Art. 15 para. 8 of the covenant were also characterized by the awareness that the norm could be taken two ways. Alf Ross, for example, expressed regret that the "disastrous" Art. 15 para. 8 had been inserted into the covenant in response to American pressure. In his assessment, the provision had enshrined a highly contested concept of sovereignty through the reference to "domestic jurisdiction," or "*domaine réservé*."[113] However, the fact that Art. 15 para. 8 established the competency of the Council to determine whether something was an "exclusive state matter" also provided an opportunity to modify this rule in practice.[114] Most writers within the reform movement interpreted Art. 15 para. 8 of the Covenant through a universalistic lens and posited a concept of state jurisdiction that depended on the legal corpus of international law.[115] Verdross, too, came to that conclusion: "With this, the League of Nations Covenant recognizes that not only the international affairs, but also the 'domestic matters' of the states depend on international law, are rooted in international law."[116]

The concept of the "exclusive internal jurisdiction" (domestic jurisdiction) that was enshrined in the positive law of the interwar period thus provided little clarity about the tenability of the thesis of the primacy of international law. Both positive international law and the judiciary remained ambiguous with respect to the primary thesis. The PCIJ, in particular, vacillated between a pre-legal concept of sovereignty and the "objective" understanding of international law that proceeded from the primacy thesis.

[110] PCIJ (*Lotus* case), Ser. A 10, 30.
[111] K. Strupp, "Les règles générales du droit de la paix," *RCADI*, 47/I (1934), 497–498.
[112] PCIJ (*Wimbledon* case), Ser. A 1, 24; (*Free Zone* case), Ser. A/B 46, 167.
[113] A. Ross, "Völkerbund und Staatssouveränität," *ZöR*, 11 (1931), 459.
[114] Ibid., 461.
[115] H. Kelsen, "Compulsory Adjudication of International Disputes," *AJIL*, 37 (1943), 406; Politis, "Le problème des limitations de la souveraineté," 47–48; Scelle, "Règles générales du droit de la paix," 502–504.
[116] Verdross, *Die Verfassung der Völkerrechtsgemeinschaft*, 173.

D The quarrel over the choice hypothesis [*Wahlhypothese*]

Uniting national law and international law into a single legal cosmos under the primacy of international law was the central theoretical project shared by Kelsen, Verdross, and Kunz. It was Vienna's most important scholarly contribution to the academic project that sought to modernize international law in the 1920s. The fact that Kelsen himself called the primacy thesis into question via the notion of the "choice hypothesis" was therefore all the more significant. According to Kelsen's argumentation underlying the choice hypothesis, it was not possible to deny that the countervailing thesis of the primacy of national law could also be argued by legal scholarship. Kelsen thought it necessary to emphasize that a view of international law that took the individual state as its central point of reference could be conclusively justified on theoretical grounds.[117]

Within this context he referred to the theory of international law as "external state law" [*äußeres Staatsrecht*] which regarded international law as merely a subset of national law.[118] From this perspective, international law was valid by virtue of its "recognition" by the individual, sovereign state. The existence of other states was likewise based merely on their "recognition" by the state's own constitutional organs. In this construct, contrary to the doctrine of the primacy of international law, national law "delegated" the norms of international law by "recognizing" all other state legal orders and the order of international law. This view thus advocated the primacy of national law. According to Kelsen, this conception fulfilled the postulate of systemic unity and was internally coherent.[119] Although it affirmed the notion of the sovereignty of the state and its essence as the highest legal community, in terms of legal theory it was defensible. And while this construct in the final analysis denied that international law was separated from national law, this theory was the "comparatively most consistent attempt" to reconcile the notion of a law of nations with the sovereign will of the state.[120]

Therefore both the objectivist view of international law as advanced by the doctrine of the primacy of international law, and the radical state subjectivism of the doctrine of external state law were conceivable.[121]

[117] Kelsen, *Problem der Souveränität*, 317.
[118] On "external state law" see Chapter 1 A 1.
[119] Kelsen, *Reine Rechtslehre* (1934), 139–142, 141; *Problems of Legal Theory*, 114–116.
[120] Kelsen, *Problem der Souveränität*, 155.
[121] H. Kelsen, *Reine Rechtslehre* (1934), 142; *Problems of Legal Theory*, 115.

The choice between these hypotheses was purely an ideological-political one and had to be left to the individual legal scholar.[122] Kelsen's choice hypothesis between the primacy of national law and the primacy of international law became a bone of contention within the School. By accepting the doctrine of the primacy of national law at least theoretically, Kelsen had relativized the doctrine of the primacy of international law, which was crucial to the program of modernizing international jurisprudence. Not least for that reason, Verdross and Kunz emphatically rejected the choice hypothesis and sought to demonstrate, by way of state practice, that the assumption of a primacy of national law was not tenable. In particular, international law clearly stood above national law for the simple reason already that a state could remain the same state in terms of international law after it had replaced its constitution and thereby had enacted a new legal order.[123] Such a legal rule could not be assumed if one proceeded theoretically from the state's legal order.

The debate over the choice hypothesis provides an important insight into the nature of the Kelsenian theory of international law. For Kelsen, purging international legal scholarship of political value judgments was a fundamental concern. As much as Kelsen sympathized with the legal-political goals of the modernization movement, he sought to keep his own theoretical constructs free of concealed value judgments. Both hypotheses were defensible in his eyes and therefore had to be accepted, with Mach's *Denkökonomie* (economy of mental effort) in mind,[124] as

[122] Kelsen, *Problem der Souveränität*, 317; *Staatsbegriff*, 99.

[123] H. Kelsen, *Reine Rechtslehre* (1934), 142; *Problems of Legal Theory*, 116.

[124] On Mach's *Denkökonomie*, the doctrine of the choice hypothesis, and its application by the School see Kunz, *Völkerrechtswissenschaft und Reine Rechtslehre*, 82; Kelsen, *Problem der Souveränität*, 99:

> In that the maxim of our value-understanding (of the normative examination) – which is analogous to the principle of the economy of thought and explanation as shown by Mach – is aimed at the greatest possible reduction of any tension that exists between Ought and Is, it tends to recognize as much as possible as valuable, that is, to recognize as much as possible of the content of Is as congruent with the content of Ought, and as little as possible as devoid of value, that is, as little as possible of the content of Is as contradicting the content of Ought. It thus represents a value-economic principle, a principle of the epistemological attainment of a value maximum.

On this see also L. Pitamic, "Denkökonomische Voraussetzungen der Rechtswissenschaft," *ZöR*, 3 (1918), 339 *et seq.*; on *Denkökonomie* in Kelsen see H. P. Rill, "Zur Methodenlehre der Rechtswissenschaft von Karl Larenz," *ÖZöR*, 13 (1964), 283.

useful tools of scholarship. As Kelsen saw it, there was no scholarly basis for deciding between the two approaches.[125] That decision could be made only in legal-political terms, whereby the pacifist would be more likely to opt for the primacy of international law and the imperialist for the primacy of national law.[126] The thrust of the Pure Theory of Law as a critique of politico-legal ideologies was visibly exemplified by Kelsen through his choice hypothesis. In spite of his cosmopolitan attitude, Kelsen, for the sake of his own credibility, had to make this concession to the theoretical "purity" of his legal theory.

Nevertheless, he repeatedly emphasized that the assumption of a primacy of national law would lead in the end to a denial of an autonomous international law.[127] The consequence of such an assumption was the superelevation of the legal order of one state. According to the doctrine of recognition, all other state legal orders as well as international law would have to be seen as derived legal sub-orders of the legal order of a single state. By putting the issue in such pointed theoretical terms, he reduced the doctrine of the primacy of national law in the final analysis to absurdity, thereby indirectly advancing the doctrine of the primacy of international law, to which he felt politically closer. The insistence on the choice hypothesis therefore primarily had a strategic function within the theoretical discourse. The interpretational openness of the choice hypothesis was meant to demonstrate the scientific objectivity of the Pure Theory of Law.

However, the choice hypothesis was more than merely demonstrative proof by Kelsen of the ideology-critical orientation of his theory of international law; it also laid bare one fundamental dilemma of the modern theory of international law. This dilemma manifested itself in the antagonism between the two seemingly irreconcilable approaches to international law. Kelsen had subjected the attempt by Jellinek and Triepel to meld the state-individualist and the universalistic approaches to a critical analysis in *The Problem of Sovereignty and the Theory of International Law*. He argued that because these two approaches often alternated, without reflection, between the objective and the subjective "epistemological standpoint," they were "scientifically" unusable.[128] In fact, the international legal mainstream had been trying since Jellinek to base its construction of international law on the empirically verifiable

[125] Kunz disagreed: *Völkerrechtswissenschaft und Reine Rechtslehre*, 82.
[126] H. Kelsen, *Reine Rechtslehre* (1934), 142. [127] Kelsen, "Souveränität," 555.
[128] On Kelsen's criticism in *Problem der Souveränität* see Chapter 2 C II.

acts of will by the "sovereign" state. This positivist method was to secure the proximity of international law to the factuality of concrete expressions of state will. At the same time, however, these writers, lest they wished to be counted among the deniers of international law, had to simultaneously proceed from the assumption that there existed an objective, binding corpus of international law that was independent from changes in individual sovereign wills. In the wake of Jellinek, German scholars tried to bring together the inherently irreconcilable lines of argumentation by integrating state sovereignty, on the one hand, and the progressive development of an objective international legal order on the other, into their doctrinal concepts.[129] The resulting alternation – often unconsidered – between the objective and the subjective epistemological standpoint formed Kelsen's chief point of criticism of the methodological approach of the then-dominant doctrine.[130]

The choice hypothesis was thus Kelsen's specific reaction to this fundamental dilemma of the modern theory of international law. For Kelsen, both the rigorously maintained thesis of external state law (i.e. the primacy of national law), as well as the conception of an objective, state-transcending law (i.e. primacy of international law), were theoretically suited to creating the postulated "unity of the legal world view."[131] The choice hypothesis thus demanded from the international lawyer a transparent political decision in favor of one of the two approaches. What Kelsen rejected was only the concealment of this decision by constantly "alternating" one's perspective. Having deconstructed the patterns of scholarly argumentation in their core, he does not succumb to the temptation to establish as absolute the construct he prefers, the primacy of international law; instead, he maintains the self-imposed critical distance to the legal-political preconditions of the opposing conceptions of international law. The choice hypothesis thus, on the one hand, outlines a central problem in the modern discourse on international law, and, on the other, shows the pains that Kelsen took to maintain his own claim to a new, non-political method for international legal scholarship.

[129] See Chapter 1 C IV. For an example from the literature after Jellinek: Nippold, *Die Fortbildung des Verfahrens in völkerrechtlichen Streitigkeiten*, 46. Nippold based his construct of international law on the sovereign will of the state, on the one hand, and on "international solidarity" as the source of an "objective" international law, on the other.

[130] Kelsen, *Staatslehre*, 142.

[131] H. Kelsen, *Reine Rechtslehre* (1934), 141.

E The opponents of the construction of a universal law and the notion of the "world state"

One criticism of the theory of international law of Kelsen and his school that was articulated by contemporaries maintained that the "objective" edifice of a universal system of law under the primacy of the law of nations invariably presupposed the establishment of a "world state" in the political sense. In fact, Kelsen had spoken positively on several occasions about the legal-political goal of the "organizational unity of the universal legal community" or the further political development in the direction of a "world state" or *civitas maxima*.[132] These utterances by the cosmopolitan Kelsen reinforced the critique of theory of international law as put forth by the Vienna School. Critics charged that it was a utopian doctrine of international law,[133] a construct of international law without the state,[134] or an unrealistic theory of international law.[135] According to this critique, Kelsen's doctrine of international law could be dismissed as the "general theory of state" of a non-existing world state. Consequently, the conception of universal law, caught in the "world state trap," was not suitable as a way to explain the reality of international relations, at least in the twentieth century. The opponents of the objective construction aimed their critique at three different levels. First, this conception of international law presupposed an already politically existing world state. Second, the construction of a universal, thoroughly coherent legal system with the international legal order overarching national law was "naked" natural law. Third, some critics rejected on principle the notion of "universality" as an ideological concept.

I Universal law, the "world state," and the civitas maxima

From the perspective of the Vienna School, international relations in the interwar period seemed increasingly caught up in a dynamic process of increasing juridification, a process for which the obsolete conceptual apparatus of the voluntaristic theories of international law was no longer adequate. The methodological destruction of the international

132 Kelsen, *Problem der Souveränität*, 320.
133 J. J. Lador-Lederer, "Some Observations on the 'Vienna School'," *Netherlands International Law Review* (1970), 126–150.
134 Carty, "The Continuing Influence of Kelsen," 344 *et seq.*
135 J. P. Haesert, "Book Review of: H. Kelsen, *Principles of International Law*," *AJCL*, 2 (1953), 579.

law positivism of the pre-war period was thus not an end unto itself, but was supposed to do justice to the rapidly changing reality of international relations in the interwar period. The Vienna School replaced the old constructs with a developmentally open model of a universal legal community. According to this model, international law was already an independent legal order with coercive character that was supraordinated to the states. This order was norm-logically prior to the state by virtue of the fact that it delegated – via individual norms of international law – the spheres of state jurisdiction as legal subsystems of the universal legal system. In the norm-logical sense, international law was the highest – i.e. "sovereign" – legal order and as such could centralize regulatory spheres on the international level virtually without restrictions. As an evolving legal order, it already possessed the necessary elementary functions of such an order, for Kelsen and Kunz believed that it had already laid down the beginnings of an international legislative, judicial, and executive branch. The legal order was still "primitive" because these three elementary functions still had to be exercised in a decentralized fashion via the individual states as organs of the order of international law.

What made this model so effective, in Kelsen's and Kunz's eyes, was the fact that it had overcome barriers to a further development and expansion of the system of international law, for example, the dogma of absolute state sovereignty. In this regard, their conception of international law followed a clear telos towards an international legal system based on centralized institutions. Nevertheless, the application of this construct of international law did not presuppose the political realization of organizational structures resembling a world state. In the following passage, Kelsen sought to clarify this subtle difference:

> The legal evolution alluded to here, tends in the end to blur the distinction between international law and the state legal system. The result is that the actual development of the law, directed as it is to increasing centralization, appears to have as its ultimate goal the organizational unity of a universal legal community – that is, the development of a world state. At the present time, however, there can be no talk of a world state. The only given is a cognitive unity of all law; that is, one can conceive of international law together with the state legal systems as a unified system of norms in exactly the same way as one is accustomed to regarding the state legal system as a unity.[136]

[136] H. Kelsen, *Reine Rechtslehre* (1934), 134–135; *Problems of Legal Theory*, 111.

Kelsen's theoretical construct of a "universal" law thus did not presuppose an organizational unity of the law in the sense of a politically realized world state; instead, it was grounded, as Kelsen put it, in a "cognitive unity." From the perspective of legal scholarship, universal law encompassed all legal norms as parts of a unified legal system. The norms of international law and national law were grounded in a unified theoretical conception of the law. This conception reduced law to its "pure" form, which, from the perspective of legal science, could take on any possible content. Freed from their a priori ethical and political limitations, international law and national law could be employed as a medium of potentially unlimited social change. The horizon was opened up – everything was possible. This included the realization of world state structures as a possible goal of international politics. Kelsen's use of the word "universal" can thus be understood in a twofold sense: "universal" stands for both the unity of international law and national law, and the unrestricted content of the medium of law as a "form" that could be used in any conceivable way.

Universal law was therefore born out of the destruction of the traditional and – in Kelsen's view – ideologized theoretical apparatus with the help of a "pure" methodology, on the one hand, and the construction of a unified legal system under the primacy of international law, on the other. "Pure method" and "objective construction" thus form the basic pillars of this theory of international law. This was not a conceptual anticipation of the organizational unity of a world state; rather, it was intended to conceptually prepare legal scholarship for the further political development of a "universal legal community" that many were hoping for in the interwar period.

In *The Problem of Sovereignty and the Theory of International Law*, Kelsen had also drawn on Wollf's formulation of the *civitas maxima*, and had regarded it as one possible designation for an encompassing universal legal system that was overarched by the higher-ranking system of international law.[137] If the state was nothing other than a personified legal system, it was for Kelsen in principle also possible to conceive of the overall legal system as a *civitas maxima* or a "world state" (Kelsen used these terms interchangeably). At the same time, however, Kelsen repeatedly made clear that one could not yet speak of a universal organizational unity with functionally divided legal organs, analogous to the modern constitutional state.[138] Still, given the mere existence of international

[137] Kelsen, *Problem der Souveränität*, 249.

[138] Ibid., 258. At the end of the Second World War, at the height of the debate over the post-war order, Kelsen addressed – *de lege ferenda* – the political feasibility of a world

legal norms, there was at least an "unorganized order," which, assuming the primacy of international law, constituted a universal legal community.[139]

The construction of universal law thus did not presuppose either a world state in the political sense, nor a world society in the sociological sense, nor a "humanity" in the Christian-natural law sense, that was bound together by shared values. As a legal-theoretical construct, it inferred from the existence of international legal norms the existence of a still-rudimentary universal order that encompassed all state legal systems. The question about the current sociological and political foundations of a universal legal community were certainly relevant for the legal sociologists, but not for the legal "scientist" in the narrower sense. The minimum empirical precondition for the theory of universal law was thus not the existence of a sociologically or politically realized world state or world society, but the real existence of international legal norms as such. The scholarly use of Kelsen's construct of international law was therefore independent of the actual realization of the organizational structures of a world state.[140] To put it in somewhat exaggerated terms, it presupposed merely the real existence of a single international legal norm as the nucleus of an evolving order. As a still largely unorganized legal system, international law for Kelsen possessed the developmental possibilities inherent in every legal system. Given the monistic overall architecture, this also included the possibility of directly empowering and obligating individuals through the international legal system, a circumstance that endowed international law with universal legislative authority also in terms of the entities to which its laws were addressed.

The vehement opposition that this developmentally-open theoretical approach encountered within the discipline was grounded, for one thing, in the nineteenth-century tradition of positivist international law, which had declared the existence of a "despotic" world state incompatible with

federation, and arrived at the following conclusion: "At present, however, such a World State is not within the scope of political reality, for it is also incompatible with the 'principle of sovereign equality' upon which, according to the Declaration signed by the governments of the United States, United Kingdom, the Soviet Union and China on November 1, 1943, at Moscow, the international organization to be established after the war shall be based." Quoted from Kelsen, *Peace through Law*, 12. The next possible step was at most a new international organization grounded in international law. Still, a world federation for him remained a desirable goal in terms of legal policy: ibid., 9.

139 Kelsen, *Problem der Souveränität*, 249.

140 In his writings on the primacy of international law, Kunz tended to come out against the establishment of a *civitas maxima* in the political sense: Kunz, "La Primauté de droit des gens," 593.

the freedom of the state. For another thing, skepticism toward a more strongly institutionalized world order received a boost from the current of realism that emerged in the discipline of international law in the middle of the 1930s.[141] To not only reflect theoretically on a superordinated international law, but to question on the level of legal policy the categorical rejection of the world state idea, amounted to the conscious breaking of a taboo. After the First World War, Kelsen and his students countered the intricate attempts of a Jellinek or Oppenheim to arrive, by building on the sovereign will of the state, at an international law that was binding on but not above the states, with a construct that not only incorporated international law into a unified notion of the law, but placed it above national law. After Germany's defeat and under the "Diktat of Versailles," many scholars in Germany and Austria were highly skeptical toward the constructed autonomy of international law, understood as the free availability of the medium of the law for the new experiments of the interwar period, such as the international administration of the Saar region, the League of Nations mandate over Danzig, or the novel system of minority protection.[142] Given the hegemonic position of the Council of the League of Nations and its institutions at the beginning of the 1920s, over which Germany and Austria had no control, the fact that the movement to modernize international law was a cosmopolitan departure in the direction of an organized system of world law was that much less suited to promoting its acceptance in these countries.

II The universal system of law as natural law?

Universal law in the Kelsenian sense dispensed with grounding itself in sociological insights, a canon of universal values, or the allegedly shared interests of states. It made itself independent of all of these and sought, through the application of logical deductions, to place the normative material into a unified and coherent conception.

John Herz, who had studied under Kelsen's supervision at the Graduate Institute in Geneva, regarded this transfer of the notion of the law as a system of hierarchical delegations to the system of international law, and the assumption of an international monopoly of force as

[141] Schiffer, *The Legal Community of Mankind*, 155–165; see Kelsen's analysis of the critics of the world state idea in *Problem der Souveränität*, 249–257.

[142] Stolleis, *A History of Public Law in Germany*, 60–64, and the discussion below, Chapter 5 D 1.

dangerous fictions.[143] The disparate and highly contested stock of norms of customary international law and treaty law could not be interpreted as a legal system endowed with coercive power.[144] For Herz, who later emigrated to the United States and became a professor of international relations, the theory of international law propounded by his former teacher Kelsen was, in its constructive orientation, the "most sophisticated natural law theory" of international relations.[145]

I will take a closer look at the natural law character of Kelsen's and Kunz's conception of international law by demarcating it from other proponents of the modernization movement. Nicolas Politis and Georges Scelle, for example, following Duguit, saw international law as a given, complete legal system, whose validity was grounded not in the sovereign will of the state, but in international solidarity. It had to be merely recognized and interpreted by international jurisprudence. The belief in universal law here found a basis in assumed "social facts."[146] Verdross, too, though in his case against his own Catholic-conservative background, referred back directly to the teachings of the Spanish late scholastics and the contemporary social theory of Othmar Spann. In that regard his theory of international law had its roots openly in natural law.[147]

143 J. H. Herz, "Kelsen's Doctrine in the Nuclear Age" in S. Engel and R. A. Métall (eds.), *Law, State and International Legal Order. Essays in Honor of Hans Kelsen* (Knoxville: University of Tennessee Press, 1964), 108. Likewise, Sir A. Zimmern, in his famous monograph *The League of Nations and the Rule of Law 1918–1935* (1st edn. London: Macmillan, 1936; reprint of the 2nd, revised edn. of 1939, New York: Russel & Russel, 1969), already influenced by the nascent "realism" within international political discourse, revealed a skeptical attitude toward international law:

> There is in fact, whatever the names used in the books, no system of international law – and still less, of course, a code. What is to be found in the treatises is simply a collection of rules which, when looked at closely, appear to have been thrown together, or to have been accumulated, almost at haphazard. Many of them would seem to be more appropriately described as materials for the etiquette book for the conduct of sovereigns and their representatives than as elements of a true legal system (98).

144 Herz, "Kelsen's Doctrine in the Nuclear Age," 109 *et seq.*

145 Ibid., 108; G. Man, *L'école de Vienne et le développement du droit des gens* (Paris: Librairie technique et économique, 1938), 119.

146 On the theory of international law of Scelle and Politis see Chapter 4 B. II.

147 A. Verdross, "Die allgemeinen Rechtsgrundsätze des Völkerrechts" in *Gesellschaft, Staat, und Recht. Untersuchungen zur Reinen Rechtslehre. Festschrift für Hans Kelsen* (Vienna: J. Springer, 1931), 358; A. Verdross, "Grundlagen und Grundsätze des Völkerrechts in christlicher Schau," *Schönere Zukunft*, XIII (1938), 385 *et seq.*; A. Verdross, "Les principes generaux de droit comme source du droit des gens,"

These substantive conceptions of unity, however, differed clearly from the Neo-Kantian, systemic construction of "universal law" in Kelsen, which had also been promoted by Hersch Lauterpacht as another one of Kelsen's students.[148] Lauterpacht, who had emigrated to England after his studies in Vienna, emphasized throughout his life the necessity of seeing international law as a complete system of norms whose application must not be blocked by the political interests of states.[149] This view of international law was to limit the loopholes for actions by states that were not regulated by international law.[150]

Lauterpacht, Kelsen, and Kunz shared the neo-Kantian call for the unity of cognition and the belief that the system-rationality of the law could be given a "scientific" foundation. The shaping force of the cosmopolitan liberalism of the enlightened Jewish bourgeoisie in Austria in the second half of the nineteenth century, which Marti Koskenniemi has convincingly demonstrated in the case of Hersch Lauterpacht,[151] showed itself not only in these authors' shared confidence in the effectiveness of the law, but also in the undaunted belief in progress that comes through in their writings.[152] To be sure, anchoring the law in morality and natural law was in principle closer to Lauterpacht's way of thinking than the assumption of an abstract basic norm emptied of all material content. However, Verdross's break with the Pure Theory of Law was much more far-reaching than the very restrained critique by Lauterpacht, who, it was said, kept a picture of Kelsen alongside one of his later teacher McNair in

Annuaire de l'Institut de droit international, 40 (1937), 183 *et seq*.; and later A. Verdross, *Statisches und dynamisches Naturrecht* (Freiburg: Rombach, 1971). On this see A. Truyos y Serra, "Verdross et la théorie du droit," *EJIL*, 6 (1995), 55–69.

148 On the complex, theoretical proximity between Kelsen and Lauterpacht see M. Koskenniemi, "Lauterpacht: The Victorian Tradition in International Law," *EJIL*, 2 (1997), 217–218; A. Carty, "The Continuing Influence of Kelsen," 352–354.

149 Lauterpacht, *The Function of Law*, 3–4, 9–25; on this see Koskenniemi, *From Apology to Utopia*, 131–154.

150 In the wake of the First World War, which was experienced as a rupture of civilization, the rule of international law was supposed to tame the irrational forces of nationalism. Throughout his life, Lauterpacht, in agreement with Kelsen, saw as the goal of such a development of the law "the gradual integration of international society in the direction of a supranational Federation of the world – a development which must be regarded as the ultimate postulate of the political organization of man," quoted in H. Lauterpacht, *International Law and Human Rights* (London: F. A. Praeger, 1950), 46.

151 Koskenniemi, "Lauterpacht: The Victorian Tradition," 257–258.

152 On the bourgeois-liberal imprint on Kelsen see Jabloner, "Kelsen and his Circle," 369–371; on the liberal attitude of the Austrian-Jewish bourgeoisie see Beller, *Vienna and the Jews*, 123; on the prevailing belief within these circles in social progress through scientific understanding see Schorske, *Fin-de-Siècle Vienna*, 6.

his study throughout his life.[153] Although Lauterpacht rejected the radical value-relativism of the Pure Theory of Law as an unnecessary expulsion of "ultimate values" from jurisprudence,[154] his self-conception as a legal scholar was decisively shaped by the system-concept of Neo-Kantianism.[155]

In Verdross as well as Scelle, the universal community of humankind was a given biological or socio-ethical phenomenon from which the existence of a universal legal order was derived.[156] Kelsen, Kunz, and Lauterpacht, by contrast, derived from the mere existence of a stock of international legal norms the progressive formation of a universal legal system. The assumption of a complete universal legal system was an a priori postulate of legal knowledge and thus *not* an ethical or biological category that preceded the law. For Verdross and Scelle, legal theory merely reflected an already given substantive community of values or solidarity. Kelsen, Kunz, and Lauterpacht, on the other hand, restricted themselves, in their constructive orientation, to the stock of empirical norms, reconstructing them through scholarly abstraction as a unified system of rules. Because of its system-building character, this conception of the law could be described as "natural law," though it was diametrically opposed to the conventional notions of natural law with respect to

[153] H. Lauterpacht, "Kelsen's Pure Science of Law" in E. Lauterpacht (ed.), *International Law. Being the Collected Papers of Hersch Lauterpacht, systematically arranged and edited by E. Lauterpacht* (Cambridge University Press, 1977), vol. 3, 404 *et seq.*

[154] Ibid., 424 *et seq.*

[155] Koskenniemi, "Lauterpacht: The Victorian Tradition," 223.

[156] In 1925, Verdross expressed regret that German international law positivism in the nineteenth century had lost its grounding in natural law universalism. Drawing on Othmar Spann, he emphasized the value of humanity as a whole and its precedence over individual nations: "For Spann, this higher-ranking nature of the community of states arises from the realization that a nation [*Volkstum*] does not constitute an ultimate entity, but itself appears as the member of higher entities, in the final analysis, of humanity . . . Although the community of states is logically prior, the whole precedes the part, the community of states precedes the state community," quoted from A. Verdross, "Die gesellschaftswissenschaftlichen Grundlagen der Völkerrechtstheorie," *ARWP*, XVIII (1924/1925), 428–429. On the relationship between Verdross and Spann see Carty, "Alfred Verdross and Othmar Spann." In his 1937 textbook on international law, however, Verdross used a theological argumentation to highlight not the unity, but the now sudden differences between nations and the value of the individual ethnic community: "The natural division of humanity cannot be abrogated even by those religious communities that are in their conception religions of humanity. Added to this is that even the endeavor to abrogate the multiplicity of nations would go against Christian doctrine," quoted from A. Verdross, *Völkerrecht* (Berlin: Springer, 1937), 40. On Verdross and Lauterpacht see Koskenniemi, "Lauterpacht: The Victorian Tradition," 225.

its epistemological premises. In this context, Kelsen readily conceded as early as 1928 that an a priori understanding of the law secured by the concept of the basic norm transcended, as a system free of contradictions, the boundaries of positivism:

> With the postulate of a meaningful order (i.e. one devoid of contradiction), jurisprudence is already transcending the boundary of pure positivism. However, relinquishing this postulate would be tantamount to its self-dissolution. If one wishes to see in the basic norm, which has been shown here to be the necessary precondition of every positivistic understanding of the law, natural law, in spite of the fact that it dispenses with every element of material justice, one could not object to this any more than one could if someone were to describe the categories of transcendental philosophy as metaphysics, because they are not given by experience but condition it.[157]

Specifically with respect to establishing international law as a higher-ranking order based on a hypothetical basic norm, Kelsen – drawing on Christian Wolff – had spoken about the dissolution of the boundary between legal positivism and natural law as early as 1920:

> The 'natural law' character of such a grounding of international law cannot and should not be denied. However, to the extent that this 'natural law' foundation, as a juridical hypothesis, is merely limited to making possible a legal system between coordinated subjects that must be developed by and filled with content through *positive* legislation [*Satzung*], the legal system of the individual state, as well, premised as sovereign, cannot do without such a natural law grounding.[158]

With this, Kelsen was conceding the constructive character of the postulate of unity and of the theory of the basic norm. All in all, the problem that I have laid out reveals that a blanket differentiation between natural law and legal positivism is inadequate for describing the Neo-Kantian, system-oriented conception of the law in Kelsen, Kunz, and Lauterpacht.

III The abuse of the idea of universalism

For John Herz, Kelsen's concept reduced the perception of the reality of international relations to the tendencies toward greater

[157] H. Kelsen, *Die philosophischen Grundlagen der Naturrechtslehre und des Rechtspositivismus* (Charlottenburg: A. Heise, 1928; also printed in *WRS* I, 281 *et seq.*), 66.

[158] Kelsen, *Problem der Souveränität*, 252 (emphasis original).

institutionalization and juridification. This lopsided focus on the progress that had been achieved in the establishment of international organizations, international adjudication, and the introduction of collective sanctions to enforce the law, anticipated developments that still clashed strongly with reality.[159] The danger of this approach, as Herz saw it, lay in endowing the aggressive quest for power by states with the semblance of normativity by way of the theory of the *bellum iustum* and a system-oriented understanding of international law. However, international law was not a system of higher-ranking norms with coercive force; Kelsen's exaggeration of these trends reinforced the cynical attitude toward the "irreality of international law" and brought about the opposite of what was originally intended.[160]

Carl Schmitt had spelled out such a critical attitude toward international law impressively in his concept of the political. Invoking Hobbes, he rejected the "normativization" or "rule of law" in international relations through the notion of a sovereign, higher-ranking legal order as a fiction:

> Hobbes has drawn these simple consequences of political thought without confusion and more clearly than anyone else. He has emphasized time and again that the sovereignty of law means only the sovereignty of men who draw up and administer this law. The rule of a higher order, according to Hobbes, is an empty phrase if it does not signify politically that certain men of this higher order rule over men of a lower order.[161]

The juridification of war as a form of sanction by the international legal community was for Schmitt also impossible, given the "political" nature of war: "War as the most extreme political means discloses the possibility which underlies every political idea, namely, the distinction of friend and enemy. This makes sense only as long as this distinction in mankind is actually present or at least potentially possible. On the other hand, it would be senseless to wage war for purely religious, purely moral, purely legal, or purely economic motives."[162] Similar to John Herz, Schmitt

159 Herz, "Kelsen's Doctrine in the Nuclear Age," 108.

160 Ibid., 109.

161 C. Schmitt, *Der Begriff des Politischen* (1932) (reprint of the 1963 edition, Berlin, 1979), 66; English trans. G. Schwab, *The Concept of the Political* (New Brunswick: Rutgers University Press, 1976), 67. On this see A. Carty, "Interwar German Theories of International Law: The Psychoanalytical and Phenomenological Perspectives of Hans Kelsen and Carl Schmitt," *Cardozo Law Review*, 16 (1995), 1251–1257.

162 Schmitt, *The Concept of the Political*, 35–36.

emphasized the danger of abuse that was inherent in the cosmopolitan project of normativization:

> When a state fights its political enemy in the name of humanity, it is not a war for the sake of humanity, but a war wherein a particular state seeks to usurp a universal concept against its military opponent . . . To confiscate the word humanity, to invoke and monopolize such a term probably could have certain incalculable effects, such as denying the enemy the quality of being human and declaring him to be *hors-la-loi* and *hors l'humanité*.[163]

Schmitt gave an impressive illustration of how the idea of universality in connection with the concept of law could be put to political use for an aggressive national quest for power.[164] However, this critique could not affect Kelsen's and Kunz's construct of international law, since they did *not* base their conception of universal law on a "humankind" that preceded the law as an assumed community of value or solidarity.

From the perspective of Kelsen, Kunz, and Lauterpacht, the danger of cynical abuse also did not discredit the project of universal law; on the contrary, it confirmed the necessity of establishing neutral institutions that were able, as centralized organs of the international legal system, to prevent the abuse of the "name of law" by any single party. As they saw it, the universal legal system could be protected against political misuse only by international bodies capable of overseeing and guaranteeing adherence to the law in international relations. To that extent, the belief in universal law necessarily included the belief in institutionalized procedures, that is, the belief in international institutions established by law as neutral representatives of an international legal community.

[163] Ibid., 54.

[164] On the anti-Semitic meaning of Schmitt's critique of the concept of universality see R. Gross, "'Jewish Law and Christian Grace' – Carl Schmitt's Critique of Hans Kelsen," in D. Diner and M. Stolleis (eds.), *Hans Kelsen and Carl Schmitt: A Juxtaposition* (Gerlingen: Bleicher, 1999), 107–108.

PART II

The outlines of the cosmopolitan project – the actors, sources, and courts of universal law

Kelsen had put forth his postulated "purity of method" above all in opposition to the dogma of sovereignty, the voluntaristic foundation of international law, and the dualism of international law and national law. As demonstrated in Part I of this book, his own "objective" construction of international law arose for the most part out of the destruction of traditional doctrinal distinctions, out of the assertion of what had previously been widely seen as impossible. Thus, duality becomes unity, state sovereignty becomes a sovereign order of international law, or a legal system between states becomes a supraordinated law that can directly grant rights to, and impose obligations on, not only states, but also individuals. Behind this revision of traditional doctrine stood, as I will continue to show in Part II, Kelsen's own cosmopolitan project. The outlines of that project become especially clear in his writings during the Second World War that were focused on questions of a new world order. This project included new actors, that is, international organizations and individuals, who take their place next to the state as the classic subject of international law. On the whole, Kelsen sought a thoroughgoing juridification of international relations. Having witnessed two world wars, he advocated a global monopoly of force that was legally controlled and enforced by an effective system of collective security. Moreover, international law was to be led from the "primitive" principle of collective liability to a more highly developed legal system in which individual liability under international law was the rule.

Kelsen did not pursue this project only through policy proposals and sociological writings, however. To be sure, on the outside it would appear that Kelsen consistently maintained the separation of legal "science" and politics – imposed by the postulate of purity – by clearly identifying writings on legal policy, on the one hand, and "purely" legal arguments, on the other. Closer examination, however, reveals a line of connection between the two goals of Kelsen's theories of international law that only appeared to be running along parallel tracks. Kelsen could promote his political project also as a legal scholar by aiming his writings on the doctrine of international law at a fundamental critique of those doctrinal constructs that could impede his desired goal, namely the further institutional development of the international legal community. To deconstruct these dogmas, he deployed his "critical" toolkit with deliberation. In this way, the initially "neutral," purely "scientific" methodological critique also served to further his own political goals. This becomes especially apparent in Kelsen's ideas on the legal sources of international law. For the political implementation of his ambitious cosmopolitan projects, Kelsen favored the instrument of the treaty as a materially unlimited, statute-like form of legislation in international politics. To that end, he sought to unmask the axiom of freedom underlying the traditional theory of treaties as an ideologically motivated restriction on the reach of the instrument of the treaty, and to expel it from international law theory as "unscientific." The leeway for action in international politics was to be expanded by destroying traditional doctrinal beliefs and constructs. Because of the tension between "purity of method" and his own political convictions, Kelsen could only to a limited extent engage in politically motivated interpretations of the legal material at hand, for doing so would have made him vulnerable to the accusation that he himself was "politicizing" international legal scholarship. It is also against this background that one should understand his "choice hypothesis" described in Part I: To maintain his own claim of being non-political in his legal writings, he allowed this hypothesis to fundamentally relativize even his own constructive project that gave primacy to international law over national law.

As a way out of this dilemma, Kelsen used the critical force of his juridical methodology to selectively destroy those conceptions that could pose a threat to his own cosmopolitan project. In this way, the self-limitation to methodological "purity" demanded by Kelsen was intended to increase the constructive maneuvering room of the politically authorized organs in the further institutional elaboration of the community of states. Kelsen's writings on doctrinal issues thus amounted almost exclusively to a large-scale critique. This destructive thrust represented the link between his political project and the postulate of "pure" scientific cognition. However, this inherent synthesis of Kelsen the cosmopolite and Kelsen the politician led, in its destructive orientation, to a considerable restriction on the sphere of activity of the legal scholar. It is no accident that Kelsen, during the Second World War, devoted himself increasingly to questions of sociology and legal policy so as to be constructively active, without constraints, in the role of legal policymaker and sociologist.

The contours of the cosmopolitan project repeatedly hinted at in Part I of the book will be drawn out more carefully in Part II. To that end, I will take a close look at Kelsen's contributions to three fields of international law that were especially sensitive for the elaboration of an institutionalized community of states. Continued attention will be given especially to the methodological approaches that Kelsen and his like-minded contemporaries used in an effort to advance their shared, highly political project.

4

The new actors of universal law

Kelsen and Kunz had conceptualized international law as a substantively unrestricted means of guiding society on the world level, that is, as "universal law." This reflected the high expectations that the cosmopolitan elites placed in the medium of international law during the interwar period. They believed that the phenomenon of European nationalism had driven the nations into the First World War. In the "new world order," aggressive nationalism was to be countered by new institutions that secured the peace. From the perspective of the liberal modernization movement, the passionate forces of nationalism could be rationalized and defused only via the law of nations in international procedures and processes. That required new actors, who were to take their place beyond the sovereign nation state as the organs of universal law. The politically created new organs of the community of states were especially the League of Nations and the individual as a bearer of rights and obligations under international law.

This new way of looking at international law was intended to do justice to its growing importance as a pacifying medium in international relations. The political conflicts created by the territorial reorganization of Europe in the wake of the First World War were to be resolved through the new world organization and through international "legal experimentation,"[1] such as novel treaties protecting minority rights or internationalized zones like the "Free City of Danzig." In the eyes of the cosmopolitan scholars, the specter of nationalism had not yet been banished. The great hopes in what international law could accomplish were directed above all at resolving the political tensions and clashes of interests underlying the Treaty of Versailles. In its pathos of reconstruction, Wilson's "new world order"

[1] I have taken this term from Nathaniel Berman, who spoke of forms of "advanced legal experimentation" in the interwar period: "But the Alternative is Despair: European Nationalism and the Modernist Renewal of International Law," *Harvard L. R.*, 106 (1993),1819; and "A Perilous Ambivalence," 377.

had invoked contradictory political principles that the League of Nations, in particular, was expected to bring into alignment.[2] In addition, some of the "principles" mentioned in the famous Fourteen Points and promises made in them to the peoples of Europe had fallen victim in the Versailles peace conferences to tactical concessions and compromise formulas. Largely one-sided reparations, which contradicted the Fourteen Points, were imposed on defeated Germany. Although the principles proclaimed by Wilson, as for example the "right of self-determination," were not yet customary international law, through their immense influence on public opinion during the war, they had crucially shaped the expectations that the world public placed in the "new world order." The League of Nations, in particular, was therefore expected to resolve the political contradictions and make true the unfulfilled promises of the post-war settlement."[3] Its authority and capacity to act as a new and influential actor in international relations were to be strengthened through a new scholarly approach to international law.

Whether on the issue of minority protection or international administration of multinational territories, there was – from the perspective of the modernization movement – a universal need for new legal procedures and institutional arrangements that would make it possible

[2] Wilson's Fourteen Points, which were issued even before the war was over, contained the following basic principles of a post-war order: full sovereignty for the Central and Eastern European states; the right of self-determination; protection of minorities; mutual guarantees for political independence and territorial sovereignty; equality of trade conditions; relinquishing the balance of power; general restrictions on armaments and no punitive war reparations. In part the Fourteen Points, as a political guide for the peace negotiations, had already carried within them unresolvable clashes in what they were trying to achieve: the promise of full "political sovereignty" for Czechoslovakia and Poland, for example, stood from the beginning in a relationship of tension to the obligation of an "effective protection of minorities" demanded from the new states. The protection of national minorities, in turn, stood in a contradiction (unresolvable by objective criteria) to the proclaimed "self-determination of nations," which could be interpreted as allowing a minority to break away from a multinational state. For its part, the guarantee of the "territorial integrity" and "political independence" of the newly created states could be achieved only by reducing the territories and limiting the political independence of the defeated Central European states. On the relationship between the right of self-determination and the protection of minorities in the interwar period, with an extensive evaluation of the contemporary literature, see Berman, "But the Alternative is Despair," 1821–1859; on the minority problem see B. Schot, *Nation oder Staat? Deutschland und der Minderheitenschutz* (Marburg/Lahn: J. G. Herder-Institut, 1988).

[3] On the varied expectations that were placed in the League of Nations see D. Kennedy, "The Move to Institutions," *Cardozo L. R.*, 8 (1987), 911–913; on the German perspective see E. Fraenkel, "Idee und Realität des Völkerbundes im deutschen politischen Denken," *Vierteljahreshefte für Zeitgeschichte*, 16 (1968), 1–14.

to counteract the subversive phenomenon of European nationalism. In the 1920s, international law was thus needed as a "social technique" of "a universal world community of law" and it was in fact deployed by international politics, often in novel ways.[4] The cosmopolitan scholars of the (numerically rather small) modernization movement were hoping to counter the latent threat to the interwar order from the "irrational" forces of European nationalism with new legal experiments. As part of that movement, the Vienna School sought, from a scientific perspective, to provide a theoretical basis for new international legal experiments and actors through a theory of the subjects of international law that was in keeping with the times and took account of the new forms of political organization.

A Legally organized communities above the state

Although the state was no longer the only subject of international law in the theory of the Vienna School, it remained the most important one.[5] Its organs are authorized by international treaty law to create new norms of international law. The states are therefore the central law-creators of the international legal system. However, according to the theory of the primacy of international law, they do not represent a sovereign entity that precedes the law, but a subordinated legal sphere that is integrated into the universal legal system.[6] The material, territorial, and temporal validity of the state legal systems is regulated by the higher-ranking norms of international law.[7] In this way, Kelsen and Kunz desanctified the state and integrated it into the universal legal system.

In the international law theory of the Vienna School, however, the state was joined by other "organized communities" as actors of the "universal community of world law."[8] The writers of the interwar period directed their attention especially at the new organizational forms that international politics had given itself, especially through the League of Nations.

[4] Berman, "But the Alternative is Despair," 1874–1898.

[5] H. Kelsen, *Auseinandersetzungen zur reinen Rechtslehre: Kritische Bemerkungen zu Georges Scelle und Michael Virally*, ed. K. Ringhofer and R. Walter (Vienna and New York: Springer, 1987), 95.

[6] H. Kelsen, *Reine Rechtslehre* (1934), 150–153.

[7] H. Kelsen, *Reine Rechtslehre* (1934), 147–153; in the process, the international legal order generally left it up to the state legal system to identify the individuals who are empowered and obligated by the norms of international law.

[8] Kelsen, *Problem der Souveränität*, 280–294.

Although the term "international organization" can be traced back to the nineteenth century,[9] in the 1920s it was not yet a widely used concept in legal scholarship. The legal discussions surrounding the "nature" of the League of Nations, meanwhile, were carried out largely on the basis of the theory of unions of states [*Staatenverbindungen*].[10] As part of the movement to modernize international law, Kelsen and Kunz also sought to provide a scientific foundation for the authority of the League of Nations and its capacity to act. The experiments in international law during the interwar period could be carried out only under the aegis of a united and "neutral" institutional actor. The international organization endowed with the authority of the law became the rallying point for hopes in a post-nationalist, more peaceful world order. The Vienna School's theory of international law, which was especially receptive to the processes of international integration, mirrored the great hopes that the authors were projecting onto the new organizational forms.

I Unions of states as a dynamic continuum of legal integration

The Vienna School, building on Kelsen's fundamental critique of the conventional notion of sovereignty and the doctrine of the primacy of international law, developed its own theory of unions of states in the 1920s. In 1929, that is, nearly half a century after Jellinek's groundbreaking work on this issue,[11] Kunz published (as part of Fritz Stier-Somlo's series of handbooks on international law) another comprehensive monographic analysis of all legal questions relating to the issue of unions of states.[12] Although he distanced himself from Kelsen on a number of specific theoretical points, his essay was grounded in the fundamental

9 P. A. Potter, "The Origin of the Term International Organisation," *AJIL*, 39 (1945), 803–806. On this issue in general see P. A. Potter, "Le développement de l'organisation internationale 1815–1914," *RCADI* 64/II (1938), 71 *et seq.*; K. Dicke, *Effizienz und Effektivität internationaler Organisationen. Darstellung und kritische Analyse eines Topos im Reformprozeß der Vereinten Nationen* (Berlin: Duncker & Humblot, 1994), 44–53. On the contribution of international organizations to the development of international law see J. A. Frowein, "Der Beitrag der internationalen Organisationen zur Entwicklung des Völkerrechts," *ZaöRV*, 36 (1976), 147 *et seq.*

10 Highly controversial, especially in Germany dating back to the founding of the German Confederation, was the demarcation between the concept of the federal state and the confederation of states. On the contemporary debate in the literature see Stolleis, *Public Law in Germany*, 341–344.

11 Jellinek, *Die Lehre von den Staatenverbindungen.*

12 Kunz, *Die Staatenverbindungen.*

positions of the Vienna School. Kelsen had worked out the basic outlines of an integration-friendly theory of unions of states as early as 1920 in his *Problem of Sovereignty and the Theory of International Law*, and had developed it further in his *Allgemeine Staatslehre* in 1925.[13] As he saw it, the entire theory of unions of states was to be reworked "from the perspective of a Pure Theory."[14]

1 Unions of states as a particular international legal community

The starting point for a theory of unions of states was for Kelsen the assumption of a monistic legal system based on the primacy of international law. As we have seen, Kelsen understood sovereignty as a formal attribute in the sense of "being the highest"; under the assumption of a primacy of international law, this attribute should be assigned to the international legal system.[15] Added to this was the assumption that the state was identical with the legal system. Proceeding from the primacy of international law, this gave rise to a universal legal cosmos in which the order of international law represented the highest and therefore "sovereign" edifice. The notion of a "community of international law" meant for Kelsen that "polities described as states" are "legally connected" through precisely that edifice.[16] Even if only a few states come together to constitute themselves as a common legal entity, this was done via the system of international law. In such a case they would constitute a particular international legal community [*Völkerrechtsgemeinschaft*].[17] These kinds of communities arose by way of the international treaty, through which the theory of unions of states became a theory of the typical content of such treaties.[18] As Kelsen saw it, the specific treaty order established by the states was part of the superordinated edifice of international law and was thus able to constrain, in any way it desired, the regulatory competencies of states in their capacity as legal systems.

The move to look at unions of states exclusively through the lens of international law broke with the distinctions in traditional doctrine between unions of states based on national law and those based on international law. Kelsen maintained that this distinction rested on

[13] Kelsen, *Staatslehre*, 163–180. [14] Kelsen, *Problem der Souveränität*, 275.
[15] On the concept of sovereignty in Kelsen see Chapter 2 C I.
[16] Kelsen, *Problem der Souveränität*, 276. [17] Ibid., 276–278.
[18] By way of example of the problem of federal state/confederation of states: Kelsen, *Problem der Souveränität*, 280 *et seq.*

the erroneous premise that unions of states should be differentiated according to the manner in which they came about.[19] In conventional theory, unions of states created by a constitutional law should be seen as "national law" unions, and those created by treaty should be seen as "international law" unions. This doctrinal distinction had been introduced into the discourse by Laband in connection with the controversial differentiation between a confederation of states and a federal state, and had been developed further by Jellinek.[20] According to this view, a confederation was an entity of international law created by treaty, whereas the federal state was described as a state based on constitutional law.[21] To that extent, the confederation was for Jellinek only a "legal relationship" which, in contradistinction to the federal state, could not be thought of as a legal person. For a legal person, Jellinek argued in his theory of unions of states, could always be the creation only of a legal system "that must stand above those through whose will it can be created."[22] This was not the case, however, with international law, which in his view derived its validity precisely from the sovereign will of the state. Since international law was seen merely as law between the states, it could not create a system of government that transformed the contracting parties into member states of a sovereign federal state.

For Kelsen, in contrast to Jellinek's conception, there was no significant theoretical difference between the terms "treaty," "constitution," or "statute" with respect to the foundational document of the new entity.[23] Moreover, historically federal states had often been created through international treaties.[24] In fact, in the case of originally unaffiliated states, i.e. states subject only to international law, this was the necessary procedure for creating a federal state. Traditional theory had tried to resolve this problem via the notion of the "constitutive treaty."[25] Like the conventional distinction between treaty and "agreement," this was an attempt to construct a special legal instrument that could subordinate the contracting states. According to the prevailing concept of sovereignty, that could be, in the final analysis, only a legal instrument derived from constitutional law. The theory of the "constitutive treaty" was based on

[19] Ibid., 280 *et seq.* [20] Jellinek, *Die Lehre von den Staatenverbindungen*, 178 *et seq.*

[21] On this, with a survey of the literature, see Jellinek, *Die Lehre von den Staatenverbindungen*, 178 *et seq.*

[22] Ibid., 179. [23] Kelsen, *Problem der Souveränität*, 282. [24] Ibid., 281.

[25] With an extensive review of the literature: G. J. Ebers, *Die Lehre vom Staatenbunde* (Breslau: M. & H. Marcus, 1910), 287.

the following line of thought: in a federal state, the member states are subject to the federal power. The conveyance of previously sovereign states into such a system must therefore be done through a law that stands above the formerly independent states. Because international law was traditionally regarded as a law *between* sovereigns, it could not fulfill that function. The "constitutive" treaty had therefore been doctrinally constructed as an exceptional case, in which an international legal instrument had the capacity to create a system of government superimposed upon the member states. That legal order, however, should not have the character of international law, but of constitutional law. For the individual states could be subordinated as member states only to a state legal system. It was thus not the order of international law (which operated only between states, after all) that had transformed the sovereign state into a member state, but the exceptional "constitutive treaty" that had created a new state constitution. Public law scholars during the German Empire sought to grasp this exceptional circumstance with additional concepts, such as that of the "agreement" (Binding) or the "national act" (Jellinek). The premise shared by all of these approaches was articulated by Jellinek as follows: "For by way of a treaty one cannot bring forth a higher will above oneself and no independent will alongside oneself."[26]

But there had also been voices of opposition to this intricate scholarly construction during the Empire. Haenel had been the first to point out critically that the "content and nature of a system is one thing, the basis for its creation another."[27] The Vienna School revived this differentiation between the process by which a legal order was created and its legal nature. Proceeding from the primacy of international law, Kelsen regarded the international treaty as a specific legal order superimposed upon the states, which could readily transform the original states into member states. From this perspective, every international legal treaty created a particular legal order, which derived its binding force over and above the states from the international legal maxim *pacta sunt servanda* or from the postulated basic norm of international law. A strict theoretical distinction between a confederation and a federal state was not compelling for Kelsen.[28] Both could be created by either constitutional

[26] Jellinek, *Die Lehre von den Staatenverbindungen*, 257.
[27] A. Haenel, *Die vertragsmäßigen Elemente der Deutschen Reichsverfassung. Studien zum Deutschen Staatsrecht* (Leipzig: H. Haessel, 1873), vol. 1, 38.
[28] Kelsen, *Problem der Souveränität*, 288.

law or an international treaty. Independent of whether one spoke of a constitution, a statute, or an international treaty, both entities constituted a particular legal order that was binding upon the states in question.[29]

As Kelsen saw it, the methodological reason behind the distinction made by the prevailing doctrine lay in an impermissible switch in the vantage point from which the issue was examined. If the talk was of a confederation, the conventional view looked at the new legal order from an international legal perspective. The particular legal order was then traced back to a treaty and thus to the basis of validity for international law, which endowed the treaty with its binding force. By contrast, with the term federal state, the prevailing doctrine assumed a vantage point that proceeded from the state.[30] In this case, the dimension of international law was blocked out. This was done with the goal of being able to describe the federal state as a sovereign entity and the confederation as a non-sovereign union of multiple states that preserved their identity: "The political postulate: conceiving of a certain constitution created by way of an international treaty as a 'state,' compels jurists beholden to the dogma of sovereignty to presuppose that this legal order set up by way of treaty is the highest, sovereign order. And only the presupposed sovereignty can make the federal state appear not to be a confederation."[31]

For Kelsen, the distinction drawn by the prevailing theory between confederation and federal state was thus based simply on a switch between the assumption of the primacy of international law and the assumption of the primacy of national law. His call for the unity of legal cognition and for a de-politicized notion of science thus allowed Kelsen to completely abolish the distinctions made by conventional doctrine.

2 The doctrine of centralization and decentralization

In his *Allgemeine Staatslehre*, Kelsen for his part invoked the concepts of confederation and federal state to illustrate his own theory of unions of states: "Confederation and federal state, these two main types of state unions differ only in the degree of centralization and decentralization."[32] For Kelsen, there was no "qualitative" but only a "quantitative" difference between the two types of union. The entire theory of state unions, he argued, was a theory of forms of union that could be differentiated merely by their divergent degrees of centralization. In

[29] Ibid., 286. [30] Ibid., 287. [31] Ibid., 287. [32] Kelsen, *Staatslehre*, 194.

this context, a legal community that was – conceptually – completely centralized was one whose order consisted exclusively of norms that claimed validity for the entire legal sphere.[33] By contrast, the completely decentralized legal order consisted of legal norms that were only valid for partial areas. The federal state differed from the confederation only in that the federal government in the federal state possessed a greater number of centralized powers. And in this setup, the transitions from the less centralized confederation to the more strongly centralized federal state were fluid.

Every form of legal union between territorially demarcated territories, Kelsen argued, could be described as a particular stage of centralization situated between the two extremes:

> Likewise, the connection of individual states to the system of international law as such, as well as to individual, particular communities such as confederacy, union, and federal state, can be assessed only from the perspective of centralization and decentralization. In fact, the international legal community does not even represent the greatest possible degree of decentralization. So-called general international law, the product of customary law, is a stock of enacted norms that are valid for the entire geographic area of the international legal system.[34]

For Kelsen, the international legal order in 1925 was still a fairly decentralized legal community. Within the legal system construed as a single entity, the various forms of union were, in this theoretical approach, distinguished only in terms of their legal content and thus different only by degree.

The Kelsenian theory of decentralization and centralization was a developmentally open concept, one that did not link the transition from a less centralized form to a more centralized one to any formal or doctrinal preconditions. This theoretical approach thus provides a deeper insight into Kelsen's conception of international law. The radical questioning of doctrinal categories such as the sovereignty dogma and the theory of the "constitutive treaty" was supposed to pave the way for a theory of international law that was "integration friendly."[35] In Kelsen's view, this eliminated the doctrinal barriers for new forms of international integration on a regional or universal level. Opening the theory of international law to the phenomenon of legally established processes of integration is the essence of the Kelsenian doctrine of unions of states.

[33] Ibid., 164. [34] Ibid. [35] H. Kelsen, *Reine Rechtslehre*, 154.

3 Sovereignty as the state's direct subordination to international law [*Völkerrechtsunmittelbarkeit*]

It was on this theoretical basis that Verdross and Kunz for their part approached the doctrine of state unions.[36] However, as a supplement to Kelsen's notion they sought to introduce another distinguishing characteristic between a federal state and a confederacy of states. Verdross wanted unions of states differentiated on the basis of whether – according to the constituent document – the reciprocal relationship among the interconnected states had to be judged definitively by the federal constitution or still by the rules of general international law. Only the first case, that is when general international law was no longer applicable with respect to the reciprocal relationship of the states, constituted a federal state.[37] The member states were then in an exclusive relationship of delegation to the federal constitution and vanished as independent subjects under international law.[38] With this, the legal systems of the individual member states moved down to the level below the state constitution. To that extent, the member states were also no longer "directly subject to international law" [*völkerrechtsunmittelbar*].[39] In his monograph *Die Verfassung der Völkerrechtsgemeinschaft* [*The Constitution of the International Legal Community*], Verdross had defined "sovereignty" as the attribute of a legal order of being *directly* subordinated to the international legal order. With this, Verdross supplemented Kelsen's notion of the sovereignty of the international legal system with a notion – derived from the law of state unions – of state sovereignty, understood as the direct subordination of a legal system to international law.

Kunz joined Verdross on this point and introduced on this basis the distinction between "genuine" and "false" unions of states:[40] Genuine unions were legal unions of states "in the sense of international law"; false unions like the federal state, by contrast, were unions of states "in the sense of national law." Genuine unions, like the confederation, were created by the international law treaty and, according to Kunz, left the *Völkerrechtsunmittelbarkeit* of the states untouched. In this regard,

[36] A. Verdross, "Zur neuesten Lehre von den Staatenverbindungen," *Niemeyers Zeitschrift für internationales Recht*, XXXV (1926), 257–275; Kunz, *Die Staatenverbindungen*.

[37] Verdross, "Zur neuesten Lehre von den Staatenverbindungen," 273. [38] Ibid., 272.

[39] Verdross, *Die Verfassung der Völkerrechtsgemeinschaft*, 118; in the same vein Kunz, *Die Staatenverbindungen*, 37.

[40] Kunz, *Die Staatenverbindungen*, 113.

the states remained sovereign. False unions, like the federal state, on the other hand, could be created both by treaty and constitutional law and resulted in the loss of the *Völkerrechtsunmittelbarkeit* of the created member states.[41] The additional differentiation between confederacy and federal state introduced by Verdross and Kunz in this way allowed the School to retain the concept of sovereignty as the demarcating criterion for the law of state unions without having to put its own doctrine of the primacy of international law in jeopardy.

II The legal nature of the League of Nations

As an utterly novel union of various sovereign states, the League of Nations stood at the center of scholarly attention during the interwar period. Once international politics had created a completely new kind of legal text with the Covenant of the League of Nations, international law experts around the world began to discuss the legal nature of the new political entity that had been established.[42] The new institution in Geneva offered a first screen onto which progressive international lawyers could project their hopes for a system of international law endowed with its own organs and central coercive authority. The international law discourse of the interwar period initially sought to classify the League of Nations doctrinally.[43] To that end, scholars had recourse primarily to the traditional theories about unions of states. Georg Jellinek, in his internationally influential monograph on state unions, had subsumed the confederation, the international administrative union, and the real-union [*Realunion*] under the term "organized state unions."[44] Demarcating the confederacy of states from the international administrative unions, Jellinek had defined it as an organized state union that was highly political in nature.[45] Because of the highly political purpose

41 Ibid.

42 With a good overview of the literature from the early years of the League of Nations: P. E. Corbett, "What is the League of Nations?" *BYIL*, III (1924), 119–148.

43 Ibid., 119–148. 44 Jellinek, *Die Lehre von den Staatenverbindungen*, 158 *et seq*.

45 On the confederation: Jellinek, *Die Lehre von den Staatenverbindungen*, 172–194. With this conceptualization, Jellinek had made the formation of organs the criterion that set the confederation apart from the "non-organized" alliances and protectorates. Within the organized unions of states, he saw a crucial difference between the non-political administrative unions and the highly political confederation created to jointly secure territory internally and externally. In this view, administrative unions, like the World Postal Union and the international river commissions, fulfilled non-political administrative tasks, while a confederation represented for Jellinek and the prevailing theory after him the product of political and security interests.

of the League of Nations, which was characterized above all by the goal of securing world peace, only a small group of authors now resorted to drawing a theoretical parallel with the international administrative unions,[46] while the majority relied on the concept of confederation, which had been the central concept in German public law scholarship to describe looser unions of states, such as the German Confederation (1815–1866). This raised the question to what extent it was possible to use the traditional concept of confederation to make sense of the new universal organization established by the Covenant. Through the Covenant of the League of Nations, the members of the League had transferred to the organs of the League a number of competencies they had previously exercised on the level of the nation state. The most urgent goal of the League was to preserve the peace.[47] That goal, mentioned in the Preamble, was served by the possibility accorded to the Assembly in Art. 3 para. 3, and to the Council in Art. 4 para. 4 to deal with all issues related to global peace. To achieve that goal, all members of the League agreed to respect the territorial integrity and political independence of all other members (Art. 10), in cases of dispute to submit to the arbitration procedures provided for and under no circumstances to proceed to war until three months after a decision had been rendered (Art. 12 para. 1, Art. 13 and Art. 15 para. 1), and to respond to violations of these procedures by imposing sanctions (Art. 16). Added to this were also a series of administrative obligations in the area of international social and humanitarian collaboration by members of the League (Arts 23 and 25).

Following upon the unprecedented degree of obligations imposed upon the member states by an international legal text, the discussion over the nature of the League revolved around the question of the relationship of the individual states to the newly created entity. Was the organization in Geneva an independent legal subject or merely a continuation of the alliances of the great European powers, excluding Germany and the Soviet Union? Was the transfer of powers – some of them highly political – to the organs of the League at all compatible with the existence of sovereign nation states?

On the one hand, the League of Nations differed from the political alliances of the nineteenth century by having its own, legally established organs. On the other hand, it was also distinct from the international

[46] On the proponents of this view see Kunz, *Die Staatenverbindungen*, 500–501.

[47] W. Schücking and H. Wehberg, *Die Satzung des Völkerbundes*, 2nd revised edn. (Berlin: Vahlen, 1924), 91.

administrative unions that had always been limited to a specific administrative sphere by virtue of its highly political purpose. At the same time, the assumption that this was a world state in the making was countered by statements from diplomats and high-ranking politicians, who during the founding phase had repeatedly emphasized that the League was not to be a "Super-État" or "Super-State."[48]

The overwhelming majority of international law jurists therefore described the organization in Geneva as a confederation of states.[49] In spite of the repeated assertion that the League of Nations was unique, this theoretical designation proved especially capable of establishing a consensus view. According to the previously described doctrine that went back to Jellinek, a confederation of states was precisely *not* a state, but a union of states under international law: "The confederacy is the lasting, agreement-based union of independent states for the purpose of protecting the federal territory externally and securing the peace internally between the allied states, to which end the pursuit of other goals can also be agreed upon. This union requires a lasting organization to realize the purposes of the federal state."[50] According to this view, the confederation was a union of sovereign states that usually also served highly political purposes and had its own organs. Herbert Kraus was the first who, on the basis of the traditional German doctrine of state unions, qualified the new organization in Geneva as a confederation of states;[51] Schücking and Wehberg followed suit. However, behind the seemingly uniform doctrinal classification as a "confederation," to which – as we shall see – the authors of the Vienna School also had recourse, there stood varying theoretical conceptions of the new organization. The diverse positions mirror the diverse political-ideological and theoretical approaches to international law during the interwar period. The Vienna School's "integration-friendly" conception of international law can be

48 The delegate Hymann declared during the first session of the Assembly of the League: "Il est bon de l'affirmer une fois de plus, la Société des Nations n'est et ne saurait être un super-État qui absorberait les souverainetés ou méditerait de les reduire en tutelle." Quoted in Kunz, *Die Staatenverbindungen*, 499.

49 Kunz, *Die Staatenverbindungen*, 501–504, with extensive references. Another group described the League as a union of states "sui generis." On the general debate over its legal nature see Corbett, "What is the League of Nations?"; and Kunz, *Die Staatenverbindungen*, 498–506.

50 G. Jellinek, *Allgemeine Staatslehre*, revised 3rd edn. by W. Jellinek, incorporating handwritten notes (reprint of the 1914 edn. Berlin: Springer, 1922), 762.

51 H. Kraus, *Vom Wesen des Völkerbundes* (Berlin: Deutsche Verlagsgesellschaft für Politik und Geschichte, 1920), 12 *et seq.*

explicated in greater detail against the backdrop of other approaches developed during the interwar years to resolve these issues.

1 The League of Nations as a personified sub-order of international law

Building on Kelsen's doctrine of state unions, Kunz classified the League of Nations as follows: "The League of Nations is a genuine union of states, a permanent, organized political union of sovereign states that retain their *Völkerrechtsunmittelbarkeit* and of certain non-state legal communities. It is in its essence a confederation of states."[52]

With the theoretical consequences that flowed from this classification, the writers of the Vienna School took a position opposed to the conventional doctrine and developed out of the theory of the primacy of international law: the League of Nations did not embody the world legal order, but represented merely a particular order of international law. The members of the League thus remained *völkerrechtsunmittelbar* and therefore sovereign, since their legal relationships were not regulated exclusively by the Charter, but in addition also by general international law.[53] For Kunz, that followed from the Preamble of the Covenant, in which the members of the League accepted the obligation to abide by general international law. Kunz explicitly opposed the notion of Jahrreiß, who argued that only those states who were not members of the League of Nations, such as for example the United States, Russia, and Turkey, remained sovereign states.[54] Kunz maintained that the member states of the League did not lose their sovereignty because of the competencies yielded by the international law treaty, any more than the United States, for example, did through international legal obligations entered into in some other form.[55]

To the Vienna School, the League of Nations was thus a sub-system of international law. Like any other legal order, it could be legally personified.[56] And since the personality of international law was for the School not tied to a state quality of whatever kind, it was possible – in deviation from Jellinek's doctrine – to describe the League of Nations as a subject of international law.[57] Jellinek had still strictly denied that a confederation,

[52] Kunz, *Die Staatenverbindungen*, 505; see also Verdross, *Die Verfassung der Völkerrechtsgemeinschaft*, 111–112.
[53] Kunz, *Die Staatenverbindungen*, 498; Verdross, *Die Verfassung der Völkerrechtsgemeinschaft*, 112.
[54] Kunz, *Die Staatenverbindungen*, 498. [55] Ibid., 500. [56] Ibid., 505. [57] Ibid.

let alone an international administrative union, constituted a legal person.[58] For Jellinek, international law could not bring about any other legal subjects than the states.[59] As Jellinek saw it, contrary to Lorenz von Stein,[60] Robert von Mohl,[61] and Albert Haenel, endowing the confederation with a legal personality of its own contradicted the concept of

[58] Jellinek, *Die Lehre von den Staatenverbindungen*, 179.

[59] Ibid., 178. This was also apparent in Jellinek's restrictive understanding of the federal power in the confederation: "Rule over sovereign states is a contradiction in terms and both theoretically and practically impossible ... However, the notion of the ruling position of the federal power can be justified only if one elevates the treaty, which admittedly forms the legal ground of the union, above the union and thereby turns it into something completely different." Quoted from Jellinek, *Die Lehre von den Staatenverbindungen*, 178.

[60] For Lorenz von Stein, international administrative law was a specialized area of international law that was characterized by strong restrictions on sovereignty. Accordingly, international administrative law could be delineated from pure international law understood as a "common law of a multitude of sovereignties existing side by side without law and courts" only by the aspect of sovereignty: L. von Stein, "Einige Bemerkungen über das internationale Verwaltungsrecht," *Schmollers Jahrbuch für Gesetzgebung, Verwaltung, Volkswirtschaft*, 6 (1882), 1 *et seq.*, 396 *et seq.* On von Stein see B. Richter, *Völkerrecht, Außenpolitik und Internationale Verwaltung bei Lorenz von Stein* (Hamburg: Hansischer Gildenverlag Heitmann, 1973); H. Bülck, "Zur Dogmengeschichte des europäischen Verwaltungsrechts" in *Recht im Dienste der Menschenwürde. Festschrift für Herbert Kraus* (Würzburg: Holzner Verlag, 1964), 45 *et seq.*; Dicke, *Effizienz und Effektivität.*

[61] Represented by Mohl, Martens, and Bluntschli, the international legal scholarship had already tried since the middle of the century to respond also theoretically to the broadening of societal life beyond national boundaries. They juxtaposed to the sovereign state the idea of international solidarity, shared universal values, or the concept of the community of states: "It is necessary to find the legal principles [*Rechtssätze*] that must regulate the relations between people in their highest potency, namely beyond the life of the individual states, for them to achieve their life purposes." Quoted from Mohl, "Die Pflege der internationalen Gemeinschaft," 586. On this see also Bülck, "Zur Dogmengeschichte des europäischen Verwaltungsrechts," 43–44. In the German literature, Robert von Mohl and Lorenz von Stein were initially the first to recognize the legal significance of international administrative tasks. The starting point for these reflections in Mohl had been the recognition of the growing economic and social interdependence of states. Hence, society included for him also "international, legal relations to order the coexistence of simultaneous, inherently mutually independent national organisms and to communally promote the kind of shared tasks that the individual state cannot accomplish on its own": Mohl, "Die Pflege der internationalen Gemeinschaft," 583. Influenced by the liberal belief in progress, Mohl saw the goal of state action in promoting not only the existential purposes of one's own people, but those of humanity as a whole. With a view toward this task, he sought to systematize more precisely the external powers of the state. On this see Bülck, "Zur Dogmengeschichte des europäischen Verwaltungsrechts," 43. The "cultivation of the international community" is the duty of the external administration and should take place through "the recognition of the law and the elimination of the existing obstacles to an intercourse beneficial to all": R. von

sovereignty.[62] If one started by grounding international law in the sovereign will of the state, Jellinek did not believe that one could construct an autonomous organizational order with legal personality. The majority of German international lawyers followed that view down to the First World War.[63] The theory of legal organs [*Organlehre*], with its outstanding importance for German national law, was not transferred to the interstate organizational forms, not least because of the great influence exerted by Jellinek's doctrine of the unions of states.[64]

In contrast to Jellinek's conception, for Kunz the League of Nations represented a partial legal order which, like any other bundle of rights and obligations, could readily be thought of as a legal person. Moreover, because the League of Nations also had its own organs, it was able to be a legally independent actor in international relations. To the School, the Covenant, like any treaty, had a dual function: "It is the treaty by which

Mohl, *Das Staatsrecht des Königreiches Württemberg*, 2nd edn. (Tübingen: Laupp, 1846), 233. This was a shared international task. With this, Mohl wanted to establish a systematic connection between the external powers of the state and international law for a sphere of international administration. The public law doctrine was to be expanded through the addition of the sphere of administration of the international community. Thus Mohl at this point already arrived at the assumption that international communities could have international legal subjectivity: Mohl, "Die Pflege der internationalen Gemeinschaft," 583.

62 Dicke, *Effizienz und Effektivität*, 52.

63 Ebers, *Die Lehre vom Staatenbunde*, 206; this was in 1924 still the view of Hans Nawiaski, "Staatenbund und Bundesstaat" in K. Strupp (ed.), *Wörterbuch des Völkerrechts und der Diplomatie* (Berlin and Leipzig: W. de Gruyter, 1925), vol. 2, 577 with further references.

64 On this problem see Dicke, *Effizienz und Effektivität*, 52. The progressive endeavors by Mohl or Stein on behalf of an international administrative law as a dynamic special field of international law found no successors in the late phase of the German Empire. In 1913, Karl Neumeyer defined international administrative law as "the legal statutes that delineate the administration of one autonomous community vis-à-vis other autonomous communities and provide for the promotion of foreign administration in its realm": K. Neumeyer, "Internationales Verwaltungsrecht" in K. Stengel and M. Fleischmann (eds.), *Wörterbuch des deutschen Staats- und Verwaltungsrechtes* (Tübingen: Mohr, 1911–1914), 444. International administrative law is thus seen – comparable to international private law – as a mere conflict of laws and it thus belongs exclusively to national law: "What is presented as international administrative law or something similar is a juristic delusion"; quoted in K. Neumeyer, "Vom Recht der Auswärtigen Verwaltung and von verwandten Rechtsbegriffen," *AöR*, 31 (1913), 129. Alongside Triepel's dualism, the stricter systematization of administrative law by Gerberian-Labandian positivism must be regarded as laying the doctrinal groundwork of the theoretical drought period in the law of international administration (organization) at the beginning of the twentieth century in Germany.

the confederation: League of Nations is constituted, and it is the constitution of the thusly constituted confederation."[65]

This theoretical classification of the League of Nations by the Vienna School shows the repercussions of their understanding of international law as a social technique of international relations. Independent of ideological barriers, it wanted the system of international law to be thought of as open to progressive development.[66] International organizations like the League of Nations were first off looked upon and analyzed in "purely" normative terms as legal sub-orders of international law. With the new organization constituting a sub-order on the level of the higher-ranking system of international law, every subject previously handled within a state could, at least potentially, be regulated by the League without any concern for alleged substantive boundaries drawn by notions of sovereignty.

The Vienna School's theory of international law regarded the newly created organization in Geneva as the organ of a particular community of international law capable of taking action. The limitations on the authority of the League to act were to be laid down exclusively through the organization's Covenant. From the perspective of universal law, it was precisely the constituent treaty that could endow the organization with whatever competencies it wished. That could also include material areas of regulation that had previously been dealt with exclusively within states.[67] Because of the new conception of state sovereignty, the latter did not act as an a priori barrier to integration. Rather, the international treaty instrument was able to restrict the competencies of the state legal system at will. The supraordinated edifice of international law thus decided – in a sovereign and flexible manner – on the allocation of competencies between international law and national law. Given the unitary construction of universal law under the primacy of international law, the organs of the League of Nations could also, in Kunz's view, enact norms vis-à-vis the members of the League that were valid both directly (without the requirement of ratification) and

[65] J. L. Kunz, "Die intrasystematische Stellung des Art. XI des Völkerbundpaktes," *Frankfurter Abhandlungen zum modernen Völkerrecht*, 21 (1931), 1.

[66] Nicolas Politis went so far as to argue that since the founding of the League of Nations, state sovereignty was an outdated concept which, like a long-extinguished star, was still sending its light to earth: Politis, "Le problème des limitations de la souveraineté," 10.

[67] On the discussion over Art. 15 para. 8 of the Covenant of the League of Nations and the problem of "domestic jurisdiction" see Chapter 3 C IV.

indirectly.[68] Moreover, for Kunz a direct effect on individuals through "League of Nations law" was also not ruled out in principle.[69]

2 The League of Nations as a community of joint ownership [*Gemeinschaft zur gesamten Hand*]

Other German-language authors of the modernization movement, especially the international lawyers with a pacifist orientation, continued to base their legal analysis of the League of Nations on Jellinek's theory of state unions. These authors rejected the radical break that proponents of the Vienna School made with the theory of the sovereign will of the state by positing an international law above the states. Nippold, Schücking, and Wehberg continued to work essentially from the voluntaristic theoretical model à la Jellinek and sought to develop, on this basis, a pacifist theory of international law promoting international organization. To that end, Nippold, for example, had supplemented the foundational basis of the will of the sovereign state in international law with the limiting principle of "international solidarity,"[70] while Schücking maintained that the will of the sovereign state was limited by "state reason" [*staatliche Vernunft*] or "natural law."[71]

On the question of the legal nature of the League of Nations, for reasons of legal policy, pacifist international lawyers like Schücking and Wehberg also had recourse to the "confederation" as an established category in the theory of unions of states. Turning the organization in Geneva legally into a "confederation" in the sense of the traditional doctrine allowed these scholars to accord the League of Nations a recognized doctrinal form of state union without having to posit the loss of sovereignty on the part of the members of the League. In their commentary on the Covenant of the League of Nations they were drawing on the

[68] The question of whether decisions by the organs of the League of Nations would be binding even without ratification was the subject of debate at the first Assembly meeting with respect to the decision about the establishment of a world court. On this point, Nicolas Politis had argued that the Assembly was unquestionably capable of making directly binding decisions, as long as the matter in question fell within the jurisdiction defined by the treaty, see *Actes de la première Assemblée, Séances des Commissions* (Geneva, 1921), vol. 1, 300 *et seq*., and Schücking and Wehberg, *Die Satzung des Völkerbundes*, 112.

[69] Kunz, *Die Staatenverbindungen*, 506.

[70] Nippold, *Die Fortbildung des Verfahrens in völkerrechtlichen Streitigkeiten*, 46.

[71] Schücking and Wehberg, *Die Satzung des Völkerbundes*, 146: "Of course, the point is not only to protect the historically evolved positive law, but also to help natural law prevail without violent upheavals."

work of Max Huber, who had granted the perception of the League of Nations as a "confederation" the function of a competency-expanding, forward-moving view of the new institution.[72] Following Huber, Schücking and Wehberg went on to say: "Not least for these reasons, we believe that we should retain the legal view of the nature of the League of Nations. The jurist must win over the politician to the advancement of the law."[73] It was inevitable that this openly political approach to international law doctrine would be criticized by Kelsen, who insisted on a strict separation of legal policy and "legal science," as an example of the "political tendencies" in the theory of the unions of states.[74]

In their commentary, Schücking and Wehberg sought to specify further the "legal status of the League of Nations."[75] As the starting point they used Jellinek's definition of the confederation of states. They believed that this definition was met especially with regard to the relationship of the League of Nations to its members: "The states have come together into an organization, but by virtue of the fact that this organization rests on a free, revocable contractual will, their sovereignty remains unaffected."[76] According to the classic position that went back to Jellinek, no higher law could arise from the sovereign will of the state as the ground for the validity of the international treaty. Nevertheless, Schücking and Wehberg wanted to construe the legal order constituting the League of Nations as a law that was binding upon its member states, the League as a separate legal person, and laws enacted by organs of the League as directly binding on its members.[77] In the process, however, the League of Nations could not be described as a higher legal order that took precedence over the states. To that extent, Schücking and Wehberg had accepted Jellinek's premise that the sovereign will of the state could not bring forth a legal order superimposed upon the states. But if that was the case, how could one construe a separate legal personality for the League as well as a competency on the part of the organs of the League to enact law that was binding for its member states?

[72] Ibid., 108.

[73] Ibid. On Schücking and his notion of international organization see D. Acker, *Walter Schücking (1875–1935)* (Münster in Westfalen: Aschendorf, 1970), 41 *et seq.*

[74] Kelsen, *Staatslehre*, 410. Irrespective of this, the Vienna School, from its systems-oriented perspective, also regarded the community of states as a legal order. The "juridification" of international relations was thus a goal the two approaches shared.

[75] Schücking and Wehberg, *Die Satzung des Völkerbundes*, 103. [76] Ibid., 104.

[77] The theoretical approach of the Vienna School, proceeding from the primacy of international law, had answered this question by positing a particular order of international law that stood above the states.

To escape the voluntaristic dilemma, Schücking and Wehberg resorted to the concept of the "community of joint ownership" [*Gemeinschaft zur gesamten Hand*], which came out of German private law and had been transferred to the confederation concept first by Ebers:[78] "Only this concept, which has sprung from the wealth and depth of the German idea of law, is able to explain the seeming contradiction that, on the one hand, no new state above the individual states has been created in the League of Nations, and, on the other hand, a unity exists with a special legal sphere which, as a common sphere, is sharply distinct from the special sphere to which each individual state is entitled."[79] In the individual sphere, the commentators continued, the states were left with their entire "internal and external life," to the extent that aspects of this sphere were not explicitly withdrawn from their free exercise by norms of international law.[80] The common sphere, on the other hand, consisted of the competencies allocated to the League of Nations by the Covenant. In this area, the League of Nations acted – and here Schücking and Wehberg drew on a formulation from Art. 15 of the Final Act of Vienna – as a "unitary treaty-entity" [*vertragsmäßige Einheit*].[81]

The League of Nations could thus act also toward its members as an entity endowed with rights and obligations. By using – in analogy to company law – a distinction between the individual and the common sphere, Schücking and Wehberg were trying to conceptualize a particular legal order that was autonomous vis-à-vis the will of the state. In fact, and here the commentators were departing fully from Jellinek's theoretical foundation, that entity was supposedly able to give rise to an autonomous, binding will: "In that the League of Nations in its internal life makes decisions as a unitary treaty-entity [*vertragsmäßige Einheit*] and does not conclude treaties (with the members of the League), provision has been made that a will binding upon the individual member arise within the treaty-based competency of the organization, without the need for ratification as is the case with international law treaties."[82]

The two commentators had thus given up a perspective that proceeded from the sovereign will of the state so as to be able, after all, to construct a "sphere of will" that was independent of the individual member states.

[78] Following an essay by Heilborn, Ebers, in his mongraph *Die Lehre vom Staatenbunde*, had offered a comprehensive justification for this approach: Ebers, *Die Lehre vom Staatenbunde*, 303 *et seq*.

[79] Schücking and Wehberg, *Die Satzung des Völkerbundes*, 109–116.

[80] Ibid., 110. [81] Ibid., 111. [82] Ibid.

The construct of the "community of joint ownership" thus served to "conceal" the paradoxical assumption of an entity which, regardless of its foundation in the sovereign will of the state, confronted the same states with a claim to exercise binding power over, above, and if necessary against, their will. In a similar vein to the Vienna School, Schücking and Wehberg were trying to construct a legally grounded, unitary, international authority. In the Kelsenian approach, a particular suprastate order of international law binding the states is established via the basic norm of international law, which establishes a binding legal order. However, this theoretical move was closed off to Schücking and Wehberg because of their premise that international law had a voluntaristic basis. The question that arose was how it was possible to construct, out of the sovereign wills of the member states of the League of Nations, an autonomous "will" of the organization even in opposition to the will of its members. Robert Redslob, for example, simply denied that this was possible: "La Société des Nations n'implique pas de volonté superieure planant sur les États."[83] The distinction between the individual and common sphere was the Schücking-Wehbergian attempt, specifically for the League of Nations, to arrive at an objective and binding legal order from the sovereign will of the member states. The voluntaristic dilemma, which Jellinek had sought to resolve for the general theory of international law via the recourse to the "objective nature of things" and Triepel via the construction of the "common will," thus reappeared in Schücking and Wehberg through the construct of the "community of joint ownership." In spite of different theoretical foundations, the common thrust of both the pacifist (Schücking and Wehberg) and the "objective" approach of the Vienna School was to conceptualize the new organization in Geneva as a legal entity with the capacity to impose its autonomous will on the states.

III The opponents of an "integration-friendly" theory of international law

The attempt by the Vienna School and by the pacifist movement in international law to construe the League of Nations as a legal entity that was autonomous vis-à-vis its members was sharply rejected by Carl Schmitt in his first monograph on international law. The "hair-splitting" about the question of the legal nature of the League of Nations,

[83] R. Redslob, *Théorie de la Société des Nations* (Paris: Rousseau & Co., 1927), 22.

he asserted, missed the "core question" of the problem.[84] When the attempt was made to construe the League of Nations as a legal order, the literature failed to consider the question of whether there was in fact an order that could be described as a "league" [*Bund*]: "The core question of the League of Nations, however, concerns precisely the question about the specific nature of the legal order embodied in it. It is the question of whether it can be regarded at all as the embodiment of a legal order that takes the status quo of Versailles as its basis, or merely as a political-practical purposive entity [*politisches Zweckgebilde*]."[85] International law, Schmitt maintained, did not exist in a vacuum, but was tied to the political situation. Thus, a *Bund* could be posited only where an ordering principle [*Ordnungsprinzip*] encompassed a system of states.[86]

With his political perspective, Schmitt picked up a pattern of argumentation that was common in Germany in the interwar period. The League of Nations, it was argued, represented a purposive political entity of the allied powers. In the final analysis, it was nothing other than the continuation of the Versailles peace conference. Bülow, in his famous book *Der Versailler Völkerbund* [The League of Nations of Versailles], made the instrumentalization of the League of Nations by the victorious European powers with the goal of continuing to oppress Germany the chief point of criticism of the new organization in Geneva.[87] Carl Schmitt also raised the question about the political legitimacy of the League of Nations and linked it to his concept of the *Bund* ["league"]. A real "league" presupposed concrete guarantees and a certain political homogeneity.

According to Schmitt, however, the outcome of this political-sociological study should also predetermine the question about the League of Nations as a legal order. Where there was no "league" in the political sense there was, for Schmitt, also no legal order. And so his answer to the "core question" in the year Germany joined the League of Nations was negative in his analysis, even though he did regard it as open for the future.[88] In this way, Schmitt sought to prevent an increase in the authority of the League of Nations through its theoretical juridification.

[84] C. Schmitt, *Die Kernfrage des Völkerbundes* (Berlin: F. Dümmler, 1926), 18.
[85] Ibid., 17–18. [86] Ibid., 18.
[87] B. W. von Bülow, *Der Versailler Völkerbund* (Stuttgart: W. Kohlhammer, 1924), introduction; Schmitt, *Die Kernfrage des Völkerbundes*, 22; referring to Schmitt with a similar view C. Bilfinger, "Betrachtungen über politisches Recht," *ZaöRV*, 1 (1929), 57–76.
[88] Schmitt, *Die Kernfrage des Völkerbundes*, 80–82.

He deliberately countered the division between Is and Ought through the use of substantive political arguments when dealing with the *legal* nature of the new entity. The concept of the *Bund* was defined by Schmitt's own political criteria – the argumentative conclusions he drew from the negated suitability of the term for the new organization, however, were of a legal nature. The goal was the complete deconstruction of the attempt of the reform movement in international law to endow the new institution with legal authority.

Schmitt's argumentation was thus aimed at the most vulnerable part of the League of Nations project. Dealing with the complex problems of the interwar period presupposed the construction of a uniform authority that was autonomous from the individual wills of the member states. It was only as long as the organs of the League of Nations were not perceived exclusively as a hegemonic instrument of individual states, but were regarded as representatives of a "community of states," that the clashing national interests and conflicting political principles could be managed case by case within the organs of the League of Nations.[89] The enthusiasm for the League of Nations among the cosmopolitan elites of the European public and within the modernization movement of international law had made a crucial contribution to this endeavor in the 1920s. However, this authority could be upheld only as long as the legal status of the interwar system guaranteed by the League of Nations via Art. 10 of its Charter could claim a certain political legitimacy. Furthermore, in Germany and Austria political support for the League of Nations depended on its continued ability to function as a projection screen for the hopes that the connected Versailles settlement, which was seen as being lopsided and too harsh, could be changed by it.[90]

Schmitt's "anti-normativist" view and the Vienna School's cosmopolitan project of an "integration-friendly" theory of international organizations were diametrically opposed in their thrust. Schmitt's position illustrates that a theory of international law that was responsive to the new "actor" in Geneva encountered rejection by many scholars in Germany during the interwar period.

[89] N. Berman, "Beyond Colonialism and Nationalism? Ethiopia, Czechoslovakia, and 'Peaceful Change'," *NJIL*, 65 (1996), 421 *et seq.*

[90] The possibility for a later revision laid down in Art. 19 of the Covenant still served in the 1920s to absorb these hopes and to postpone the final resolution of the conflicting political principles to a later point in time; on this see Berman, "Beyond Colonialism and Nationalism?," 432 *et seq.*

B The individual

In Kelsen's international law theory, the state and international organizations were joined by the individual as the third important actor. For Kelsen, the individual stood out because, as the only natural person, he or she was the final addressee behind the personified legal system of the state of any international organization. The legal personifications of the state and the international organization were for Kelsen pure "fictions" that must not be allowed to obscure the fact that merely a term for the unity of the legal order so described was at issue.[91] As Kelsen saw it, the law understood as a social technique could have as its object only the conduct of natural persons, that is, human beings.[92] And from his perspective, that applied equally to national law and international law. For example, even if a norm of international law was addressed to the state, in actuality it regulated the conduct of one or more individuals in their capacity as a state organ.[93] However, specifying the relevant organ is something that international law usually left to the state legal system, which for that purpose was construed as a legal person.[94] Although this merely indirect reference to the conduct of individuals was still prevalent in international law, in technical legal terms it was by no means imperative, as was demonstrated by a growing number of cases in which individuals were directly authorized and obligated under international law.[95] Thus, according to the Pure Theory of Law, behind the legal systems personified by jurisprudence stood the human being as the real addressee of all law. According to Kelsen, the individual could be authorized or obligated either indirectly or directly by the norms of universal law.[96]

I Positive law

To undergird his thesis, Kelsen, during the interwar period, invoked the few examples in positive law where individuals were directly authorized

[91] On Kelsen's "identity thesis" see Chapter 2 A II.

[92] Kelsen, *Problem der Souveränität*, 51. [93] Kelsen, "Les Rapports de Système," 284.

[94] Kelsen, *Problem der Souveränität*, 130 *et seq.*

[95] Kelsen, "The Law as a specific Social Technique," 97; examples in H. Kelsen, "Théorie générale du droit international public," *RCADI*, 42/IV (1932), 148 *et seq.*; Kelsen, *Peace through Law*, 75 *et seq.*; on this see Rub, *Hans Kelsens Völkerrechtslehre*, 372–374.

[96] This went against the prevailing notion in the German legal literature: "Individual human beings are not nor can they be subjects of international law"; quoted from Hold-Ferneck, *Lehrbuch des Völkerrechts*, 247; see also A. Zorn, *Grundzüge des Völkerrechts*, 2nd edn. (Leipzig: J. J. Weber, 1903), 28; Kohler, *Grundlagen des Völkerrechts*, 52.

or obligated through international legal treaties. By regarding the Treaty of Versailles as valid international law, Kelsen believed that there was a basis in treaty law for the punishment of the German Emperor. For that reason he also regarded the punishment of individuals by international law as fundamentally unproblematic.[97] Kelsen maintained that the extradition and punishment of the German Emperor provided for in Art. 228 para. 2 of the Versailles Treaty was not illegal, given its basis in a treaty.[98] The treaty created an exception to the immunity of the state recognized in customary law.[99] Within the monistically conceived legal cosmos, the punishment of individuals under international law did not pose a theoretical problem for Kelsen. The immunity of heads of state was not sacrosanct, since for Kelsen it was no longer derived from a concept of sovereignty that preceded the law and was untouchable by international legal norms. As a norm of customary law, it could be restricted to any degree by new, derogational treaty law. According to the theory of the primacy of international law, conflicting national law had to be annulled. Based on his conception of universal law, Kelsen became one of the first legal scholars who sought to pave the way, both theoretically and in terms of legal policy, for a criminal law that was binding on individuals. A number of publications from the time of the Second World War and prior to the Nuremberg trials pursued this topic further.[100]

On the side of rights, the main difference between the individual and the state lay for Kelsen in the fact that the individual had no capacity to create customary law and conclude international treaties.[101] However, Kelsen believed that granting individuals standing before international courts was important to the further development of international law, a step that had already been achieved in some cases:

[97] On this see, as early as 1920: H. Kelsen, "Der völkerrechtliche Strafanspruch wegen völkerrechtswidriger Kriegshandlungen," *Neue Freie Presse Wien* (September 8, 1920), 3–4.

[98] Ibid.; Kelsen came to this conclusion also with respect to the Nuremberg tribunal, for while there was retroactivity, it was not contrary to international law: H. Kelsen, *Principles of International Law* (New York: Rinehart, 1952), 137; on this see Rub, *Hans Kelsens Völkerrechtslehre*, 371–377.

[99] H. Kelsen, "Théorie générale du droit international public," *RCADI*, 42/IV (1932), 154.

[100] H. Kelsen, "Collective and Individual Responsibility in International Law with Particular Regard to Punishment of War Criminals," *Calif. L. R.*, 31 (1943), 530–571; H. Kelsen, "The Rule against Ex Post Facto Laws and the Prosecution of Axis War Criminals," *Judge Advocate Journal*, 2 (1945), 8–12, 27, 46; H. Kelsen, "Will the Judgment in the Nuremberg Trial constitute a Precedent in International Law?," *International Law Quarterly*, 1 (1947), 153–171; on this see Chapter 6 A.

[101] Kelsen, "Théorie générale du droit international public," 268; on the international legal treaty, H. Kelsen, "Contribution à la théorie du traité internationale," *Revue internationale de la théorie du droit*, 10 (1936), 262.

> For when the individual state no longer stands without exception between the individual person and the international legal community, when the international legal community with its specific organs is directly available to the individual person, even against 'his' state, when the individual state in certain cases can in fact proceed against its own subjects only through powers granted by an international court, the system of international law, that is to say, the international legal order that constitutes this specific community of international law, no longer differs significantly in terms of legal technique from the legal system of the individual state.[102]

Kelsen was here anticipating a development in state practice toward a greater participation of individuals in procedures of international law. The unmediated effect of international legal norms on individuals, combined with direct access to courts above the state, was for him the crucial breakthrough toward a more effective universal law. As soon as international legal norms directly entitled and bound individuals in a comprehensive way, it would also be possible to replace state liability under international law with individual liability.[103] International law was still characterized as "primitive" law precisely by the fact that it extended its sanctions not only to the individuals truly responsible, but to all persons subject to the state's legal system. The goal – and here Kelsen revealed his evolutionary conception of international law – was to individualize this "collective liability," which was practiced only in "primitive" legal cultures.

II The critique of Scelle and Politis

It was not only in Kelsen and his School that the individual appeared in international legal scholarship at that time. Georges Scelle and Nicolas Politis also placed the individual as a new subject of international law alongside the demystified state. Politis formulated his approach this way: "Behind the vain fiction of the state there exists only one true personhood: that of the individual."[104] For him, the deconstructed metaphysical state consisted merely of human beings endowed with the power to regulate

[102] H. Kelsen, "Die Technik des Völkerrechts und die Organisation des Friedens," *ZöR*, 14 (1934), 253.

[103] Ibid., 254.

[104] Politis, "Le problème des limitations de la souveraineté," 6; on the legal status of individuals and other non-state actors in current international law, using the example of international humanitarian law, see J. Karenfort, *Die Hilfsorganisationen im bewaffneten Konflikt. Rolle und Status unparteiischer humanitärer Organisationen im humanitären Völkerrecht* (Frankfurt am Main: P. Lang, 1998), 95–125.

collective interests.[105] Georges Scelle went so far as to see the individual as the sole subject of international law.[106] For Scelle, the "*société internationale*" consisted of individuals, who in turn belonged to a multitude of other social systems, for example, families, occupational groups, races, and cultures. These social groups were borne by the phenomenon of solidarity, and each, in its development, pursued its own politico-legal organizational forms.[107] Only one of these organizational forms was the state, which had to be seen not as uniformly structured, but as a heterogeneous entity comprising a multitude of intact social groupings. Between these organized social groups, according to Scelle's conception of the "*droit objectif*," there emerged intersocial norms that mirrored the reciprocal dependence and human solidarity. In turn, these higher-ranking, "imperative" norms were to form the foundation of larger organizational forms. For Scelle, the highest organizational form was the *société internationale*, which found its basis in the transnational solidarity between individuals.

The substance of the formal organizational forms was thus for both Scelle and Politis the individual as a social being. However, in contrast to Kelsen's norm-logical abstraction, these two thinkers sought to derive the special status of the individual from the socio-biological consciousness of human solidarity, which could be demonstrated only among humans. Kelsen subjected Scelle's theory of international law to a fundamental critique, though he never published it. In this study, Kelsen criticized Scelle's classification of the individual as the sole subject of international law as too one-sided.[108] He argued that in his exclusivity, Scelle was committing the same mistake as the prevailing notion with its focus on the state as the subject of international law.[109] By excluding the state in its mediatizing function from his reflections, Scelle's theory could define only in an imprecise manner the role of the individual in the international legal order.[110]

In its thrust, however, the discovery of the individual within Scelle's theory of international law was quite comparable to Kelsen's approach. This could also be the reason why Kelsen never published his comprehensive critique of Scelle's conception of international law. Both pursued the goal of pushing back the central place that classic positivism accorded the state. To that end, Scelle relativized the state as a heterogeneous

105 Politis, "Le problème des limitations de la souveraineté," 6; on this see Berman, "But the Alternative is Despair," 1807.

106 Scelle, *Précis de droit des gens*, 42. 107 Ibid., 29.

108 Kelsen, *Georges Scelle*, 94–96. 109 Ibid., 95. 110 Ibid., 95–108.

political organization of individuals, who were simultaneously part of other organizational forms, such as, for example, the higher-ranking *société internationale*. In the view of the Vienna School, by contrast, the state as a legal system was controlled by international law, which could restrict its sphere of power to whatever extent it desired. The law as a social technique in the sense of a cultural achievement was to become – freed from meta-legal barriers, as it were – usable as an instrument for guiding the behavior of individuals also on the universal level. Both approaches represented an effort to preserve the interwar legal order against the destructive powers of European nationalism by way of the medium of the law.[111]

C Universal law as a dynamic system of integration

As we have seen, new actors stepped onto the stage of universal law in the Vienna School's theory of international law. The bearers of rights and obligations under international law were not only states, but also unions of states (international organizations) and individuals. The normative web constructed by Kelsen and Kunz between the various actors of the universally conceived legal cosmos require a comprehensive interpretation.

The central difference between the state legal system and the international organization lay in the classification of the international organization as part of the international legal order. According to the theory of the primacy of international law, the international organization, as a particular order of international law, was placed above the state. Within the hierarchical structure of international law, the state, as a legal system directly derived from international law, ranked below the law of nations. Because of this hierarchical arrangement, the law of the international organization was potentially able to bind the states subordinated to it. On this question, then, there were no theoretical limitations regarding the content of the founding treaty. For that purpose, the barrier of a substantive concept of sovereignty preceding the law had been theoretically eliminated by the School. In addition, the international organization is potentially in a position to entitle and obligate the inhabitants of the member states directly as well. Should the law of the international organization clash with internal national law, it can claim precedence over the conflicting national law through the doctrine of the primacy of

[111] See Nathaniel Berman's studies on Robert Redslob and the juristic engagement with nationalism in the interwar period: Berman, "But the Alternative is Despair."

international law. In Kelsen's original conception, the conflicting national law is *ipso facto* null and void. Kelsen later revised this view and made the legal consequence of a collision dependent on whether the legal system in question provided for an annulment procedure. In this conception, the conflicting national law is valid but can potentially be nullified.

Another difference between the international organization and the state as a legal system is the different degree of centralization of the respective legal system. As a general rule, a union of states or international organization left a considerable number of regulatory powers at the level of the member states. An international organization was thus a less strongly centralized order than the federal or unitary state. However, through a dynamic process of integration, such an international organization was able to centralize a growing number of competencies. In this way, the international order could, in a fluid process of transition, turn into a system with as strong a degree of centralization as was otherwise displayed only by state legal systems. In Kelsen's view, the decisive contribution to a stronger centralization of the legal order lay in the establishment of compulsory jurisdiction.[112] At a certain point, which Kelsen deliberately did not define in precise terms, one was then dealing with a state legal system. The law of international organizations thus dealt with a multitude of particular international legal orders on a dynamic continuum of integration.

For Verdross and Kunz, that point was reached when, in the relationship of the member states to one another, general international law had been completely displaced by the "constitutional law" of the international organization. The confederation of states or international organization had then turned into a federal state. At that moment, the international organization not only turns into a state, but its legal order within the hierarchy of the monistic legal universe drops from the level of international law to the level of state legal systems. That did not entail a loss of status, however; rather, it allowed the state legal system to enjoy the privileges that general international law accorded to the state. They included especially the possibility of creating new international law in conjunction with other states and without any substantive restrictions. By contrast, the international organization had this privilege only with respect to the competencies granted by its particular legal order created by the treaty.

[112] On this see chapter 6.

According to Kelsen, the dynamic continuum introduced through his doctrine of centralization and decentralization could take effect in regional forms of integration as well as on the level of general international law. The crucial novelty in this conception was the understanding of and confidence in the integrational function of the medium of law. By creating a higher-ranking, autonomous legal system through the medium of international law, the states, as legal orders, subordinated themselves in their mutual relationships to the rule of law and not to a world state that devoured them.

The formalized view of the theory of unions of states under international law opened up a broad leeway for a functional application of the medium of international law in international processes of integration.[113] It sought to shield scholarship from ideological arguments opposing the rule of law in organized international relations. The cosmopolitan project of a thorough juridification of international relations required strong international actors available for regional and universal projects of integration beyond the traditional notions of sovereignty. Kelsen, Kunz, and Verdross conceived of international law as a dynamic system of law-driven integration.

[113] With an application to the European Union: Ch. Leben, "Hans Kelsen and the Advancement of International Law," *EJIL*, 9 (1998), 287–305; W. Pauly, "Concepts of Universality. Hans Kelsen on Sovereignty and International Order" in D. Diner and M. Stolleis (eds.), *Hans Kelsen and Carl Schmitt: A Juxtaposition* (Gerlingen: Bleicher, 1999), 47–49. On the continuing transformation of the system of international law through regional and universal integration projects see E. H. Riedel, "The Progressive Development of International Law at the Universal and Regional Level" in R. Wolfrum (ed.), *Strengthening the World Order: Universalism v. Regionalism* (Berlin: Duncker & Humblot, 1990), 115–144.

5

Legal sources as universal instruments of law-creation

As we have seen, the cosmopolitan project of Kelsen and Kunz included strong international organizations capable of enforcing international legal rules at the universal level. In theoretical terms, these organizations were also able to grant rights directly to individuals and impose obligations on them. As described in the last chapter, Kelsen sought to break open the doctrinal restrictions of the theory of unions of states, which was fixated on the notion of sovereignty. Not only would this make it possible to better classify new forms of legal organization doctrinally, it would also allow them to be presented vis-à-vis the states as largely autonomous legal orders. However, the creation of new forms of organization by international politics presupposed the existence of efficient instruments of law creation. To that end, Kelsen maintained, the legal sources of international law represented by custom and the treaty had to be made available to international politics as substantively unrestricted instruments of societal change. Before examining in greater detail the Kelsenian theory of treaty law and customary law, I will take a look at the general foundations of Kelsen's doctrine of legal sources.

A Sources beyond metaphysics and consensus

Kelsen's theory of the sources of international law was based on the assumption of the hypothetical character of the law. That international law found its objective basis neither in posited meta-legal values, nor in a consensus of sovereign state wills. Instead, Kelsen traced international law back to a merely hypothetically presupposed basic norm and in so doing positioned his theory of legal sources beyond the traditional foundation of international law in consensus or natural law. Although Kelsen undergirded the hypothetical character of the law in his so-called "classical phase" with neo-Kantian arguments,[1] his theory of sources consisted mainly in a critique of the traditionally assumed foundations of international law. The postulated "objective" character of international law is a result of the repression of subjective notions of justice, on the one hand, and the uncoupling of the legal sources from the consensus of the sovereign will of the states, on the other.

I The critique of metaphysical dualism

Various doctrines about the sources of international law had been developed during the interwar period. The reform movement in international legal scholarship regarded the assumption of the sovereign will of the state as the foundation of international law as an outdated doctrine of the nineteenth century. This retrospective critique reduced the complex combination of psychological self-obligation, the willful acceptance by the state, and its limitation by the objective "nature of the community of states" as articulated by the likes of Georg Jellinek[2] to a nationalist obsession with sovereignty. New sociological or natural law foundations were to take the place of these doctrines from the "dark age" of international law.[3]

In the course of the 1920s, Verdross moved increasingly away from Kelsen's methodological premises and eventually came out unambiguously in favor of a natural law foundation, in the spirit of the Spanish late scholastics Vitoria and Suarez. Regardless of this move to moral substance, he continued to argue that he was at the same time advocating a doctrine of positive international law, of an "international law of experience."[4] Verdross saw a close connection between Christian natural law and positive law in general, which he believed to be constitutive also for international law: "For on the one hand, its positive validity is based on

[1] See the particularly clear account in S. L. Paulson, "On the Kelsen–Kant Problematic" in E. Garzón Valdéz (ed.), *Normative Systems in Legal and Moral Theory. Festschrift for Carlos E. Alchourrón and Eugenio Bulgyin* (Berlin: Duncker & Humblot, 1997), 209–213.

[2] On Jellinek see Chapter 1 C IV 1.

[3] Duguit, *Souveraineté et liberté*, 105–110. In his lectures, Duguit compared the German doctrine influenced by Jellinek to the French doctrine of the basic rights of states: "[. . .] la doctrine allemande était plus brutale. J'en trouve surtout l'expression dans les ouvrages d'un juriste allemand eminent, dont on ne saurait méconnaitre le rôle at l'influence, le professeur d'Heidelberg, aujourd'hui décédé, Jellinek." Ibid., 107–108.

[4] On Verdross's theory of international law see Simma, "The Contribution of Alfred Verdross to the Theory of International Law," 55–69.

the moral idea, grounded in God, of a uniform humanity divided into a multitude of states; on the other hand, however, that idea can only become realized if it has an effect on the actions of the states . . . Thus, for a complete comprehension of positive international law, it is necessary to both fathom the ideas that underlie the fact of international law, and to probe the actions in which they have an effect . . . Positive international law arises only from their synthesis."[5]

According to Verdross, the international jurist could understand the norms of natural law only through the analysis of positive law. At the same time, however, the understanding of positive international law presupposed insight into the eternal ideas of natural law. Verdross could escape this circular argument only with a Hegelian sleight of hand: In his view, the real object of cognition that is "international law" lay in the dialectical sublation of the duality of positive international law and Christian "laws of humanity" [*Menschheitsrecht*].

According to the theory of *droit objectif* developed by Duguit and Scelle, custom and treaty were merely the emanation of a pre-existing *solidarité sociale*. As such, they did not produce any law but were merely, in a declaratory way, the reflection of an international law rooted in "international solidarity." The goal of positing a law already pre-existent in Christian values or international solidarity was a construct of international law that was uncoupled from the sovereign will of the state. Duguit and Scelle, in particular, sought to achieve advances in methodological objectivity through recourse to "social facts" (Durkheim). In their self-perception as modern international lawyers, they had left behind the "apologetic" legal positivism of the nineteenth century and had developed a more objective foundation for the law of nations, one that incorporated social consciousness and social reality.[6]

Kelsen did not accept this strategy of objectification. To him, Scelle's conception, for example, was not modern at all, but no less antiquated than classic natural law. He compared the conception of a sociological source of the law underlying positive law with the idea of the "national spirit" [*Volksgeist*] articulated by the German historical school of law.[7] In the final analysis, he argued, both approaches had a natural-law character, because both assumed that the "right" law could be brought forth only from the "nature" of a "people" or from some kind of societal "consciousness." In the end, "nature" thus became the legislator

[5] Verdross, "Die allgemeinen Rechtsgrundsätze des Völkerrechts," 358.
[6] On Scelle see Chapter 4 B II. [7] Kelsen, *Principles of International Law*, 2nd edn., 443.

behind positive law. The jurist's task, when analyzing positive law, was then to analyze whether particular norms were in conformity with the pre-existing "right" law. The doctrine of an "international legal consciousness," which was already frequently encountered in the nineteenth century, and which Heinrich Drost revived in the 1930s under the concept of "latent international law," was for Kelsen likewise based on the assumption of a pre-existing, extra-positive source of law.[8]

To Kelsen, all of these conceptions reflected an understanding of the law that bore the imprint of metaphysics. As with every metaphysical construct, in this case, as well, the object of cognition was doubled in that a kind of prototype of this object was projected onto a level not accessible to experience. The object accessible to cognition (positive law) was then seen as a reproduction of the ideal prototype (natural law). Kelsen argued that this metaphysical way of thinking reproduced the Platonic dualism of idea and reality from the parable of the cave.[9] In that sense, the assumption that positive law was only a reflection of a law already pre-existing in a social consciousness or international solidarity was for Kelsen a "juridical dualism" [*juristischer Dualismus*]. This dualism was implied by the word "source," which, according to a later statement of Kelsen, was a "figurative and highly ambiguous expression" which led to confusion and should be dropped altogether.[10] The legal system posited as underlying positive law was for him a "metaphysical" construction intended to endow the existing law with absolute legitimacy.[11] However, the assertion of these absolute norms lying at the back of the law was not objectifiable, but usually a move motivated by interests and ideology. As Kelsen saw it, the world legal community created by the law of nations was too heterogeneous, the interests and ideas of solidarity of the actors were too diverse to speak of a scientifically verifiable "shared consciousness of law," "shared interests," or an "international solidarity."[12]

For Kelsen, the metaphysical categories projected behind positive law were thus too subjective, too irrational, and in the end not concrete enough to constitute a scientifically verifiable source of international law. Kelsen criticized these doctrines,[13] which had – like the Pure

[8] H. Kelsen, "Théorie du droit international coutumier" in *Festschrift für Franz Weyer* (Prague, 1939), vol. 2, 8; H. Kelsen, "Zur Grundlegung der Völkerrechtslehre. Eine Auseinandersetzung mit Heinrich Drost," *ÖZöR*, 1 (1946/1948), 53.

[9] Kelsen, "Théorie du droit international coutumier," 8.

[10] Kelsen, *Principles of International Law*, 2nd edn., 437.

[11] Kelsen, "Théorie du droit international coutumier," 9. [12] Ibid.

[13] Rub, *Hans Kelsens Völkerrechtslehre*, 310.

Theory of Law – sought a methodological way of placing the theory of the legal sources of international law on a foundation that was uncoupled from the sovereign will of the state, precisely at their most vulnerable point: the requirement that the law be concrete.[14] For the positivist Kelsen, as for his student Kunz,[15] a theory of the legal sources of international law would have to be based on positive law as enacted by formally verifiable procedures.

II The critique of the positivist consensus model

Kelsen, however, was also opposed to the conventional positivist theory of sources, which had traced the binding force of the law back to the consensus of the sovereign will of the state. With his rejection of the consensual foundation of international law, Kelsen was moving within the orbit of the general modernization movement in international law theory during the interwar period.[16] For Kelsen, the conventional positivist doctrine of sources was nothing more than an indirect application of the theories of self-obligation: "Toute cette théorie de sources n'est q'une paraphrase de la théorie bien connue de l'autolimitation de l'État, suivant laquelle l'État ne pourrait être obligé que par sa propre volonté" ["This entire theory of the sources is nothing but a restatement of the well-known theory of the self-limitation of the state, according to which the state can be obligated only by its own will"].[17]

In actual fact, however, Triepel and Oppenheim, working from a critique of Jellinek's theory of self-obligation, had tried at the beginning of the century to develop a consensual foundation of international law that went beyond the will of the individual state.[18] The goal was a more

[14] On the analysis of the oscillating movement inherent in the source discourse between binding but not sufficiently concrete natural law (justice), and the concrete but not sufficiently binding positivist recourse to the will of the state (consent), see Koskenniemi, *From Apology to Utopia*, 270 *et seq*.; D. Kennedy, *International Legal Structures* (Baden-Baden: Nomos, 1987), 99–107.

[15] J. L. Kunz, "The Nature of International Customary Law," *AJIL*, 47 (1953), 662–669, 336–337.

[16] For a critique of the consensual foundation of international law see Verdross, *Die Einheit des rechtlichen Weltbildes*, 37; L. Le Fur, "Règles générales du droit de la paix," *RCADI*, 54/IV (1935), 21–32; J. L. Brierly, *The Basis of Obligation and Other Papers* (Oxford: Clarendon Press, 1958), 11; on this see Koskenniemi, *From Apology to Utopia*, 270; J. Boyle, "Ideals and Things: International Legal Scholarship and the Prison House of Language," *Harv. ILJ*, 26 (1985), 337.

[17] Kelsen, "Les Rapports de Système entre le Droit Interne et le Droit International Public," 285.

[18] On what follows see the account in Chapter 2 D.

objective foundation of international law, though without having to break completely with the doctrine of the sovereign will of the state, which guaranteed in their view the concreteness of the law. What was needed was a construct that did not depend on the continuous consent or approval of each individual legal subject. With their endeavour, Triepel and Oppenheim were also searching for an answer to the question of how a tacit state – or a newly created state – could be bound to general international law. The binding compulsory nature of international law as a legal system should not be dependent on explicit consent of all legal subjects. Recourse to the externally discernible will of the state as the guarantor of the concreteness of international law was not, by itself, able to satisfy the need for the binding character of international law.[19] For that reason, Triepel and Oppenheim had taken recourse to the "common will" or "common consent" of the states as the foundation of international law.[20] It stood for the objective sum of the individual sovereign wills of the states. According to Oppenheim, common consent could come about even without the explicit approval of all states and create legal normativity. In the absence of verifiable utterances of state organs individual consent was construed as *tacit* approval, and the validity of general international law was traced back to a *pactum tacitum*.[21] By positing a consensus that could be established also by silence, scholars could get by without explicit consent by all states. With the help of the construct of the *pactum tacitum*, the consent of the overwhelming majority of the states was seen as sufficient for establishing a general, normativity-creating consensus. That consensus could be held up as binding on both the new and the silent states. With this argumentative strategy, the lack of verifiable consent by individual states was to be pushed aside in favor of gains in normativity.

Kelsen rejected these constructs as untenable fictions. As he saw it, both the doctrine of self-obligation and Triepel's theory of the common will of the states went back to the liberal basic assumption of an a priori

[19] Upon closer examination, Triepel's critique of Jellinek's grounding of international law via the latter's doctrine of "objective international law" was itself such a strategy of mediation between the concretely verifiable will of the state, on the one hand, and the assumption of a normativity-creating "objective international law," which in Jellinek was derived from the "nature" of state relations, on the other. On this see Chapter 2 D.

[20] Oppenheim, *International Law*, 15; on Triepel see Chapter 2 D.

[21] On this, Oppenheim: "Entry into the international community of states entails the implied condition that the new member subordinates himself to all of the generally valid law of the community." Quoted from L. F. Oppenheim, "Zur Lehre des internationalen Gewohnheitsrecht," *Niemeyers Zeitschrift für internationales Recht*, XXV (1915), 8.

freedom of the individual state. According to that basic principle, the individual state could not be legally obligated against its will.[22] As a way out of this dilemma, Rousseau had already sought to derive the construct of a binding social order from a contract between free individuals. For Kelsen, Rousseau's doctrine of the *contrat social* was also behind the attempt to ground the sources of international law in consensus.[23] In international law theory, the place of the free individual was taken by the sovereign and personified state, and the legal order grounded in consensus was thus the assumption of a *contrat social* between states.[24]

These liberal intellectual traditions, Kelsen argued, also gave rise to the doctrine which posited that the norm *pacta sunt servanda* should be seen as the basic norm of international law. It became the normative basis for the international legal system that bound the sovereign state via consensus.[25] Kelsen believed that the contract theories, long obsolete in the general doctrine of the state, were still causing mischief in the theory of international law.[26] As was previously the case in state law, they served in international law to conceal or legitimize the subjection of the addressee of the law to the legal system. Although the contract theories bathed this relationship of subordination and superordination in a more benign light through the fiction of the general consensus of free individuals, Kelsen argued that they could not belie the fact that the free will of the subjects of international law was not able, by itself, to establish the binding nature of international law.

Kelsen was also unsparing in his criticism of the doctrine of tacit consent as pure fiction.[27] In point of fact, he argued, the consensus foundation of general international law had to collapse if only a single state withheld its consent. The doctrine of the *pactum tacitum* was nothing other than the old, fictitious distinction between the *volonté générale* and the *volonté de tous*, by which the consent of all individuals was, in the final analysis, replaced with the consent of the majority.[28]

[22] Kelsen, *Principles of International Law*, 2nd edn., 446–447.
[23] Kelsen, "Théorie du droit international coutumier," 21–22; *Principles of International Law*, 2nd edn., 446–447.
[24] Kelsen, "Théorie du droit international coutumier," 21; *Principles of International Law*, 2nd edn., 447.
[25] Ibid. [26] Ibid.
[27] Kelsen, "Théorie du droit international coutumier," 19; *Principles of International Law*, 2nd edn., 448.
[28] Kelsen, *Principles of International Law*, 2nd edn., 448.

In Kelsen's view, a binding social order can never be based on the consent of all individuals or states concerned. In the final analysis, every legal system was a relationship of domination [*Herrschaftsverhältnis*] that could be established and claim validity also against the will of individual targets of the law. For Kelsen, although the consensus-based doctrines of legal sources did satisfy the requirement of concreteness through reference to the sovereign will of the state, they could establish the normativity of international law only through untenable fictions.[29]

III The hypothetical character of international law: the basic norm of international law

Following Kelsen's critique outlined above, in the debate over the "source" or the "validity ground" of international law, neither an argumentative strategy based solely on natural law or socio-biological or psychological assumptions, nor one based solely on positivism and consensus, was sustainable by itself. The doctrine of the a priori "*droit objectif*" (Scelle) or of Christian natural law (Verdross) were too vague, and to become concrete they had to resort after all to "declaratory" positive law through a kind of metaphysical doubling. The doctrine of the consensus of the sovereign will of the states for its part required extra-positivistic standards to establish an objectivized, binding nature of international law vis-à-vis the will of individual states.[30] To that end, it had developed the constructs of an "objective international law" derived from the nature of the community of states (Jellinek), the doctrine of the "common will" (Triepel), and the "common consent" arising from silence (Oppenheim). Kelsen had thus attacked both the natural law and the consensus foundations of international law at their respective Achilles heels: the lack of concreteness for natural law, and the absence of a binding normative nature in the voluntaristic–consensual theories.

The path that Kelsen chose to escape the "justification dilemma"[31] of the sources of international law was not to lay out a new, mediating

[29] On Kelsen's critique of Oppenheim's model see his "Théorie du droit international coutumier," 19–21.

[30] For a comprehensive theoretical analysis of international law's "justification dilemma" between natural law and legal positivism, using human rights as an example, see E. H. Riedel, *Theorie der Menschenrechtsstandards* (Berlin: Duncker & Humblot, 1986), 170–181; for a fundamental language-analytical study of the various argumentative strategies concerning the "basis of obligation," see Koskenniemi, *From Apology to Utopia*, 268.

[31] Riedel, *Theorie der Menschenrechtsstandards*, 180–181.

strategy of objectification, but to dissolve the tension between binding normativity and an empirically verifiable positivity of the law into the construct of a hypothetical basic norm of international law.[32] For Kelsen, the basic norm of international law is the presupposed hypothetical rule according to which states should act the way they have customarily acted.[33] We are thus dealing with the idea of normativity underlying customary international law, which must be applied to the facticity of international politics for us to be able to think international law in the first place. This basic norm is hypothetical in the sense that it derives the validity of positive, enacted norms not from absolute metaphysical values or alleged "social facts," but from a specific mental operation of the legal scholar. The positive legal norms that are established by acts "naturally occurring in reality"[34] are thus not considered to be intersubjectively valid, but merely of a hypothetical validity.[35] The positive enactment of law cannot substantiate the normativity of international law on its own, but requires for that purpose a further theoretical presupposition – namely the abstract idea of a particular legal normativity that is captured in the figure of the basic norm.[36] It is thus only the intellectual presumption of a hypothetical basic norm that turns the concrete Is-acts of law making, its textual basis, into legal norms.

Kelsen worked out the exclusively hypothetical and thus neo-Kantian character of the basic norm of international law only over the course of the 1920s in a give and take with Kunz, Métall, and Verdross. The hypothetical approach I have sketched is not yet found with this clarity in his 1920 work *The Problem of Sovereignty.* Here he had countered what he regarded as the failed attempt by the "voluntarists" to constitute an objective international law with a conception of the basic norm that

[32] Kelsen, "Théorie du droit international coutumier," 4; *Reine Rechtslehre* (1934), 130.

[33] Kelsen, "Théorie du droit international coutumier," 4. On the basic norm of international law in the contentious debate between natural law and positivist approaches see H. Isak, "Bemerkungen zu einigen völkerrechtlichen Lehren Hans Kelsens" in: O. Weinberger et al. (eds.), *Reine Rechtslehre im Spiegel ihrer Fortsetzer und Kritiker* (Vienna and New York: Springer, 1988), 270–273.

[34] H. Kelsen, *Reine Rechtslehre* (1960), 614.

[35] Kelsen, *Die philosophischen Grundlagen der Naturrechtslehre*, 286; on the hypothetical character of the law in Kelsen see: Dreier, *Rechtslehre*, 196–204, and on the positivity of the law, 159–166; K. Engisch, "Vom Sinn des hypothetischen juristischen Urteils" in his *Beiträge zur Rechtstheorie* (Frankfurt am Main: V. Klostermann, 1984), 196 *et seq.*; Julius Kraft spoke in this regard of the "irreality of the law," quoted from "Paradoxien des positiven Rechts," *Internationale Zeitschrift für Theorie des Rechts*, 9 (1935), 280.

[36] On the norm as an interpretive scheme see H. Kelsen, *Reine Rechtslehre* (1934), 4–5.

was still hazy.[37] Although Kelsen, in this early version, already spoke of an "original hypothesis" [*Ursprungshypothese*] or a hypothetically presupposed "original norm" [*Ursprungsnorm*],[38] in his understanding at that time, the basic norm of international law referred to as the *Ursprungsnorm* was still to be given a constitutive content [*Vorsatzung*] that was independent from the will of those to whom the norm was addressed. This "proto-constitution" included also the international legal rule *pacta sunt servanda*: "And specifically the international legal rule *pacta sunt servanda* fully deserves, along with the other basic principles of international law, the name of a statute, that is, a legal statute in the sense of an objectively necessary prerequisite for legal norms, a hypothesis through which an international law becomes possible in the first place as the constitution of a community of coordinated polities."[39]

[37] H. Kelsen, *Problem der Souveränität*, 262. On the basic norm in Kelsen's early work: S. L. Paulson, "On the Early Development of the Grundnorm" in F. Fleerackers (ed.), *Law, Life and the Images of Man. Festschrift for Jan M. Broekman* (Berlin: Duncker & Humblot, 1996), 217–230. Although Kelsen, in the Introduction (VIII), already refers to Kant's transcendental philosophy, the basic norm is here not yet turned into the transcendental condition of jurisprudential cognition. On this see Paulson, "On the Early Development of the Grundnorm," 228–230. According to Paulson, at the beginning of the 1920s, Kelsen was in a transition between the Constructivist Phase and the subsequent Neo-Kantian period: "Four Phases in Hans Kelsen's Legal Theory? Reflections on a Periodization," *Oxford Journal of Legal Studies*, 18 (1998), 157, 161. In the first edition of *Reine Rechtslehre*, the basic norm was then the transcendental condition of legal cognition: Kelsen, *Reine Rechtslehre* (1934), 67 and *Grundlagen*, 12; on the transcendental turn in Kelsen see Paulson, "On the Kelsen-Kant Problematic," 197–213; on the two theoretical approaches associated with the basic norm, the Neo-Kantian and the "thought-economical" [*denkökonomische*] approach to hypothesis-formation in Ernst Mach see Paulson, "Die unterschiedlichen Formulierungen der Grundnorm," 55–56.

[38] The peculiarity of international law, Kelsen argued, was that this *Ursprungsnorm* did not establish a kind of constitution, but endowed inter-state norms directly with a binding nature, *Problem der Souveränität*, 262: "What characterizes international law – like any primitive law – is the circumstance that between the necessarily hypothetically presupposed *Ursprungsnorm* – and in its presupposition lies the only pure statute not linked to any act of law-making – and the act of norm-creation through treaties or agreements, no intermediate stage that serves general law-making is inserted, no legislative process to be undertaken by a special organ, as one is used to in the legal system of individual states."

[39] Kelsen, *Problem der Souveränität*, 217; on the basic norm in international law: H. Thévénaz, "Kelsen et le droit international" in B Dutoit and E. Grisel (eds.), *Mélanges Georges Perrin* (Lausanne: Diffusion Payot, 1984), 318; L. Pitamic, "Die Frage der rechtlichen Grundnorm" in F. A. von Heydte (ed.), *Völkerrecht und rechtliches Weltbild. Festschrift für Alfred Verdross* (Vienna: Springer, 1960), 207 *et seq.*

There was disagreement within the School about the precise content of the basic norm of international law. As we have seen in *The Problem of Sovereignty*, Kelsen had originally posited a kind of hypothetical proto-constitution (*Vorsatzung*) that was to at least include the rule *pacta sunt servanda*. Beginning in 1926, Verdross then directly invoked *pacta sunt servanda* as the basic norm in international law, though he noted at the same time that the basic norm would, in the final analysis, have to be anchored in "the realm of values."[40] Anzilotti and Strupp likewise regarded *pacta sunt servanda* at this time as the content of the basic norm.[41] In his own theoretical approach, Kunz initially replaced the basic norm with a "basic norm complex" that was to contain additional basic principles of international law.[42]

However, resistance to positing *pacta sunt servanda* as the content of the basic norm arose within as well as outside the School.[43] Métall and Kunz rejected such a move with the argument that *pacta sunt servanda*

[40] Here we can already see the beginnings of Verdross's active embrace of the natural law doctrines of the Spanish late scholastics. See Verdross, *Die Verfassung der Völkerrechtsgemeinschaft*, Preface and 21–23. Previously, Verdross had attempted, on convoluted pathways, to specify the content of the basic norm of international law more precisely. In his work *Die Einheit des rechlichten Weltbildes*, he initially tried to demonstrate the existence of a supra-state stock of norms – referred to as "supra-state series of laws" – through state practice. The "constitution" of international law was to contain all those legal tenets that were the condition of all others without themselves being conditioned by them. This version, which drew on Kelsen's early conception of the basic norm in *Problem der Souveränität*, was a cognitively necessary, presupposed original constitution: Verdross, *Die Einheit des rechlichten Weltbildes*, 59, 119 *et seq*. In his second mongraph, *Die Verfassung der Völkerrechtsgemeinschaft*, the concept of constitution was then uncoupled from the question of the basic norm. In this work, Verdross derived its "constitution" from customary international law. To that end, he abandoned the constitutional concept he had still advocated in 1923 in *Die Einheit des rechlichten Weltbildes*, and replaced it with a material notion of constitution in the sense of general principles of international law. For Verdross, only the tenet *pacta sunt servanda* now fulfilled the function of a cognitively necessary, presupposed basic norm. From this point on, he used the notion of constitution only in a material sense with reference to the most important positive norms of customary international law. See Verdross, *Die Verfassung der Völkerrechtsgemeinschaft*, Preface, 21–23, 32; on the discussion within the School see J. L. Kunz, "The 'Vienna School' and International Law" [1934] in Kunz, *The Changing Law of Nations*, 402–404.

[41] Anzilotti, *Lehrbuch des Völkerrechts*, 49–50; Strupp, *Grundzüge des positiven Völkerrechts*, 11.

[42] J. L. Kunz, *Die Anerkennung der Staaten und Regierungen im Völkerrecht* (Stuttgart: Kohlhammer, 1928), 4; on this see Rub, *Hans Kelsens Völkerrechtslehre*, 342; Man, *L'école de Vienne et le développement du droit des gens*, 106.

[43] In Germany, this doctrine was strongly criticized in Walz, *Völkerrecht und Staatliches Recht*, 122 *et seq*.

was a norm of customary international law, that is, positive law, and as such could not be the content of the basic norm. Given its hypothetical character, the basic norm must not have any substantive legal content.[44] Subsequently, Verdross, too, moved away from *pacta sunt servanda* as the basic norm. In the 1931 Festschrift for Kelsen, he declared the general principles of international law to be the content of the basic norm of international law.[45] Kelsen, meanwhile, arrived at the position outlined above, which asserted that the content of the basic norm was the norm that the states should act in the way they have customarily acted.[46] With this, Kelsen had declared the hypothetical assumption of legal scholars that custom creates legal normativity as the basic norm of international law.[47] As Kelsen, Kunz, and Métall saw it, the basic norm of international law must not contain any specific rule of customary international law (*pacta sunt servanda*), for otherwise one would have to explain the legal validity of customary law on the basis of customary law itself.[48] Through the hypothetical formulation of the basic norm, these authors sought to capture this paradox in the abstract idea of an – intellectually presupposed – binding nature of the law. Through the hypothetical articulation of the basic norm, international legal scholarship was to be freed from the need for an ultimate extra-legal foundation of the law. In their eyes, the hypothetical basic norm, as a placeholder[49] for the idea of a specifically

[44] Kunz, "The 'Vienna School' and International Law," 403–404; R. A. Métall, "Skizzen zu einer Systematik der völkerrechtlichen Quellenlehre," *ZöR*, XI (1931), 420.

[45] Verdross, "Die allgemeinen Rechtsgrundsätze des Völkerrechts," 354–365.

[46] Kelsen, *Reine Rechtslehre* (1934), 130.

[47] The question of whether this formulation of the basic norm of international law, which still contained a material "remnant," can be at all reconciled with the transcendental interpretation of the basic norm propounded by Kelsen in his Neo-Kantian phase, cannot be further investigated within the context of the present work. Kelsen maintained the conception of the basic norm as a hypothetical *Einsetzungsnorm* of international law after the Second World War: Kelsen, *Principles of International Law*, 2nd edn., 446.

[48] Kunz, "The 'Vienna School' and International Law," 403–404; Métall, "Skizzen zu einer Systematik der völkerrechtlichen Quellenlehre," 420; Kelsen, *Reine Rechtslehre* (1934), 130.

[49] Here is the precise explanation of this by Joseph Raz, "Kelsen's Theory of the Basic Norm" in Paulson and Litschewski Paulson (eds.), *Normativity and Norms*, 67: "He [Kelsen] is able to maintain that the science of law is value-free by claiming for it a special point of view, that of the legal man, and contending that legal science adopts this point of view; that it presupposes its basic norm in a special, professional, and uncommitted sense of presupposing. There is, after all, no legal sense of normativity, but there is a specifically legal way in which normativity can be considered."

legal validity, secured the "objectivity" of the scholarly understanding of the law.[50]

B *The legal sources of international law and the hierarchical structure of the law*

According to Kelsen, working from the basic norm of international law, it was possible to place the legal sources of international law in turn into a hierarchical self-referential system. Adolf Merkl's hierarchical structure of the law [*Stufenbau der Rechtsordnung*],[51] which Kelsen had adopted in his Pure Theory of Law, proceeded from the assumption that the legal system was made up of a continuous process of law-creation arranged in a hierarchical structure.[52] The law is increasingly concretized as it moves in descending order to the next level of the legal pyramid. The act of creation on each level is authorized and procedurally constrained by the higher-ranking normative level (e.g. the constitution), and it creates a more concrete norm belonging to its own lower-ranking level (e.g. a statute). Within the hierarchical model, the application of the higher norm is thus at the same time the creation of a more concrete norm

[50] Deryck Beyleveld and Roger Brownsword believe that while the "doctrine of presupposition" underlying the notion of the basic norm is compatible with Kelsen's value-relativism, it is incompatible with a positivist doctrine of the law, since the combination of a hypothetically presupposed basic norm and a value-relativistic conception of jurisprudence leads to a "relativized legal idealism" and was *not* able to establish an objective legal science in the sense of legal positivism. See D. Beyleveld and R. Brownsword, "Methodological Syncretism in Kelsen's Pure theory of Law" in Paulson and Litschewski Paulson (eds.), *Normativity and Norms*, 143–144. A. Ross speaks in this context of Kelsen as a "quasi-positivist": "Validity and the Conflict between Legal Positivism and Natural Law" in Paulson and Litschewski Paulson (eds.), *Normativity and Norms*, 159–161.

[51] Merkl, "Prolegomena einer Theorie des rechtlichen Stufenbaus," 1311 *et seq.*, and "Die Rechtseinheit des österreichischen Staates," *WRS*, I (1918), 1115 *et seq.*; "Das Recht im Lichte der Anwendung," *WRS*, I (1918), 1167; "Das doppele Rechtsantlitz," *WRS*, I (1918), 1091 *et seq.*

[52] On the hierarchical structure see W. Ebenstein, "The Pure Theory of Law: Demythologizing Legal Thought," *Calif. L. R.*, 59 (1971), 643; Dreier, *Rechtslehre*, 129–136; Th. Öhlinger, *Der Stufenbau der Rechtsordnung* (Vienna: Manz, 1975), 9 *et seq.*; W. Krawietz, "Reinheit der Rechtslehre als Ideologie?" in W. Krawietz, E. Topisch, and P. Koller (eds.), *Ideologiekritik und Demokratietheorie bei Hans Kelsen* (Berlin: Duncker & Humblot, 1982), 413; N. Luhmann, "Positivität des Rechts als Voraussetzung einer modernen Gesellschaft" [1970] in his *Ausdifferenzierung des Rechts. Beiträge zu einer Rechtssoziologie und Rechtstheorie* (Frankfurt am Main: Suhrkamp, 1981), 121 *et seq.*

belonging to the lower level.[53] Kelsen took this doctrine, which had originally been created for constitutional law, and applied it also to the legal sources of international law.

As a result, customary international law established by the hypothetical basic norm was for Kelsen not on the same level as international treaty law, but was seen as constituting a normative layer above it.[54] Just as constitutional law regulated the generation of lower-ranking laws in national law, the higher-ranking customary law determined the generation of international treaty law. The most important customary legal norm in this context was *pacta sunt servanda*. This norm, Kelsen argued, created international treaty law by endowing international treaties with binding legal force. Kelsen described this view of law creation with respect to the hierarchically structured legal sources as a "dynamic" perspective. The opposing "static" view arranged the various norms hierarchically, based on the question of the ground of their validity. From this "static" perspective, the customary legal norm of *pacta sunt servanda* was for Kelsen the basis for the validity of all treaties under international law;[55] from the "dynamic" perspective it was also the generative norm of international treaty law.[56] The treaties produced through the application of international customary law were subordinated to the latter within the hierarchical structure of the law.

For the School, international treaty law was thus not only a law that was subordinated to customary law, but also a more concrete and individualized form of law. While general international customary law was applied to all states, most treaties were valid only between a certain number of states.[57] Within national law, administrative acts or decisions by the courts constituted the lowest normative level. The statute as the higher-ranking law regulated the generation of the administrative act, which, as a lower-ranking norm, applied a general statutory rule to a particular situation. Through the complete transfer of the hierarchical model to the legal sources of international law, the decisions of

[53] From the dynamic hierarchical model one must distinguish the derogatory structure, which regulates the destructibility of individual norms: R. Walter, *Der Aufbau der Rechtsordnung* (Graz: Leykam, 1964; 2nd edn., Vienna: Manz, 1974), 53 *et seq.*; R. Hauser, *Norm, Recht und Staat. Überlegungen zu Hans Kelsens Theorie der Reinen Rechtslehre* (Vienna and New York: Springer, 1968), 67 *et seq.*

[54] Kelsen, *Reine Rechtslehre* (1934), 129–130.

[55] Kelsen, "Contribution à la Théorie du Traité Internationale," 255.

[56] Kelsen, *Reine Rechtstheorie* (1934), 129–130.

[57] Kelsen, "Contribution à la Théorie du Traité Internationale," 254–256.

international courts or other organs created by treaties formed the most concrete normative level of international law. As a result, Kelsen maintained that it was possible to arrange the legal sources of international law – beginning with the basic norm of international law, moving on to customary law and treaty law, and all the way to individual court decisions – into a hierarchically structured context of creation.

I Customary law

Kelsen's theory of international customary law[58] is shaped by the critique of Scelle's *droit objectif* and natural law doctrines, on the one hand, and the rejection of the consensual foundation of international law, on the other. This dual differentiation had a direct impact on his position regarding the creation of international customary law and on the question of the binding normative force of this legal source. Moreover, from the perspective of the hypothetical character of the law, Kelsen had to answer the question of which empirically demonstrable Is-acts are "transformed" into customary legal norms under the application of the hypothetical basic norm of international law. This issue does not arise within state law, because the political system of modern societies has largely formalized procedures of norm creation, and thus calls (denominates) the Is-acts that can claim legal validity "constitutional document" or "law gazette" for example. In contrast to law-creation through central state organs, customary law was for Kelsen a decentralized form of law-making. However, as a "primitive" form of law-making, custom does *not* possess a formal characterization of legally relevant Is-acts (i.e. acts encompassed by the hypothesis of legal validity).

For the project of a post-metaphysical doctrine of international law, however, a scientifically verifiable stock of statutory norms was of crucial importance. Consequently, international custom, too, was for Kelsen not the expression of an invisible, presupposed external law, but was to be regarded, in spite of its decentralized nature, as a formal process of positive law-making. He argued that the concept of custom described both the factual process of law-creation and the created norm. From the perspective of the doctrine of the legal sources of international law,

[58] From the secondary literature: H. Thévénaz, "À Propos de la Coutume" in S. Engel and R. A. Métall (eds.), *Law, State, and International Legal Order. Essays in Honor of Hans Kelsen* (Knoxville: University of Tennessee Press, 1964); Rub, *Hans Kelsens Völkerrechtslehre*, 316–319.

however, only the ascertainment of the actual norm-creating process was relevant.[59]

Since the end of the nineteenth century, the prevailing doctrine of international law had divided the norm-creating process into two elements: first, the practice of states extending over a long period of time, and second, a legal conviction on the part of the states accompanying that practice (*opinio iuris sive necessitatis*).[60] This theoretical combination – dominant also in the twentieth century – of objective practice and subjective legal conviction allowed the international lawyer to handle customary law in a flexible way. Moreover, the requirement of state practice offers the scholar an objectivity-guaranteeing, empirical anchor in determining new norms. What is more, by negating the existence of a subjective element in concrete cases, the international lawyer can contest the strengthening of an ongoing practice into a norm.

1 Dispensing with the *opinio iuris*

In his 1939 theory of customary law, Kelsen regarded the assumption that an *opinio iuris* was a constitutive element of international customary law as erroneous.[61] The *opinio iuris*, he argued, was a reflection on a legal norm through state organs that the same state was about to create through its conduct. This norm therefore did not yet exist at the time, when the "legal conviction" [*Rechtsüberzeugung*] had to be demonstrated. Hence, the "legal conviction" was either an error on the part of the norm-creating state organ, or the reflection on a presupposed, invisible law to which the state felt bound to adhere in its conduct. In the latter case, the assumption of a subjective element rested on the "metaphysical doubling" of the law carried out by natural law doctrines and the *droit objectif*. But as long as the norm-creating process was under way, states could not be bound either objectively or subjectively to a norm that did not yet exist.

[59] Kelsen, "Théorie du droit international coutumier," 10; on this see N. Bobbio, "Kelsen and Legal Power" in Paulson and Litschewski Paulson (eds.), *Normativity and Norms*, 445–446.

[60] On the emergence of the doctrine of customary law see P. Guggenheim, "Contribution à l'histoire des sources du droit des gens," *RCADI*, 94 (1958), 52; W. G. Grewe, "Vom europäischen zum universalen Völkerrecht," *ZaöRV*, 42 (1982), 449–479; on various approaches to the theory of the sources of law: E. H. Riedel, "Standards and Sources. Farewell to the Exclusivity of the Sources Triad in International Law," *EJIL*, 2 (1991), 58–83.

[61] Kelsen, "Théorie du droit international coutumier," 11.

Because Kelsen conceived of customary law as a purely law-creating process, the *opinio iuris* could not be for him a legal, but at most a moral, sense of obligation, one that could not be allowed to play a role in determining positive law.[62] Kelsen's adverse stance toward the need for a subjective element in establishing international customary law was the expression of a general skepticism about the objectifiability of mental legal convictions: "Il est presque impossible de prouver l'existence de l'élément psychique, à savoir l'existence des sentiments ou des pensées des individus qui ont accomplis les actes constituant la coutume dans le passé."[63] Kelsen evidently regarded the mental element as the point of entry for the subjective value judgments of the international lawyer ascertaining the international customary-law norm. The establishment of the *opinio iuris* is difficult to objectify, and as such it did not, for Kelsen, meet the demands of a "scientific" jurisprudence.

As another argument, Kelsen pointed to the other norm-creation processes of international law. International legal scholarship dispensed with the demonstration of a legal conviction also when it came to the theoretical foundations of treaty law as another source of international law. By referencing other legal sources, Kelsen was suggesting to his readers that the additional *psychological* element of the legal conviction was pointless. There was a good reason why doctrine with regard to other sources of international law did without the *opinio iuris*. For example, when an international legal treaty was entered into, the notion that the contracting parties assumed that they were already obligated by another source of the law made no sense at all. If that were the case, there would be no need for them to sign a treaty, since the very function of the treaty was to create new law between the signatories. With respect to a court decision, as well, which – according to the Pure Theory of Law – created a new individual norm, it would not occur to anyone to verify the legal conviction of the judges.[64] Because Kelsen posited not only customary law, but also the treaty and the decision of the court as law-creating processes of at least limited autonomy, the assumption of an *opinio iuris* that could be verified by jurisprudence struck him as a limitation on the freedom of the law-creating organs. For Kelsen, law-making was a central function of the political system, and jurisprudence must not restrict the degree of liberty required to fulfill that function.[65] Precisely that danger existed, however, if the international lawyer sought to determine the legal consciousness of political organs. This argument reflected

[62] Ibid., 12. [63] Ibid. [64] Ibid., 12–13. [65] Ibid., 14.

Kelsen's ideology-critical skepticism toward legal scholarship. His implicit criticism was that the manipulable demonstration of an *opinio iuris* by the scholar in the final analysis put the jurist in the place of the established law-making organs. Kelsen rejected this kind of interference in the autonomy of the political system. Once again, he demanded that international legal scholarship impose limitations on itself.

2 The replacement for the *opinio iuris*

However, Kelsen's renunciation of the demonstration of an *opinio iuris* (motivated by his critique of ideology) thrusts the international lawyer into an even greater conundrum on the question of positive customary law. If she follows Kelsen, all she has for now to demonstrate positive law is the practice of states. In the absence of the *opinio iuris*, how does one deal with the constant violation of rules that are part of the secure stock of customary norms? Does such violation constitute a law-destroying exercise, or merely deviant behavior that does not question the normative quality of the rule? Without an additional regulatory element, it is no longer possible to exclude certain Is-acts on principle by invoking the lack of legal consciousness. If one dispenses with the second regulatory element, every action by the state is initially an act that carries equal weight for the creation of norms. The unavoidable process of selecting and weighing state Is-acts in the scientific demonstration of customary law remains highly subjective, however.

Kunz criticized the move to dispense with the *opinio iuris*, which was also advocated by Guggenheim, by arguing that it was no longer possible to distinguish the rules of international courtesy from binding international customary law.[66] The qualification of an international legal norm as binding or non-binding occurred for customary law doctrinally via the concept of legal conviction. Without the counterbalance of the *opinio iuris*, every act engaged in by a state with greater frequency would solidify into customary law.

This problem did not arise for Kelsen in 1939, since his "theory of customary law" must be seen as strongly fixated on international adjudication at that time.[67] The decisions by international organs, and here especially the decisions by international courts, were for Kelsen the most

[66] J. L. Kunz, "The Nature of Customary Law," *AJIL*, 47 (1953), 665.

[67] Thévénaz was the first to point out this link: "À Propos de la Coutume," 325.

important pillar in determining customary law.[68] Together with the practice of international treaties, international adjudication formed an objectifiable criterion for determining international customary law. In Kelsen's theory of customary law, the treaty and court judgments, which were more formalized and thus for him "more objective," replaced the uncertain *opinio iuris*. In his search for formalizable criteria for determining international customary law, Kelsen thus fell back on empirically demonstrable treaties and court decisions. This made it less easy for international legal scholarship to ideologically distort the stock of norms than is the case with the demonstration of a legal conviction by the acting states.

By contrast, the idea of invoking the views of eminent international jurists – a kind of *opinio communis doctorum* – as a norm-relevant factor did not occur to Kelsen. Revealingly enough, for Kelsen international lawyers participated in the creation of customary law only by advising governments. They contributed to the emergence of customary law by influencing the actual conduct of states in this way. To *determine* customary law, Kelsen favored decisions and treaties as formally verifiable material created by competent law-making organs.

The hierarchical logic of the law-generating sources becomes circular, however, if the lower law-generating levels become the most important proof of the highest normative level, that is, customary law. This effect results when Kelsen almost completely blocks out the application function of the subordinated legal sources in the hierarchical structure in favor of a focus on the law-creating function. In Kelsen's reconstruction, the court is not primarily applying international customary law, but is itself creating new customary law. Since court decisions – alongside state practice – are drawn upon to determine customary law, they move the development of customary law along in the Kelsenian conception. But this makes it look as though the decisions of international courts, and not customary law, stand at the apex of the hierarchy of sources. As a result of the posited reciprocal influence exerted by legal sources on one another, the model of the hierarchical structure encounters its limitation here.

Kelsen also emphasized that when international judges applied customary law, they usually dispensed with proof of an *opinio iuris*.[69] But if customary law itself can be given its real shape only from the material of individual court decisions and international treaties, what is the normative basis on which international courts actually render their decision

[68] Kelsen, "Théorie du droit international coutumier," 15–16. [69] Ibid., 16.

when they invoke customary law? In determining customary law, an international judge can draw only upon earlier decisions of international courts, in addition to the ambiguous practice of states. In the final analysis, the theory of customary law that Kelsen published in 1939 was conceived for an international legal order with compulsory jurisdiction. Given the uncertain stock of norms, courts rendering binding decisions would have to largely create new, individual law. A multitude of concrete court decisions would then create sufficient normative material that scholars could draw upon instead of the *opinio iuris* in demonstrating the general norms of customary law.

It was probably no coincidence that Kelsen did not reintroduce the *opinio iuris* as an element of customary international law until 1967 in the second edition of his book *Principles of Public International Law*, after the hope in the establishment of compulsory jurisdiction which he had articulated in the 1930s and 1940s had been dashed.[70] Still, even here he did not hold back with a more than critical commentary about the great uncertainties that attached to the traditional scholarly determination of customary law.[71] Moreover, even in 1967, Kelsen made it very clear that the problem of customary law could not be resolved by international legal scholarship, but only by international courts: "It may be readily granted that for the most part these uncertainties would not arise if international tribunals had the same role in the interpretation and development of international law that national courts have in the interpretation and development of national law. But in the absence of a system of compulsory jurisdiction the many uncertainties attending customary law must be expected to persist."[72]

II *An objective doctrine of treaties*

While Kelsen's doctrine of customary law is directed against the natural-law assumption of given legal principles behind positive law and the resulting entry points for the jurist's subjective value judgments, his doctrine of the treaty hinged on a critique of the doctrine of the free will of the state as the central constructive principle of the prevailing theories of treaty law. According to the conventional view, the binding nature of the treaty was

[70] Kelsen, *Principles of International Law*, 2nd edn., 440; in the second edition of the *Pure Theory of Law*, Kelsen had pointed to the *opinio iuris* in his general discussion of customary law: *Reine Rechtslehre* (1960), 232; on this see Thévénaz, "À Propos de la Coutume."

[71] Kelsen, *Principles of International Law*, 2nd edn., 451–452. [72] Ibid., 452.

based on the voluntary consensus of the sovereign wills of states. In this view, the instrument of the treaty, in its respect for the autonomy of the individual state, reflects the special structure of international law, which is profoundly different from the state legal order. In contrast to the authoritative relationship of the state legal order to the citizen, international law was not based on supra-state laws, but on voluntary treaties between equal sovereigns. By way of negative demarcation from the state's "authoritative law" [*Herrschaftsrecht*], international law was called "coordination law," "horizontal legal order," or "inter-state law."[73] These attempts at a definition served the endeavor to harmonize the idea of a binding international law and the assumption of the sovereignty of states. The state was equated with an individual who is not subject to any state legal order, but is legally bound exclusively by treaties entered into freely with other individuals of equal standing.

Kelsen's "Contribution à la théorie du traité international" of 1936 was directed against this grounding of international treaty law in the sovereign will of the state and the resulting differentiation of international law from "authoritative" state law. With his "*conception objectiviste*" of international treaty law, Kelsen was trying to unmask the "*conception individualiste ou subjective*" of international law as a construct that rested on fictions.[74] The association between the treaty and the principle of freedom was for Kelsen a liberal ideology stemming from private law. Just as private autonomy was the basis of the contract in private law, he argued, sovereignty was made the basis of the treaty in international law. If one dissolved this link, the international treaty became a particular authoritative order [*Herrschaftsordnung*] comparable to national public law. From a legal-theoretical point of view, for Kelsen the difference between an international treaty and national law was not one of kind, but merely of degree.[75] Kelsen sought to substantiate this view by looking at the way in which international treaties arose and worked.

1 The creation of the treaty-based legal order

As with national legislation, the creation of law through international treaties was for Kelsen a central function of the legal system.[76] This law-creating

[73] On the interstate structure of international law see Oppenheim, "Zur Lehre des internationalen Gewohnheitsrecht," 3.
[74] Kelsen, "Contribution à la Théorie du Traité Internationale," 264. [75] Ibid., 270.
[76] Ibid., 261.

procedure is regulated by higher norms, that is, in state law by the constitution and in international law by customary law. Thus, the international treaty created a new norm of international law by applying the customary rules that rank above the treaty in the hierarchical structure of legal sources, among which was also the central norm *pacta sunt servanda*.

In keeping with the customary law prevailing at the time, the contracting parties were for Kelsen chiefly states. However, alongside states, other legal communities in his view also possessed the capacity to create law by virtue of customary law or special treaty law. Here Kelsen pointed to the Vatican and international organizations like the League of Nations.[77] Moreover, an expansion of subjects empowered to create law beyond this circle was by no means ruled out. For Kelsen, however, this assumption could not conceal the fact that in the final analysis it was expressions of will by individuals that were made the basis of the treaty. From a legal perspective, these individuals were initially seen as organs of a state legal order.[78] This was the classic "subjective" perspective of the treaty, which regarded the acting individuals as constitutionally appointed organs of individual states.

According to Kelsen, however, one could juxtapose to the "subjective" view of the treaty that proceeded from the individual state an "objective" perspective that proceeded from the international legal order. In that perspective, the treaty-concluding individuals are not only organs of the state, but at the same time also part of an organ of the international legal community. In fact, they formed first and foremost a composed, particular organ of the international legal order, and only secondarily organs of their respective states: "Car c'est le droit des gens qui les appelle à la fonction de créer du droit des gens. C'est sur un principe du droit des gens que repose leur compétence pour la création du droit des gens."[79]

Even if prevailing international law left it up to the states to determine the organs authorized to conclude a treaty, this was an allocation of competency that emanated from international law. According to Kelsen, then, international law made use of individual state legal systems in putting together its own law-creating organs.[80] In a perspective that proceeded consistently from the international legal order, that is, which applied the doctrine of the primacy of international law, the parties to a treaty become sub-organs of a specialized legislative process of the international legal community.

[77] Ibid., 262. [78] Ibid., 263. [79] Ibid., 262. [80] Ibid., 261–262.

In equating the international treaty with national legislation, Kelsen, however, went even a step further in 1936: With respect to the substantive structure of the declarations of will, as well, he saw no essential difference between the treaty and the statute. Kelsen's argument was directed against the traditional definition of the treaty, which stated that it came about through two or more substantively different, but related, declarations of will. Even in a private law contract, Kelsen did not see the presence of two different declarations of will promising the respective performance. Instead, Kelsen conceived of a treaty as several substantively aligned declarations of will with respect to establishing a common treaty-based order. In this model, the parties state their willingness through their identical declarations of will to establish a legal order, which can then obligate the treaty partners to different factual actions. For Kelsen, however, the exchange of different actions envisioned by the treaty did not in any way alter the fact that the declarations underlying the treaty should be seen as parallel in the alignment of their wills.[81]

With this, the distinction between "*traités-contrat*" and "*traités-lois*" treaties (i.e. between those that involved legal transactions and those that created law), disappeared in Kelsen's theory. It was Triepel who had applied the distinction – originating with Binding – between a law-creating "agreement" and the legal transaction [*rechtsgeschäftlicher Vertrag*] to international law.[82] Only the agreement was created by identical declarations of will aimed at establishing a legal order. It created new law, while the contractual treaty involved only the application of the general norms by means of the treaty, that is, chiefly the norm *pacta sunt servanda*.[83] For Kelsen, by contrast, every treaty, in keeping with the hierarchical structure described above, was simultaneously the application of existing law and the creation of new law. Through the treaty, the higher-ranking customary norms are applied via the conclusion of the

[81] Ibid., 258.

[82] Triepel, *Völkerrecht und Landesrecht*, 35–62, with a general discussion of the concept of agreement [*Vereinbarung*] and of the treaty with reference to the theory of agreement of Karl Binding, to whom Triepel's famous monograph is also dedicated.

[83] Triepel on agreement and treaty, *Völkerrecht und Landesrecht*, 65: "Since, on the other hand, as must be restated once again, a substantial portion of all so-called 'state treaties,' namely all true 'treaties' in the sense explained above, are simply incapable of creating objective law, there arises the task of examining which state treaties are true treaties, which are true agreements, and which among the latter are capable of producing international law." On the declarations of will in the "law-creating" agreements see ibid., 67: "Here, too, the declarations of will must be, in contrast to the treaty, declarations of equal will [. . .] aimed at the same undertaking."

treaty and at the same time a new, concrete normative order is created. Thus, in contrast to Triepel's conception, every treaty is a "law-creating" treaty. As an interim conclusion we can note that Kelsen considered every international treaty a particular order of international law created by the aligned declarations of will by sub-organs of the international legal community.

Working from this, Kelsen was able to expand the analogy to national law: in the constitutionally created two-chamber system, as well, a law came about through two aligned declarations of will by the two constitutional sub-organs.[84] In their interaction they could be seen, comparable to the parties to a treaty in international law, as a composed legislative organ. By seeing the treaty and the statute as law-creating processes established by the legal system, Kelsen brought them very close together from an abstract-theoretical perspective. Theoretically speaking, the parties to a treaty are no more free than the legislative organs of the state constitution, since both organs are empowered to create law within a formal and material framework prescribed by the supraordinated legal system. Kelsen deconstructed the conventional doctrinal distinction between the treaty based on the principle of autonomy on the one hand and the statute as the exercise of public authority, on the other, so as to make his specific view of the international treaty conceivable in the first place. This made the international treaty appear to be an instrument of law-creation of a post-sovereign universal law that was comparable to legislation within a state.

2 The international treaty's mode of action

Kelsen also analyzed the international treaty's mode of action against the foil of national legislation. His argument was directed against the notion that the treaty bound only the signatories to it and could not create any rights and obligations for third parties.[85] Given the principle of autonomy, the treaty, in the traditional doctrine, could impose reciprocal obligations only on the state parties, whereas national law was capable of imposing unilaterally binding obligations on citizens who were not involved in its creation. We are thus dealing once more with the dichotomy between freedom and authority underlying the doctrinal distinction between treaty and statute, which Kelsen was trying to expel from the

[84] Kelsen, "Contribution à la Théorie du Traité Internationale," 264. [85] Ibid., 265.

theoretical analysis of these law-creating instruments as a form of ideology.

For Kelsen, an international treaty obligated the individual states as legal systems. However, positing the legal person of the state as the reference point of the treaty obligations must not conceal the effect of the treaty on the individuals affected. In the final analysis, the international treaty obligated and authorized not a "suprahuman state person," but, via the state legal system, state organs that were in turn composed of individuals.[86] In the process, there was not necessarily a direct personal correspondence between the individuals involved in concluding the treaty and those who were in fact obligated by it. From the perspective of the affected individuals, it is therefore possible that persons uninvolved in bringing the treaty about could be empowered and obligated by an international treaty.[87] By excluding the legal person as the common point of reference of all state actions from his reflections as a "fiction," Kelsen was trying to question the doctrine that a treaty was prohibited from creating obligations for third parties.

As Kelsen saw it, international law generally obligated individuals by way of the state legal system. It was left to the latter to determine which organs had to fulfill the obligations of the treaty and in which form. In that sense, the normal case was an effect of international law on individuals that was mediated through the state legal system.[88] This mode of action, however, was for Kelsen not a phenomenon specific to international law. This mediated effect of a contract emerged also within intrastate law, especially in collective wage agreements. In this instance, the effect of the contract was mediated, from the perspective of the affected workers and employers, by the directly obligated organizations as legal persons.[89]

For Kelsen, however, the mediated effect of the international treaty was not a compelling necessity. Positive international law had already brought about a direct obligation and empowerment of individuals, even if that was still the exception. As a consequence of the erroneous assumption that international law could obligate and empower individuals only indirectly, Kelsen argued, international legal scholarship had eventually come up with the doctrine of the absolute necessity of the "transformation" of international law into national law. But the necessity of "transformation" stood in contradiction to positive

[86] Ibid., 268. [87] Ibid. [88] Ibid., 271. [89] Ibid., 269.

law.[90] In this way, Kelsen relativized the traditional doctrine's emphasis on the special nature of the mediated effect of international law in two ways: first, the phenomenon was also found in national law in the form of so-called "collective contracts," and, second, while the mediated effect was the normal case, it was by no means an absolute theoretical necessity. According to Kelsen, then, the international treaty could not only unfold its effect vis-à-vis the signing parties, but also, independent of this, empower and obligate individuals directly as a particular legal order.[91]

As the final step of his analogy to national law, Kelsen asked himself whether the treaty could also bind the organs and legal subjects of states not involved in concluding the treaty; that is, whether a "genuine" treaty benefitting and burdening third parties was theoretically possible. Using the example of contemporary forms of international treaties, the Treaty of Versailles and the Covenant of the League of Nations, Kelsen sought to demonstrate the extent to which the international legal order was already making use of agreements at the expense of or for the benefit of third parties.[92] He concluded that especially the empowerment of third-party states and their citizens was practically and theoretically possible: "Ce ne sont pas seulement des traités en faveur d'États tiers, ce sont aussi des traités en faveur des particuliers, c'est à dire des particuliers en tant que sujets d'États tiers, qui sont possibles, mais pas encore parfaitement réalisés en droit international positif."[93]

With the positive law demonstration of treaties benefitting and burdening third parties, Kelsen wrapped up the theoretical approximation of the international treaty and national law: "En ce qui concerne la possibilité d'accorder des droits à des tierces personnes, la création du droit par traité peut se rapprocher dans une certaine mesure de la création du droit par la voie legislative."

Kelsen could succeed in his far-reaching analogy between the international treaty and national law only by negating all doctrinal constructs derived from the principle of liberty or sovereignty. In creating the treaty, the state or its organs were acting as part of a legislative organ of international law. By concluding the treaty, this composed organ established a particular suprastate order of international law that asserted

[90] Ibid., 271; on this see especially his detailed study, Kelsen, "La transformation du droit international public." For this problematic see Chapter 3 A III.

[91] Kelsen, "Contribution à la Théorie du Traité Internationale," 271.

[92] Ibid., 271–292.

[93] Ibid., 286.

validity independent of the momentary "will" of the parties to the treaty. The binding force of this legal order was not limited to the signing parties in the narrower sense, but could extend also to individuals and third states not involved in the process that gave rise to the treaty. The doctrine of the autonomy principle as the foundation of the treaty had, according to Kelsen, led to the erroneous classification of international law as "interstate" law and to the doctrinal prohibition against so-called treaties burdening third parties.

The ideologically grounded notion of liberty thus posed, in the form of the sovereignty doctrine, a barrier to the further development of the international legal community. Purified from the dross of the doctrine of sovereignty, the international treaty functioned, in Kelsen's view, as a flexible and substantively unlimited instrument of law-creation. Through the instrument of the treaty, Kelsen opened up for international politics quasi-unrestricted spheres of action. To what extent the spheres of liberty of individual states were preserved or certain extra-judicial values were realized was left entirely to the parties to the treaty – acting potentially without restrictions – in their role as legislative organs of international law. According to Kelsen, the development and implementation of political programs must not be constrained by the doctrine of international law. Kelsen's theory of the hypothetical character of international law rested in this regard on an ideology-critical self-limitation of legal scholarship.

C The theory of legal sources as a self-limitation of legal scholarship

Kelsen's primary concern in ousting natural law and the social contract as the foundation of international law was to draw a clear boundary between the scholarly description of legal norms and political legislation by the authorized organs. To that end, the Pure Theory of Law deliberately restricted the analytical and interpretive horizon of international legal scholarship, and deconstructed traditional doctrinal concepts. The spheres of action granted to political organs in the norm-creating process by the doctrine of the hierarchical structure were to be protected. At the highest level of the hierarchy of norms there existed no predetermined substantive limits constraining the legislator. The latter could transport the most diverse moral, ethical, religious, or political ideas into the form of law. It was only at the lower, concretizing levels that the organs chosen by the legal system were restricted by the higher-ranking law. Still, at every level there existed a certain discretionary leeway, which Merkl had called the "autonomous determinant."[94] The formal application of the law and the politically creative act of legislation merged in the specific concretization of norms.

Kelsen's theory of legal sources sought to protect the finely tuned relationship between politics and the law, achieved by the doctrine of the hierarchical structure, against interference from a politicized public law scholarship. Kelsen's theory of legal sources thus became primarily a critique of those doctrinal constructions whose application put the jurist in the place of the authorized organs of law-creation. That was the reason why Kelsen's criticism of the traditional doctrine of customary law was directed against the difficult-to-objectify element of the *opinio iuris* as an alleged entry point for the jurist's ideological premises. With regard to the doctrine of treaty law, Kelsen located the central ideological element in the principle of sovereignty. However, the protection of a political space for law-creation was for Kelsen not an end in itself, but served to stabilize the medium of the law within international relations. By granting scope for political action only to organs authorized by the legal system, the law was to be protected against ideological influences from legal scholarship that went beyond this. According to Kelsen's theory of legal sources, international law accepted the exercise of political influence only via the level of legally established organs regulated by formal procedures. The specific normativity of the law as a "congealed form of politics"[95] was stabilized by rejecting "pseudo-scientific" distortions. Failure to do so would, in Kelsen's eyes, prevent international law from effectively performing its function as a universal medium of social change. In the process, Kelsen's criticism was directed especially against those ideological premises that contradicted his own ideal of a largely institutionalized system of universal law. It was no accident that the suppression of customary law in favor of decisions by international courts and the "reshaping" of the instrument of the treaty into a statute-like form of law-making were in line with Kelsen's own cosmopolitan ideal of the rule of law in

[94] A. Merkl, *Allgemeines Verwaltungsrecht* (Vienna: Springer, 1927), 142; Kelsen, *Staatslehre*, 232; on this see N. Achterberg, "Kelsen und Marx. Zur Verwendbarkeit der reinen Rechtslehre in relativistischen und dogmatischen Rechtssystemen," *Politik und Kultur*, 2 (1975), 48, and N. Achterberg, "Hans Kelsens Bedeutung in der gegenwärtigen deutschen Rechtslehre," *DÖV*, 27 (1974), 454; Dreier, *Rechtslehre*, 133.

[95] Ibid., 114.

international relations, secured by formalized legal sources and international courts.[96]

D The opponents of a "dematerialized" doctrine of legal sources

The strict rejection of moral, ethical, and political criteria when conceptualizing the doctrine of sources met with criticism during the interwar period, especially from German international lawyers. This criticism was chiefly due to the need not only to denounce the "injustices" of the Treaty of Versailles politically, but also to contest their legitimacy. The Pure Theory of the Law, with its thrust critical of ideology, struck many contemporaries not only as highly unsuitable, but as downright counterproductive to the foreign policy concerns of the Reich. The restrictions on Germany's sovereignty and the burdens from the Treaty of Versailles both regarded as "unjust," were to be opposed with the help of arguments drawn from international law.[97] In the interwar period, the Vienna School's theory of international law was accused of stabilizing the concrete order established on the basis of the peace treaties by ignoring its politically and morally reprehensible content, and undermining the Reich's efforts to revise the Treaty of Versailles.

I Rematerialization as a strategy of revision

Although Kelsen and Kunz had repeatedly criticized the peace terms imposed upon Germany as harsh and therefore as a latent threat to the entire organization of the League of Nations,[98] from a strictly legal point

[96] On Kelsen's conception of international jurisdiction see Chapter 6.

[97] These were debates over international law primarily with French and English international lawyers, which concerned, among other things, the questions of the validity of treaties concluded under coercion, war guilt, the extradition and punishment of war criminals, and the factual impossibility of fulfilling the Treaty (reparations). On this see Stolleis, *A History of Public Law in Germany*, 60–64.

[98] J. L. Kunz wrote the following in a review of a work on the League of Nations by Léon Bourgeois (L. Bourgeois, *Pour La Société des Nations*), in *ZöR*, 4 (1925), 199: "But how can one continue to speak of the cause of the Entente as the 'cause du droit et de liberté,' [. . .] seeing as the peace treaties are creating so much new injustice, claim that 'ce n'est pas au lendemain de la Victoire du droit que les grandes Puissances abandonneraient la cause du droit' in view of *these* peace treaties, in view of *this* postwar posture, especially of *France*" (emphasis original). H. Kelsen, *The Legal Process and International Order*, The New Commonwealth Research Bureau Publications (London: Constable & Co., 1934), 15.

of view they affirmed the legal validity of the Treaty of Versailles.[99] Kelsen justified his position by noting the absence of a prohibition in customary law against treaties concluded under coercion. The criticism of the School by other authors was thus directed not so much against this concrete position, as against the dematerialized "purity" of the international legal methodology postulated by Kelsen. With its theory, it was argued, the Vienna School, as an extension of French international law scholarship, affirmed the concrete status quo of Versailles.[100] As a result of the rigorous rejection of morality and politics, opponents argued, the strictly positivist theory of international law legitimated the concrete, potentially unjust and – because of the factual situation – intolerable content of the international legal system.[101]

Already at the end of the 1920s (and increasingly so in the 1930s), leading representatives of German international law felt that the strict delineation of the normativity of the law from other systems of Ought, such as morality or justice, and the strict dualism of Is and Ought were unacceptable. The basic tenor of the criticism had already been set by Carl Schmitt in 1926: the "juridification" of international politics through the alleged conspiracy between French international lawyers

[99] Kelsen, *Unrecht und Unrechtsfolge im Völkerrecht*, 600, note 1; J. L. Kunz, "Book Review of: Karl Heyland, *Die Rechtsstellung der besetzten Gebiete*," *ZöR*, 4 (1925), 196, where Kunz addressed the possibility of contesting the Treaty on the ground of *exceptio doli* because of the non-compliance with Wilson's Fourteen Points (as *lex contractus* by virtue of the Lansing Note), but left the question open as still unresolved.

[100] In the period after the Second World War, the proponents of state law positivism during the Weimar period were frequently criticized on the grounds that a positivist theory of law inevitably leads to the affirmation of a given, concrete legal order, and that it had in this way contributed to the acceptance of the National Socialist regime in Germany. This view was refuted by later historical research on Nazi law and scholarship, which illustrated that scholars who defended and helped to establish the new Nazi regime used to attack opponents as "positivists" and "bourgeois formalists" for not embracing new political concepts, such as the "*Volksgemeinschaft*" and the "*völkischer Führerstaat*" in their publications. It was in fact the liberal "formalists" who defended the rule-of-law principles of the Weimar legal system, which was not formally abolished in the first years of Nazi rule, but only gradually erased by new interpretations of existing laws through scholarship and practice and new legislation. On affinities with and opposition to National Socialism among individual German public-law scholars and the complex relationship between theory and a changing political context, see M. Stolleis, "In the Belly of the Beast" in his *The Law under the Swastika: Studies on Legal History in Nazi Germany* (Chicago University Press, 1998), 87 *et seq.*, and *History of Public Law*, 249 *et seq.* For a theoretical rejection of the charge that the Pure Theory of Law affirmed a particular state order see Dreier, *Rechtslehre*, 159–228.

[101] Schmitt, *Die Kernfrage des Völkerbundes*, 50; C. Bilfinger, "Zum Problem der Staatengleichheit im Völkerrecht," *ZaöRV*, 4 (1934), 487.

and the Vienna School served the goal, in the final analysis, of cementing Germany's unjust situation under the Treaty of Versailles. Schmitt argued that the modern doctrine of international law, by expelling the question about the material principles for revising an unjust status quo from the objective realm of a scientific jurisprudence, "essentially avoids such questions of principle, possibly with the excuse that it is positive. Needless to say, this kind of positivism is nothing other than the most impotent legitimation of the prevailing status quo."[102] According to this argument, the "objective construction" of international law sought by the School affirmed the "humiliation" of the German people suffered in Versailles.

Other influential German international lawyers, the likes of Viktor Bruns[103] and Carl Bilfinger,[104] also insisted in the 1930s on a stronger rematerialization of international jurisprudence. To that end, great currency was given to the notion of equality, which the status quo created by the peace treaties was seen as having seriously violated:

> Equal treatment and reciprocality in rights as well as obligations is the foundation of the Covenant of the League of Nations, as it is of the system of international law as such. The one-sidedness of the permanent burdens

[102] Schmitt, *Die Kernfrage des Völkerbundes*, 50. In this quote, given below in full, Schmitt was referring to the problem of Art. 19 of the Covenant of the League of Nations, which provided for the possibility of revising the peace treaty in case of a threat to peace:

> A state with a rising population and growing expansion, whose vital force is wearing itself out against unnatural, torn borders and oppressive tribute payments, a disarmed and dishonored people is not helped by this . . . If things are to be done truly lawfully, it could be helped only by a recognized, concrete principle of change that can be categorically applied by international entities. Where is such a principle to be found? The modern theory of international law essentially avoids such questions of principle, possibly with the excuse that it is positive. Needless to say, this kind of positivism is nothing other than the most impotent legitimation of the prevailing status quo.

On the points of contact and differences in the thought of Carl Schmitt and Hans Kelsen see H. Hofmann, *Legitimität gegen Legalität. Der Weg der politischen Philosophie Carl Schmitts* (Berlin: Duncker & Humblot, 1964), 41–56; on the biographical points of contact see B. Rüthers, "On the Brink of Dictatorship. Hans Kelsen and Carl Schmitt in Cologne 1933" in D. Diner and M. Stolleis (eds.), *Hans Kelsen and Carl Schmitt: A Juxtaposition* (Gerlingen: Bleicher, 1999), 115 *et seq.*

[103] On Bruns see Stolleis, *A History of Public Law in Germany*, 425–427.

[104] On Bilfinger see ibid., 430–432. On Bilfinger's relationship to National Socialism see the illuminating comments by L. Becker, *'Schritte auf einer abschüssigen Bahn.' Das Archiv des öffentlichen Rechts (AöR) und die deutsche Staatsrechtswissenschaft im Dritten Reich* (Tübingen: Mohr Siebeck, 1999), 86–90.

> and restrictions that the Versailles Treaty imposes upon the German Reich therefore stands in unresolvable contradiction to the principles of the Covenant of the League of Nations and to the system of international law.[105]

These observers denounced the divergent starting conditions and thus the materially "unjust" status quo created by the instrument of the treaty. A concept of justice that was not only formal but material was used to question the lawfulness of the central treaties of the interwar system.[106] As Bilfinger said about this methodological strategy: "It would appear that scholarship, by means of the abstract and normativistic method, has turned equality and equal rights [*Gleichberechtigung*] into virtual concepts devoid of substance. The newer practice, by contrast, has taken the path to the synthesis of Ought and Is by raising the question, precisely in connection with the equality of states, about the actual characteristics of an independent state."[107] Through a substantive charging of the concepts of equality and sovereignty, it was possible to not only politically criticize the concrete manifestation of the system of international law, including the Charter of the League of Nations, but also to depict it as unlawful from a scholarly perspective.[108] Through a materialization of concept-formation, the legal-political question about the legitimacy of the interwar order could be turned entirely into a legal question in the narrower sense. The "purity" of legal cognition that Kelsen sought by separating Is and Ought was rejected in favor of a repoliticization of international legal scholarship. Schmitt, Bilfinger, Berber, and Bruns believed that only a materialization of central international legal concepts would allow

105 V. Bruns, "Bund oder Bündnis," *ZaöRV*, 7 (1937), 300.

106 D. F. Vagts, "International Law in the Third Reich," *AJIL*, 84 (1990), 686–690. On the specifically National Socialist critique of Kelsen's theory of law see Y. Englard, "Nazi Criticism Against the Normativist Theory of Hans Kelsen – Its Intellectual Basis and Post-Modern Tendencies" in Diner and Stolleis (eds.), *Hans Kelsen and Carl Schmitt*, 133–154. On the landscape of international jurisprudence in Germany in the 1920s and 1930s see I. Hueck, "Die deutsche Völkerrechtswissenschaft im Nationalsozialismus" in D. Kaufmann (ed.), *Geschichte der Kaiser-Wilhelm-Gesellschaft im Nationalsozialismus. Bestandsaufnahme und Perspektiven der Forschung* (Göttingen: Wallstein, 2000), 490 *et seq*.

107 Bilfinger, "Zum Problem der Staatengleichheit," 487.

108 Especially revealing is Bilfinger's 1938 lecture in The Hague, in which he described practically the entire Covenant of the League of Nations as unlawful because of violations against the "principle of equality" and against the "principle of state independence": C. Bilfinger, "Les bases fondamentales de la Communauté des États," *RCADI*, 63 (1938).

them to help a materially "just" international legal order achieve a breakthrough.[109]

II Pure Theory of Law and the "unjust" status quo

From a perspective of legal policy, Kelsen was not uninterested in the question of revision and the "unjust" status quo of the interwar period:

> Every day the need is felt more strongly for some means of modifying and developing existing international law . . . for some means other than the cumbersome method of obtaining the agreement of all those persons deriving duties or rights from the rule which is desired to change. The need is particularly appreciated for some way to escape from the status quo laid down by the peace treaties, regarded by many people as unjust and, indeed, intolerable. Of this need almost everyone is persuaded today.[110]

Kunz, too, engaged – from a legal-policy perspective – in the debate over revision, which became increasingly heated as the 1930s wore on.[111]

Still, neither Kelsen nor Kunz[112] believed that there was an "objective," i.e. scientific, answer to the question about a "more just" international

[109] As Berber said in 1934 in his *Sicherheit und Gerechtigkeit* (Berlin: C. Heymann, 1934): "It will be of crucial importance for the fate of Europe whether the neo-vitalist forces, which have achieved a breakthrough especially in Italy and Germany, are able to move creatively beyond this technical rationalism."

[110] Kelsen, *The Legal Process and International Order*, 15.

[111] In 1939, shortly before the outbreak of the war, Kunz wrote, looking back over the importance of the revision debate for the interwar period: "It is hardly an exaggeration to state that the whole post-war history of Europe is made up of the struggle against the status quo." Quoted from J. L. Kunz, "The Problem of Revision in International Law," *AJIL*, 33 (1939), 34. Initially, the international legal discussion revolved – parallel to Germany's political fight against Versailles – around the requirements of the revision article (19) in the Covenant of the League of Nations. In the 1930s, when the revision problem became more urgent in the face of a militarily reviving German Reich, there began a debate over "collective security." It revolved chiefly around the question to what extent a violation of the territorial status quo could be prevented through collective military sanctions within the framework of the League Covenant (Art. 16). As the danger of war became more acute, the revision debate in international law – which seemed increasingly desperate – was then carried on during the second half of the 1930s under the slogan of "peaceful change."

[112] For Kunz, the "peaceful change" debate was a question of law-making. Resolving this question required a "supranational legislation" that did not yet exist with the League of Nations. Such a procedure entailed the problem, however, that positive law made the revision of treaties – and thus of the status quo of international law – contingent upon the consent of all involved parties: "The real problem of revision arises when one of the parties, usually the beatus possidens, does not consent; and this is, in such conflicts, a typical situation. In such cases, practically the most important cases, should war as an

order.[113] Even if it were possible to achieve agreement about the goals of a social order encompassing humankind, there was not scientifically objectifiable understanding on the question of the correct deployment of the means for achieving those goals.[114] The different, contradictory principles that were being put forth in the name of "international justice" were evidence for the unknowability of an objective concept of justice in international relations.[115] Although the notion of justice did have for Kelsen an irreplaceable function for human coexistence, the different values transported by this notion were, in the end, always relative in nature. A relativistic theory of values did not mean for Kelsen that values did not exist, "only that there are no absolute but only relative values, no absolute but only a relative justice, that the values that we constitute by our norm-creating acts and make the basis of our value judgments cannot assert the possibility of ruling out contrary values."[116]

For Kelsen as well as for Kunz, notions of justice, values, and natural law manifest their relevance at the level of norm-creation.[117] They were useless, however, for a scholarly analysis of positive law once it had been established.[118] In the Pure Theory of Law, notions of justice and values

instrument of revision be excluded, overriding supra-national legislation alone remains a suitable procedure": Kunz, "The Problem of Revision in International Law," 51. Kunz destroyed this idealistic vision with the resigned statement that such supranational legislation was a practical impossibility at the moment and in the near future: "For supra-national legislation implies, of course, a super-state" (p. 52). Because the voluntary consent also of members benefiting from the status quo remained the prerequisite of peaceful change, it was inevitable, as Kunz explicitly noted, that every argument in the direction of "overriding legislation" fell into the "world-state trap." For a world-state legislative entity based on majority decisions contradicted the traditional liberal axiom of the fundamental independence of states.

113 H. Kelsen, "The Essential Conditions of International Justice," *Proceedings of the Thirty-fifth Annual Meeting of the American Society of International Law, April 24–26*, 1941, 70.

114 Ibid., 71. 115 Ibid.

116 Kelsen, *Reine Rechtslehre* (1960), 69. On the separation of law and justice in Kelsen see the discussion and extensive references in Dreier, *Rechtslehre*, 160–166.

117 For Kunz, the problem of the just international order was a political problem, one that confronted not the jurist, but the organs of law-creation. International legislation had to break with the individual notions of states and make the common interest into the "guiding line." That had been the idea of the Spanish late scholastics, to whose natural-law doctrines one should, according to Kunz, certainly give consideration, *de lege ferenda*: Kunz, "The Problem of Revision in International Law," 51.

118 For Kelsen the value-relativist, as for Weber, the principle of freedom from value judgments becomes the precondition for any scientific understanding; on this see F. Loos, *Zur Wert- und Rechtslehre Max Webers* (Tübingen: Mohr, 1960), 49; Dreier, *Rechtslehre*, 162.

were already excluded as legal criteria[119] through the formulation of the basic norm and the concept of "imputation" as a specific interpretive scheme.[120] The object realm of legal scholarship remains limited to positive law. The objects of research are therefore positive legal norms, understood as acts laid down by humans,[121] regardless of whether they were ethically reprehensible or were felt to be unjust by those to whom they were addressed. As Horst Dreier has noted, the law in its dematerialized form in the Pure Theory of Law becomes "a methodologically neutralized means for purposes that lie beyond it and are juristically of no consequence."[122] For Kelsen, therefore, the legitimacy problem, as a question about the "right" or "just" law, cannot impair the validity of legal norms, and it is not open to a binding resolution through legal scholarship.[123] The separation of legal cognition from the question of justice, a stance motivated by a critical view of ideology, eliminates in this way the possibility of an extra-legal critique of the law dressed up in jurisprudential garb.

If this self-limitation of legal scholarship with the described critique is already taken as an affirmation of the existing law, the simultaneous relativizing function of the posited contingency of the law is left out of the equation.[124] For the stabilizing assumption of a general conformity of the prevailing law with the "right law" or with "justice" is equally eroded in the Pure Theory. The acceptance of the complete contingency of the legal medium not only allows, but actually strengthens, a distancing from positive law on the basis of individual political and moral motives, which can increase the pressure for reform.[125] However, the fact that positive law is in need of political or moral criticism does not lead to an altered scholarly assessment of the legal material by international lawyers. From a scholarly perspective, the moral reprehensibility of its content cannot impair the legal quality of formal law. The alternative would be the denial of the quality of law on the basis of politically and morally reprehensible content. That, however, would be tantamount to downplaying the politically reprehensible coercive order established by the legal form. By contrast, the scholarly determination that an "unjust" coercive order has the quality of law could increase political pressure in the direction

[119] Chapter 2 A. [120] Kelsen, *Reine Rechtslehre* (1960), 3f. [121] Ibid., 614.
[122] Dreier, *Rechtslehre*, 195. [123] Kelsen, *Reine Rechtslehre* (1960), 360.
[124] Dreier, *Rechtslehre*, 195.
[125] As an example see the suggested reforms in Kunz, "The Problem of Revision in International Law," 51.

of individual disobedience, political reforms, or an overthrow of the legal status quo.[126] According to the Pure Theory of Law, the demystified medium of the law had lost the dignity of a law that was divinely established or morally superior because of the authority of the state or other extra-legal foundations. In Kelsen's view, the accusation of affirming an "unjust" status quo could not affect the Pure Theory because it remained absolutely indifferent as to the material content of the legal norms.

III *Replacing the ideal of justice with the ideal of peace*

Kelsen expanded on his critical reflections upon the ideal of justice, for while he rejected any jurisprudential designation of a concrete order as "just" or "unjust," from a sociological perspective he accorded a higher chance of survival to social orders that structurally pursued the reconciliation between conflicting interests. Only these kinds of social orders were in a position to realize their true goal of securing peace.[127] This hints at what Kelsen presupposed as the legal-political goal of any social order: it is the ideal of peace, which could replace the ideal of justice to some extent.[128] At the same time, the concept of justice, freed from the uncertain basis of subjective value judgments, was to be transformed into a formalized basis of every social order: "Justice in this sense means legality; it is 'just' for a general rule to be actually applied in all cases where, according to its content, it should be applied. It is 'unjust' for it to be applied in one case and not in another similar case."[129] With this, Kelsen reduced the concept of justice to the principle of legality.

Kelsen does something similar with the concept of equality, which he also wants to be understood jurisprudentially in purely formal, and not in substantive terms. For under international law, it was certainly not the case that all states – on the basis of treaties and particular customary law – had the same material duties and rights. As a result, equality could refer only to the fundamental ability to be a carrier of rights and duties: "Equality is the principle that under the same conditions States have the same duties and the same rights."[130] Formal equality was thus fully

126 Ibid. 127 Kelsen, "The Essential Conditions of International Justice," 72.

128 Ibid., 72; "Die Idee des Naturrechts," 266, 276 *et seq.*; *Grundlagen*, 343 *et seq.*; *General Theory*, 22 *et seq.* On this, with an illuminating differentiation from the legal theory of Hart, see Pawlik, *Die Reine Rechtslehre und die Rechtstheorie H. L. A. Harts*, 28–35.

129 Kelsen, "The Essential Conditions of International Justice," 72.

130 H. Kelsen, "The Principle of Sovereign Equality of States as a Basis for International Organization," *Yale L. R.*, 53 (1944), 209.

compatible with material inequality. The principle of equality was merely a tautology of the legal principle that a legal norm must be applied in all cases in which, according to its content, it should be applied.[131] Like the principle of justice, the concept of equality is relevant for the legal scholar only in its formal shell as the expression of the legality principle or the "rule of law."

For Kelsen, the law as an empty form could take on any and all content, it served exclusively to erect social "order" and thus the ideal of peace. International justice therefore meant to him peace through international law. The international legal "order" had to be maintained in the sense that the always necessary social change was brought about not by violence, but by peaceful procedures of conflict resolution.[132] The procedural transformation of "international justice" into the ideal of peace that Kelsen hinted at prompted Verdross to the criticism that the Pure Theory of Law, contrary to the postulated absolute value-neutrality, also rested on a "value-philosophical foundation."[133] Even if Kelsen posited only a "relative peace," given the possibility of forcible sanctions,[134] peace through legal procedures does indeed become the central function of law in international relations.

For Kelsen order through law meant the securing of peace. Kelsen's value relativism dissolved the material principles of justice and equality in the empty form of the law, which could, in this way, serve to restrain violence and war, that is, to pacify societies. In that sense, the demarcation against the natural law foundations of international law and the concept of equality and sovereignty, which could be given whatever political charge one wanted, was not an end in itself, but served to preserve the functionality of the law with respect to the goal of securing peace. That was the meaning behind the hypothetical character of international law and the strict reduction of the concept of justice, equality, and sovereignty to the formal principle of legality. It was only in its neutralized formalism that the law could function as the ordering and guiding medium of a heteronymous plurality of social interests. This sociologically motivated faith in the peace-creating function of the medium of law thus did not break with the value-relativistic claim to a

[131] Ibid. [132] Kelsen, "The Essential Conditions of International Justice," 72.

[133] A. Verdross, "Rechtstheorie Hans Kelsens," *WRS*, II (1930), 1307, and "Zum Problem der völkerrechtlichen Grundnorm," *WRS*, II (1956), 2204. B. Horvarth had already observed much the same: "Comment on Kelsen," *Social Research*, 18 (1951), 322; on this see Dreier, *Rechtslehre*, 165.

[134] Kelsen, "The Law as a specific Social Technique," 81.

"scientific" jurisprudence; rather, it presupposed the same.[135] After the civilizational rupture of the First World War, and against the looming reality of new violent interstate conflict, pacifying the world community of universal law became for Kelsen the central function of international law.

[135] On this see J. L. Kunz, "Die definitive Formulierung der Reinen Rechtslehre," ÖZöR, 11 (1961), 383.

6

The international judiciary as the functional center of universal law

From the middle of the 1930s to the end of the Second World War, Kelsen devoted most of his scholarly attention to the question of political reform of the institutional structure of the international legal community. Before the outbreak of the Second World War, his publications dealt with the discussions about the reform of the League of Nations, which had been going on since the mid 1930s.[1] Later, Kelsen's work on this topic made a contribution to the debate over a new, peace-securing world organization, which got under way during the war.[2] At the center of these publications stood the *de lege ferenda* call for the establishment of an international court charged with compulsory adjudication. Kelsen's blueprint of a constitutive document for the new world organization made the court the central organ, whose decisions would have to be enforced by a council of the great powers. The creation of such a court, rendering binding decisions, was the institutional core of Kelsen's cosmopolitan project.

A Peace through compulsory jurisdiction

Having witnessed two world wars, Kelsen saw in the rule of law in international relations, secured by courts rendering binding decisions, the only way to a more peaceful world order. The state of peace pursued

1 Kelsen, *The Legal Process and International Order*; H. Kelsen, "Les résolutions de la SDN concernant la séparation du Pacte et des Traités de Paix," *RDILC*, 1 (1939), 101 *et seq.*; with a critical revision of the various provisions of the Charter, H. Kelsen, "Revision des Völkerbundstatuts" in *Legal Technique in International Law. A textual critique of the League Covenant* (Geneva Research Center, 1939); H. Kelsen, "Sanktionen sind Sache des Gerichts," *Geneva Press Service* (July 10, 1936), 1–3.

2 H. Kelsen, "The Old and the New League: The Covenant and the Dumbarton Oaks Proposals," *AJIL*, 39 (1945); H. Kelsen, "The Strategy for Peace," *American Journal of Sociology*, XLIX (1944), 381 *et seq.*; H. Kelsen, "International Peace – by Court or by Government?" *American Journal of Sociology*, XLVI (1941), 571 *et seq.*

by compulsory jurisdiction[3] did not mean for Kelsen the complete absence of violence, but merely a state of relative peace.[4] In that sense Kelsen set himself apart from a "utopian pacifism," which he regarded as a serious threat to international politics.[5] In the future, the decision to use force would no longer remain within the competency of individual legal subjects, but would be transferred to central organs of the community for the purpose of sanctioning violations of the law. The final, binding decision about the existence of a violation of the law subject to sanction, referred to by Kelsen as a "delict," was made by a central court organ *ex officio* or at the request of the contending parties. The central place that Kelsen accorded compulsory jurisdiction within the legal system had already manifested itself clearly in the 1920s with respect to national law in his scholarly analysis of the dispute over the reach of constitutional jurisdiction in the Weimar Republic.[6] Kelsen's approach to both issues seems to share his general faith in the peace-creating function of constitutional adjudication.

The real originality in Kelsen's works on international law from this period lies in the direct combination of concrete *de lege ferenda* proposals with his own socio-historical studies, which buttressed his own policy proposals. As a constructive justifying strategy, Kelsen developed his own theory of the evolution of legal systems, which, applied to international law, made the establishment of compulsory jurisdiction seem like the next step in a progressive development of the international legal order. To further underpin his legal-political convictions, he trained his critical eye on the traditional international legal doctrine concerning the function of international courts in international relations. Kelsen thus solicited support for the establishment of compulsory jurisdiction as the central element of his cosmopolitan project on three different levels: first, through the constructive articulation of a draft charter for the new world organization; second, through the equally constructive development of his own general theory of the evolution of legal systems; and

[3] See the programmatic title of his 1944 book *Peace through Law*.

[4] Kelsen, "The Law as a specific Social Technique," 81.

[5] Kelsen, *Peace through Law*, VIII.

[6] H. Kelsen, "Wesen und Entwicklung der Staatsgerichtsbarkeit. Überprüfung von Verwaltungsakten durch die öffentlichen Gerichte" in H. Triepel, H. Kelsen, and M. Layer (eds.), *Veröffentlichungen der Vereinigung der Deutschen Staatsrechtslehrer, Heft 5, Tagung vom 23. und 24. April 1928 in Wien* (Berlin and Leipzig: W. de Gruyter, 1929), 30–88.

third, by destroying those doctrinal elements in international legal scholarship that could be marshaled against his *de lege ferenda* proposal.

I *The politico-legal approach: the Permanent League for the Maintenance of Peace*

In 1944, Kelsen published a draft charter for a "Permanent League for the Maintenance of Peace" as the successor organization to the League of Nations.[7] Kelsen's new world organization had four main organs: assembly, court, council, and secretariat.[8] The charter consisted of clear procedural rules governing the working relationships between the four organs. The only substantive regulation was a comprehensive prohibition on the use of force on the part of members of the new organization.[9] If a state wanted to enforce international legal rules through war or forcible reprisals against another member state, it was up to the court, at the request of the affected state or the council, to decide whether the charter had been violated. Only after the court had determined that the law had been broken could the council impose the necessary military and economic sanctions on the responsible member states. In Kelsen's draft charter, the council could take action on the sanction question only on the basis of, and in conformity with, the court's finding that the state conduct in question had been illegal. The court became the central organ whose actions obligated the council. The eruption of violence in international relations was hereby to be rationalized in a judicially dominated and fully institutionalized procedure.

With this, Kelsen was reviving the Hague Movement's strategy of juridifying international relations through obligatory arbitration.[10] The international pacifist movement had already made the development of the international judiciary one of its central demands during the first two decades of the century. The decisions rendered by international tribunals

[7] Kelsen, *Peace through Law*, Annex I, 127–140. [8] Ibid., Art. 2, 127.

[9] Ibid., Art. 34, 134.

[10] Much to the chagrin of the pacifist movement, the Second Hague Conference in 1907, because of the alleged obstructionist attitude of the Reich government, had been able to agree only on a voluntary form of arbitration by the Court of Arbitration in The Hague. If the pacifists were to have their way, the Third Hague Conference would finally remedy this shortcoming. On this see, from the perspective of someone involved in the pacifist movement, O. Nippold, *Die Gestaltung des Völkerrechts nach dem Kriege* (Zurich: O. Füssli, 1917), 12–27.

over legal disputes, in the view of authors such as Schücking, Lammasch, Wehburg, and Nippold, should be implemented by an international organization by way of collective enforcement measures.[11] These demands, already put forth in the German-language literature before and during the First World War by Nippold and Schücking and other authors,[12] were unable to prevail during the political negotiations over the League Covenant.[13] The call for compulsory jurisdiction[14] fell on

[11] According to the blueprint of the American "League to Enforce Peace," even disagreements touching on the "vital interests" of a participating state should be brought before at least an international commission of inquiry. However, when it came to the arbitration proposal that would be issued by the commission regarding a particular dispute, it was – according to the blueprint – left to the discretion of the parties to accept it. On the blueprint of the "League to Enforce Peace" see O. Nippold, *Der Völkerbundsvertrag und die Frage des Beitritts der Schweiz* (Bern: K. J. Wyss Erben, 1919), 5–6, and Nippold, *Die Gestaltung des Völkerrechts*, 12–27.

[12] W. Schücking, *Der Staatenverband der Haager Konferenzen* (Munich and Leipzig: Duncker & Humblot, 1912). In his 1918 monograph *Die Völkerrechtliche Lehre des Weltkrieges* (Leipzig: Veit, 1918), he was referring to the Hague treaty system when he noted, in his reform proposals: "Voluntary court of arbitration and voluntary mediation have failed, no question, the future belongs to the obligatory. Henceforth no state may be allowed to light the torch of war without the attempt having first been made to arrive at a peaceful compromise" (205). Alongside the Court of Arbitration in The Hague, an international agency was to be created that would be staffed with independent international lawyers and able to function as an obligatory and non-partisan arbitration authority: *Der Weltfriedensbund und die Wiedergeburt des Völkerrechts* (Leipzig: Verlag Naturwissenschaften, 1917).

[13] Kennedy, "The Move to Institutions," 888. Although the proposals of the "League to Enforce Peace" had initially prompted Wilson to incorporate the League of Nations project into his Fourteen Points, the influence of the so-called "East-Coast Foreign Policy Establishment," which was the driving force behind the "League to Enforce Peace," on the President waned toward the end of the war. In Paris, the old "internationalists" were no longer involved in laying out the American drafts: W. F. Kuehl, *Seeking World Order. The United States and International Organization to 1920* (Nashville: Vanderbilt University Press, 1969), 267–270.

[14] At the time of the Paris negotiations, the pacifist conception had become the basis also of the official German proposals for the League of Nations. The so-called "*Gelehrtenentwurf*" [Experts' Blueprint] (on this see Ph. Zorn, *Der Völkerbund* (Berlin: Engelmann, 1919)) was introduced into the Paris negotiations by the Reich government in slightly modified form, though it failed to have any influence on the Covenant of the League of Nations that was finally agreed upon. See "Entwurf der Reichsregierung als Note an die Pariser Friedenskonferenz vom 9. Mai 1919," printed in A. Luckau, *The German Delegation at the Paris Peace Conference* (New York: Columbia University Press, 1941), 225–233. According to this draft proposal, Montesquieu's separation of powers was to apply also to the League of Nations: Zorn, *Der Völkerbund*, 25. Compared to the so-called "Hurst–Miller Draft," the emphasis here lay on the establishment of a permanent international court and a neutral office of arbitration as a counterweight to the Council of the great powers. In Germany the hope was now for an independent,

deaf ears in Paris and Geneva after the First World War.[15] The influential British draft by General Smuts, on which Wilson had based the revision of his own first draft, which he had brought to Paris, opted instead for a strong council of the great powers, which was to come up with and implement political solutions to disputed issues. Compulsory adjudication was seen as an unnatural superstructure that was not in accord with the reality of the coexistence of sovereign states: "The new institution must not be something additional, something external, superimposed on the existing structure. It must be an organic change; it must be woven into the very texture of our political system. The new motive of peace must in future operate internally, constantly, inevitably, from the very heart of our political organization, and must, so to speak, flow from the nature of things political."[16]

The Covenant of the League of Nations subsequently enshrined the primacy of politics over international law institutionally with the powerful organ of the Council.[17] Agreement could be reached only on the formula in Art. 14 of the Covenant, which charged the Council with drafting a plan for the establishment of a Permanent Court of International Justice.[18] In effect, then, the new institutional arrangement

obligatory international jurisdiction that would make it possible for Germany to take its place as an equal partner alongside the great powers in spite of the defeat. After the defeat in the war, Germans favored neutral legal entities as the guarantor of a just order of peace and a counterweight to the Council as the political organ of the victorious allied powers. At this time, Germany's foreign-policy interests were congruent with the demands of the international peace movement that came out of the Hague Movement.

[15] In the response (composed by Robert Cecil) of May 22, 1919, the conference rejected the German proposals for obligatory arbitration and a permanent international court as not practical at that time. Response in D. H. Miller, *The Drafting of the Covenant* (New York: G. P. Putnam's Sons, 1928), vols. I–II, 539–541.

[16] Smuts Plan in Miller, *The Drafting of the Covenant*, 46. The decision to dispense with obligatory arbitration was a concession by Wilson to the British Smuts Plan. The top French negotiator, Léon Bourgeois, had himself argued repeatedly for at least a legal connection between the arbitration procedures of the Covenant and the Court of Arbitration in The Hague. This time, however, it was the Americans, and among them especially Wilson and Miller, who rejected any link between the Covenant and the "failed" Hague system. Wilson believed that the new world order must not be connected in any way with the pre-war institutions: Kuehl, *Seeking World Order*, 278; Kennedy, "The Move to Institutions," 890.

[17] The institutional structure of the Paris blueprint of the League of Nations envisioned three main organs: the assembly of all members states, the council of the five great powers, and the secretariat. In other words, there were two political organs and one administrative organ.

[18] On the history of the creation of the Permanent Court of International Justice (PCIJ) see Schücking and Wehberg, *Die Satzung des Völkerbundes*, 2 edn., 556–568.

failed to institutionalize the encompassing and compulsory judicial controls of political decisions taken in and outside the new institution demanded by the internationalists.[19] To be sure, the Covenant itself, in Art. 12, provided for a process of dispute settlement, which obligated the members of the League, in case of a dispute, to submit the matter to "either arbitration or judicial settlement or to enquiry by the Council." And the contending parties could not resort to war until three months after the announcement of the decision.[20] Still, in this case as well, given the fact that states could choose between political settlement by the Council and judicial proceedings or arbitration, the contending parties were not obligated to subject themselves to a binding legal decision.[21] A later attempt to introduce compulsory jurisdiction by amending the Covenant, in the form of the so-called "Geneva Protocol," failed in 1924 when Britain eventually did not ratify the document.[22] And while the arbitration treaty from 1928, which supplemented the Covenant of the League of Nations, (the so-called 'General Act') did introduce compulsory jurisdiction in a differentiated procedure,[23] it limited it through

[19] The statute for the PCIJ was adopted only by a decision of the General Assembly on December 13, 1920. However, through Art. 13 of the Covenant, the jurisdiction of the court was linked to the voluntary declaration by the state in question to abide by the decision. The attempt, especially by South American states, to enshrine obligatory arbitration in the statute proposed by the Council did not find enough support in the first session of the General Assembly. The majority of the states joined the opinion of the Council that the time for such a provision was not yet ripe; on this see Schücking and Wehberg, *Die Satzung des Völkerbundes*, 2 edn., 563. On the compatibility of an obligatory jurisdiction with the Covenant of the League of Nations see P. J. Baker, "The Obligatory Jurisdiction of the Permanent Court of International Justice," *BYIL*, IV (1925), 68–102.

[20] On Art. 12 see Schücking and Wehberg, *Die Satzung des Völkerbundes*, 2 edn., 501–514.

[21] H. Wehberg, "Der Weltschiedsvertrag der Generalakte," *Völkerbund. Monatsschrift der Dt. Liga für Völkerbund*, 2 (1929), 39.

[22] Even with this ambitious project, the preparatory commission, in the unanimously adopted report to the General Assembly of the League of Nations, maintained that conflicts involving territorial issues and the revision of treaties should remain excluded from the system of arbitration. See the report by N. Politis to the Assembly on 1 October 1924, printed in *Niemeyers Zeitschrift für Internationales Recht* 33 (1924–1925), 172–201 (185–186); on this see E. H. Carr, *The Twenty Years' Crisis 1919–1939* (London: Macmillan and Co., 1939), 185. On the "Protocol for the pacific settlement of international disputes," see P. J. Baker, *The Geneva Protocol* (London: P. S. King & Son, Ltd., 1925). On the dispute settlement procedures in Arts. 3, 4, and 6 see W. Schücking and H. Wehberg, *Die Satzung des Völkerbundes.* 3rd, revised and extended edn. (Berlin: Vahlen, 1931), 176, 184.

[23] Following the failure of non-judicial dispute settlement, a party to the treaty could no longer avoid judicial proceedings: See Arts. 17 and 21 of the General Act, printed in W. H. Grewe (ed.), *Fontes Historiae Iuris Gentium. Quellen zur Geschichte des Völkerrechts*, vol. 3/2, 1815–1945 (Berlin and New York: W. de Gruyter, 1992), 1067–1078.

the possibility of making reservations allowed for in the Treaty (Art. 39).[24]

Kelsen's own draft of a charter in 1944 was based on the conviction that the absence of a global court rendering compulsory decisions about any dispute brought to it by states or organs of the League had permanently weakened the international legal order in the interwar period. In his blueprint, the jurisdiction of the court extended to all disputes that arose between members. As laid out above, that included also the question regarding the legality of the use of force in international relations. In Kelsen's conception, war and reprisal were possible only as legally authorized sanctions against a state that was violating the charter. However, carrying out the sanction presupposed the decision by a court that the member had in fact broken the rules. To that extent, not only did the monopoly of force lie with the world organization, but the use of force was possible only to enforce international law on the basis of a court decision. Within his vision of universal law, war and reprisals became acts of law enforcement of the international legal community. As such, this legal community was in need of a central organ that determined the illegality of the behavior being remedied and that reviewed the legality of the applied sanction. In Kelsen's eyes, only a judicial organ was able to exercise that function.

The substantively unlimited competence of the court also reflected Kelsen's conception of universal law. The political sphere to be regulated by international law was not restricted by a pre-legal concept of sovereignty. A rigid conception of the "*domaine réservé*" or "domestic jurisdiction" in the sense of an untouchable core area of state sovereignty was incompatible with the objective construction of international law by the Vienna School.[25] According to the doctrine of the primacy of international law, the latter could lay hold of and regulate any matter previously regulated by national law. If the judicial organ was to decide all disputes between members brought before it, its jurisdiction could not be subject to any a priori substantive limitations. In another Annex to his draft statute, Kelsen added procedural rules on how to punish those

[24] "The General Act is the first instrument which aims at institutionalizing obligatory arbitration in the case of failure of previous conciliation as a means of settling non-legal disputes." Quoted from K. Oellers-Frahm and N. Wühler, *Dispute Settlement in Public International Law* (New York: Springer, 1984), 61, with additional references. On this see J. L. Brierly, "The General Act of Geneva 1928," *BYIL*, XI (1930), 119 *et seq.*; Wehberg, "Der Weltschiedsvertrag der Generalakte," 40; Carr, *The Twenty Years' Crisis*, 185.

[25] On this see Chapter 3 C IV.

individuals who, as organs of their states, were responsible for the violation of the charter.[26] This jurisdiction in criminal matters of the court included the possibility, upon the request by a member state or the council, to also prosecute and try war crimes committed or ordered by governments.[27] Members of governments should be punished by the international court as they would have been according to their own state law if they had acted as organs of the state.[28] Member states were obligated to hand over individuals prosecuted by the court.

Kelsen, in light of the indescribable horrors committed during the Second World War upon the orders of individuals, did not believe that the doctrine of the functional immunity of state organs was in any way sacrosanct. He argued that the immunity of heads of states could be completely revoked by the new charter as a treaty under international law. Direct obligations of individuals, as well as individualized prosecution, indictment, and conviction through international courts, were perfectly in line with the concept of international law as articulated by the Vienna School.[29] The court envisioned by Kelsen, composed of five criminal lawyers and twelve international lawyers, thus not only had the power to decide any dispute brought before it by the organs or individual member states, but it also functioned as a two-tiered criminal court for individual representatives of governments who could be charged with violations of international law.

The proposed powers of the new international court were a political reaction by Kelsen to the "failure" of the League of Nations and the impending legal processing of war crimes and the Holocaust. From a theoretical point of view, Kelsen based the proposed establishment of a central international court on a socio-historical doctrine of the evolution of law.[30]

II The socio-historical approach: compulsory jurisdiction as a necessary step toward a centralized, universal legal system

The formation of an institutionalized and encompassing legal system was for Kelsen the result of various prior developmental stages. As he saw it,

[26] Kelsen, *Peace through Law*, Annex II, Art. 35a, 144; excluded from this, according to Art. 35c of the draft, were representatives of states belonging to the Council of the organization, 145.

[27] Kelsen, *Peace through Law*, Annex I, Art. 35b, Section 1, 144. [28] Ibid.

[29] On the individual within Kelsen's doctrine of international law see Chapter 4 B.

[30] On what follows see Rub, *Hans Kelsens Völkerrechtslehre*, 293; C. Jabloner, "Menschenbild und Friedenssicherung" in R. Walter and C. Jabloner (eds.), *Hans Kelsens Wege sozialphilosophischer Forschung* (Vienna: Manz, 1997), 59–62.

the first, primitive stage of legal organization of a given political community was characterized by the fact that law enforcement was not individualized, but still fell upon the entire tribe or the collective.[31] In addition to the achievement of individual liability based on guilt, a highly developed legal system was also characterized by a higher degree of centralization of legal functions. By contrast, the primitive legal system was still in a state of complete decentralization.[32] For example, at the primitive evolutionary stage, neither the creation nor the application of the law was undertaken by common organs, but exclusively by the individual subjects of the legal system.

Kelsen applied this insight gained from the historical analysis of "primitive" local or early state forms of legal systems to international law.[33] In international law, as well, it was usually not individuals who were entitled and obligated by the international legal order, but the entire state as a collective entity. Comparable to the institution of the blood feud, the punishment of a head of government fell not only upon him as the criminal individual, but by way of war upon the entire population. The sanctions of the legal community were thus not yet individualized. Also, the decision on whether to impose sanctions, again comparable to other primitive legal systems, was not yet made by a joint organ of the legal community. Instead, it rested within the competence of the individual states as legal subjects.[34]

The first and – for Kelsen – decisive step in the direction of a centralization of the implementation of law was the establishment of a judge who decided disputes as an organ independent of the contending parties.[35] The judge could decide cases on the basis of general norms derived from customary law or norms already laid down as positive law. If the judge found that a breach of the law existed, the legal remedy had to be determined and its implementation ordered.

According to Kelsen, at this evolutionary stage, however, the implementation of the sanction was still organized in a decentralized fashion.[36] In this early phase of centralization, then, the court functioned as a kind

31 Kelsen, "The Law as a specific Social Technique," 92. 32 Ibid., 93.

33 The demand for the establishment of an obligatory international jurisdiction during the Second World War was in Kelsen based on the notion of international law as an evolving, still "primitive legal system," a viewpoint which – as described above – had also played an important role in the nineteenth century, for example in Fricker under the label of the "becoming law."

34 On this see O. Pfersman, "De la justice constitutionelle à la justice internationale: Hans Kelsen et la seconde guerre mondiale," *Revue française de droit constitutionnel*, 16 (1993), 773.

35 Kelsen, "The Law as a specific Social Technique," 93. 36 Ibid., 94.

of arbitral tribunal, with the implementation of its decision left to the parties by way of self-help. The implementation of the sanction by the community organs required a mighty administrative apparatus, but such an apparatus had to be seen as the typical achievement of the more developed state legal system.[37] A special characteristic of the modern constitutional state as the highest known evolutionary stage of the legal system was for Kelsen the centralization also of the law-creating function carried out by common organs, which followed upon the centralization of the function of the application of the law.

In the Kelsenian "theory of civilization,"[38] the introduction of compulsory jurisdiction thus marked the transition from a primitive and decentralized legal system to a centralized one. The application of the law by the judge was the first evolutionary step, which could be followed later by the centralization of the organs of implementation and law-creation. To bolster the argument that the system of international law was subject to the same evolutionary conditions as other primitive legal systems, Kelsen introduced a parallel phenomenon from contemporary biological research, the so-called "biogenetic law." According to this theory, the embryo in the womb recapitulated in a kind of time lapse all of humankind's evolutionary stages. In the same way, international law, as a still primitive law, had to recapitulate the evolutionary achievements of national law step by step.[39]

Kelsen thus applied to the system of international law the sociological insights gained from a study of primitive legal communities. As he wrote in 1942: "The fact that the application is centralized much earlier than the creation of law is of greater importance. It seems to manifest a certain regularity of evolution originating in the sociological and especially in the sociopsychological nature of the law. We may therefore presume with a certain degree of possibility that the development of international law has the same tendencies as the development of national law."[40] As a still primitive legal system, international law was for Kelsen in a stage of

[37] Ibid., 95.

[38] C. Jabloner, "Verrechtlichung und Rechtsdynamik" in: *ZöR*, 54 (1999), 263–265.

[39] H. Kelsen, *Law and Peace in International Relations. The Oliver Wendell Holmes Lectures, 1940–1941* (Cambridge, MA: Harvard University Press, 1942), 149. The newer secondary literature has noted that the general theses on the evolution of the law and the central role played by the courts in it have been confirmed by recent socio-legal research: Jabloner, "Menschenbild und Friedenssicherung," 62; N. Luhmann, *Das Recht der Gesellschaft* (Frankfurt am Main: Suhrkamp, 1993), 258 *et seq*.

[40] Kelsen, *Law and Peace in International Relations*, 148.

evolutionary transition.[41] To be sure, it was still states as collectives that were held responsible for breaches of the law, and not single individuals according to the extent of their individual responsibility. Moreover, individuals were generally entitled and obligated only indirectly, that is, via the state legal systems. In addition, neither the application of the law nor its creation had been transferred to specialized central organs. However, the practice of arbitration under international law could already be seen as a harbinger of the transition to a more highly evolved stage of legal evolution. It confirmed the thesis of the primary development of judicial functions. Still lacking, though, was a court that rendered binding decisions as a centralized organ authorized to control the encompassing application of the laws of the international legal system. In the sense of legal policy, that was the necessary next step toward the creation of a more strongly centralized international legal order.

The notion of first advancing central law-creation through a codification of international law[42] or through a world parliament, in order to then introduce obligatory international jurisdiction in a second step, ran counter to Kelsen's evolutionary model. In that case, the crucial function of centralized, compulsory jurisdiction as an evolutionary stage of transition cannot take effect; the inherent course of the evolution of the law would be violated. International law was in a kind of transition stage toward becoming the law of the universal legal community. Compulsory jurisdiction as an evolutionary accomplishment would give rise to further centralized organs for the application and creation of law at the universal level. When that happened, international law, as a "social technique" of the world community, would be increasingly able to directly entitle and obligate individuals and to involve them as individuals in international judicial proceedings. However, the further development of the international legal system – which is shaped by international politics – will only proceed in this direction if attention is paid to the legal-historical insights about the evolution from "primitive" legal systems. International law is law, and as such it is therefore subject to the general evolutionary rules of the law, according to which the establishment of a centralized and compulsory jurisdiction plays the central role in overcoming the primitive stage of legal development. Kelsen thus sketched out theoretically the development of

[41] Kelsen, "The Law as a specific Social Technique," 97.

[42] On the efforts at codification in the interwar period, with an extensive survey of the literature, see Garner, "Le développement et les tendances récentes du droit international," 626–640.

international law into a highly evolved medium for the creation of a stable societal order on the global level.

In the approach of the Vienna School, the differences between international law and state law, long regarded in the legal literature as "weaknesses" and "deficiencies," were transcended as phenomena that were evolutionarily temporary.[43] Moreover, by taking an evolutionary view of international law, Kelsen refuted the contrary conclusion that Bergbohm had drawn from the "primitive" nature of the international legal system, namely that the establishment of a central, obligatory jurisdiction contradicted the foundation of international law in the sovereign will of the state, and that international law "by its nature" could bring forth only voluntary, bilateralized arbitration procedures.[44] Even Kaltenborn had not regarded the situation of self-help and the role of the states as judges over their own affairs as a problem. In fact, in his eyes, the establishment of compulsory jurisdiction even contradicted the "nature" of international law.[45] By contrast, Kelsen's diagnosis of "primitive law" underscored the evolutionary necessity for the establishment of a centralized court system on the world level that rendered obligatory decisions.

Kelsen based his call for compulsory jurisdiction not only on his evolutionary theory of the law, but also on a critique of the doctrinal objections against compulsory jurisdiction. The prevailing doctrine of international law had posited a limitation on the judicial function, which arguably emanated from the very "nature" of international law. This position found its expression in various doctrinal constructs, the most important of which Kelsen tried to refute in order to lend greater weight to his own postulate.

[43] It is likely that the parallelism between primitive legal communities and the international legal system in the formation of courts of arbitration as the first central communal organs, and the discernible recourse to customary law in the legal systems that were compared, prompted Kelsen to spell out this analogy. See Kelsen, *Law and Peace in International Relations*, 149. However, the application of historical insights into primitive legal communities to international law seems particularly problematic given that some of the actors of the international community in the twentieth century were themselves highly evolved legal cultures. Because of the interrelationship between international law and the more highly developed normative state systems, the evolutionary conditions of the international legal system can be compared only to a limited extent with the evolution of largely isolated "primitive" legal communities. However, Kelsen did not examine the aspect of the clash of different stages of legal evolution in the monistic legal cosmos and its effect on the presumed laws of legal evolution.

[44] Bergbohm, *Staatsverträge und Gesetze*, 24–32.

[45] C. Kaltenborn von Stachau, "Zur Revision der Lehre von den internationalen Rechtsmittlen," *ZStW*, 17 (1861), 87; Heller, *Die Souveränität*, 157.

III The doctrinal approach: the fundamental critique of the doctrinal limitation on the judicial function in international relations

In Kelsen's view, it was above all the "dogma" of the "non-justiciability of political disputes" and the closely allied assumption of the "incomplete nature of the international legal system" that misled the literature into an overblown theoretical limitation on the function of jurisdiction in international politics. The demand for compulsory jurisdiction fundamentally questioned the assumed limitations – presented by scholars as "nature-given" – on the role of law within international relations. Hersch Lauterpacht's *The Function of Law in the International Community* of 1933 had subjected both the literature and the practice of arbitration in the nineteenth and twentieth centuries to a critical analysis from the same point of view.[46] In the process, he had already clearly emphasized the harmful effects on state practice of the theoretical perpetuation of the doctrines of the distinction between legal and political disputes and the incompleteness of the international legal system.[47]

In the tradition of the modernization movement in international law in the 1920s, Kelsen and Lauterpacht sought to create a new theoretical foundation for a "rule of law" in international relations. This included a comprehensive critique of the traditional theories of international law concerning the "limits" of international jurisdiction, theories that they regarded as apologetic. For them, obligatory judicial decision-making was not only theoretically conceivable, but also desirable in terms of legal policy. Even if the two men differed noticeably in their argumentative style, their contributions to this issue bore a striking resemblance in terms of their critical thrust. What follows is a closer look at their critique of the "dogma" of non-justiciable disputes.

Kelsen's draft of the charter did not envision any material restriction on the jurisdiction of the judicial organ: "The Court is competent to decide any dispute between Members of the League submitted by one of the parties to the dispute."[48] Kelsen did not provide for the possibility of rejecting a case as a "purely political" dispute.[49] In this, his draft differed from the jurisdiction clause of the PCIJ statute from 1920, in which the

[46] Lauterpacht, *The Function of Law in the International Community*; on Lauterpacht's theory of international law see Koskenniemi, "Lauterpacht: The Victorian Tradition in International Law."

[47] Lauterpacht, *The Function of Law in the International Community*, 435.

[48] Kelsen, *Peace through Law*, Annex I, Art. 31, Section 2, 137. [49] Ibid.

Court's jurisdiction had been made dependent on a voluntary declaration of the member state and had been restricted to "legal disputes" through the chapeau of Art. 36. The classes of legal disputes were subsequently enumerated in this provision.[50] According to Art. 36, the jurisdiction of the PCIJ encompassed: (1) "the interpretation of a treaty"; (2) "any question of international law"; (3) "the existence of any fact, which, if established, would constitute a breach of an international obligation"; and (4) "the nature or extent of the reparation to be made for the breach of an international obligation."[51]

The limitation of jurisdiction to "legal disputes" could be read as reflecting the conventional international-law doctrine of the non-justiciability of political disputes. In this view, all disputes qualified as "highly political" were by definition outside the legal system and could therefore not be decided by an international court or arbitral tribunal.[52] The conventional doctrine regarded the sphere of "high politics" and "national honor"[53] as lying outside the boundaries of international law as drawn by state sovereignty.[54] As positive law, the distinction between "political" and "legal" disputes was found in a multitude of arbitration treaties in the nineteenth and early twentieth centuries.[55]

[50] In the statute of the International Court of Justice, as well, we find the same four-fold enumeration (Art. 36, para. 2) and the reference to "legal" disputes in the chapeau of that paragraph.

[51] The enumeration in Art. 36 of the statute of the PCIJ stemmed from Art. 13 of the Covenant of the League of Nations; on this basis in the League Covenant see Schücking and Wehberg, *Die Satzung des Völkerbundes*, 2nd, revised edn., 517.

[52] As early as 1870, Friedrich Adolf Trendelenburg had sought, in his famous book *Lücken im Völkerrecht*, to establish the impossibility of settlement by arbitration in those cases in which a historical development had fundamentally altered interstate relations. The major nineteenth-century textbooks of international law also regarded questions of great national import as non-justiciable, political matters: F. A. Trendelenburg, *Lücken im Völkerrecht. Betrachtungen und Vorschläge aus dem Jahre 1870* (Leipzig: S. Hirzel, 1870), 21; on this see Lauterpacht, *The Function of Law in the International Community*, 1–25.

[53] On the reserve clauses on questions of the state's "vital interests" and questions of national honor, which are frequently encountered in the nineteenth century, but which hardly appeared any more between the two world wars, see F. Münch, "Das Institut de droit international und die obligatorische Gerichtsbarkeit" in W. Wengler (ed.), *Justitia et Pace. Festschrift zum 100jährigen Bestehen des Institut de droit international* (Berlin: Duncker & Humblot, 1974), 119.

[54] Lauterpacht, *The Function of Law in the International Community*, 12, with extensive references; R. Redslob, *Das Problem des Völkerrechts* (Leipzig: Veit und Comp., 1917), 319; Trendelenburg, *Lücken im Völkerrecht*, 21; U. Fastenrath, *Lücken im Völkerrecht* (Berlin: Duncker & Humblot, 1991), 238; G. Dahm, *Völkerrecht* (Stuttgart: Kohlhammer, 1961), vol. II, 491.

[55] Fastenrath, *Lücken im Völkerrecht*, 236.

Kelsen criticized both the doctrinal distinction between legal and political disputes,[56] and the argument advanced in the literature against compulsory jurisdiction to the effect that international conflicts were usually economic or political in nature and could therefore not be decided by legal criteria.[57] For him, the assumption that there were non-justiciable disputes was logically untenable. As soon as a legal system existed, he maintained, any societal action, including economic or highly political conduct, could be subjected to a legal assessment.[58] The international legal system encompassed every disputed behavior as either lawful or unlawful. This view led Kelsen to the unmistakable pronouncement: "A positive legal order can always be applied to any conflict whatever."[59]

In Kelsen's neo-Kantian understanding of the law, there could be no gaps in a legal system. If international law was seen as a system of binding norms for the regulation of international relations, it was no longer possible to construe behaviors that lay outside the law. Kelsen tried to illustrate this with an example: if international law did not obligate State A to allow residents of State B to enter the country, State A was, in legal terms, free to grant entry or deny it. In that case, the relations between State A and State B were subject to a regulation just as much as if an international legal norm obligated State A to grant residents of State B free entry.[60] For if there was no obligation, the state was simultaneously legally permitted to behave in this matter as it pleased. In this way, the sphere of what was legally permitted was as much encompassed by the legal system as the sphere of prohibited behaviors.[61]

56 Kelsen, *Peace through Law*, 22. 57 Ibid., 24. 58 Ibid., 26.

59 Ibid., 29. 60 Ibid., 27.

61 Ibid., 27. The PCIJ applied the principle of the general freedom of action by states outside of clearly defined law in its famous "Lotus" decision (1927). On the general freedom of action, see A. Bleckmann, "Die Handlungsfähigkeit der Staaten. System und Struktur der Völkerrechtsordung," *ÖZöR*, 29 (1978), 173 *et seq.*; H. Mosler, "Völkerrecht als Rechtsordnung," *ZaöRV*, 36 (1976), 6 *et seq.* In its decision, the PCIJ did not, however, explicitly invoke the logical conclusion of the "negative norm," but the independence or sovereignty of states: "International law governs the relations between independent states [. . .] restrictions upon the independence of states cannot, therefore, be presumed" (Series A, No. 10, 18). The court used a similar line of argument in "Wimbledon" (1923) and later in "Free Zones" (1932) (Wimbledon: Series A, I, 24; Free Zones: Series A/B 46, 167). The "Lotus" decision has often been criticized – especially from a natural-law perspective – on the grounds that it accorded the states an excessively large leeway of action while neglecting the values underlying the system of international law. The value of liberty, it was argued, was set up as absolute, and the possibility of balancing it against other values was ruled out: Lauterpacht, *The Function of Law in the International*

By obligating those to whom norms were addressed to behave in a certain way, the legal system, according to the Pure Theory of Law, granted them freedom beyond the clearly stipulated legal obligations.[62] For the Neo-Kantian Kelsen, as for Radbruch, the legal system already contains the following logical premise: "[W]here one is not obligated to do or to forbear from doing, there one is free."[63] It was this negative norm that was applied in a decision rejecting a claim to a certain behavior that did not correspond to a specific legal duty.[64] Because of the assumption of a negative norm for those spheres of conduct in which no legal obligations had been stipulated, the existence of gaps was theoretically ruled out for Kelsen.[65] With this argument, Kelsen rebuffed, from a

Community, 97; V. Bruns, "Völkerrecht als Rechtsordnung I," *ZaöRV*, 1 (1929), 35; R. Bernhardt, "Ungeschriebenes Völkerrecht," *ZaöRV*, 36 (1976), 59; Fastenrath, *Lücken im Völkerrecht*, 241. Other weighty arguments have been marshaled against the effectiveness of the principle of the general freedom of action in completing the system of international law. See: Koskenniemi, *From Apology to Utopia*, 220–223; Fastenrath, *Lücken im Völkerrecht*, 248–252. The most convincing point of criticism is the weak significance of the negative principle of freedom in the case of "conflicts of freedom." If several states make excessive use of their freedom of action within an area not regulated by international law, the result – e.g. on the question of the use of the seas and space, or in case of unclear borders – can be conflicting exercises of freedom which cannot be resolved solely through the application of the negative norm. On this see Koskenniemi, *From Apology to Utopia*, 100.

62 Kelsen, *Reine Rechtslehre* (1934), 100; *Problems of Legal Theory*, 84.

63 "The so-called 'gap,' then, is nothing but the difference between the positive law and a system held to be better, more just, more nearly right." Quoted from Kelsen, *Reine Rechtslehre* (1934), 101, *Problems of Legal Theory*, 85. In that sense, recourse to the incompleteness of a legal system was a veiled desire for a reform of the law: Kelsen, *Law and Peace*, 164; G. Radbruch, *Rechtsphilosophie*, ed. E. Wolf and H. P. Schneider, 8th edn. (Stuttgart: K. F. Koehler, 1973), 294. On this, with further references, see Fastenrath, *Lücken im Völkerrecht*, 240–244.

64 Kelsen, *Reine Rechtslehre* (1934), 101; *Problems of Legal Theory*, 85.

65 In the debate over an obligatory jurisdiction at the beginning of the 1950s, Julius Stone questioned the conclusiveness of the thesis of the negative norm for international law: J. Stone, *Legal Controls of International Conflict* (London: Stevens, 1954), 159–162. He argued that the division of the legal cosmos into statutory legal obligations, on the one hand, and a sphere of permitted, free conduct, on the other, was based on a false dichotomy. The conclusion that the international judge would either have to find the defendant guilty on the basis of a legal obligation, or, in the absence of a norm obligating the defendant, decide the case in favor of the defendant, was not correct, since these were not two mutually exclusive options. Rather, one could always construct a *tertium quid*, which was for the international judge the *non liquet* because of the absence of legal norms. Moreover, Stone pointed to the soliciting of expert opinions by international courts, in which the contradictory logic of the negative norm no longer worked given the absence of the plaintiff/defendant scheme (162). In terms of legal theory, the argumentation by Kelsen and Stone has come in for criticism. Critics have maintained that it is a

theoretical perspective, the argument of non-justiciable disputes that was marshaled against compulsory jurisdiction in international law.[66]

The main thrust of the doctrinal distinction between political and legal disputes lay, for Kelsen, in the political desire to exclude the establishment of judicial decision-making powers from certain areas of

bivalent, ontologically justified logic, which was already based on the premise that a legal system had to contain a rule for every conceivable situation. From this was inferred the exclusivity of the distinction lawful/unlawful, and this in turn was used to substantiate the coherence of the legal system. The logical conclusion of completeness thus rested on a *petitio principii* and could not rule out the use of a third category of what was legally "unregulated." On this see Fastenrath, *Lücken im Völkerrecht*, 242–243, with further references. For a critique of the logic used see, in addition to Stone, K. Engisch, "Der Begriff der Rechtslücke. Eine analytische Studie zu Wilhelm Sauers Methodenlehre" in *Festschrift für Wilhelm Sauer* (Berlin: W. de Gruyter, 1949), 94 *et seq*., and Tammelo's studies on the logical structure of the law: "There appears to be no a priori reason why a legal order could not be a logically open normative system. Hence it is objectionable to refer to the negative legal maxim as a principle of legal logic or legal ontology." Quoted from I. Tammelo, "The Logical Structure of the Law Field," *ARSP*, XLV (1959), 100. See also his essay "On the Logical Openness of Legal Orders," *AJCL*, 8 (1959), 191–203; W. Fikentscher, *Methoden des Rechts in vergleichender Darstellung. Band IV: Dogmatischer Teil* (Tübingen: Mohr, 1977), 116 *et seq*.; Chr. Weinberger and O. Weinberger, *Logik, Semantik, Hermeneutik* (Munich: C.H. Beck, 1979), 114 *et seq*. The attack on legal-theoretical grounds was joined by the natural-law critique, according to which unregulated "injustice" must not be permissible, as it presumably would be under the negative norm. Ulrich Fastenrath, in his monograph *Lücken im Völkerrecht*, subjected the validity of the "negative postulate of freedom" within international jurisprudence to another critical examination and called it, with respect to the realization of the most just order possible, potentially "dysfunctional": "With a view to the realization of values that the legal order is charged with, and to the fact that the legal order itself establishes values, it is easier to tolerate that it behaves indifferently toward unjust acts, than that it affirms them." Quoted from Fastenrath, *Lücken im Völkerrecht*, 252. On the negative norm see C. Cossio, "Egologische Theorie und Reine Rechtslehre," *ÖZöR*, 5 (1952), 19; on Kelsen's revision of the norm-logic in his later work see O. Weinberger, "Kelsens These von der Unanwendbarkeit logischer Regeln auf Normen" in *Die Reine Rechtslehre in wissenschaftlicher Diskussion*. Schriftenreihe des Hans-Kelsen-Instituts (Vienna: Manz, 1982), vol. 7.

66 Kelsen's "negative norm" is not only a theoretical *modus ponens*, but the liberal correlate of his scheme of the legal proposition [*Rechtssatzschema*], which was oriented toward sanction. The law is not only a coercive apparatus, but it also grants freedom from the law beyond the clearly established legal norms. This paradoxical construct of a legally granted freedom from the law is based on the Kantian definition of the law as the embodiment of the conditions under which (conflicting) individual freedoms can be reconciled under the general laws of freedom, Kant, *The Metaphysics of Morals* (*Metaphysik* 1798, 337). Based on this view, for Kelsen and Radbruch, sanction-backed interference in the a priori freedom of the individual was possible only through positive legal norms. In terms of national law, this approach provided protection against arbitrary actions on the part of the state. On this see Fastenrath, *Lücken im Völkerrecht*, 241.

international relations. That did not change the fact, however, that the relations in question had to be seen as regulated by international law.[67] The exclusion of political disputes in treaties on the establishment of arbitral tribunals, as for example in the Pact of Locarno, created the false impression that it was possible to distinguish between legal and political conflicts on the basis of objective criteria.[68] According to the Pact of Locarno (Art. 3), legal disputes were to be brought before the court of arbitration, whereas political disputes had to be submitted to a conciliation committee.[69] The separation between arbitration procedures for legal disputes and conciliation or mediation procedures for political disputes was thus an undeniable element of state practice during the interwar period.[70]

Kelsen emphasized the subjectivity of the criteria for distinguishing between political and legal disputes, which allowed the parties to avoid an undesired decision by an arbitral tribunal in any given case. If a treaty establishing a tribunal thus recognized a distinction between political and legal conflicts, it empowered the parties to withhold disputes from the jurisdiction of the court whenever they believed that the expected application of international law would be subjectively unsatisfactory.[71] The doctrine of the distinction between political and legal disputes thus produced an effect that was analogous to the *clausula rebus sic stantibus*. Just as the *clausula* de facto invalidated the customary law maxim *pacta sunt servanda*, excluding the court of arbitration's competence from extending to political disputes repealed the treaty obligation of taking a dispute to the court of arbitration.[72] For Erich Kaufmann and other German authors, however, such restriction clauses flowed from the

[67] Kelsen, *Peace through Law*, 27. [68] Ibid., 28.

[69] Art. 3, Sections 2 and 3 of the Rhine Pact of Locarno state: "Any legal question with regard to which the Parties are in conflict shall be submitted to a judicial decision, and the parties undertake to comply with such decision. All other questions shall be submitted to a conciliation commission. If the proposals of this commission are not accepted by the two Parties, question shall be brought before the Council of the League of Nations, which will deal with it in accordance with Article 15 of the covenant of the League."

[70] Fastenrath, *Lücken im Völkerrecht*, 236. [71] Kelsen, *Peace through Law*, 29–30.

[72] Ibid., 30. Kelsen radicalized the demand for compulsory jurisdiction also compared to other authors who regarded themselves as "progressive" in that matter. Schücking, for example, expressed himself much more moderately in 1924 on the question of the distinction between political and legal disputes: "Only in lay circles could one advocate the opinion that it is possible today to submit all international conflicts simply to one and the same agency of arbitration. Those knowledgeable of the problems knew: there are some disputes that are non-justiciable . . . These pure conflicts of interest, which cannot thus be solved by an actual court of arbitration, are joined by the category of disputes

very essence of state sovereignty as the central theoretical cornerstone of international law and keep international law in touch with political reality.[73]

The strict distinction between mediation procedures for so-called "purely political" disputes and judicial procedures for legal disputes was not well received by Kelsen. Although he recognized the necessity of political mediation processes, he believed that the failure of an attempt at mediation had to trigger a judicial procedure.[74] The exclusive assignment of a dispute to a political organ, which – like the Council of the League of Nations – decided unanimously, bore the danger that the dispute would in the end not be resolved at all.[75]

The result of Kelsen's critique was thus the same as Lauterpacht's fundamental attack on the international legal "dogma" of non-justiciable disputes. In his well-known 1933 monograph, Lauterpacht had initially provided a thorough assessment of the practice of the court of arbitration and the decisions of the PCIJ with respect to this question.[76] In the process, he used well-known arbitration cases – like the British Guiana–Venezuelan Boundary case,[77] the Alabama dispute,[78] the North Atlantic Fisheries case,[79] and the Behring Sea controversy[80] – as

which can be seen formally as legal disputes because they have some kind of legal side to them, but which today are in fact regarded by the nations not as legal questions, because they have a strong political element." Quoted from Schücking and Wehberg, *Die Satzung des Völkerbundes*, 2nd edn., 580.

73 Kaufmann, *Das Wesen des Völkerrechts*.

74 Kelsen, *Peace through Law*, 32. 75 Ibid., 31.

76 Lauterpacht, *The Function of Law in the International Community*, 139–201. Given his Neo-Kantian bent, Lauterpacht based himself also on the assumption of a formal "completeness" of the legal system. On this basis to his critique, which he shared with Kelsen, see Koskenniemi, "Lauterpacht: The Victorian Tradition in International Law," 225. However, there were distinct differences between Lauterpacht and Kelsen on the question of a material unity of the epistemologically complete legal system. Kelsen structured the legal system into interconnections of delegation, that is, as a logical system that was as much as possible free of contradictions. Lauterpacht, by contrast, saw in the recourse to general legal principles or in the ingenious use of classic juridical argumentative devices, e.g. analogy, the most important resources for creating the material completeness of the legal system. See Lauterpacht, *Private Law Sources*, 83–84, and H. Lauterpacht, "Some Observations on the Prohibition of 'Non Liquet' and the Completeness of the Law" in *Symbolae Verzijl* (The Hague: Nijhoff, 1958), 196 *et seq.*

77 Lauterpacht, *The Function of Law in the International Community*, 148.

78 Ibid., 147; see also K. Strupp, *Wörterbuch des Völkerrechts und der Diplomatie* (Berlin and Leipzig: W. de Gruyter, 1924–1929), vol. I, 16–19; Liszt, *Völkerrecht*, 342.

79 Lauterpacht, *The Function of Law in the International Community*, 149.

80 Ibid., 150; Strupp, *Wörterbuch des Völkerrechts und der Diplomatie*, 128–129; Liszt, *Völkerrecht*, 185.

examples where a legal settlement of the dispute had been achieved in spite of the presence of many vital political and economic interests. Lauterpacht interpreted the frequent recourse by statesmen to the contested distinction between political and legal disputes, with the goal of preventing a procedure in a court of arbitration, as confirmation of the baleful effect of this dogma, which international legal theory continued to entertain:

> It is embarrassing to note the resignation with which most international lawyers, fully conscious of the juridical unsoundness and confusing effect of the traditional distinction between the two classes of disputes, justify the perpetuation of this distinction in international conventions on the sole ground that Governments attach importance to it. But Governments, it has been shown, attach importance to it, not only because it is a convenient means of substituting an apparent for an effective obligation, but also because of the encouragement which it receives from international lawyers.[81]

From the fact that dozens of arbitration treaties since the first Hague Conference contained an exemption clause for matters of "high politics" or if "vital interests" were at stake, Lauterpacht thus did not infer the existence of a relevant principle of international law; instead, he attributed this state behavior also to the constant affirmation it received from an apologetic international law scholarship.[82] For him, one could infer from state practice *not* the acceptance of a corresponding legal principle, but instead the necessity of a scientific questioning of this notion with a view toward a future change in state practice. This view was typical of the self-understanding of the modernization movement in international legal scholarship between the wars, which saw itself as progressive. To Lauterpacht, the task of the international lawyer was not to affirm the status quo by providing a legal mirror to state practice, but to subject state conduct to an evaluative interpretation with a view toward the rule of law in international relations. In his eyes, the theory of international

[81] Lauterpacht, *The Function of Law in the International Community*, 435.

[82] On the bilateral treaties of arbitration that were set up in the wake of the first Hague Conference: Lauterpacht, *The Function of Law in the International Community*, 29–31. A "compulsory" arbitration of disputes was established by Art. 36, Section 2 of the Statute of the PICJ by way of a facultative declaration that the parties would abide by the decision of the court. See Münch, "Das Institut de droit international," 116–118. Still, in spite of the declared willingness to submit to the court, it was possible to see in the wording of Art. 36, Section 2, a limitation of the competence of the court to "legal" disputes, in accordance with the doctrine of the distinctions between political and legal conflicts. On this see Lauterpacht, *The Function of Law in the International Community*, 34–37.

law had for too long spread the doctrinal blanket over an international politics that was compromising international law.

In his theoretical reflections on the question of completeness, Lauterpacht took a less categorical position than Kelsen. To that end, he distinguished between a formal and a material "completeness" of the international legal system.[83] Only in formal terms could the existence of gaps be ruled out; material gaps arising from the teleological examination of a norm, however, were a normal phenomenon of every legal system.[84] Lauterpacht solved the problem of reconciling a compulsory jurisdiction with a legal system that had material gaps through recourse to juristic argumentative devices such as analogy in conjunction with general legal principles. The judge could invoke general legal principles, and using analogy and general deduction, he could arrive at an individual decision in every dispute.[85] Lauterpacht refuted the doctrine of the non-justiciability of certain disputes by means of examples in which international judges and arbitrators filled in a material gap by applying classic techniques of juristic argumentation.[86]

The divergent argumentative strategy of the two men is striking. Lauterpacht invoked counter-examples from judicial practice to prove that it was possible to solve even politically explosive disputes.[87] Kelsen,

[83] For Lauterpacht, too, the "completeness" of the legal system is an a priori principle of law: *The Function of Law in the International Community*, 63–65. The correlate to this principle is the prohibition of *non liquet* for the international judge. If the legal system as a whole cannot be incomplete, then the judge could not leave a case brought before him undecided (64). As a doubled-sided principle, it was, according to Lauterpacht, a general legal maxim of the civilized nations in the sense of Art. 38, Section 1 of the statute of the PICJ (66). This was corroborated by the practice of international courts, which had not pronounced a *non liquet* in any known case.

[84] Lauterpacht criticized the recourse to a general negative norm as a simplification of the complex problematic:

> It is easy to say that there is no gap in the law, its silence in a particular case must be regarded as having a negative effect on the claim before the court. Such reasoning may frequently be correct. But at times, it may be an expression of intellectual inertia or short-sightedness. It is the idea that there do exist gaps in the law – material gaps in the teleological sense as judged from the point of view of the general purpose of the law, and as distinguished from formal gaps identical with a break in the continuity of the legal order.
>
> *The Function of Law in the International Community*, 86–87.

[85] Ibid., 101–102, 110 *et seq.* [86] Ibid., 110 *et seq.*

[87] Koskenniemi, *From Apology to Utopia*, 26–27, with further references; on Lauterpacht and Kelsen see p. 35.

by contrast, argued on a strictly theoretical basis. To him, the distinction between legal and political disputes could not be made in an objective manner. It therefore constituted a doctrinal doorway through which international lawyers could bring their political opinions to bear on the issue. Moreover, to his mind it could be logically refuted. In brief: By hewing close to actual practice in his argumentation, Lauterpacht defeated the traditional doctrine with its own weapons, while Kelsen applied his critique on a more abstract level. Lauterpacht and Kelsen criticized the unreflective and one-sided adoption of treaty practice into international legal doctrine. Merely because states, by excluding "political" disputes, had in practice often reserved for themselves the possibility of avoiding judicial settlement, that distinction must not be perpetuated by the doctrine of non-justiciable disputes. As Kelsen and Lauterpacht saw it, nothing from the perspective of either legal theory or legal practice stood in the way of an international jurisdiction that rendered compulsory decisions on matters political.

B The theoretical classification of the judicial decision

I The function of the judicial decision within the hierarchical structure of the law

Kelsen's desire to foster the establishment of compulsory jurisdiction in international law must be analyzed more closely against the backdrop of the theoretical function of courts in the Pure Theory. The outstanding significance that Kelsen accorded the courts was based not only on his evolutionary theory of the law, but also on his concept of the dynamic legal system that was derived from the theory of the hierarchical structure of the legal system.[88]

For Kelsen, the decision of the court served to concretize abstract general norms.[89] It thus had by no means only a declaratory character, in the sense of merely pronouncing already existing law. Rather, it had a constitutive, law-creating function: "That there is held to be a concrete material fact at all, which is to be linked with a specific legal consequence, and that this concrete material fact is indeed linked with concrete legal consequences – this entire connection is created by the judicial decision."[90] As Kelsen saw it, the decision by the court created an individual legal norm

[88] See the discussion of the hierarchical structure in Chapter 5 B.
[89] Kelsen, *Reine Rechtslehre* (1934), 79; *Problems of Legal Theory*, 68. [90] Ibid.

by concretizing a norm of customary law or an international legal treaty. According to the previously described hierarchical structure of the law [*Stufenbau*], the application of a higher-ranking norm within the hierarchy of norms was simultaneously the creation of a lower-ranking norm by the authorized legal organ. In this way, following Kelsen, the application could be seen as the dynamic process of concretizing norms.

Law-making was always an empirical act, the performance of which created a norm by having the act satisfy the conditions for the creation of a norm as laid down in a higher norm.[91] For Kelsen there was, however, no guarantee that the concrete decision by a court was still in accord with the general norm that was being applied.[92] Yet in such a case this individual norm still had the force of law.[93] This was the institution of the *res iudicata*, which was central to every legal system.[94] The theory of the hierarchical structure adopted from Merkl allowed Kelsen to see the application of the law by the courts simultaneously as law-making. Moreover, because this was law-making at the last level of concretization, the court decided in the final analysis what was law.[95] Only the application of the law to the individual case, which laid claim to being valid even if it departed from the abstract rule, formed the concrete corpus of law: "One should not overlook the important fact that in the last analysis the law is not what the legislator more or less clearly sets forth or what the rule of custom more or less comprehensibly implies. The law is what the court finally decides."[96]

By emphasizing the crucial function of the judiciary within the legal system, Kelsen sought to demonstrate that the importance of a centralized legislature – in the sense of a world parliament – was secondary to that of the courts. Not only was the concretization of the law by the courts the first step – in his theory of legal evolution – toward a modern, centralized legal system, even within the more highly evolved legal systems it remained functionally the most important organ of the legal order. For Kelsen, the still decentralized law-making by treaties and customary law created a sufficient material basis for the introduction of a compulsory jurisdiction. The stronger centralization of general law-making could then follow in a

[91] Kelsen, *Reine Rechtslehre* (1934), 82 *et seq.*; *Problems of Legal Theory*, 70. On this see Heidemann, *Die Norm als Tatsache*, 78–79.

[92] Kelsen, *Law and Peace*, 162–163.

[93] On the problem of judge-made law as a source of law in the Continental European and the common-law tradition see Luhmann, *Das Recht der Gesellschaft*, 304–310; J. Esser, "Richterrecht, Gerichtsgebrauch und Gewohnheitsrecht" in J. Esser (ed.), *Festschrift für Fritz von Hippel* (Tübingen: Mohr, 1967), 95 *et seq.*

[94] Kelsen, *Law and Peace*, 163. [95] Kelsen, "International Peace," 575. [96] Ibid.

later step.[97] By contrast, Kelsen believed that the effort to create a comprehensive codification of international law by a kind of world parliament before establishing compulsory jurisdiction was potentially dysfunctional. One must not overestimate the function of the legislator. But if one considered the eminent importance of the courts, it becomes clear "why there can be no legislator without a judge, even though there can very well be a judge without a legislator."[98]

II The nature of judicial decision-making

If one sees the courts as the central organ of the legal system, as Kelsen did, the question about the nature and method of the judge's act of decision takes on special relevance. I shall therefore take a closer look at Kelsen's theory of interpretation for what it has to say about the boundaries or guiding principles of individual law-making by the person who applies the law.

According to Kelsen, the process of law-making as it moves from a higher to a lower norm is guided by the mental procedure of legal interpretation.[99] In addition to this mental process, the higher norm – to a certain extent – also predetermines the content of the lower norm. But this higher norm formed only the frame, within which the lower norm had to be established.[100] Because the content of the lower norm was thus never completely "determined," the interpretation of the norm served to choose one possible concretization of the more general framework provided by the higher norm. In addition, for Kelsen there was no "method according to which only one of the several interpretations of a norm could be distinguished as 'correct.'"[101] As he saw it, all methods of interpretation developed by the traditional doctrine lead to a possible, but never to the only, correct result. The possibility of interpretation arose precisely from the openness of the norm to various methods of interpretation.[102] It was futile to try to establish "legally" one correct concretization by excluding the others.[103] For Kelsen,

[97] On the evolutionary theory of law see Section A II above.

[98] Kelsen, "International Peace," 575.

[99] Kelsen, *Reine Rechtslehre* (1934), 90; *Problems of Legal Theory*, 77. On the theory of interpretation see Heidemann, *Die Norm als Tatsache*, 78–79.

[100] Kelsen, *Reine Rechtslehre* (1934), 91; *Problems of Legal Theory*, 78.

[101] Kelsen, *Reine Rechtslehre* (1934), 96; *Problems of Legal Theory*, 81.

[102] Kelsen, *Reine Rechtslehre* (1934), 97; *Problems of Legal Theory*, 81.

[103] Kelsen, *Reine Rechtslehre* (1934), 96; *Problems of Legal Theory*, 81.

objectively "right" results of interpretation could not be arrived at either from judicial interpretive techniques such as *analogy*, or from the *argumentum e contrario*, or from the so-called weighing of interests.

In his *Pure Theory*, Kelsen thus demystified the "objectivity" of these methods of interpretation along with other classic techniques of legal argumentation. From a scholarly perspective, the only remaining purpose of interpretation was to determine an external semantic framework; one could speak here of the "*Wortlautgrenze*" ["semantic boundary"] that circumscribed the subjective act of the judge's decision.[104] In the second edition of his *Pure Theory*, Kelsen spoke with respect to interpretation by legally authorized organs of "authentic interpretation."[105] With this, he demarcated this form of interpretation sharply from scholarly interpretation. Neither the judge as the one applying the law, nor the legal scholar, could claim that he alone was able to determine the only correct way of applying the norm. But in the case of the subjective decision of the judge, we are dealing with an application-act authorized by the legal system, whereas for Kelsen the legal scholar was not embedded within such a functional context.[106] He had to limit himself to demonstrating the various decision options of the one applying the law and place them side by side as equals.[107]

In this way, the application of the norm was largely disconnected from the problem of jurisprudential cognition: "For if there can be an interpretation of a norm, then the question as to which is the 'correct' choice from among the possibilities given within the frame of the norm is hardly a question of cognition directed to the positive law; it is a problem not of legal theory but of legal policy."[108] The individual creation of a norm thus becomes a subjective act of will on the part of the judge:

> In applying a statute, there may well be room for cognitive activity beyond discovering the frame within which the act of application is to be confined; this is not cognition of the positive law, however, but

[104] In this critical view of the traditional methods of interpretation, Kelsen was in agreement with the realistic theory of international law of McDougal and Schwarzenberger; see M. S. McDougal, "International Law, Power and Policy: A Contemporary Conception," *RCADI*, 82 (1953), 149–157; G. Schwarzenberger and E. D. Brown, *A Manual of International Law*, 6th edn. (Milton: Professional Books, 1976), 135–137; on this parallelism see Koskenniemi, *From Apology to Utopia*, 298.

[105] Kelsen, *Reine Rechtslehre* (1960), 350; Heidemann, *Die Norm als Tatsache*, 136–137.

[106] Kelsen, *Reine Rechtslehre* (1960), 353.

[107] It was in this way that Kelsen was trying to write his commentary on the charter of the United Nations; see the final chapter of the present book.

[108] Kelsen, *Reine Rechtslehre* (1934), 98; *Problems of Legal Theory*, 82.

> cognition of other norms, which can now make their way into the law-creating process, the norms, namely, of morality, of justice – social value judgments customarily characterized with the catchphrases "welfare of the people," "public interest," "progress," and so on. From the standpoint of the positive law, nothing can be said about their validity and whether or not they can be identified.[109]

The judge, unlike the legal scholar, was thus free to incorporate personal value judgments, political maxims, and ideas of justice into his decision – according to Kelsen, he could not but do so. This brings us to a critical point of the Pure Theory, one to which the more recent secondary literature about the now "classic" 1931 Weimar dispute over the limits of constitutional adjudication[110] has called attention.[111] Critics see in the possibility granted by Kelsen of a largely free and thus political law-making by the constitutional court a contradiction to the limitation on politics by the courts that he actually desired.[112]

What Kelsen asked the enlightened jurist to confront through his view of the court decision, however, was not so much a contradiction in the theoretical approach of the Pure Theory, as one of the central paradoxes of the law. The legal sociologist Kelsen was aware of the central role that binding decisions by courts have for the ability of the legal system to function, but he was realistic enough not to resolve the paradox of the "undecidability of the decision."[113] Instead, the Pure Theory of Law sought to constructively capture the objectively uncontrollable and, in the final analysis, irrational character of the court decision through the dynamic view of the creation of law. That was also the reason why Kelsen

109 Kelsen, *Reine Rechtslehre* (1934), 98–99; *Problems of Legal Theory*, 83.

110 H. Kelsen, "Wer soll Hüter der Verfassung sein?" *WRS*, II, 1873 *et seq.*

111 See the critical approaches by M. Troper and D. Dyzenhaus: in M. Troper, "Kelsen und die Kontrolle der Verfassungsmäßigkeit" in A. Carrino and G. Winkler (eds.), *Rechtserfahrung und Reine Rechtslehre* (Vienna and New York: Springer, 1995), 15–39, and M. Troper, "'The Guardian of the Constitution' – Hans Kelsen's Evaluation of a Legal Concept" in D. Diner and M. Stolleis (eds.), *Hans Kelsen and Carl Schmitt: A Juxtaposition* (Gerlingen: Bleicher, 1999), 81 *et seq.*; D. Dyzenhaus, *Legality and Legitimacy. Carl Schmitt, Hans Kelsen and Hermann Heller in Weimar* (Oxford University Press, 1997), 102–160.

112 Troper, "Kelsen und die Kontrolle der Verfassungsmäßigkeit," 15–39; Dyzenhaus, *Legality and Legitimacy*, 149, 157; on this criticism see Jabloner, "Verrechtlichung und Rechtsdynamik," 270–278.

113 On the paradox of the "undecidability of the decision" see Luhmann, *Das Recht der Gesellschaft*, 317: "Courts must also decide in cases where they cannot decide; or at least, not within tenable standards of rationality. If the law cannot be found, it must simply be invented." On the "affliction of the undecidable" see J. Derrida, *Gesetzeskraft. Der mystische Grund der Autorität* (Frankfurt am Main: Suhrkamp, 1991), 49.

did not need to restrict the subjectivity of the court decision through a purified theory of interpretation. The intrusion of the judge's subjective value judgments into decisions of the court should *not* be glossed over by the seeming objectivity of the theories of interpretation. Instead, Kelsen construed the scientifically uncontrollable factor as an act of law-making of the judge that was authorized by the legal system.[114] The degree of freedom granted to the judge by the dynamic idea of law-creation allows the court to adjust the law to the current needs of society.[115]

It thus no longer comes as a surprise that Kelsen was more than receptive to the use of general legal principles and decisions *ex aequo et bono* by international courts and arbitrators. In an analysis of Art. 38 of the statute of the PCIJ, Kelsen noted the outstanding possibilities of the court to account for the demands of justice and equity through the application of general legal principles.[116] Reference to general legal principles always allowed the court in practice also to apply considerations of equity, even though *ex aequo et bono* decisions by statute require the special consent of the contending parties.[117] In fact, for Kelsen, considerations of fairness – in the sense of the adjustment of the abstract norm to the specific circumstances of the case – by a court rendering compulsory decisions were unavoidable: "A court which really has compulsory jurisdiction, that is to say, which is competent to decide finally all disputes without any exception, inevitably will adopt positive law in its concrete decisions gradually and imperceptively to actual needs; in other words, will decide on the basis of equity, even if it is not expressly empowered to apply principles other than those of law."[118] The application of general legal maxims, considerations of equity, and notions of justice, which Kelsen

[114] To that extent, the court, like any other legal organ, can be seen simultaneously, according to Kelsen, as a "political" organ. But it remains a legal organ only if, in the political act of applying the law or making law, it adheres formally and materially to the framework established by the legal system: H. Kelsen, "Science and Politics," *American Political Science Review*, XLV (1951), 660.

[115] Kelsen, "International Peace," 575.

[116] Kelsen, "Compulsory Adjudication of International Disputes," 406. [117] Ibid.

[118] Ibid. In contrast to Kelsen, Lauterpacht, in his argumentation, had shied away from describing the administration of the law as law-making. For him, the judge was applying existing law in a creative process. There was no need to depict the function of the judge as a purely automatic, formal deduction from the law, nor cause for the assumption that the decision of a court was the highly subjective affair of a judge who was guided by emotion: Lauterpacht, *The Function of Law in the International Community*, 103. The judge's freedom to decide should not be overestimated, especially in the international arena, since the competence of the court was grounded in the voluntary agreement of states (104). For Lauterpacht, the subjective element inherent in the decision

sought to prohibit the legal scholar from using, was not only permitted to the judge, but from a functional point of view necessary. That subjective value judgments and political preferences flowed into the rendering of a decision and in the end were also cast into the form of the court's decision was the precondition for the necessary, continuous reform of the law. Thus, they found their justified function not in the jurisprudential determination and analysis of the law, but on the level of law-creation by the organs set up for that purpose by the legal system.

III The postulate of compulsory jurisdiction as the consequence of a system-oriented conception of the law

And yet doubts remain. Does the desired establishment of a compulsory judicial organ at the head of the world organization not end up replacing a political organ of government representatives with an equally politically, but less legitimated, organ of legal experts? The political dimension of the judicial decision that Kelsen made clear would seem to suggest as much. However, the simple equating of a court rendering compulsory decisions with a political world government obscures the special nature of the judicial organ and the desired reciprocal relationship between "political" and "legal" organs. Above all, this perspective would fail to consider the specific legal rationality inherent in judicial proceedings, which sets it apart from a purely political organ. Judges render their decisions in the form of the law, and their justification is based on legal forms of argumentation. Although the Pure Theory of Law destroys the myth that the judge pronounced objective law, that does not turn the judgment of the court into nothing more than a political "decision." The formal procedure of arriving at a judgment forces the judge to engage in juristic argumentation, which means that the legal corpus has to be

encountered its limit in the respect for the rule of law. The judge's freedom to decide remained a freedom within the law (103). Julius Stone criticized Lauterpacht for what he believed was an inconsistent construct. He maintained that in order to justify a prohibition of *non liquet* or an obligatory jurisdiction, one had to eventually posit a law-creation activity on the part of the judge: J. C. Stone, "Non Liquet and the Function of Law in the International Community," *BYIL*, 25 (1959), 137. Lauterpacht was concealing this when he pointed in his argumentation to the fruitfulness of the general legal maxims in the judge's finding of law (133–137). Because a judge always had a choice between various legal maxims, he did not apply existing law, but in the end created new law (159). On the debate between Lauterpacht and Stone see I. G. M. Scobbie, "The Theorist as a Judge: Hersch Lauterpacht's Conception of the International Judicial Function," *EJIL*, 2 (1997), 274–298.

constantly part of the reflections. Moreover, in the choice of personnel there is also a fundamental difference to a genuinely political decision-making organ like the Council of the League of Nations. Under Kelsen's proposal, the judges are chosen in a complicated procedure on the basis of their specific legal qualifications. In addition, they are organizationally and financially independent of their home countries.[119] In spite of the irrational element that is an inherent part of the process of arriving at a judicial decision, Kelsen trusted the professionally trained, neutral personality of the judge, who developed the law further in a procedure that adhered to the law.[120] The court thus does not act as a world government, but is placed alongside the purely political organs, such as the Council, as the guarantor of a final, legal constraint on politics.

The political demand for a court with compulsory jurisdiction sprang from Kelsen's belief in universal law. If that law, from a methodological perspective, was to have a specific "Ought," that is, a specific inherent rationality, it required the greatest possible concretization of this "Ought" by organs that apply the inherent logic of the legal system at least to some limited degree. A binding law above the state can be truly established only through a judicial decision about what is valid law, that is, about the precise content of the sphere of the law that is often non-codified and based on customary law.

At this point it makes sense to take a look at the more recent research on systems theory, which, in spite of a completely new concept of system, has, like no other sociological theory of the twentieth century, emphasized the inherent rationality and self-referential nature of functional societal subsystems' communicative processes following a specific inner rationality. For Luhmann courts have a central position in any institutionalized legal system:

> That courts must decide is the starting point for the construction of the legal universe, for legal thought, for juristic argumentation. *That is why* "legitimation" in the sense of a value-reference that transcends the law ultimately cannot play a role in the law. *That is why* everything depends on respecting earlier decisions one can take guidance from, unless they are changed. *That is why* the res iudicata is unassailable, unless rules of exception provided for in the law take effect. And *that is why* the law must

119 See the proposed regulation concerning the selection and compensation of judges in Kelsen, *Peace through Law*, 129–135.

120 Kelsen, "The Essential Conditions of International Justice." For Koskenniemi, the Kelsenian system collapses for lack of its own theory of interpretation: *From Apology to Utopia*, 473.

> be seen as a self-referential, self-contained system, in which even under extreme social tensions the "purely juristic argumentation" can be practiced, which decides on its own which interpretive leeway it can afford and where the demand for a distortion must be turned away.[121]

According to Kelsen and Lauterpacht, the desired evolutionary achievement of the medium of law as a technique for guiding societal processes requires also on the international level a central legal institution that renders obligatory decisions on the question of the lawfulness of disputed actions. Compulsory jurisdiction thus becomes the functional equivalent of the epistemological postulate of the unity or self-referential nature of the legal system. It is the institutional keystone in a theoretical construct that conceives of international law as a universal societal medium that is becoming at least gradually autonomous from politics.

C Realist opposition to the quest for a strong international judiciary: compulsory jurisdiction as another "distinguished international lawyer's dream"

In the 1940s, the demand for an international court that rendered compulsory decisions came increasingly under the suspicion of being a utopian aspiration, out of step with political realities. As early as 1939, E. H. Carr, in his famous book *The Twenty Years' Crisis, 1919–1939*, noted, with reference to Kelsen and Lauterpacht, that the view of international law as a legal system that was institutionally completed by compulsory jurisdiction was another "distinguished international lawyer's dream of an international community whose center of gravity is in the administration of international justice."[122] For Carr, this approach fails to grasp the political foundations of the legal system. It turned the judge into a legislator, and this caused international politics to be theoretically absorbed into the law. A resolution to international conflicts through a non-partisan judicial organ on the basis of equity and common sense would dissolve the boundary between law and politics. That is precisely why there existed clashing views when it came to assessing British interests in Egypt, American interests on the Panama Canal issue, the future of Danzig, and the borders of Bulgaria, "because there is no political agreement even of the vaguest kind as to what equity and

[121] Luhmann, *Das Recht der Gesellschaft*, 317–318.
[122] Carr, *The Twenty Years' Crisis*, 186. The book has been reprinted to this day.

common sense mean in relation to such questions."[123] On issues of high politics the world was dealing with issues aimed at bringing about a change in the law, and as such they could not be handed over to a judge to decide.[124]

From this perspective, Kelsen's and Lauterpacht's assumption that courts would be able to adjust international law to pressing societal needs in individual cases overtaxed the legal system. For Carr, a legal process is fundamentally different from a political one in that it blocks out the question of power. Before the law the parties are equal, regardless of the asymmetries of power. This fiction contradicted the inherent logic of international politics, where the strength of the individual states had to be considered a crucial factor in the solution of conflicts of interest: "Nothing is gained, and the proper function of law is debased and discredited, if this political function is entrusted to a tribunal, whose constitution and procedure are deliberately assimilated to those of a court of law."[125] From this point of view, the capacity of the law is exceeded with a compulsory international jurisdiction.

For Carr, the possibility of legally arbitrating every conflict between states by a court of law therefore ran counter to the nature of international politics and was typical of a utopian legal view of interstate relations. This "realistic" argument from a work often considered the "bible" of international relations studies was persuasive to experts on international politics not only in 1939. In the wake of this argumentation, a separate scholarly discipline consolidated itself after the Second World War, which was embraced above all by disillusioned former German international lawyers such as Morgenthau, or the former Kelsen student John Herz. Within the discipline of international law itself, the realist critique of the systems-oriented view of the law was advanced after the

[123] Ibid., 188.

[124] Ibid., 187–188. James Leslie Brierly also believed that a great many disputes involved a weighing of the political and economic interests of the parties, and this was thus a task for which statesmen were more qualified than international judges: Brierly, "The Judicial Settlement of International Disputes," 106. For Julius Stone, as well, the critical question directed at Lauterpacht was whether the pacification of international relations was in fact well served by asking the international judge to continue the development in every conceivable case of what Stone regarded as the completely inadequate stock of international legal norms: "At what point does a legal judgment 'settling' a case on an inadequate basis of knowledge and experience only serve to exacerbate the process of conflict by prematurely entrenching one side behind a bastion of vested legal right?" Quoted from J. C. Stone, "Non Liquet," 160.

[125] Carr, *The Twenty Years' Crisis*, 188.

Second World War especially by Georg Schwarzenberger. He based his approach on the factual conditions of international politics, and advocated an "inductive" methodology to international law.[126] The desired juridification of international relations through international courts was rejected as a deductively misguided utopian argumentation, and judicial rationality was subjected to the power constraints of politics.[127]

For Lauterpacht and Kelsen, the problem of international jurisdiction before and during the Second World War revolved above all around the future institutional development of international relations. That development could be achieved only by way of an international treaty and thus via international law. With the theoretical insight of the legal scholar into the specific inherent rationality of highly evolved legal systems, they favored to this end the creation of a court that rendered binding decisions. The transfer of their system-oriented approach to the law to international law was for them beyond questioning. If international law had the quality of law, it had to be conceptualized as a complete system of norms. In this respect, the relatively small number of general international legal norms was no obstacle to the creation of a compulsory jurisdiction. Had the League of Nations not given excessive consideration to the power logic of politics in the structure of its organs? As they saw it, the existing international legal framework was in dire need of better judicial support. Irrational power politics had brought war, now a unified international legal system was to bring peace. International legal validity, which came with the criticized notion of formal equality, had an irreplaceable function and value for taming and civilizing the irrational forces of nationalism and unrestrained pursuit of alleged national interests. The last sentence of the lectures on "Law and Peace in International Relations," which Kelsen delivered at Harvard in 1942, remained programmatic for this thinking during the Second World War: "The idea of law, in spite of everything, seems still to be stronger than any other ideology of power."[128]

Kelsen's postulate of a compulsory jurisdiction seems to clash headlong and irreconcilably with the arguments of the "realists." In fact, the sociologically motivated belief in universal law was discredited after the

[126] G. Schwarzenberger, *The Inductive Approach to International Law* (London: Stevens, 1965).

[127] Ch. De Visscher, *Théories et réalités en droit international public* (Paris: A. Pedone, 1953), 90–91.

[128] Kelsen, *Law and Peace*, 170.

war as utopian. Under attack by the "realists," the mainstream of international law after the Second World War sought to escape the suspicion of being utopian by increasingly dispensing with a system-oriented perspective. Instead, many international lawyers presented themselves as more pragmatic in their analysis of international norms and institutions and dressed higher aspirations in vague neo-scholastic natural-law oriented concepts,[129] while the discipline of international relations focused predominantly on the question of power.[130] It was only in the 1980s that a scholar like Georges Abi-Saab gave Kelsen's system-oriented approach to international law a prominent position in his Hague lectures.[131]

But the distinction between realism and utopianism I have laid out is too narrow, too self-sufficient, and in the end too simplistic to do justice to the significance that this controversy between Kelsen and Lauterpacht, on the one side, and Carr and Morgenthau, on the other, had for the discipline of international law. The clash of brilliant legal-theoretical analyses of the inherent value and institutional requirements of international legal validity, on the one hand, and the sober analysis of the antagonistic political interests and ideologies dominating the interwar period, on the other, gives rise to the question of how, in the institutional development of international relations, both the specific inherent rationality of the "judicial" and the "political" can be taken into account.

A closer look also reveals that the realist critique itself must be differentiated with regard to the role the protagonists accorded international legal validity. While Carr conceded that law cannot be reduced to the mere exercise of power,[132] Morgenthau – inspired by Carl Schmitt – inaugurated an approach to law which tended to reduce international legal validity to a phenomenon that was always dependent on its congruence with the interests of the strongest political actors.[133] For him

[129] This is one of the reasons why Verdross arguably became much more influential in the post-Second World War discipline of international law than Kelsen.

[130] It was only in the 1980s and 1990s that international relations scholars rediscovered the autonomous value and significance of law in international relations under the concept of "constructivist" approaches to international relations.

[131] G. Abi-Saab, "Cours général de droit international public," *RCADI*, 207/VII (1987).

[132] Carr, *The Twenty Years' Crisis*, 228–229.

[133] On Morgenthau and his foundational influence on the post-war discipline of international relations see M. Koskenniemi, "Carl Schmitt, Hans Morgenthau, and the Image of Law in International Relations" in M. Byers (ed.), *The Role of Law in International Politics. Essays in International Relations and International Law* (Oxford University Press, 2000), 17–34.

effective constraints on state action could only derive from common interests in a given situation or from a balance of power.[134] The idea of an autonomous legal system guiding the conduct of states was hereby theoretically ruled out.

In retrospect, the discourse transcends the superficial realism/utopianism dichotomy, and the true central issue, namely the extent to which the international institutions must open themselves to the perspective of power without relinquishing the non-instrumental belief in international legal validity moves into the foreground. From this perspective, the problem of building an international legal community becomes a question of institutional imagination, one that must incorporate and preserve the inherent and autonomous value of both international politics and international law.

[134] H. J. Morgenthau, *Politics Among Nations. The Struggle for Power and Peace*, revised by K. W. Thompson and W. D. Clinton, 7th edn. (New York: McGraw-Hill, 2006), 10 *et seq*.

7

The role of the international legal scholar after Kelsen – a concluding reflection

Throughout this book Kelsen's approach to international law has been explained as arising from the tension-filled relationship between the two crucial goals of his theories of international law: first, establishing a non-political methodology of legal scholarship, and, second, promoting the cosmopolitan project – born in the interwar period – of a thoroughly juridified and more strongly institutionalized world order. Time and again, I have pointed to the inner connection that Kelsen established between these two originally conflicting goals. That main link was found in the methodologically guided – that is, "purely" scholarly – critique of those doctrinal elements that potentially stood in the way of his own cosmopolitan project. The consequence of this critique was a not inconsiderable limitation on the role and significance of international legal doctrine in areas that were especially sensitive for his politico-legal project. Kelsen was obviously willing to accept that consequence.

In his introduction to the 1950 commentary on the Charter of the United Nations, *The Law of the United Nations*, Kelsen offered a final statement on his self-conception as an international lawyer. He had to measure his own commentary on the Charter by the role that he accorded the international lawyer in the introduction: "'Juristic' in contradistinction to 'political' has the connotation of 'technical.' It is not superfluous to remind the lawyer that as a 'jurist' he is but a technician whose most important task is to assist the law-maker in the adequate formulation of legal norms."[1] The point is a "technical" analysis of the norm text that must leave aside the jurist's subjective political ideas: "This book is a juristic – not a political – approach to the problems of the United Nations. It deals with the law of the organization, not with its actual or desired role in the international play of powers."[2]

[1] H. Kelsen, *The Law of the United Nations. A Critical Analysis of its Fundamental Problems,* 2 Impression (New York: F. A. Praeger, 1951; 1st edn. 1950), XIII.
[2] Ibid.

The task of a juristic commentary was to review the internal consistency of a legal text. To that end, all conceivable interpretations of individual norms with their respective repercussions for other statutory prescriptions had to be described and placed side by side as equal. The conventional procedure of working up a single interpretation as the correct one was based on a fiction.[3] There were always multiple logically defensible interpretations that the jurist had to lay out and provide the law-applying organs as a choice. The function of the jurist, according to Kelsen, was thus to assist the law-making and law-applying organs as a non-political "norm technician."[4] Based on his claim of "purity," Kelsen, in the preface, forbids a value-based interpretation of the normative material with a view to one's own political goals. For him, the jurist is a structural engineer, not an architect.

In his clear analysis of the most important provisions of the Charter, Kelsen sought to live up to this principle. In fact, by placing various possible interpretations side by side, he was able to achieve an advance in "objectivity" over a conventional commentary. With his postulate of logical consistency, Kelsen, as in to his critique of the conventional doctrine of international law, uncovered the weaknesses in the Charter in an almost ruthless fashion. One gets the impression that Kelsen was trying to show that there was a lack of skillful legal advice when the Charter was drafted. Large swathes of the commentary consist of demonstrating that norms or parts of norms were "superfluous," "meaningless," "unclear," or "contradictory."[5] Kelsen rejected the ingenious use of interpretative methods or a recourse to the "spirit" of the Charter to smooth out inconsistencies and ambiguities. When in doubt, his formal interpretations, which hewed close to the wording decided against a competence-expanding interpretation of the Charter in the sense of the doctrine of implied powers.[6]

A. H. Feller from the UN Legal Department was especially critical of Kelsen's approach:

> It may well be unfortunate from a 'scientific' standpoint that legal obligations must carry with them so much extraneous baggage – but such is the

[3] Ibid., XIV–XV. [4] Ibid., XIII.

[5] For an example see the commentary on Art. 35 of the Charter: Kelsen, *The Law of the United Nations*, 422–424.

[6] Ibid., 330; on this see the critique by O. Schachter, "Review of: Hans Kelsen, *The Law of the United Nations*," *Yale L. Rev.*, 60 (1951), 192; A. H. Feller, "Review of: Hans Kelsen, *The Law of the United Nations*," *Col. L. R.*, 51 (1951), 538; and L. B. Sohn, "Review of: Hans Kelsen, *The Law of the United Nations*," *Harvard L. R.*, 64 (1950–51), 518.

> nature of constitutions which live in the minds of people and are adaptable to growth along with the societies they are intended to govern. The consequence of this failure to appreciate the basic nature of the instrument is a tendency towards narrow and restrictive interpretation which in effect says that if it is not written explicitly in the Charter, it is illegal.[7]

Through the reductionist commentary, Kelsen maintained his claim to being non-political, at least outwardly. In actuality, though, one can draw, at various points of the commentary, an inner connection between Kelsen's own political ideas about a workable global organization and the "purely" technical commentary on the Charter. This is especially apparent in his discussion of the statute of the International Court of Justice. One of Kelsen's most important political concerns, the introduction of rights of the individual that are actionable before international courts, was buttressed in his commentary on Art. 34 of the statute with the "pure" argument of logical consistency: "The fact that no private individual has access to the court seems not to be consistent with the fact that the Charter – in contradistinction to the Covenant – contains provisions whose purpose is to protect the individual against the state."[8] Moreover, it was an inherent contradiction in the Charter to grant the United Nations the right to enter into international legal treaties with other states, while at the same time removing the disputes that might arise from control by the International Court of Justice through Art. 34 of the statute. The central role of international jurisdiction that Kelsen postulated (*de lege ferenda*) during the war, and his belief in universal law whose development had to be carried on by an independent judiciary, did not fail to influence the "purely" logical commentary on Art. 34. Here, too, we can see that already the choice of the criticized norms or doctrinal elements obviously represented a highly subjective act on the part of the jurist. Oskar Schachter wrote about this in his review of Kelsen's commentary: "For throughout the book there seems to be so sustained an effort to discover the maximum of inconsistency – even absurdity – in the Charter ... that one is apt to infer that Kelsen's underlying objective is the revision of the Charter and a building of a new organization closer to his own heart's desire."[9]

However, it was not only Kelsen's disappointment that his own blueprint had not been considered in the drafting of the Charter, but also the self-imposed limitation of a jurist who was critical of ideology, that led to

[7] Feller, "Review," 538.
[8] Kelsen, *The Law of the United Nations*, 484. [9] Schachter, "Review," 193.

the destructive thrust of the commentary. Because of his claim to be non-political, the only way left for Kelsen was a technical critique of norm texts and doctrine. A constructive interpretation of the provisions of the Charter that yielded to his own legal-political ideas, as Lauterpacht had undertaken with regard to the Charter norms dealing with human rights, for example, was blocked from the outset by his claim to scholarly self-restraint.[10] Time and again, the jurist Kelsen sought in logical critique the balance between a non-political legal "science" and his own cosmopolitan project. But even in his self-limitation to a technical-logical analysis, he could not do full justice to his own claim to objectivity.[11]

I set out to show that the work on international law by Hans Kelsen and his students can be explained as arising from two central, interwoven motives. For one, Kelsen and Kunz, in particular, sought to bring international legal scholarship close to the level of the "exact" sciences and thus turn it into a "pure," meaning more objective and non-political, discipline. At the same time, these men tried to advance their own cosmopolitan project of a thorough court-driven juridification of international relations. Behind these legal-political demands stood the sociologically motivated belief in the evolutionary potential of universal law, in the capacity of the medium of law to function as a valuable social technique of establishing order in international relations. Their writings on international law were thus simultaneously part of the scholarly project of the Pure Theory, and of the legal-political project. The duality of the goals is maintained externally through the fairly consistently practiced formal separation between "pure" juristic works and those writings and arguments with a political–sociological or *de lege ferenda* orientation. The inner connection between the legal-doctrinal writings

[10] Kelsen, *The Law of the United Nations*, 27–53. This is especially apparent if one compares Kelsen with Hersch Lauterpacht's contemporaneous, progressive works in the 1950s about the status of human rights protection under the United Nations Charter: *International Law and Human Rights*, 145–165. With an analysis of the proposed post-war foundations of the doctrine of human rights, Riedel, *Theorie der Menschenrechtsstandards*, and "Menschenrechte der Dritten Dimension" in *Europäische Grundrechtezeitschrift*, 16 (1989), 9–21.

[11] In the preface to the commentary, Kelsen himself conceded on this point: "It stands to reason that in dealing with legal questions the elimination of political questions is always relative, never absolute." Still, he clung to his own claim: "In a merely juristic inquiry the political ends of the law-maker, in so far as they are ascertainable in an objective way, are taken for granted, and, hence, not subjected to criticism, except to the degree that it may properly be restricted to a law as a means to these ends." Quoted from: Kelsen, *The Law of the United Nations*, XIII.

and the cosmopolitan project lay in the critique of those doctrinal elements that went against their own political concept.[12]

The starting point in Kelsen's thinking was the fundamental principles – which had already influenced his doctoral dissertation on Dante Alighieri – about the unity of cognition, logical coherence, and the hierarchical and contradiction-free system. These principles were epistemologically underpinned by a stringent conception of methodological dualism and later by the transcendental argument, both of which could be linked to neo-Kantian thinking. With the help of a novel set of methodological tools, Kelsen subjected the pillars of the traditional constructions of international law by German writers, which harked back to the end of the nineteenth century, to a fundamental critique. Especially the developed "identity thesis" and the "doctrine of fictions" allowed for provocative attacks on the traditional understanding of the sovereign will of the state, on the theory of auto-limitation, and on the dualistic separation of international law and national law.

On the basis of the critical questioning of the traditional theoretical edifice, Kelsen, Kunz, and Verdross developed their own concept of international law at the beginning of the 1920s. In contrast to Triepel, their own "objective" construction proceeded from a unitary view of the law. According to the monistic perspective, international law and national law were parts of a unitary legal system. Moreover, this understanding formed the basis of the demonstration that international law, contrary to the lamentations of the deniers and doubters, could be conceived as a law endowed with the power of coercion. To that extent, it could be subsumed along with state law into a unitary conception of the law. International law and state law were thus in the end part of a uniform system of norms endowed with binding force. In the overall legal system thus created, international law was then elevated above national law through the thesis of its primacy. This "objective" construction of international law reflected the confidence that Kelsen and his students had in the potential power of the medium of international law. Following the view of Kelsen and Kunz, the medium of the law conceived as unitary was to be put at the disposal of international politics – drained of value judgments and demystified – as an effective medium for erecting a cosmopolitan order.

[12] That could also be one of the reasons why Kelsen never published his comprehensive critique of Georges Scelle's conception of international law. For in spite of divergent methodological premises, Scelle was in the end working towards the realization of a comparable cosmopolitan project: Chapter 4 B II.

The unitary theoretical construction of national law and international legal norms under the primacy of international law did not presuppose an organizational unity of the law in the sense of a politically realized world state. Instead, it was grounded first of all merely in what Kelsen called the "cognitive unity" of all law. From the perspective of the legal science, the "universal law" conceived by this novel method and objective construction encompassed all legal norms as part of a hierarchically structured system of law. Within this framework, the norms of international and national law were based on a unitary theoretical understanding of the law. This understanding reduced the law to its "pure" form, which – from a legal-scientific perspective – could be filled with content of any kind. Freed from preconceived ethical and political limitations, international law and national law could be deployed as a potentially unlimited medium of societal change and development. Kelsen's use of the term "universal community of world law" [*universale Weltrechtsgemeinschaft*] can thus be understood in a dual sense: "Universal" stands both for the unity of international law and national law in the sense of a global systemic validity of law, and secondly for the substantively unlimited nature of the medium of law as a technique of social change that could be used in every conceivable way.

Behind the conception of a universal law stood the barely concealed desire for a thoroughly juridified cosmopolitan order to be erected by international politics. It included international organizations, individuals as subjects of international law, a global organization with a monopoly of force, and a compulsory international jurisdiction to secure the complete rule of law in international relations. Part II of the present study has shown how Kelsen, in an effort to promote his politico-legal goals, turned to the fields of the doctrine of international law, which were especially critical for his cosmopolitan project. With his doctrine of state confederations (international organizations), Kelsen construed the legal system as a dynamic integration order, in which the medium of the law was available without restrictions to realize regional and universal integration projects. For that very purpose, Kelsen also reinterpreted the sources of international law, especially international treaty law, into a post-sovereign form of law-making by the universal legal community. As a third element, Kelsen sought to provide a theoretical foundation to the hoped-for introduction of compulsory international jurisdiction by articulating his own evolutionary theory of law.

As I have shown in detail, this cosmopolitan project arose in the three selected areas of international law theory primarily through the destruction of traditional doctrinal distinctions. Kelsen made deliberate and targeted use of the destructive potential of his "critical" methodology. In that sense, the application of the outwardly neutral means of a strictly logical critique of traditional doctrine and methodology served his own political ideas. In his theory of state confederations, Kelsen criticized the complex doctrinal distinction between confederation and federal state and dissolved it into a theory of "fluid transitions" between the various forms of association. In his theory of legal sources, he attacked the axiom of freedom that underlay the doctrine of treaty law and its repercussions for the central doctrinal elements of international treaty law. On the issue of international adjudication, as well, Kelsen sought to crack open the limitations on the function of international courts established by the traditional doctrine of international law.

To be sure, the epistemological grounding of the "critical method" and of Kelsen's conceptual universe remained in many ways fragmentary, sometimes incoherent and was refuted early on. However, the critical potential of the new method, which was based not least on the often merciless precision and unadorned elegance of Kelsen`s way of expression, was able to identify and uncover the particular political and ideological core within the central concepts of international jurisprudence. In the problem areas I have examined, which were especially critical to his cosmopolitan project, Kelsen endeavoured in this way to remove "doctrinal" barriers. The creative leeway that was gained beyond traditional doctrinal constructions was to be placed at the disposal of international politics, that is, statesmen and judges, to advance the development of the cosmopolitan world order. To that extent, the destructive thrust of the abstract analyses contributed to his own cosmopolitan project. Destruction and construction can be distinguished only on the surface in Kelsen's theory of international law.

Kelsen's belief in universal law manifested itself in the hope for social progress through "objective" scientific insight, on the one hand, and in the faith in the peace-creating function of the institutionalized medium of the law in international relations, on the other. These motivations gave rise to the specific orientation of the international law theories of Hans Kelsen and his most important students.

The cosmopolitan project of the interwar period – which united these authors – has remained, in its kaleidoscopic variety, the leitmotif of modern international legal scholarship. With its value-relativistic conception of international law, aimed at the characteristics of an autonomous international legal validity with quasi-limitless functionality, Kelsen's project was noticeably different, though, from other universalistic conceptions, chiefly those based on moralistic or sociological conceptions of the law. For Kelsen, the unlimited faith in the de-substantiated and systemic conception of law presupposed a post-metaphysical and non-political handling of positivized law by legal scholarship. As a result there arose a reductionist understanding of international legal scholarship, which was supposed to disempower the jurist in favor of the "authentic interpreters," that is, the politicians and judges.

The sought-after balance between the "objective" cognition of the medium of law and the political goal of a thoroughly juridified universal order endowed the international law theories of the Vienna School with their special internal structure. It led Kelsen, the founder of this current in international law theory, to uncover the central paradoxes and ideological premises of the international law discourse of his time. The emergence of a highly political agenda from the deconstructed dogmas does not reduce the value of his insights in these writings.

POSTSCRIPT – ON KELSENIAN FORMALISM IN INTERNATIONAL LAW* (2010)

Interest in the history of the discipline of international law, in general, and in Hans Kelsen, in particular, has continued to grow in the years since the original publication of this study.[1] Various reasons seem at play here: the study of the first high phase of the modern discipline of international law in the late nineteenth and early twentieth centuries may help to reassure a discipline that finds itself under growing pressure

* The bulk of this new postscript is based on a lecture given at the Lauterpacht Centre for International Law at the University of Cambridge on October 24, 2008 during my stay as a visiting fellow at the Centre. I am grateful to the Director, Professor Crawford, and his colleagues at the Centre for providing me with this opportunity and to the participants in the lecture for helpful and inspiring comments and discussions.

[1] With a chapter on Kelsen Martti Koskenniemi's book on the history of European international law: M. Koskenniemi, *The Gentle Civilizer of Nations. The Rise and Fall of European International Law 1870–1960* (Cambridge University Press, 2001); for a recent discussion of Kelsen's legal theory see A. Somek, "Kelsen lives," *EJIL*, 18 (2007), 409–451; in the context of the Max Planck research project on the history of German international law in the twentieth century headed by Michael Stolleis, a number of monographs have recently been published in German: K. Hassel, *Kriegsverbrechen vor Gericht. Die Kriegsverbrecherprozesse vor Militärgerichten in der britischen Besatzungszone unter dem Royal Warrant vom 18. Juni 1945 (1945–1949)* (Baden-Baden: Nomos, 2009); F. Degenhardt, *Zwischen Machtstaat und Völkerbund. Erich Kaufmann (1880–1972)* (Baden-Baden: Nomos, 2008); A. Wüst, *Das völkerrechtliche Werk von Georges Scelle im Frankreich der Zwischenkriegszeit* (Baden-Baden: Nomos, 2007); H. Wiggenhorn, *Verliererjustiz. Die Leipziger Kriegsverbrecherprocesse nach dem Ersten Weltkrieg* (Baden-Baden: Nomos, 2005); B. Roscher, *Der Briand–Kellogg-Pakt von 1928. Der "Verzicht auf den Krieg als Mittel nationaler Politik" im völkerrechtlichen Denken der Zwischenkriegszeit* (Baden-Baden: Nomos, 2004); S. Steinle, *Völkerrecht und Machtpolitik. Georg Schwarzenberger (1908–1991)* (Baden-Baden: Nomos, 2002); P.K. Steck, *Zwischen Volk und Staat. Das Völkerrechtssubjekt in der deutschen Völkerrechtslehre (1933–1941)* (Baden-Baden: Nomos, 2003); F. Herrmann, *Das Standardwerk. Franz von Liszt und das Völkerrecht* (Baden-Baden: Nomos, 2001); reflecting on various approaches: A. Kemmerer, "The Turning Aside. On International Law and its History" in R.A. Miller and R.M. Bratspies (eds.), *Progress in International Law* (Leiden: Martinus Nijhoff, 2008), 71–94.

to justify its existence. What, after all, can international lawyers with their own epistemological traditions and sensibilities contribute to the conversation about global law that political scientists, economists, and sociologists cannot do equally as well or better? And when the debate revolves around the foundations of the discipline, Kelsen's name keeps cropping up and his project seems to assume new contextual relevance – after all, the awareness of a distinct legal methodology is at the heart of the Pure Theory of Law.

Or did the interest in the theoretical roots of the discipline perhaps grow out of the fact that we find ourselves since the beginning of the new millennium in a situation of political upheaval, crisis, and uncertainty, the resolution of which is still unclear when it comes to the future shape of international law? The cosmopolitan project of juridifying and institutionalizing international relations and its concrete emanations has been discussed among legal scholars with renewed – and not uncritical – vigor since the beginning of the new millennium.[2] Despite the proliferation of new institutions, Wolfgang Friedmann's 1964 vision of an "international law of co-operation," which was supposed to rescue mankind from "ruinous and destructive competition and exploitation of the resources of the earth short of war,"[3] has not come true for the majority of the world's inhabitants.

Another reason could be the potential of Kelsenian formalism as a critique of ideology during times of moralized interventionism after the paradigmatic 1999 NATO intervention in Kosovo. Moreover, the attitude of some international lawyers, "right or wrong – my country," which Kelsen and his School vigorously attacked in the interwar period, has also proved quite long-lived in certain parts of the discipline, especially as it relates to the prohibition on the use of force and the treatment of detainees in and after armed conflict.

This postscript to the English edition of *Believing in Universal Law* offers me an opportunity not only to respond to critiques expressed in reviews of the original edition, but also to summarize anew some of the central theses of the book in light of recent developments. What characterizes Kelsenian faith in universal law, what are the limitations of

[2] See J. Habermas, *Der gespaltene Westen. Kleine politische Schriften X* (Frankfurt am Main: Suhrkamp, 2004); on a change of perception regarding international organizations: J. Klabbers, "The Changing Image of International Organizations" in J.-M. Coicaud and V. Heiskanen (eds.), *The Legitimacy of International Organizations* (Tokyo: UN University Press, 2001), 221–255.

[3] W. G. Friedmann, *The Changing Structure of International Law* (London: Stevens, 1964), 94.

Kelsenian formalism within international law, and what makes it nonetheless so valuable to modern-day international jurisprudence? I will answer these questions in two steps: first, the structures and limitations of Kelsenian formalism in international law as worked out in the book will be highlighted once more. Second, some central assumptions of his writings on international law, which were contextually situated within the study, will be examined in the mirror of selected contemporary debates. As the concluding summary will spell out, I wish to capture the enduring relevance of Kelsen's ideas to modern-day international jurisprudence in the term "reflexive formalism" – not as a jurisprudential method or theory in its own right but as a scholarly sensibility for the distinctiveness of international law as a unique social medium.

A The structure and limits of Kelsenian formalism in international law

The central project of the Pure Theory of Law was the creation of an "objective" legal scholarship, the quest for the epistemological standpoint outside of the politicized clashes of interests, beyond the instrumentalization and submissive harnessing of legal science for political ends. In 1928, Kelsen described the state of jurisprudence this way:

> The discipline becomes a mere ideology of politics. The fact that scholars can be found who muster the dubious courage to make a virtue of this unfortunate situation, who, renouncing the professional ethics [*Berufsethik*] of all science, give up the ideal of an objective understanding free from all subjective interests, and defend the right of methodological syncretism by proclaiming the indissoluble bond between law and politics, is one of the characteristic signs of our times. In a society convulsed by world war and world revolution, it is more important than ever to the contending groups and classes to produce usable ideologies that allow those still in power to effectively defend their interests. That which accords with their subjective interest seeks to be presented as what is objectively right. And so the science of the state and the law must serve that purpose. It provides the "objectivity" that no politics is able to generate on its own.[4]

The "liberation" from political "bondage" postulated in the Pure Theory of Law with such Enlightenment pathos is a struggle for the inherent autonomy of legal scholarship. At the same time, Kelsen pens his main work, the monograph *The Problem of Sovereignty and the*

[4] Kelsen, "Juristischer Formalismus."

Theory of International Law, during the First World War, a historical phase in which the pacifist–liberal currents in Europe and the United States regarded the inadequate development of the international legal system as the chief reason behind the outbreak of the war. Kelsen shared this view. He saw in a reform of the international legal system the key to a more peaceful world, but with this basic cosmopolitan conviction he was not in the majority in German public law scholarship in the period between the wars.

Kelsen's self-conception as it related to international law was thus fed from two basic beliefs that were not hard to find within the liberal, German-speaking bourgeoisie in Central Europe: first, the belief in the specific rationality and pacifying force of the law in international relations; second, the belief in social progress through scientific, that is, "objective" understanding. Kelsen saw a link between an "objective," i.e. non-political, international legal scholarship and the potential of law as an autonomous medium within international relations.[5] The Pure Theory of Law regarded the supposedly ideologized jurisprudence of international law as an obstacle to the further development of the international legal system. Kelsen shared this mindset with his closest student of international law, Joseph L. Kunz, and with Hersch Lauterpacht, who had studied with Kelsen in Vienna before emigrating to the United Kingdom.[6]

The belief in progress through "objective" scientific understanding on the one hand, and in the autonomous medium of the law on the other, is a cultural phenomenon of a vanished epoch of European jurisprudence in the late nineteenth and early twentieth centuries. Emerging out of the gradual demise of the Habsburg Empire, it found its most radical champion in Kelsen. In his short autobiography Kelsen himself had depicted the Pure Theory of Law as a being decisively coined by the pre-First World War Austrian context.[7] After all, it had been the force of the law that had been perceived as holding together the multi-ethnic empire, bound to replace the missing "homogeneous" society and common cultural foundations (see Chapter 2).

[5] For all the passion with which Kelsen pursued the project of objectivization, he himself seemed to question whether it could in fact be fully realized: "If there is any point where one can take a stance outside the realm of power, it is science." Quoted from: Kelsen, "Juristischer Formalismus und Reine Rechtslehre," 9.

[6] On the relationship between Lauterpacht and Kelsen see Koskenniemi, "Lauterpacht: The Victorian Tradition in International Law," 218–225; Carty, "The Continuing Influence of Kelsen," 352–354.

[7] H. Kelsen, *Werke*, ed. Matthias Jestaedt (Tübingen: Mohr-Siebeck, 2007).

In what follows, I would like to retrace once more my assessment of Kelsen's attempt to establish an objective "science" of international law and the limits to the objectification project that I have spelled out in the study. This aspect of the book, which sees Kelsen as a political individual and reconstructs a close link between his own cosmopolitan project and the Pure Theory of Law, was the main critical point voiced in some of the reviews.

I *Formalism as a quest for objectivity*

According to Kelsen, the quest for the epistemological Archimedean point outside of politicization and subjectivity could succeed only through the formalization of jurisprudential concepts. Kelsen maintained that objectivity and a scientific nature as the overarching goals of jurisprudence presupposed a formal method that was to be given an epistemological grounding in the Pure Theory of Law. In this context, he drew a categorical distinction between a formalistic legal practice and a formal theory of the law as a science. The sweeping charge of "formalism" that contemporaries levied against the Pure Theory of Law, in his view unjustly equated it with a formalistic application of norms by the courts. Kelsen argued that the Pure Theory of Law could not be criticized as a variant of the formalistic "*Begriffsjurisprudenz*" [conceptual jurisprudence] that had been attacked since the late nineteenth century, especially by the German Free Law movement – that was a charge he rejected.[8] The Pure Theory of Law regarded the application of the law as a process that, while prestructured, could not, in the final analysis, be completely grasped jurisprudentially in its creative dimension. For example, Kelsen regarded the decision of a court not as a formalistic and immediate application of the law, but as the creative generation of an individual norm.[9] And that was the reason why, according to Kelsen, the Pure Theory of Law could not be associated with a formalistic legal practice.[10]

By contrast, Kelsen explicitly embraced formalism when it came to the scholarly cognition of the law, which he sought to separate sharply from the creation and application of the law. This separation of cognition and will, of "pure" theory and "political" practice, was intended to secure the objectivity of jurisprudence as a formal science. The task of the legal

[8] Kelsen, "Juristischer Formalismus," 9. [9] See below 13.
[10] Kelsen, "Juristischer Formalismus," 6–7.

scientist was to establish a formal system of concepts.[11] The formality of this conceptual apparatus is simultaneously evidence of its distance from politics and proof of its scientific nature:

> That this system of concepts must have a relatively formal character is self-evident to anyone to whom the principles of logic and method theory are not entirely alien. For it is through the concepts of a general doctrine of law that the immense wealth of positive legal material is to be epistemologically mastered. Like every form of cognition, legal cognition, too, must formalize its subject matter. For precisely in this formalism lies what is held up as a virtue against the "formalism" denounced as a vice: its objectivity.[12]

Expelling the political could succeed only in a conceptual world that is subject to its own objectifiable laws. The latter entailed the basic principles of the unity of cognition, logical coherence, and a systematic interconnection free of contradictions. The heightened level of abstraction was to make possible an "objective" grasp of the "law" that was comparable to the natural sciences. The desire to associate jurisprudence with the natural sciences, which were seen as particularly progressive, can be observed as a phenomenon within the German legal discipline as early as the nineteenth century.[13]

To achieve this end, the newly acquired conceptual apparatus had to demonstrate a certain independence from the current content of the historically conditioned positive law. Kelsen referred to these concepts, which "proved themselves in every legal system" as *Rechtsformbegriffe*.[14] For Kelsen, the law, because it engaged in normative appeals, belonged – like theology or ethics – to the realm of "Ought," whereas "nature," for example, as an empirically verifiable act, belonged to the realm of "Is." The task of the disciplines of science, understood as specific doctrines of normative Ought, on the one hand, and of empirical Is, on the other, was to systematically understand the respective laws governing Ought and Is.[15] The *Rechtsformbegriffe* were for Kelsen concepts that were able to capture the specific Ought structure of the law. With respect to the

[11] Kelsen has this to say about this distinction: "Cognition of the law cannot be anything other than 'conceptual jurisprudence' [*Begriffsjurisprudenz*]. How could one understand without concepts? Of course, the generation of the law is something else. It is not aimed at concepts; it must create legal norms, it is the function of the will, not cognition; it must create the material in the first place which the science of the law strives to understand." Quoted from: Kelsen, "Juristischer Formalismus," 6.

[12] Ibid., 6–7. [13] On this see Chapter 1.

[14] Kelsen, "Juristischer Formalismus," 6. [15] Kelsen, *Hauptprobleme*, VI.

"classical phase" of the Pure Theory of Law, we must therefore proceed on the assumption that the *Rechtsformbegriffe*, as central concepts of jurisprudence, are derived as a pure, transcendental category from the so-called "normative imputation" [*normative Zurechnung*], that is, from the Ought that is specific to the law.[16] The *Rechtsformbegriffe*, which Kelsen at times also referred to as *Rechtsvorraussetzungsbegriffe* [a priori legal concepts], share in the "transcendental" status and are thus classified as the conditions of correct legal cognition that precede any experience. In this way, they must be seen as a conceptual world that is totally separate from the respective content of positive law.[17] Consequently, the concept of sovereignty, for example, becomes, as a *Rechtsformbegriff*, a condition for recognizing a legal system as a uniform, hierarchically structured system of norms derived from a supreme layer of norms. The loaded concept "sovereignty" thus is reduced to being the scholarly attribute of the highest level of norms in a given legal order.

Kelsen provided ex-post facto theoretical support to his own "science" of legal cognition by introducing "transcendental legal categories." The laws of the world of *Rechtsformbegriffe* are the principles of the unity of cognition, hierarchy, strict rationality, and logic. These basic structures of Kelsenian thinking, which could already be demonstrated in his doctoral dissertation on Dante Alighieri in 1905,[18] had been methodologically secured by the transcendental argument. The "objective" science postulated by Kelsen, which was to be achieved through the constructive uncoupling of the abstract concepts from the current content of the norms, already offered contemporary critics a two-fold point of attack under the slogan of a "radical-logicistic metaphysics."[19] Because of their distance from current law, the concepts generated by Kelsen's approach seemed to have little usefulness, not only for those who applied

[16] Thus Kelsen, explicitly with respect to the new "transcendental" concept of the state, which he wanted to put in place of the "metaphysical" idea of the state: Kelsen, *Hauptprobleme*, V.

[17] Kelsen, *Reine Rechtslehre* (1934), 3–5; *Staatsbegriff*, 200. [18] On this see Chapter 3, AI.

[19] Contemporary examples of this critique: Kaufmann, *Gesammelte Schriften*, 198; Sander, *Rechtsdogmatik*, 30; Schwind, *Grundlagen und Grundfragen des Rechts*, 26, 29; and Kelsen's response, *Rechtsgeschichte*, 11. Kelsen distanced himself from logical approaches in norm theory in his later work; on this see Pawlik, *Die Reine Rechtslehre und die Rechtstheorie H. L. A. Harts*, 146; Weinberger, *Normentheorie als Grundlage der Jurisprudenz und Ethik*, 94; Walter, "Das Problem des Verhältnisses von Recht und Logik," 299 *et seq*.

the law, but also from the perspective of many legal scholars.[20] Moreover, as Erich Kaufmann and Wilhelm Jöckel noted early on, they were not truly "pure" in the sense of the Kantian categories. Both authors had pointed out that Kelsen's *Rechtsformbegriffe* were not transcendental legal concepts in the sense of pure legal categories, but merely highly abstracted "general empirical concepts" of jurisprudence, which were by no means situated before any kind of experience.[21] However, Kelsen's conceptual world had abstracted itself more radically from the concrete legal experience on which it was based than was the case with the traditional concepts of a general doctrine of state law and international law. As a result, these concepts could be arranged into a system aimed at coherence, unity, hierarchy, and logic.

II International legal scholarship as a transcendental system of formal concepts

What then, was this system of formal concepts that was supposed to render the science of international law immune to politics? The crux of the Kelsenian understanding of international law was the elimination of the prevailing notion of the personified state, understood as a de facto unit of power. From the perspective of a "pure" jurisprudence, the state is for Kelsen identical with the state's legal system. This so-called "identity thesis" is based on two intertwined lines of argumentation. First, there is the postulate of methodological dualism described above, according to which jurisprudential cognition could extend only to Ought systems and not to causal (Is) structures;[22] second, there is Kelsen's "theory of the juristic fiction." Drawing on Vaihinger's *The Philosophy of 'As If'*, Kelsen recognized in the juristic use of the concept of the "state person capable of will" [*willensfähige Staatsperson*] a doubling or "hypostatization."[23] Kelsen argued that in the misguided juristic thinking, the proper function of the legal person as the unity-creating point of attribution of norms was turned into a living, human-like figure, a state organism.

[20] Alfred Verdross, an early student of Kelsen's, who then went his own way from the beginning of the 1930s at the latest, therefore tried time and again to immunize himself against this kind of criticism and to present his central teachings as congruent with the "international law of experience"; see Verdross, *Die Verfassung der Völkerrechtsgemeinschaft*, V–VI; on Verdross's final theoretical break with the Pure Theory of Law see chapter 5.

[21] Kaufmann, *Gesammelte Schriften*, 193; Jöckel, *Hans Kelsens rechtstheoretische Methode*, 162.

[22] Kelsen, *Hauptprobleme*, XVI.

[23] Kelsen, *Problem der Souveränität*, 18.

This critical assumption was a rupture with the late nineteenth-century German public law doctrine, which, represented by Georg Jellinek, had always maintained the voluntaristic foundation of international law and had been in the process, since the end of the nineteenth century, of elaborating this perspective through sociological theories.[24] With the identity thesis, international law was supposed to be disconnected from the notion of the state as a "person" capable of will. To all previous constructs of the state, which, often proceeding from Hobbes's ambiguous notion of the state, regarded the latter as a mythical creature, a mortal god, or a rationalistic mechanism, a machine or apparatus, Kelsen counterposed a radical-normativistic understanding of the state.

Building on this concept of the state, international law could now be construed as part of an all-encompassing, unitary legal system. International law and state law were parts of a single legal system. Kelsen resorted to the notion of "delegation" as a unity-creating structural principle.[25] According to the norm-logical delegation scheme introduced in his book *The Problem of Sovereignty and the Theory of International Law*, every norm could be traced back to a supraordinated norm that created it. This supraordinated norm constituted the basis for the validity of the delegated norm and regulated the formal requirements for the creation of the subordinate norm.[26] By incorporating Adolf Merkl's so-called "doctrine of the hierarchical structure" [*Stufenbaulehre*], Kelsen was thus able to arrange the legal norm into a unitary context of creation and validity.[27] The Basic Norm completed the legal system as the final, "hypothetically presupposed" source. For Kelsen, international law and state law were thus a single system that could be traced back to a single basic norm.[28] This concept of the basic norm not only stopped the unavoidable *regressus ad infinitum* of any

24 C. Schönberger, "Introductory Note" in H. Kelsen, *Werke*, ed. M. Jestaedt (Tübingen: Mohr-Siebeck, 2008), vol. 2, 39.

25 Hart described the unity of the norms established via delegation as the "weaker version" of the unity argument in Kelsen. The "stronger version" was the concept of unity epistemologically presupposed; see H. L. A. Hart (ed.), *Essays in Jurisprudence and Philosophy* (Oxford: Clarendon Press, 1983), 309 *et seq.*

26 H. Kelsen, *Reine Rechtslehre* (1960), 228.

27 A. Merkl, "Prolegomena einer Theorie des rechtlichen Stufenbaus," 1339; on the doctrine of the hierarchical structure see Behrend, *Untersuchungen zur Stufenbaulehre Adolf Merkls und Hans Kelsens.*

28 We are here thus also dealing with the function of the basic norm as the highest authorization to create law or delegate other norms.

hierarchical structure, but also dissolved the question about the final ground of the validity of the law into epistemology. Recourse to any of the other assumed foundations of international law that were common at the time was thus blocked. The binding power of international law could no longer be traced back to the self-obligating will of the state, the common will of the states, their shared interests, or divine law.[29]

This raised the question of how international law and state law were related within the monistic legal system. According to Kelsen, international law and state law had to be placed into a hierarchical context of delegation. That end was served by the primacy thesis, which, within the monistic legal system, situated international law above state law. By means of the principle of effectiveness rule, international law determined the geographic and temporal sphere of validity of state legal systems. In addition, international law also defined the material sphere of validity for state legal systems. Because international law was able to regulate every conceivable form of human conduct through the instrument of the treaty, it could potentially be used for all circumstances of life that had previously been regulated solely by state legal systems.[30] From this perspective, international law determines not only the creation and end of the state legal order, but also the territorial and material realm in which it is valid. With respect to the temporal, territorial, and material validity of its norms, a given state legal system was merely a "partial system" subordinated to international law. When creating new international law, states should be seen as organs of the supraordinated international legal community, which were authorized by customary international law to engage in such activities.[31] Within this constructive re-interpretation of existing recognized rules of customary law, the notion of sovereignty was reduced to its norm-logical core, that is, to the question of determining the "highest normative level" in the unitary legal system. According to the doctrine of the primacy of international law, that level was the international legal system, which had the attribute of sovereignty. Very much in the spirit of the interwar movement to modernize international law, the monumental "dogma" of the sovereignty of the individual state was emphatically knocked off its pedestal by Kelsen and especially by his students. Kelsen's transcendental system of

[29] For a historical summary of various approaches to theoretical justification in the nineteenth century see Chapter 1.

[30] Kelsen, *Reine Rechtslehre* (1934), 147–149; *Problems of Legal Theory*, 120–121.

[31] Kelsen, *Reine Rechtslehre* (1934), 152; *Problems of Legal Theory*, 122.

Rechtsformbegriffe created an international law without substantive state sovereignty; its place was taken by a legal cosmos which, hierarchical and structured through delegation, elevated international law philosophically above the state. As I try to show in the book, Kelsen, in his construction of this legal universe, relies on Christian Wolff's concept *civitas maxima* (through Kaltenborn) and not on Kant's essay on eternal peace, because Kant still retains a strong notion of substantial state sovereignty.

A closer look reveals that Kelsen's central concern, to free jurisprudence from the stranglehold of the political, was achieved through a theoretical move that remained unavoidably unstable: Kelsen postulated a strict separation between scientific, "objective" legal cognition, on the one hand, and the political creation and application of the law, on the other. This rigorous separation fails to recognize that there is, sociologically, a discursive connection between theorists and practitioners, a connection that is in fact institutionalized through universities. We are dealing here with a reciprocal stimulation and influence, which was in fact not unwelcome to Kelsen with an eye toward the political impact of the Pure Theory of Law. The law, as later communicative approaches to legal theory have brought out more clearly, is a communicative context that unites theorists and practitioners, with eminently political consequences.[32]

III The limits of objectivity

Kelsen's Neo-Kantian formalization of jurisprudence does not contain its own doctrine of interpretation. For Kelsen, the process of the interpretation of a norm by the legal practitioner and the legal theorist defied complete objectification. When it comes to the realm of the application of the law, the Pure Theory of Law dispensed entirely with its own substantive theory of interpretation. Instead, such a theory is completely absorbed into the doctrine of the hierarchical structure of the legal system [*Stufenbaulehre*]. According to the "dynamic" variant of this theory, norm-application was considered a dynamic intellectual process moving from a higher to a lower norm in the hierarchical structure of the legal system. Applying a norm to a specific case creates an individualized lower norm through the reference to the text of a "higher" norm. Kelsen

[32] On the discursive connection between legal practice and legal theory see P. Bourdieu, "The Force of Law: Toward a Sociology of the Legal Field," *Hastings Law Journal*, 38 (1987), 805–853.

describes this "intellectual activity" of legally authorized courts and public officials as the act of "authentic" interpretation.[33] In this process, the higher norm only to a limited extent predetermined the content of the new lower norm. Norm-application by authorized organs, such as courts or public officials, thus involved an act of interpretation. The input by the higher level of norm-production created merely the semantic "framework" that had to be respected by the lower norm. This act of interpretation by law-applying organs, which chose one of the possible readings within the outer semantic limits, was conceptualized as a creative act, as individualized legislation. As a theoretical consequence of this assumption, Kelsen erases the conceptual difference between adjudication and legislation.[34] Moreover, for Kelsen there was no "scientific" method by which only one of the several readings of a norm could be identified as the "correct" one. There was no "objectively correct" interpretation of norms.[35] With interpretation came an unavoidable intrusion of subjectivity, politics, values, and idiosyncratic preferences. While exposing the dilemma of interpretation, Kelsen stopped short of contributing to its methodological containment. Instead, he completely removed methodological questions regarding the act of interpretation from the Pure Theory's realm of cognition.[36]

The lack of compulsory jurisdiction in most areas of international law, however, renders this problem particularly acute in international law. The Pure Theory provides no guidance to practitioners on how to interpret the law. The reappearance of the "political" in the application of the law that Kelsen accepted as unavoidable is another way of describing the central conundrum of the law, which Jacques Derrida described as the "*Heimsuchung durch das Unentscheidbare*" and Niklas Luhmann as the "*Entscheidung des Unentscheidbaren*."[37] But how does the law fulfil its function of creating order if its application remains, in the final

[33] Kelsen, *Reine Rechtslehre* (1934), 90; *Problems of Legal Theory*, 77.

[34] Through his doctrine of the dynamic application of the law, Kelsen comes closer to the communicative paradigm of later legal theories, such as those of J. Habermas, P. Bourdieu, and N. Luhmann, than all other contemporary legal theories, though he artificially excludes the scientific examination of the interpretation of the law because of his inflated claim of objectivity.

[35] Kelsen, *Reine Rechtslehre* (1934), 96; *Problems of Legal Theory*, 81; this has important repercussions for the notion of democratic legitimacy; see for international adjudication A. von Bogdandy and I. Venzke, *In Nome di Chi? Giurisdizione Internazionale e Teoria del Discorso* (Turin: Trauben, 2010).

[36] On this and the critique see Chapter 6.

[37] Derrida, *Gesetzeskraft*, 49; Luhmann, *Das Recht der Gesellschaft*, 317.

analysis, political? Kelsen trusted in the practice of the courts, even as he ascertained an element of irrationality in the application to any given case. As a judge of the Austrian constitutional court, Kelsen had practical insight into the political dimension of constitutional adjudication, but it did not cause him to lose his confidence in a specific kind of judicial rationality. How else could one explain his lifelong advocacy of compulsory adjudication in constitutional and international law? Despite its political dimension, individual law-creation by the judge was, for Kelsen, denatured politics because it was to some extent constrained by the cognitive process of the concretization of norms. In the language of systems theory, the decision of the court is, in spite of its political dimension, still a communication internal to the (legal) system. With a common-law background Dworkin and Raz, for instance, have tried to demonstrate that there are technical (coherence)[38] and institutional limitations[39] to the court's interpretation of the law, adherence to which – notwithstanding the unquestioned existence of political maneuvering room – can be seen as an inherent demand of the system. Despite Kelsen's illuminating theoretical equation of adjudication and legislation, it remains problematic within this context that the Pure Theory of Law, as a theory of law, promotes the civilizational function of a specific judicial rationality without being able to explain it.

The issue of interpretation arises, however, not only in the area of the application of the law, but also on the level of international legal scholarship. To the question of from which angle the legal scholar should interpret the monist legal system created by Kelsen, the latter has a particular answer, one that grants an unexpected amount of room to the "political" with regard to the structure of the legal system. According to Kelsen, the make-up of the hierarchically structured legal system depends fundamentally on a basic interpretational decision that is prior to legal "science," meaning it is "political" in Kelsen's understanding. The question here is whether the monistic legal cosmos is constructed on the foundation of the primacy of national law or the primacy of international law. If state law is given primacy, it forms the highest

[38] R. Dworkin, *Law's Empire* (London: Fontana Press, 1986).

[39] J. Raz, *The Authority of the Law: Essays on Law and Morality* (Oxford: Clarendon Press, 1979), ch. 10; on various attempts to solve the application problem in the common-law tradition: D. Kennedy, *A Critique of Adjudication, fin de siècle* (Cambridge, MA: Harvard University Press, 1997), 26–39.

level of norms, and international law is conceived as a subordinated system of norms derived from the respective national constitution. By contrast, if international law is given primacy, the state legal systems are subordinated sub-systems of international law and are coordinated by it. For Kelsen, the primacy question is based on a fundamental political decision that cannot be answered by legal "science."[40] Looking at international law, the structure of the created transcendental world of scientific legal cognition itself depends, according to Kelsen, on a fundamental "political" value-decision by the jurist.

Kelsen was thus trying to describe the political dimension of every form of international legal scholarship – i.e., the question whether a norm is interpreted from the standpoint of a supraordinated system of international law, or from the perspective of the sovereign individual state to which any binding norm that binds it must be traced back – by way of the so-called "choice hypothesis." If one considers that the doctrine of the primacy of state law entails, according to Kelsen, a denial of international law as an autonomous legal system, it becomes clear that Kelsen's construct of international law is subject to the proviso of a fundamental political decision. The reason why Kunz and Verdross openly dissented from the choice hypothesis was that central aspects of their shared cosmopolitan project – such as direct rights and obligations of the individual under international law and the post-sovereign empowerment of international organizations – depended on how this choice was made.

However, Kelsen's formalized and deductive conceptual apparatus described above, that is, the claim to unity of cognition and hierarchical system-building, forced Kelsen to acknowledge that both primacy assumptions were inherently consistent. In a paradoxical way, Kelsen's formal understanding of legal scholarship, which sought to expel the political from the realm of legal cognition, generated in the choice hypothesis the far-reaching theoretical concession that legal cognition in international law at its basis was also subjective and political in character.[41] In order to rescue his claim to objectivity, Kelsen demanded the jurist's transparent decision whether the norms of international law

[40] Kelsen, *Rechtsgeschichte*, 317; on the so-called "choice hypothesis" and the controversy about it within Kelsen's "school" of international law see Chapter 3D.

[41] It would be 1989 before Martti Koskenniemi, following David Kennedy, was able to reformulate Kelsens's critique of the continuous and unreflected change between the two epistemological standpoints [*Wechsel des Erkenntnisstandpunktes*] in international law with the help of the linguistic distinction between "ascending" (primacy of national

should be interpreted on the basis of the primacy of state law or that of international law. To him, a "science" of international law was still possible, in spite of a fundamental political decision on the part of the jurist about the posited total construct. Scientific objectivity thus – in a more abstract sense – lay in making political preferences transparent and pursuing a strict deductive construction of the system on this basis.

IV Formalism as creative destruction: the cosmopolitan project

Kelsen's epistemological critique of the traditional conceptual apparatus of international law, spelled out in the book *The Problem of Sovereignty and the Theory of International Law*, was worked out during the First World War, which historians refer to as the "*Ur*"-catastrophe of the twentieth century. Contemporaries experienced the corpse-strewn battlefields and trenches filled with poison gas as a fundamental rupture of civilization. Especially the theory of the primacy of international law revealed Kelsen as an ardent internationalist, who saw in the creation of legally supported institutions by a new international law the only way to tame the murderous irrationality of European nationalism.

Kelsen's theory conceived of international law as "universal law." And it was not only in regard to the territorial sphere of validity that he regarded it as a universal medium. Kelsen accorded international law universality also in its subjects and in potential purposes of its regulation – Kelsen spoke of law as a "social technique."[42] Beyond the theoretical barriers erected by the traditional notions of sovereignty, international law was to hold regulatory competency that was potentially unlimited also in substantive terms. In his functional understanding, law was therefore "universal" in the two-fold sense of that adjective. Behind the conception of a universal law stood Kelsen's desire – openly articulated as early as 1920 – for a thoroughly juridified cosmopolitan order that was to be established by international politics. It included international organizations capable of taking action, individuals as subjects of international law, a world organization with a monopoly on the use of force, and compulsory international jurisdiction to secure the complete

law – apology) and "descending" (primacy of international law – utopia) arguments in international legal discourse: Koskenniemi, *From Apology to Utopia*; D. Kennedy, "Theses about International Law Discourse," *German Yearbook of International Law* (1980), 353–391; on Koskenniemi and Kelsen see J. v. Bernstorff, "Sisyphus was an International Lawyer. On Martti Koskenniemi's *From Apology to Utopia* and *The Place of Law in International Politics*," *German Law Journal* 7/12, (2006), 1015–1035.

42 Kelsen, *Problem der Souveränität*, 75 *et seq*.

rule of law in international affairs. These political projects unquestionably assumed the features of a world federation governed by public law, which Kelsen affirmed early on as morally desirable.[43]

As I have noted at various places in the book, inherent in Kelsen's theory of international law is a connection between the destructive critique of the traditional, "political" – i.e. unscientific – conceptual apparatus of international law, and this simultaneously highly political project, which was aimed at a fundamental revision of international relations. It was no accident that the approach to international law that was critical of jurisprudential methodology created room for a thorough juridification of international relations yet to be created by statesmen. A few reviews of the German edition of this book questioned or rejected this thesis.[44] At the same time, the assumption of an eminently political dimension within the Pure Theory of Law has in the meantime been advanced by other authors.[45] By way of clarification of my interpretation of the Kelsenian theory of international law, it should be noted that the point is not to retrospectively impute dishonest motives to Kelsen because of this link between the cosmopolitan project and the Pure Theory of Law. Rather, it is my contention that the tension-filled connection between "scientific" methodology and political project is crucial to an understanding of the Kelsenian theory of international law. At various places in his corpus of work, Kelsen himself spoke indirectly about the political dimension of the Pure Theory. He emphasized repeatedly that the expulsion of the politicized concepts of jurisprudence created new maneuvering room for the "authentic" interpreters, that is,

[43] See Chapter 3EI.

[44] Bardo Fassbender has criticized the link drawn between Kelsen's own political project and his UN Charter Commentary, B. Fassbender, "Die Friedens-Warte," *Journal of International Peace and Organization*, 78 (2003), 297–302; András Jakab more fundamentally denied the existence of any link between these two dimensions in Kelsen's works: A. Jakab, "Kelsen's doctrine of international law between epistemology and politics," *Austrian Review of International and European Law*, 9 (2006), 49–62.

[45] Martti Koskenniemi argues that the Pure Theory of Law was by no means politically "innocent." See Koskenniemi, *The Gentle Civilizer of Nations*; H. Brunkhorst, "Kritik am Dualismus des Internationalen Rechts" in R. Kreide and A. Niederberger (eds.), *Transnationale Verrechtlichung* (Frankfurt: Campus Verlag, 2008), 40–42; J. Klabbers – covering the middle ground – in his review of the German first publication of this work found it "of course far from implausible to presume a relation between the cosmopolitan and the purist": J. Klabbers, "Book Review of J. von Bernstorff, *Der Glaube an das universale Recht. Zur Völkerrechtstheorie Hans Kelsens und seiner Schüles*," *EJIL*, 14 (2003), 614; L. Vinx in his book speaks of an institutional "utopia of legality" pursued by the Pure Theory of Law: L. Vinx, *Hans Kelsen's Pure Theory of Law* (Oxford University Press, 2007), 215–216.

those who applied the law.[46] With this, the Pure Theory of Law, as a critical theory, aimed at making possible a reshaping of the prevailing political conditions. The scientific critique was to enhance the functionality of the medium of the law and its use for new purposes by political actors. The destruction of certain jurisprudential concepts in this sense was not meant to remain a purely "scientific" project. The call for the theoretical end to state sovereignty, for example, was to influence politicians and judges in the creation and application of international law and thereby exert a political effect, which Kelsen intended in just that way. Translated into Kelsen's terminology, new concepts created by legal scholarship [*Rechtsformbegriffe*] thus also led to the emergence of new concepts within positive law [*Rechtsinhaltsbegriffe*] through newly enacted law, which had emancipated itself from the prevailing ideological distortions of legal concepts. For example, if the attacked distinction between justiciable "legal" and non-justiciable "political" disputes is theoretically dissolved by international legal scholarship as a whole, this increases the likelihood that the statute of a new international court would likewise abandon this distinction.

Kelsen's utter determination to do justice to his own claims of objectivity in terms of legal constructivism only left room for hierarchical, logically structured system-building. The direct influence on international legal doctrine occurs in Kelsen's writings almost exclusively via the destruction of what he regarded as "ideologized" conceptualizations. In the process, what becomes continually and clearly visible behind the critique of international law is Kelsen's own desire that the politics of the interwar period create a thoroughly juridified international system. That, however, is a highly political project. Moreover, in the final analysis the "realm of the Ought" that Kelsen had philosophically created cannot, in spite of its level of abstraction, defend itself against what it so vigourously fought against: the irruption of the political. As I tried to highlight above, taking a stance "outside of power," by way of philosophical formalization, has its own limits.

Martti Koskenniemi, in his fundamental historical reconstruction of European international legal scholarship, denies the lasting value of Kelsenian formalism, while at the same time arguing for a "culture of formalism" within international law: "The way back to a Kelsenian formalism, a formalism *sans peur et sans reproche* is no longer open."[47] Even if I

[46] Kelsen, *United Nations*, XIII.
[47] Koskenniemi, *The Gentle Civilizer of Nations*, 495.

agree with his verdict, in view of the limitations to the Kelsenian project that I have spelled out above, in what follows I would like to articulate more clearly a Kelsenian legacy beyond his quest for objectivity. It would appear that Koskenniemi himself, with his sensitive account of a vanished "culture of formalism," wants to build a bridge to an existing tradition that is inconceivable without Kelsen.[48] It is not so much the constructive result of the ultimately unsuccessful Kelsenian search for objectivity, as the search itself that leads to a changed perspective on international law. His methodological search for an autonomous category of legal validity in international relations and the confidence in its potential are elements of Kelsenian formalism that deserve to be examined in more detail.

B The continuing relevance of Kelsenian formalism in international law

The essence of Kelsenian formalism is the critique of jurisprudential methodology, and its central political driving force is a critique of ideology. Hegemonic political forces use charged legal interpretations to consolidate political power structures. For Kelsen it was the self-destructive forces of European nationalism and authoritarianism that could be found in the contemporary doctrinal structures of international and state law, and which he set out to destroy. To this day, scholarly debates mirror and promote certain hegemonic projects by opening themselves up willingly to certain political rationalizations on the level of conceptualization – be they moral ideas, economic rationalizations, or the de facto prevailing power-asymmetries. In what follows I seek to illustrate once more the significance that can be attached to Kelsenian formalism in a completely altered historical–cultural context.

I Formalism and morality

In the Pure Theory of Law, Kelsen separated the law radically from morality: "Here, above all, the task is to unfetter the law, to break the connection that is always made between the law and morality."[49] The law is a man-made coercive system that does not have moral character per se.

[48] See ibid., 179–265; on the question of the political importance of Kelsenian formalism see his *From Apology to Utopia*, reissue with new Epilogue (Cambridge University Press, 2005), 602; on Koskenniemi and Kelsen see Bernstorff, "Sisyphus was an International Lawyer," 1015–1035.

[49] Kelsen, *Reine Rechtslehre* (1934), 12; *Problems of Legal Theory*, 14.

With his strict separation thesis, Kelsen took on many of his contemporary international lawyers who deemed a strict separation of law and morality to be counterproductive. Even his most influential students did not agree with him on this issue. Alfred Verdross and Hersch Lauterpacht, for instance, advocated a close theoretical connection between positive international law and principles derived from natural law. Both had been influenced by Hans Kelsen at the beginning of their academic careers, but later distanced themselves from him intellectually precisely because of his moral agnosticism. For both men, morality assumed a foundational role in international law, though in different ways.

Verdross in fact became the most influential early advocate of the notion of *ius cogens* and international legal constitutionalism based on the assumption of existing universal moral values.[50] For him the divine idea of "humanity" lies at the basis of the international legal order and informs positive international law.[51] After the First World War, Verdross began to have direct recourse to the writings of the Spanish late-scholastic writers de Vitoria and Suarez, who had promoted a construction of international law based on Christian religious principles. Verdross later deemed it necessary to recognize that the divine idea of humankind lies at the basis of the international order and to assess the acts of states as expressions of this idea.[52] International law for him was a synthesis of natural-law concepts and actual utterances of state representatives. Verdross also was the first modern international lawyer who advocated the concept of a constitution of the international legal order to comprise its most fundamental laws.[53] Ever since, the notion of foundational legal principles of humanity has animated a strong and heterogeneous field of international lawyers, who interpret legal developments with a manifest moral dimension as signs of an increasing constitutionalization of the international legal order. *Ius cogens* norms, *crimes against humanity*, and other elements of international legal practice

[50] On his theoretical contributions to the international legal debate Simma, "The Contribution of Alfred Verdross to the Theory of International Law," 33–54.

[51] On notions of morality in international law, see J. von Bernstorff and I. Venzke, "Ethos, Ethics and Morality in International Relations" in R. Wolfrum (ed.), *The Max Planck Encyclopedia of Public International Law* (Oxford University Press, 2010 – online edition [www.mpepil.com]).

[52] Verdross, "Die allgemeinen Rechtsgrundsätze des Völkerrechts," 354 *et seq.* (358).

[53] The notion of the "*Verfassung*" changed considerably over time in his works; see for an early version, Verdross, *Die Verfassung der Völkerrechtsgemeinschaft.*

and doctrinal debate with a strong moral dimension are considered emerging foundational norms.[54] According to this approach, an existing moral consensus can and does influence the creation and development of international law, in particular by way of custom. Thriving on the notion of an international community, a set of fundamental principles are said to acquire or to have acquired a constitutional status, distinguishing them from other norms of international law.[55] The current world order is conceived as based on a priority of values reflecting a hierarchy of norms;[56] hereby many of these approaches promote a constitutionalism that does not necessarily presuppose an institutional backing of the respective constitutional norms.[57]

For Lauterpacht – in contrast to Verdross – direct recourse to foundational religious principles was no longer an option. He understood morality as natural justice that *always* remained in the background of the positive legal order. Morality for him played a vital part through filling gaps and directing legal development towards the ends of universal

[54] As a prominent example of this scholarly trend C. Tomuschat, "International Law: Ensuring the survival of mankind on the eve of a new century," *RCADI*, 281 (1999), 9–438. At times, this is made explicit and finds support in international legal practice. For instance, in the *Corfu Channel Case* the ICJ has based its legal findings on "certain general and well-recognized principles, namely: elementary considerations of humanity," [1949] ICJ Rep 4, 22; and in the *Barcelona Traction Case* in which the ICJ embraced the notion of *erga omnes* obligations, [1970] ICJ Rep., 3, 32; a more recent example is the interpretation of the prohibition of genocide as *ius cogens* in the *Armed Activities on the Territory of the Congo Case* (New Application: 2002) [2006] ICJ Rep 1, paras 64 and 125. Another expression of the force of moral foundations may be found in Art. 53 of the Vienna Convention on the Law of Treaties (1982), which stipulates that treaties violating *ius cogens* norms are null and void.

[55] J. A. Frowein, "Konstitutionalisierung des Völkerrechts," *Berichte der Deutschen Gesellschaft für Völkerrecht*, 39 (2000) 427–447; A. Peters, "Global constitutionalism revisited," *International Legal Theory*, 11 (2005), 39–67; using the notion of general principles, S. Kadelbach and T. Kleinlein, "International Law – A Constitution for Mankind? An Attempt at a Re-appraisal with an Analysis of Constitutional Principles," *German Yearbook of International Law*, 50 (2007), 303–348; with a constitutional approach based on the UN Charter see B. Fassbender, "The United Nations Charter as Constitution of the International Community," *Columbia Journal of Transnational Law*, 36 (1998), 529–619; commenting on constitutional approaches, A. von Bogdandy, "Constitutionalism in International Law. Comment on a Proposal from Germany" in *Harvard ILJ*, 47 (2006), 223–242.

[56] See *Arrest Warrant of April 11, 2000 (Democratic Republic of the Congo v. Belgium)*, Joint separate opinion of Judges Higgins, Kooijmans, and Buergenthal [2002] ICJ Rep 3, 85, para. 73, stating "the emergence of values which enjoy an ever-increasing recognition in international society."

[57] A. Bianchi, "Human Rights and the Magic of Jus Cogens," *EJIL*, 19 (2008), 491–508.

justice. It entered legal discourse through recourse to general legal principles and related notions of natural justice rather than as a matter of hierarchical religious foundations. He conceded that natural justice is in fact frequently invoked to disguise selfish interests, but maintained that this was not a reason to dispense with natural justice altogether: "We would rather err in the pursuit of a good life for all than glory in the secure infallibility of moral indifference."[58] Arguably these two former students became much more influential within the post-Second World War discipline of international law than Kelsen himself, which has to do with a general revival of natural-law theories after the Second World War.

The main reason for Kelsen's separation thesis was his relativistic approach to international morality itself. For Kelsen there is no such thing as an absolute and uncontested notion of universal values and justice. Kelsen argued that due to the plurality of interests and divergent moral claims in international politics, no "objective" insight into the nature of "justice" can ever be obtained. The diverging values that are advocated under the term of "justice" in the international arena are only relative and therefore cannot play a foundational role for international law. There is no harmony of interests in international politics that would be expressed by international law – international politics is a deeply antagonistic affair.[59] But Kelsen had a further concern regarding the use of moral arguments in international legal discourse. It is the potentially ideological use of morality. Claims to morality in legal discourse can serve as a disguise for ulterior motives and interests, they overexploit the legal discourse, and can be used to justify ideological distortions of positive law by way of the moral argument. Hence, appeals to morality can be used by powerful actors in order to align a sense of what is right and good with their interests, thereby cementing hegemony.

The current use of moral arguments within international legal discourse goes far beyond the philosophical question about the ultimate foundation of the law, which was one of the theoretical obsessions of German international lawyers in the nineteenth century. It also goes beyond the enduring inclination of international legal scholarship to perceive international law in its entirety as a means for implementing humanitarian concerns, which also emerged as a strong discursive undercurrent during this time. Recent military interventions prove that recourse to humanitarian sentiments as a justification for a breach of

[58] Lauterpacht, "Kelsen's Pure Science of Law," 418–419.
[59] Kelsen, "The Essential conditions of International Peace," 70 *et seq.*

legal rules and standards is alive as ever.[60] Despite necessary political and legal differentiations between these cases, recent Western interventions in Kosovo (1999), Afghanistan (2001), and Iraq (2003) all had in common that their official justifications made ample references to the negative human-rights record of the invaded country.[61]

Those constitutional approaches that – in the neo-scholastic natural-law tradition – proceed from a legal system grounded in morality are in danger of endowing, out of well-intentioned motives, certain morally charged norms of international law with greater scholarly weight than they have in legal practice. In the attempt to advance the development of the law in a progressive direction, they can unwittingly abet the rhetorical misuse of these norms within international politics. Certain legal norms, elevated into constitutional rank, can thus turn into a facade without lasting effects on legal practice, a facade behind which international politics and unrestrained economic structures continue to operate as usual.[62] Or to put it differently: at what point do moral idealizations of international law become so far removed from the concrete human effects of law and politics that they themselves, for all their good intentions, take on affirmative characteristics? Charles de Visscher in 1971 held that the international community "est un ordre en puissance dans l'esprit de l'homme; dans les réalités de la vie internationale elle en est encore à se chercher, elle ne correspond pas à un ordre effectivement établi."[63] Despite the subsequent move from "bilateralism to community

[60] On the evolution and the current perspectives of international law from a Kantian point of view: Habermas, *Der Gespaltene Westen*, 113–193.

[61] US President George W. Bush justified his "war on terror" in 2004 before the UN General Assembly by stating: "Our security is not merely found in spheres of influence or some balance of power. The security of our world is found in advancing the rights of mankind," UN Doc. A/59/PV.3, 7–11; on human rights and the "war on terror" see A. Anghie, "On Critique and the Other" in A. Orford (ed.), *International Law and its Others* (Cambridge University Press, 2006), 389–400; on the turn to ethics before the Iraq war see M. Koskenniemi, "The Lady Doth Protest Too Much. Kosovo and the Turn to Ethics in International Law," *Modern Law Review*, 65 (2002), 159–175; on the intervention in Kosovo see also B. Simma, "NATO, the UN and the Use of Force: Legal Aspects," *EJIL*, 10 (1999); for an assessment of the illegality of the 2003 US intervention in Iraq see R. Wolfrum, "The Attack of September 11, 2001, The Wars Against The Taliban and Iraq: Is There A Need To Reconsider International Law on the Recourse to Force and the Rules of Armed Conflict?" in *Max Planck United Nations Yearbook 7* (2003), 1–78; on the Bush doctrine See G Nolte, "Die USA und das Völkrecht" in Journal of International Peace and Organization 78 (2003), 119–140.

[62] I have tried elsewhere to describe in greater detail the basic dilemma of the turn to rights: J. v. Bernstorff, "The Changing Fortunes of the Universal Declaration of Human Rights: Genesis and Symbolic Dimensions of the Turn to Rights in International Law," *EJIL*, 19 (2008), 903–924.

[63] C. De Visscher, "Positivisme et 'jus cogens'," RGDIP, 75 (1971), 8.

interests"[64] in a number of areas of positive international law, deep-seated conflicts over what the common interests actually are continue to persist. Recently, Andrew Hurrel, in the tradition of Hedley Bull's prudent concept of international law as "minimal standards of co-existence," has also warned that overly ambitious conceptions of global order might unduly endorse a "premature global solidarism."[65]

Kelsen's cosmopolitan project also had a strong constitutional dimension in its attempt to empower international institutions to develop and enforce global rules addressing the most pressing political issues of his time; this project, however, remained realistically grounded and legally formalized – a constitutional approach that denied the foundational character of an alleged harmony of interests, universally shared moral values, or an accomplished international community.

II Formalism and realism – Hans Kelsen, Carl Schmitt, and the Weimar constellation

For Kelsen, the radical separation of law and morality turned the Pure Theory of Law into a "radically realistic legal theory."[66] Through the realistic view of the law, the Pure Theory refused to serve political interests by supplying them with ideologies by which the social order is legitimized or disqualified. Somewhat unexpectedly, Kelsen had a powerful intellectual ally in his critique of international moralism: his great opponent Carl Schmitt, who sided with him on the issue of international moralism. Hans Kelsen and Carl Schmitt were on opposite sides of the Weimar political spectrum in the interwar period. Kelsen was a committed social democrat, supporter of the Weimar Republic and the League of Nations, whereas Carl Schmitt detested liberal democracy and the interwar move into international organization, which in his view had betrayed Germany in the Versailles settlement.[67]

64 See the comprehensive and early study of B. Simma, "From Bilateralism to Community Interests in International Law," *RCADI*, 250/IV (1994), 217–384.

65 A. Hurrell, *On Global Order. Power, values, and the constitution of international society* (Oxford University Press, 2007), 55; on Hedley Bull and his concept of international order see Bernstorff and Venzke, "Ethos, Ethics and Morality in International Relations."

66 Kelsen, *Reine Rechtslehre* (1934), 17; *Problems of Legal Theory,* 18.

67 His theoretical insights into the ideological nature of international political discourse did not stop Carl Schmitt from openly endorsing the racially motivated exclusion of German international lawyers of Jewish origin from the German academic landscape in the 1930s, or from collaborating intensively with the Nazi government in the first years of Nazi rule in Germany.

Interestingly, Schmitt developed his critique of international moralism as a response to the move to international institutions, which he saw as a hegemonic project of the United States, United Kingdom, and France directed against Germany, concealed under a universalist rhetoric of the international rule of law. Schmitt's critique of international moralism is epitomized in his pointed statement he adapted from Pierre-Joseph Proudhon: "whoever invokes humanity wants to cheat."[68] In his *Concept of the Political*, Schmitt sees a close connection between political violence and moral claims to universal justice. For him, states attempt to wage wars in the name of *humanity* in order to justify political violence. By invoking terms such as "humanity" the political opponent is rendered an outlaw outside humanity and outside the law. Even though Kelsen and Schmitt share a realistic perspective on claims to morality in international legal discourse, they draw different conclusions from this insight. Kelsen upholds the potential value of an international legal order, which has the capacity to pacify and rationalize international disputes.

In contrast, Carl Schmitt dismissed the civilizing function of the legal form in international relations as a fictitious and unrealistic construction. His notion of realism was driven by the fundamental assumption that every type of legal system must be juristically conceptualized from the vantage point of the authority that has the power to establish and abolish it. However, not only does this understanding relate to the foundational act itself, it also has far-reaching consequences for the understanding of legal validity and the formation of juristic concepts. The law is thus conceived as constantly facing the latent threat of being suspended. Consequently, its validity is conceptually completely dependent on non-juridical factors. To that extent, the validity of the law is of no value in and of itself, but has a derivative and therefore always dependent character; the law is at all times subject to the proviso of a political decision about its validity.[69] By virtue of this fixation on a total

[68] C Schmitt, *The Concept of the Political*, trans. and with an introduction by G. Schwab (New Brunswick: Rutgers University Press, 1976), 54.

[69] Where Kelsen looks at politics and the law from the ideal of a system of peace, war – that is, the life-threatening, radical questioning and suspension of the legal system – becomes the central orientation point of legal thinking in the "realistic" argument. Carl Schmitt is undoubtedly the best-known representative of this current of thinking. In his work *Politische Theologie*, Schmitt said the following about this:

> The decision frees itself from every normative tie and becomes absolute in the true sense. In the exceptional case, the state suspends the law, by virtue of its right to self-preservation, as they say. The two elements of the

political proviso, this kind of realistic argument tends toward an interpretation of legal concepts that is guided by notions of power. The law is conceptualized from the vantage point of the concrete order outside the law, the de facto realm of political influence, and specific historical power constellations. Concepts like hegemony, sphere of influence, or the emerging *Großraum* are not seen as challenges to international law, but as the constitutive characteristics of the legal concept derived from them.[70] In addition, the political vanishing point of the Schmittean understanding of society is not the law and its institutions, but the subjection and destruction of the enemy as the essence of politics.

In spite of these fundamental differences, the conceptions of international law held by Hans Kelsen, Carl Schmitt, and their student Hans Morgenthau was based on a shared, antagonistic understanding of politics. This realistic notion of politics, which was shaped by the "Weimar constellation" and looked at politics not in a harmonizing sense as the identity of shared interests, but as an existential struggle between conflicting claims to power,[71] made Kelsen and Schmitt into the most important and influential legal theoreticians with a Weimar background.[72] Both authors' writings on this issue have been a reference point for international legal scholars ever since. In my view, the fundamental skepticism toward any assertion of a substantially moral basis of international law within a world marked by the clash of political and economic interests, conflicting cultural sensibilities, and asymmetries of power is of lasting importance for the theory of international law. However, in radical distinction to Schmitt, Kelsen believed in the conflict-solving potential of the law within international relations. The

> concept of "legal order" confront each other here and prove their conceptual independence. Just as in the normal case the independent moment of the decision can be pushed back to a minimum, in the exceptional case the norm is destroyed.

C. Schmitt, *Politische Theologie. Vier Kapitel zur Lehre von der Souveränität*, 2nd edn. (Munich and Leipzig: Duncker & Humblot, 1934), 18–20.

70 The *Großraumtheorie* [theory of spheres of influence] is the best-known example of such a conceptual formation; on this see M. Schmoeckel, *Die Grossraumtheorie. Ein Beitrag zur Geschichte der Völkerrechtswissenschaft im Dritten Reich, insbesondere der Kriegszeit* (Berlin: Duncker & Humblot, 1994).

71 Koskenniemi, "Carl Schmitt, Hans Morgenthau and the Image of Law in International Relations."

72 Chantal Mouffe bases her antagonistic theory of democracy for that very reason on Schmitt even though Kelsen would have been the more appropriate choice given the nearness of his democratic theory to the project Mouffe has recently advanced, see C. Mouffe, *On the Political* (London, New York: Routledge, 2005).

Kelsenian conception of international law juxtaposes to the moral and the realistic argument a formal understanding of the law as a neutralized medium of guidance and conflict-resolution. For Kelsen, the principle of law takes the place of the principle of justice and the principle of power. The core of this legal principle is the maxim of formal equality: "Equality is the principle that under the same conditions States have the same duties and rights."[73]

The equality principle understood in this way was to Kelsen a tautology of the legal principle that stated that a legal norm had to be applied in those cases in which it was supposed to be applied according to its content.[74] Herein lies for Kelsen the specifically formal justice of the law, which demanded its general and predictable application independent of power resources and morality.[75] As he saw it, the law could function as a medium for ordering the global plurality of interests only in its neutralized formality. Substantial justice within international relations thus remained a contingent utopia. A contextual approximation to this utopian goal is only possible via international law and legally supported institutions, though it can also be prevented by the concrete outcome of a given global legislative process. From this perspective, international law thus becomes a means to address and argue about shared standards and fundamental experiences of injustice within the only available communicative medium that – by way of its formality – is capable of transcending power asymmetries and idiosyncratic preferences.

III The belief in systemic unity of international law in the age of fragmentation.

Kelsen used his anti-ideological toolkit at the beginning of the 1920s to defend two highly political, nascent projects against strong political forces opposing them: a strong world organization to secure world peace, and the strengthening of the still-young democratic institutions in Weimar and Vienna. Despite his technical critique of the Covenant of

[73] Kelsen, "The Principle of Sovereign Equality," 209. [74] Ibid.

[75] On the value of formal equality in times of hegemony, see J. L. Cohen, "Sovereign Equality vs. Imperial Right: The Battle over the 'New World Order'" in W. Breckman et al. (eds.), *The Modernist Imagination: Intellectual History and Critical Theory: Essays in Honour of Martin Jay* (New York, Oxford: Berghahn Books, 2008), 346–367; see on sovereign equality also B. Kingsbury, "Sovereignty and Inequality," *EJIL*, 9 (1998), 599–625 and P. Weil's classic piece "Towards Relative Normativity in International Law?" *AJIL*, 77 (1983), 413–442.

the League of Nations and its connection to the Versailles settlement, Kelsen considered its adoption a civilizational break through. As the currents of autocratism and fascism grew stronger in Germany, Austria, Italy, Spain, and other European countries during the interwar period, the institution of the League of Nations came under increasing pressure. To counter this, Kelsen and Hersch Lauterpacht pursued a reform-oriented project of a public-law-based world federation. Central for Kelsen in this context was the introduction of compulsory adjudication at a universal level. The reformed, new world court was to institutionally secure and further develop the rule of the law within international relations. As his theoretical basis, Kelsen was working in this regard with a dual assumption of unity: first, the unity of law as a complete system of norms that regulated all conflicts; second, the assumption that the institutional creation of unity through a growing centralization of the legal function on the international level constituted an evolutionary achievement.

Georges Abi Saab has convincingly stated that "Kelsen est peut-être l'auteur qui a plus contribué à asseoir la vision du droit comme système au cours du XXe siècle."[76] For Kelsen the legal order must be construed as a complete and unified system of legal rules. From a scholarly perspective there can only be one legal order, which is endowed with the attribute of legal validity. There is only one single code of legal normativity. It is a "scientific" postulate to conceive international law and national law in that way. Lauterpacht shared Kelsen's conviction that the international legal order had to be conceptualized as a complete system of legal rules.[77] As a consequence, both authors dismissed the notion of gaps in the international legal order. For Lauterpacht, however, completeness was a question of substantive unity, which had to be achieved by the ingenious application of natural-law principles by the legal craft. For Kelsen it was a philosophical (neo-Kantian) postulate. For him, non-legal forms of behavior could no longer be construed. Where no explicit rule existed, the legal system created degrees of freedom for those subject to the law through the so-called negative norm, according to which everything that was not prohibited was allowed. This somewhat irritating insight still seems valuable, in spite of its problematic philosophical justification. For the law is always present also through non-regulation and makes value judgments by its silence. For example, if international legal norms do not

[76] Abi-Saab, "Cours général de droit international public," 108.
[77] See Chapter 6AIII.

explicitly forbid certain practices in international trade or financial markets with potentially disastrous economic and social consequences, as a legal system it allows state and private actors to engage in these activities.

Regarding the question of institutional unity, Kelsen – towards the end of the Second World War – published numerous articles on the question of the new world order after the Second World War. His main proposal was the establishment of a universal system of compulsory adjudication controlling the use of force in international relations. A centralized judicial body, the new world court, was meant to adjudicate all disputes between states as well as over war crimes committed by individuals, without the possibility for states to limit or withdraw their obligatory acceptance of the jurisdiction of the court. In 1944 Kelsen even drafted a statute for an international criminal court as well as a blueprint for a new world organization. Interestingly, Kelsen developed his own historical theory of legal evolution in order to justify his political proposals. He claimed that European medieval primitive legal orders were marked by a decentralized system of application and enforcement of the law, whereas more developed "civilized" legal orders tend to centralize these functions. According to Kelsen's historical observations, medieval European societies are characterized by a multitude of organs that create and enforce the law. Instead of one centralized legislator and a hierarchical system of courts, these various actors create and enforce the law locally without recourse to the notion of an overarching system of law. These primitive legal systems are based on locally produced customary law, which is enforced locally through self-help or self-appointed powerful local actors.[78]

Kelsen used these historical insights into the nature of medieval pre-state legal orders to describe the nature of the international legal order in the 1940s. International law also relied on decentralized norm-production through custom and it lacked centralized adjudication and enforcement. Kelsen – despite his belief in the potential of international legal development – actually was quite critical of its current state of development. For him it could already be termed law, but it still had the inherent tendency to give in to political power, for instance through the principle of effectiveness. Kelsen held that the first step to a more centralized and less primitive legal order historically was the centralization of the judicial function. For once you have courts in place, they can

[78] See Chapter 6AIII.

develop a system of law regulating the exercise of authority in an ever more centralized legal community. For Kelsen, courts were the institutional center of every mature legal system. The establishment of compulsory adjudication on the international level, including the general acceptance of its jurisdiction over all disputes by all states, would be the next evolutionary step for international law. The centralization of legislation and enforcement of legal rules through global institutions would then follow. Kelsen operated here with an analogy between the emergence of the modern European state and international legal development. Independent of these dubious borrowings from evolutionary theory, Kelsen thus recognized the functional importance of the courts for a dynamic development of international law, which was confirmed by the proliferation of ever more influential international judicial bodies in the second half of the twentieth century.

However, in institutional terms the trend toward institutional centralization predicted by Kelsen has not happened, at least not on a global level. Instead of the predicted evolutionary path toward a judicially controlled world federation based on international law, the second half of the twentieth century has brought about the establishment of ever more sophisticated issue-related international regimes that rely on their own mechanisms of adjudication and enforcement. There is no hierarchichal system of courts that judicially guarantees the systemic unity of international law. Moreover, the United Nations has failed to become the final, judicially controlled arbiter of the authorization to use force in international relations. Instead of world state structures, we face the challenges of issue-related fragmentation in an institutionally decentralized legal order, where individual regimes like the World Trade Organization [WTO] have their own independent dispute-settlement mechanisms. To that extent, while the evolutionary tendencies toward centralization through judicial bodies as described by Kelsen are occurring within individual regimes, these partial regimes are only inadequately tied together into a comprehensive legal system institutionalized through centralized courts. Although there is no formal hierarchy, the sectorial regimes that assert themselves globally in legal terms are those that are endowed with the strongest implementation mechanisms. Legal practice hereby gives rise to institutional hierarchies caused by the varying institutional endowment of the regimes. On its own, the WTO, for instance, will accept rationalities of other international legal regimes, such as human rights claims, only to a limited extent and always under the diktat of its own free-trade rationality. International law, thus, is under a threat of being colonized by specific sectorial subsystems of the international society, in particular in those areas where it has been built around the preferences of strong economic actors.

For Kelsen there was, from a legal perspective, no categorical distinction between international organizations and states as legal systems. In his monistic legal cosmos, the individual is a legal subject of various subsystems, which differ legally only by their varying degrees of centralization. The state legal system is a strongly centralized legal order, while international law on the whole represents a complex of norms with little centralization. Like states, international organizations constitute legal subsystems within the monist system. They are less strongly centralized than state law, but in theory they can also directly empower and obligate individuals. The transitions between organizational forms depend on the respective degree of centralization of the legal subsystem and are thus conceived as fluid processes in a politico-legal continuum. Thus, an international organization or a confederacy of states can – through continuous transitory reforms – become a federal state, and vice versa. From a legal point of view, treaty and constitution do not constitute categorical differences. The European Union has become the prime example of Kelsen's doctrine of the evolutionary centralization of legal systems. From this perspective, the notion of the supranationality of the EU[79] seeks to conceptually grasp a transitional stage on the fluid continuum of centralization and decentralization. Kelsen predicted in this context that through increased production and implementation of norms by international organizations, international law would slowly assume the functions of administrative law as we know it on the national level with the capacity to directly regulate individual behavior through international legal norms. International law would increasingly function like national law, be it criminal law or administrative law (see Chapter 4). A current example at the UN level, which confirms Kelsen's predictions in this regard, are the Security Council resolutions on individualized sanctions against terror suspects and other individuals.[80] These resolutions work like national administrative law, unfortunately without due process and without a centralized judicial organ to turn to. His critical

[79] On this notion: A. von Bogdandy, "The European Union as a Supranational Federation," *Columbia Journal of European Law*, 6 (2000), 27–54.

[80] On the human rights implications of the sanction regime, M. Bulterman, "Fundamental Rights and the United Nations Financial Sanction Regime. The Kadi and Yusuf judgments of the Court of First Instance of the European Communities," *Leiden Journal of International Law*, 19 (2006), 753–772.

stance on the lack of judicial controls of the UN Security Council seemed correct: In order for a legal order to acquire a higher "civilizational" status, independent judicial controls must be in place before a centralized legislative or administrative body takes action.[81]

To be sure, during the interwar period Kelsen was not yet able to recognize the potential democracy problem created by increasing norm-production in international institutions, although in the UN Charter commentary he emphasized the importance of legally (de-)limited powers of the individual organs of the organization.[82] Kelsen proceeded on the assumption that the exercise of authority in the international realm had to be linked to concrete legal powers subject to judicial review. To him, the medium of the treaty was here the crucial source of law. Within the framework of the current debate over "global law" and "global governance," there is a growing emphasis on the potential of private, special regulatory regimes outside the realm of formal international law. These are supposedly more flexible than traditional international organizations – examples are the global regulation of the Internet, the *lex mercatoria*, and global banking regulation.[83] As I have shown in this book, Kelsen placed great hopes in the medium of treaty law and sought to render it more effective theoretically.[84] In recent years, treaty instruments have been seen with growing frequency as too rigid and resistent to change to be able to provide adequate guidance to global

[81] Referring to the reaction of the UN Security Council to the failure of Libya to hand over the Lockerbie suspects for trial in Scotland James Crawford noted: "The point is that in the absence of an *ultra vires* doctrine, and some institutional expression of it, the Security Council under Chapter VII has the appearance of an unrestrained collective executive power. That is dangerously close to the definition of a tyranny, limited only by the possibility of disagreement between the collective bearers of the power, the permanent and temporary members of the Security Council." Quoted from: "Negotiating Global Security Threats in a World of Nation States: Issues and Problems of Nation States" in J. Crawford (ed.), *International Law as an Open System* (London: Cameron May, 2002), 95–121 (106–107).

[82] On the so-called global democracy deficit and international law: J. Crawford and S. Marks, "The Global Democracy Deficit: An Essay in International Law and its Limits" in Crawford (ed.), *International Law as an Open System*, 137–155.

[83] W.H. Reinicke, *Global Public Policy. Governing Without Government?* (Washington, DC: Brookings Institution Press, 1998). On various phenomena of so-called "global law": G. Teubner (ed.), *Global law without a state. Studies in modern law and policy* (Brookfield: Dartmouth, 1997); claiming a fundamental change in international regulation A.-M. Slaughter, "Global Government Networks, Global Information Agencies, and Disaggregated Democracy," *Michigan Journal of International Law*, 24 (2003), 1041–1075; on new governance phenomena and the limiting role of law C. Joerges (ed.), *Transnational Governance and Constitutionalism* (Oxford: Hart, 2004).

[84] See Chapter 5BII.

regulatory developments. However, these disadvantages of existing treaty instruments should not obscure a central achievement of the treaty concept. Flexibility is not a value in and of itself. The treaty secures formal equality in the creation and application of global rules. It can also be used to better coordinate the various treaty regimes through more sophisticated treaty provisions regulating conflicts. Moreover, the treaty concept carries an unlimited potential for experimentation with new forms of participation and transparent politicization, as well as for enhanced flexibility without entirely relinquishing the achievement of formal equality.[85] Kelsen's theory of the treaty, by virtue of its uncoupling from substantive notions of state sovereignty, furnishes provocative avenues for pursuing precisely a more experimental approach to treaty law. By contrast, informal regimes often favour strong actors who, in looser unions with self-chosen partners, secure and further expand their technological, economic, and scientific lead by creating new standards.[86]

Institutional fragmentation and de-formalization are not the inevitable fate of modern international law. These developments are based on intentional decisions by strong actors with no interest in a functioning, cross-sectorial political generalization of interests. Fragmentation is the result of the deliberate withdrawal by stronger states from such multilateral institutions in which developing countries and organizations of civil society are capable of politicizing sector-spanning aspects and issues.[87] For that reason it is also unlikely that individual specialized regimes will, in the future, incorporate sector-spanning rationalities into the operation of the regime of their own volition.[88] The philosophy on which they are founded is based

[85] A. Spiliopoulou Åkermark and O. Mårsäter, "Treaties and the Limits of Flexibility," *Nordic Journal of International Law*, 71 (2005), 509–540; J. Klabbers, "Book review of: A. Aust, *Modern Treaty Law and Practice*," *NJIL International Law*, 71 (2002), 203–205; C. Tietje, "The changing legal structure of international treaties as an aspect of an emerging global governance architecture" in *German Yearbook of International Law*, 42 (1999), 26–55.

[86] On strategic institutional choices of powerful states when it comes to creating new institutions and leaving old ones: E. Benvenisti and G. W. Downs, "The Empire's New Clothes: Political Economy and the Fragmentation of International Law," *Stanford Law Review*, 60 (2007); On the US and strategic instrumentalization of international law: N. Krisch, "More Equal than the Rest? Hierarchy, Equality and US Predominance in International Law" in M. Byers and G. Nolte (eds.), *United States hegemony and the foundations of international law* (Cambridge University Press, 2003), 133–175.

[87] Ibid.

[88] This, however, seems to be the hope expressed in A. Fischer-Lescano and G. Teubner, "Regime collisions: the vain search for legal unity in the fragmentation of global law," *Michigan Journal of International Law*, 25 (2004), 999–1046.

precisely on the exclusion of such aspects, usually in favour of an effective – meaning politically unimpeded – promotion of particular interests. It is only in exceptional cases that specific regimes, which are uncoupled from general political forums, can be influenced by critical reactions of the general public to the effects of their operations. Such ad-hoc politicization always depends on the highly selective and short-lived attention span of global media. As a reaction to such selective, media-driven political protests against specific institutions strong actors tend to move to enforce their interests through bilateral law as for instance in international investment law.

Kelsen's theory of international law was created during and between two world wars and was aimed at securing world peace through a strong world organization with a global monopoly of force controlled by courts. The second half of the twentieth century was not characterized by a new world war, but by many warlike conflicts, often internal in nature. Moreover, the world finds itself in a permanent state of social "war," caused by extreme poverty, a crisis in which the death toll has by now exceeded that of the two world wars many times over. Since the last decades of the twentieth century, broad swaths of Africa have been depopulated by diseases that have been curable for quite some time. The structurally exclusionary character of the "international community"[89] was long obscured within the Western public by the nuclear confrontation of the two superpowers. The post-Second World War institutional set-up was from the very beginning a politically fragmented one. It never had the structures in place to effectively develop and coordinate cross-sectorial activities of the growing number of largely autonomous international organizations belonging to the UN system. Sectorial international organizations and UN special agencies managed to become ever more independent from both their member states and from the central UN organs, making cross-sectorial political coordination almost impossible to achieve. Moreover, the hopes for profound change through a de-formalized and network-based multilateralism following the end of the cold war have also been disappointed.[90]

[89] On the various versions and theoretical foundations of the notion of the international community: A. L. Paulus, *Die internationale Gemeinschaft im Völkerrecht. Eine Untersuchung zur Entwicklung des Völkerrechts im Zeitalter der Globalisierung* (Munich: Beck, 2001).

[90] As Andrew Hurrell states:

> For many states and other groups, the rhetoric of liberal multilateralism covered the reality of its top-down, prescriptive, and often coercive character. The substantive outcomes appeared to be stacked in favour of the most powerful: collective security had become selective security; the

The phenomena of the heterarchy, sectorialization, de-formalization, and privatization of global rule that have been identified by sociological approaches should, however, be regarded as a challenge to international law, not as a confirmation of its ineffectiveness. To be sure, Kelsen's deductively derived and hierarchically structured norm system seems of little doctrinal use today to resolve complex legal situations, in which various special international treaty regimes and one or more national laws may be at play. Still, to me that is no reason to banish the belief in the unity of the law from international legal scholarship. Not only because this approach qua theory encapsulates a high sensibility for the interconnectivity of the various global, regional, and national legal orders and the emergence of individuals and international organizations as legal subjects.[91] In spite of the apodictic, Neo-Kantian foundation of the postulate of unity in Kelsen, its constructivist character continues to emphasize an important aspect of the craft.[92] According to Kelsen, the unity of the law ultimately is in the eye of the legal beholder. In a time of fragmentation it seems important, if not vital, that international legal scholars do not give up the notion of systemic unity of international law so close to the hearts of Kelsen and Lauterpacht. If unity has not been achieved institutionally, it needs to be upheld intellectually by lawyers in international legal practice. The unity of the law stands for the possibility of a deterritorialized legal discourse connecting the various functional subsystems. It is only within such a sector-spanning legal discourse that fundamental experiences of injustice and exclusion can be effectively articulated. For law must always be both a medium in the service of functional imperatives of sectorial subsystems *and* a communicative medium that remains accessible for discursive engagement through the lifeworld [*Lebenswelt*].[93]

> agenda of human rights favoured democracy and civil and political rights but neglected social and economic rights, and ignored calls for greater economic justice; and although economic globalization was heavily promoted, there was little attention to its discontents and downsides. The hard line hegemonist "we can do it alone" is certainly wrong. But the liberal hegemonist version "we can do it together" depends on who "we" are, and what "it" is, and what is meant by "together."

Hurrell, *On Global Order*, 283.

91 A historical development, which has led to a more "open-textured" international legal system as described by J. Crawford, "International Law as an open System" in J. Crawford (ed.), *International Law as an Open System* (London: Cameron May, 2002), 17–38 (21).

92 On this see Chapter 3A.

93 This is of course the approach to law developed by Jürgen Habermas in *Faktizität und Geltung* (Frankfurt am Main: Suhrkamp, 1992).

Unity thus assumes an *aspirational* character, representing the hope for a new cross-sectorial global polity, based on transparent and continuously politicized rules, and revising the institutional arrangements that intentionally unleashed the forces of economic, financial, and scientific globalization, and with them also their exclusionary potential.[94] This does not have to be the discredited world state (whatever that is), but experimental institutional arrangements that allow for the egalitarian formulation of cross-sectorial policies based on legal procedures, allowing for transparent rule-making regarding the most urgent issues at stake.[95] The role of international law in this vein would also be to reconnect global rule to national publics through new institutional procedures, for unless that happens, executive global rule-making remains isolated from non-institutionalized local and national discursive structures.[96]

If we abandon the aspiration of systemic unity, however, we will have given in to the tyranny of the strongest subsystems of the global society [*Weltgesellschaft*] and international law might eventually turn into a flexible set of sectorial standards, a mere facade when it comes to the generalization of interests, and a highly effective instrument when cementing particular preferences of strong actors; a truly hegemonic project. Interestingly, Kelsen's and Lauterpacht's old-fashioned belief in the systemic unity of international law has also been reaffirmed in the International Law Commission [ILC] fragmentation report.[97] From this perspective, an admittedly aspirational belief in the validity of international law as a unified system of legal rules seems to become ever more relevant.

[94] For – as Joseph H. H. Weiler noted – "despite the 'progressive' values with which the turn to Community is normally associated – notably human rights and the environment – the absence of true polity is highly problematic." Quoted from: J. H. H. Weiler, "The Geology of International Law – Governance, Democracy and Legitimacy," *ZaöRV*, 64 (2004), 558.

[95] Christoph Möllers speaks of "*freiheitsgefährdende Parzellierung*" through fragmentation; see Ch. Möllers, *Gewaltengliederung. Legitimation und Dogmatik im nationalen und internationalen Rechtsvergleich* (Tübingen: Mohr, 2005), 223; with a similar argument for the field of migration see J. Bast, "Das Demokratiedefizit fragmentierter Institutionalisierung" in H. Brunkhorst (ed.), *Demokratie in der Weltgesellschaft*, Soziale Welt-Sonderband Nr. 18 (Baden-Baden: Nomos, 2009), 185–193.

[96] J. von Bernstorff, "Zivilgesellschaftliche Partizipation in Internationalen Organisationen: Form globaler Demokratie oder Baustein westlicher Expertenherrschaft?" in Brunkhorst (ed.), *Demokratie in der Weltgesellschaft*, 277–302.

[97] M. Koskenniemi, *Fragmentation of international law. Difficulties arising from the diversification and expansion of international law.* Report of the Study Group of the International Law Commission (University of Helsinki, 2007).

In the preceding section I have highlighted some aspects of Kelsen's international law theory, which I consider a lasting contribution to international legal discourse: his sensibility regarding attempts at hegemonic instrumentalization of the law, his skepticism towards moral foundationalism, his antagonistic perception of politics and his defense of the systemic validity and unity of international law. Proceeding from this analysis, I can now conclude with a sketch of the legacy of Kelsenian formalism.

C Conclusion – from Kelsen to reflexive formalism in international law

Kelsen did recognize the dynamic and self-referential structure that generates law, as well as the relative indeterminacy of the law in the process of its concretization. Moreover, in the notion of the choice-hypothesis [*Wahlhypothese*], he ruthlessly exposed the political character of the international legal discourse. However, he did not relinquish his own claim to objectivity; instead, to preserve the purity of his Pure Theory, he took refuge in the transcendental realm of a logically coherent articulation of concepts and system. At the same time, this claim to objectivity – philosophically underpinned and in its radical nature doomed to failure – led him to a critical stance toward then prevailing theoretical foundations of international law. Kelsen's legacy thus is neither his German nineteenth-century obsession with a "scientific" legal methodology, nor his concrete interwar blueprints for world state structures. Instead his legacy is the demystification of international law by stripping it of its alleged external foundations. In a radicalized modernist spirit, international law becomes a social technique that can be used for any purpose. There are no inherent limits to international legal experimentalism. Using an Arendtian metaphor, international law can now become the city wall of a global polis, in which political deliberation can take place in an egalitarian form.[98]

Kelsen saw, however, that in order to enable the legal form to fulfill this function, the notion of an international legal validity needs to be preserved; it needs to be defended against ethical, political, and economic attacks on its societal autonomy. Kelsen's legacy is thus the belief in the

[98] H. Arendt, *The Human Condition* (Chicago University Press, 1958), 194–195.

potential value of systemic international legal validity, as a notion that cannot be fully dissolved into power, utility, morality, or any other external rationality.[99] His description and critique of various scholarly de-formalization strategies constitute the real value of the Pure Theory of Law. What remains is an irritation which, independent of epistemological foundations, generates an element of self-criticism. The "standpoint outside of power" that Kelsen sought for international law can be interpreted as the quest for a level of reflection that defends the law's inherent rationality against political, economic, and other social rationalities.

At a time when many writers on international law are trying to provide the discipline with a "more objective" basis in economic models, interest analyses, or ethical categories, this approach seems exceedingly timely. These other approaches make the mistake of attributing the validity of the law to normatively charged categories such as "rational interests," "moral norms," and "power." In so doing, they apply external criteria to the validity of the law: And while these criteria unquestionably play a significant role in international relations, their projection onto international law deprives the legal medium of the potential of transcending these particularistic rationalities in the form of shared formal rules.[100] It is one of the fundamental insights of the classic debate over positivism in sociology that the unreflective scientific selection and reproduction of certain societal rationalities – as, for example, economic-utilitarian rationality – tends to scientifically transfigure and thus promote particular societal forces. Given how weakly institutionalized the international legal system is, the temptation seems especially acute for the international lawyer to equate a specific, societal sub-rationality, like, for instance, economic rationality, with legal rationality. The very moment one takes this step, the particularistic project has asserted itself juridically and has thereby also cemented itself politically.

Moreover, the law is then denied the openness to incorporating, for example, content that is irrational or oblivious to power, thereby turning it into a binding international legal rule. If that happens, the law,

99 I have made this argument elsewhere: J. von Bernstorff, "Kelsen und das Völkerrecht. Rekonstruktion einer völkerrechtlichen Berufsethik" in R. Walter, C. Jabloner, and Klaus Zeleny (eds.), *Kelsen und das Völkerrecht, Schriftenreihe des Hans Kelsen Instituts Band 26* (Vienna: Manz, 2004).

100 This is one of the categorical mistakes made by E. A. Posner and J. L. Goldsmith, *The Limits of International Law* (Oxford University Press, 2005).

in its relative interpretational indeterminacy, is subjected to the diktat of a hegemonic sub-rationality with a universalistic facade. This intellectual temptation is countered by Kelsen's image of the empty legal form, which can conceptually incorporate any kind of content – including an anti-hegemonic one. Kelsen seemed right in forcefully reminding the discipline that approaches based on interests, power, and morality can neither generate a higher scientific objectivity, nor conceptually model an autonomous validity of international law. In addition, moralist approaches tend to endow concrete international legal rules with a dignity they often do not deserve.

Kelsen's belief in the potential of the legal form in international relations remains – in terms of legal theory – the most radical counter-assumption to these approaches. To me, Kelsenian formalism is therefore a radicalized project of international legal modernity, which initiated a central theoretical shift. Kelsen created a reflexive element in international legal theory,[101] according to which the law, for one, was never entirely absorbed into a different societal rationality; it is never merely a reflection of power, economic preferences, or moral ideas. And while it is indissolubly linked to politics through its interpretational indeterminacy,[102] it is always both more and less. For another thing, this reflexive element creates a self-critical distance toward the hegemonic instrumentalization of the notion of law in a given historical situation. The international lawyer's reflexive awareness that I have traced out here combines methodological skepticism with a context-dependent critique of hegemony, without relinquishing the faith in the possibilities of universal law. In that sense, the image of the empty universal legal form is for the law what Habermas refers to as the "reflexive" potential of modernity, its capacity for critical self-examination and correction under conditions of social contingency.[103] For international law, this step means – precisely on the basis of the insight into the relative interpretational indeterminacy of the law – to hold on to the potential value of its formality, without idealizing the concrete content of the law. This can be a strategy to cope with the eternal problem of how

[101] Bernstorff, "Kelsen und das Völkerrecht."

[102] On the politics of international law see Koskenniemi, *From Apology to Utopia*, reissue with new Epilogue.

[103] J. Habermas, in G. Borradori (ed.), *Philosophy in times of Terror, Dialogues with Jürgen Habermas and Jacques Derrida* (Chicago University Press, 2003), 42.

international law can be a means to fend off the menace of hegemony, if it itself is used as a vehicle of that menace.

The Pure Theory of Law thus marks the transition to a reflexive modernity in international jurisprudence. International law can become a universal, communicative practice with the goal of institutionalizing legitimate institutions, in which the way transnational public authority is exercised can be meaningfully discussed and politically challenged.[104] That a reflexive formalism must today acknowledge its own lack of an objectifiable theoretical foundation is no obstacle to its potential societal value as a foundationless emancipative practice in the Rortyan sense. On the contrary, the missing objectifiability of its basic assumptions can increase the self-critical distance from the specific contextual repercussions of such a communicative practice.

Kelsen's philosophical attempt at establishing an objective "science" of international law was condemned to failure. The reflexive distance, however, that has been created by his image of the empty, universal legal form is needed now more than ever.

[104] See Rainer Forst for a political conception of transnational justice: R. Forst, *Das Recht auf Rechtfertigung: Elemente einer konstruktivistischen Theorie der Gerechtigkeit* (Frankfurt am Main: Suhrkamp, 2007), 343–356.

CAREER SKETCHES: HANS KELSEN, ALFRED VERDROSS, AND JOSEF LAURENZ KUNZ

Hans Kelsen (1881–1973)

Hans Kelsen was a Viennese legal theorist and constitutional and international lawyer of Jewish background who is often described as the most important legal mind of the twentieth century. His chief work was *Die Reine Rechtslehre* [The Pure Theory of Law], first published in 1934. The purity of jurisprudential method postulated in it, understood as a "scientific" positivism, was a fundamental critique of the voluntaristic positivism [*Staatswillenspositivismus*] that dominated the public-law mainstream in the German Empire, and simultaneously a radicalized response to the opening, at the beginning of the twentieth century, of public-law scholarship to the young disciplines of sociology and psychology. Kelsen himself, however, was not only a constitutional and international lawyer, but also a legal theorist, legal sociologist, and legal historian. Throughout his life, he championed parliamentary democracy and compulsory constitutional adjudication, which he helped introduce in Austria, as well as the juridification of international relations and their law-based institutionalization.

Kelsen's main work on international law was his 1920 monograph *Das Problem der Souveränität und die Theorie des Völkerrechts* [The Problem of Sovereignty and the Theory of International Law]. He wrote it during the First World War in a historical phase when the pacifist-liberal current in Europe and the United States regarded the inadequate institutionalization of the international legal system, including compulsory jurisdiction, as the chief reason for the outbreak of the war. Kelsen shared this view. He saw in the reform of the international legal system the key to a more peaceful world and tried to destroy central assumptions of the voluntaristic foundation of international law – that is, assumptions based on the will of a sovereign state – in nineteenth-century German-language international legal scholarship. In later years, as well, his work continued to deal with basic questions of the discipline, for example in his two Hague lectures and in his textbook *Principles of International Law* (1952). In addition, there were numerous publications on individual issues of international law, with legal issues from the law of international organizations and international jurisdiction forming a central focus. Finally, there was the comprehensive commentary on the UN Charter, *The Law of the United Nations* (1951).

Kelsen's academic biography is at the same time a tragic story from what Eric Hobsbawm has called "The Age of Extremes." His eventually extremely successful academic career, crowned by many honorary doctorates, in the period before, between, and after the two world wars took him from Vienna, Cologne, and Geneva to Harvard and Berkeley. However, nearly all his moves and the emigration were involuntary and came in response to life-threatening perils, persecution, or political defamation and had an anti-Semitic background. The following career sketch is based largely on Kelsen's own autobiographical writings.[1]

The period before and during the First World War – education and scholarly imprinting in the Austrian monarchy (1881–1919)

Hans Kelsen was born in Prague in 1881. His father, Adolf Kelsen, hailed from Brody in Galicia; at age fourteen he had relocated to Vienna and then Prague, where he ran a small workshop for lamps and lighting fixtures. His mother, Auguste Loewy, was German-speaking and came from Bohemia. After the family had moved back to Vienna, Kelsen attended the *Gymnasium* there. By his own admission, he was a mediocre student.[2] Even during his school days, he began to take an interest in philosophy, especially Kant's transcendental philosophy.[3] After his *Abitur* (1900) and a subsequent year of military service (1900–1901), he decided, more out of practical considerations than for any other reason, to study law with the intent of becoming a lawyer or judge. The study of philosophy, so he reasoned at the time, would have led him into a teaching career, something his own schooling had turned him firmly against.[4]

[1] Autobiography in: M. Jestaedt (ed.), *Hans Kelsen Werke* (Tübingen: Mohr Siebeck, 2007). The only biography of Kelsen by one of his students is R. A. Métall, *Hans Kelsen. Leben und Werk* (Vienna: Deutike, 1969).

[2] Kelsen, Autobiography in: M. Jestaedt (ed.), *Hans Kelsen Werke*, 31.

[3] Ibid., 33. [4] Ibid., 34.

During his years at university, Kelsen continued to study philosophical issues on his own, reading, among other things, the works of Herman Cohen, the head of the Marburg School of Neo-Kantianism. The only class he attended regularly during the first years of his studies, by his own admission, was that taught by Professor Leo Strisower, an international lawyer known beyond Vienna, on the history of the philosophy of law. There he learned about the political-philosophical writings of Dante Alighieri and decided, against the advice of Strisower, to write a monograph about Dante's work *De Monarchia*.[5] In this book, which he himself, looking back, called an "unoriginal schoolboy's piece," one can already see the basic intuitions and preferences which shaped his understanding of law and international politics. During the second half of his studies, he also participated in the seminars on state law taught by Professor Edmund Bernatzik, who was regarded as a keen and eloquent interpreter of Austrian constitutional law. It was here that the idea of studying a topic in public law under Bernatzik for his *Habilitation* matured. However, during the years Kelsen was working on his *Habilitation*, Bernatzik made clear to him that he had little prospect of an academic career, and he advised him to become a lawyer or bank official. Kelsen, however, would not be deterred from his undertaking. With a scholarship he went to Heidelberg for his *Habilitation*, where Georg Jellinek was teaching at the time.

At the beginning of the twentieth century, Georg Jellinek's doctrine on state law was the measure of all things in German-language public law. Georg Jellinek, the first dean of the Heidelberg law faculty who was of Jewish background, had retained the Hegel-inspired assumption of the will of the sovereign state as the law's ground of validity, but enriched his theory of public law with sociological and psychological elements. His work symbolizes the transition to a modern broadening of perspectives in German legal scholarship toward the integration of insights from the new neighboring disciplines, such as for example the emerging field of sociology. In Heidelberg, Kelsen attended Jellinek's seminar and felt repelled by the devoted band of disciples he felt Jellinek had gathered around himself. By now obsessed with the idea of putting legal positivism on a more objective scientific basis, he worked out a theoretical approach that turned against Jellinek's theoretical approach in two ways.[6] First, it displaced the

5 Ibid., 35–36.

6 This is what Kelsen had to say in his autobiographical sketch (41): "I was completely intoxicated by the feeling of embarking on a new path in my discipline."

Hegelian notion of will and the personification of the state as a subject capable of an exercise of will. Second, it radically rejected Jellinek's broadening to include sociological and psychological questions, which Kelsen wanted to purge entirely from the subject matter of jurisprudence.

With his monograph *Die Hauptprobleme der Staatsrechtslehre, entwickelt aus der Lehre vom Rechtssatze*, which was published in 1911, Kelsen successfully defended his *Habilitation* at the faculty of law and political science in Vienna. However, he was not offered a professorship at the faculty, probably because of his Jewish background. Kelsen had converted to Catholicism at the age of 24 (1905) and to Protestantism at the age of 31 (1912). In 1912 he married Margarete Bondi; the marriage lasted sixty-one years. The couple had two daughters. During the last three years before the First World War, Kelsen taught at the University of Vienna as a private lecturer and founded the *Österreichische Zeitschrift für Öffentliches Recht* [Austrian Journal for Public Law], though without acting as the editor in a way that was apparent on the outside. Shortly before the outbreak of the war, he became an official lecturer at the Vienna Export Academy, today's Economic University of Vienna.

Soon after the outbreak of the war, Kelsen was declared "fit only for office work" by the military authorities because of a serious lung infection and was transferred to the Ministry of War. There, Minister Colonel General Stoeger-Steiner became aware of him through an essay on military law that Kelsen had published, and he appointed him his personal advisor on questions of military and international law, especially on the question of separating the Hungarian army from the joint Habsburg military forces. At this time, Kelsen also started to work on his central monograph on international law, *Das Problem der Souveränität und die Theorie des Völkerrechts*, which was not published until 1920. An anecdote recounted in his autobiography provides insight into the political situation during the final weeks of the Habsburg monarchy:[7]

> I can still vividly remember one of my last conversations with the minister. I had been summoned to the minister via phone in the middle of the night. He received me in his dressing gown in his private office in the official residence he had in the building of the Ministry of War. He handed me the text of a telegram that President Wilson had sent in response to the offer by the Austro-Hungarian government to grant the nationalities of the monarchy the right of self-determination, and he asked me to comment on Wilson's statement. While I was reading

[7] Ibid., 49–50.

> Wilson's response, the minister put on his uniform jacket and invited me to go into his office. On the way there we had to pass the ball room that was part of the minister's residence. At that point the minister said to me that it was embarrassing to live in such splendid chambers during such a terrible time. "Especially, Your Excellency, if one knows that one is the last Minister of War of the monarchy." "You are crazy," he responded, "how can you say something so awful!" To the very last moment, the old officer, even though he had no illusions about the magnitude of the military defeat, could not believe it possible that an empire of four hundred years could simply vanish from the stage of history. When I took my leave in person a short time later, he stood there in his office deathly pale. On the drive into the Ministry, the mob had pelted his car with stones, a shard of glass had injured him on the cheek. He shook my hand and said with emotion: "You were right. I am the last Minister of War of the monarchy."

Kelsen himself, through his position in the ministry, was directly involved in the various plans to save, reform, and liquidate the Habsburg monarchy. He composed an internal, and in the end unsuccessful, memorandum intended to persuade the Emperor to transform the monarchy into a federation of independent nation states on the basis of the right of self-determination of nations.[8]

During the war, Kelsen also began to gather around himself in Vienna a circle of young jurists who, in the interwar period, became known beyond Vienna as the "Vienna School of Legal Theory."[9] In the area of international law they included above all Alfred Verdross, Leonidas Pitamic, Josef Laurenz Kunz, and Rudolf Aladár Métall, later Leo Gross and John Herz, and, from a broader sphere, also Hersch Lauterpacht and Hans Morgenthau. The public-law scholar Adolf Merkl, the creator of the concept of the hierarchical structure of the law [*Stufenbaulehre*], also belonged to the circle as one of Kelsen's oldest students. However, Kelsen's school was characterized more by the shared questions prompted by Kelsen than by shared positions on the same. Contradicting the teacher's theses, even in published form, and scholarly debate and critique seem to have been the uniting element.

After the war – Kelsen as professor and constitutional court judge in Vienna (1919–1933)

Kelsen's early scholarly renown, and especially his work as personal advisor to the minister in the Imperial Ministry of War during the First

[8] Ibid., 50. [9] Ibid., 55–56.

World War and the high-ranking political contacts this entailed, made it possible for him to obtain a regular professorship at the faculty of law and political science in Vienna after the war (1919).[10] In 1918, Kelsen had been asked by the State Chancellor of the provisional Austrian government, the Social Democrat Karl Renner, to participate in the drafting of the new Austrian constitution, for which the Weimar Constitution was to serve as the model. Kelsen worked out several drafts, and with the new constitutional court he created the first judicial body in constitutional history to be given the power to overturn laws on the grounds of unconstitutionality with an effect that was general and not limited to the specific case. One of the drafts worked up by Kelsen was adopted, with changes, by the constituent National Assembly. The section on constitutional adjudication had passed the parliamentary process without alteration.[11]

Notwithstanding his sharp critique of the political theory of Marxism, Kelsen, by his own account, drew ideologically ever closer to socialist ideas during this time and openly embraced social democracy. This is what Kelsen said looking back:[12]

> From the very beginning, I was in complete agreement with the democratic program of the Austrian Party, which did stand fundamentally on the ground of Marxism, but which had practically nothing to do with the anarchistic state theory of Marx and Engels. As an individualist, I was originally opposed to its economic program of nationalizing the economy. Later, especially under the impression of the economic upheavals that the war had brought with it, I became more and more inclined to acknowledge that the system of economic liberalism, the way it was being realized under the given circumstances, provided no guarantee for the economic security of the mass of the have-nots. [. . .] I was and am fully aware of the difficulty combining the nationalization of production with the political freedom of the individual; but I believe I must be objective enough to acknowledge that economic security for the great mass is more important than anything else, and that I do not have the right to be politically active for the preservation of an economic system in which I and those like me do well, and to act against an economic system of which I had to assume that it was in the interest of the great mass.

As professor for state and administrative law at the University of Vienna between 1919 and 1929, Kelsen published fundamental monographs that constitute the central pillars of his public-law oeuvre. It

[10] Ibid., 54. [11] Ibid., 66–67. [12] Ibid., 58–59.

began in 1920 with *Das Problem der Souveränität und die Theorie des Völkerrechts* [The Problem of Sovereignty and the Theory of International Law], followed by *Der soziologische und der juristische Staatsbegriff* [The Sociological and the Legal Concept of the State, 1922], *Die Allgemeine Staatslehre* [General Theory of the State, 1925], *Die philosophische Grundlagen der Naturrechtslehre und des Rechtspositivismus* [The Philosophical Foundations of the Theory of Natural Law and of Legal Positivism, 1928], and *Wesen und Wert der Demokratie* [The Nature and Value of Democracy, 1929]. During that time he also delivered his first Hague Lectures, "Les Rapports de Système entre le Droit interne et le Droit international" (RdC 1926, Tome 14, 227–331). In these years, Kelsen's school became known beyond Vienna as the Vienna School of Legal Theory. One of his students from those days was Hersch Lauterpacht, who was probably the most influential international lawyer in the world during the first two decades after the Second World War.

In the fall of 1929, Kelsen left Vienna to accept a professorship at the legal faculty in Cologne. This move had been preceded by a defamation campaign from Catholic-conservative circles and their press organs against Kelsen as constitutional judge. Since 1920, Kelsen had been a member of the constitutional court he himself had conceived, and in 1928 he had been part of a decision that abolished so-called *Dispensehen* by the regular courts. This decision was intended to put an end to the ultra vires repeal by regular courts of official permissions for remarriage following a divorce. According to Austrian constitutional law, this power of repeal belonged only to the administrative court, not the regular courts. The Conservative government, which opened itself increasingly to Fascist influences from the end of the 1920s, used this decision to abolish the independent status of constitutional court judges, who were replaced by a panel of politically appointed judges. Deeply embittered by the destruction of the independent constitutional court and the anti-Semitic defamation campaign against him personally, Kelsen went to Cologne with his family, where the University had offered him a full professorship. Here he devoted himself to an intensive study of positive international law, since in Cologne, as the director of the seminar on international law, he lectured on positive international law for the first time.

Only a few months after Hitler came to power, Kelsen was one of the first law professors to be dismissed by the Nazi government. On the same day in Germany, the renowned legal scholars Hermann Heller (1891–1933),

Hermann Ulrich Kantorowicz (1877–1940), Karl Loewenstein (1891–1973), and Hugo Sinzheimer (1875–1945), among others, were put on a "leave of absence" effective immediately.[13] The faculty intervened in favor of Kelsen through a written petition to the Reich Commissioner for the Prussian Ministry of Science, Art, and Popular Education, and asked for his reinstatement. All professors of the university signed the petition, with the exception of Carl Schmitt.[14] The latter had been newly appointed to the faculty that same year, with Kelsen's support. At this time, Carl Schmitt stood at the beginning of his rapid rise to becoming the "crown jurist" of the Nazi regime in the first years after the takeover of power.

Emigration experiences – Kelsen in Geneva and the United States (1933–1973)

After his dismissal in Cologne, Kelsen left Germany with the help of a local Nazi official who worked in the university administration and procured an emigration visa for him. Back in Vienna, the university was no longer willing to offer him an academic post in 1933. Moreover, in 1934 he was forced, because of his Jewish background, to relinquish the editorship of the journal *Zeitschrift für Öffentliches Recht*, which he had founded in 1914.[15] This caused a falling-out with his former student Alfred Verdross, who henceforth appeared in the journal as the editor-in-chief without Kelsen's participation. That same year, Kelsen accepted an offer at the Institut de hautes études internationales in Geneva, where, as he would write later, he would spend "seven years of satisfying work in an ideal environment."[16] He rejected job offers from the London School of Economics and the New School of Social Research in New York because he regarded his knowledge of English as inadequate.[17]

Kelsen's time in Geneva saw the publication of the first edition of the *Pure Theory of Law*, an extremely condensed and stylistically brilliant summation of the Kelsenian theory of law, state, and international law. In Geneva, Kelsen devoted himself to an intensive study of the history of natural law, which led him to the ancient belief in the soul in pre-Homeric Greek culture and in the so-called "primitive" religions; in that belief he saw the key to understanding the development of all natural-law thinking. Only parts of this sociological-anthropological work, which was heavily laced with references to the history of philosophy and encompassed more than 2,000 manuscript pages, were

[13] Ibid., 79, note 240. [14] Ibid. [15] Ibid., 45. [16] Ibid., 89. [17] Ibid., 81.

published by Kelsen much later.[18] Another work published during his early years in Geneva was *The Legal Process and International Order* (translated by Horsfall Carter, London, 1934). Well-known students and up coming scholars who studied with Kelsen at the Institut de hautes études internationales were Hans Morgenthau, John H. Herz, and Umberto Campagnolo.[19] During this time, Kelsen was also given an additional professorship at the German-speaking university in Prague, which he sought to combine with his job in Geneva. However, his work in Prague did not last long. Once again, anti-Semitically motivated attacks on him personally prevented sustained work. This is what Kelsen said about this time in his autobiography:[20]

> In the middle of October 1936, I went to Prague alone, without my family, to begin my lectures. I had taken a leave of absence from the institute in Geneva. On the day of my inaugural lecture, the university building was occupied by National Socialist students and by members of non-student, German-national organizations. . . . Already after my first few words, the cry was heard: "Down with the Jew, all non-Jews must leave the hall." . . . My very small audience in fact consisted of only a few Jewish and socialist students. Added to this was that I received several anonymous letters signed with the swastika, which threatened my life in case I did not give up my work at the university. That such threats had to be taken very seriously was shown by the murder some time ago of Professor Theodor Lessing, who, to escape the persecutions of the Nazis, had fled to Czechoslovakia, where he had been assassinated in Karlsbad.

When the situation in Czechoslovakia became more and more tense politically in 1938 due to the increasingly open aggression on the part of the German-national, largely National Socialist-organized, forces in Prague, Kelsen was unable to continue his teaching at the university. Back in Geneva, Kelsen feared, when war broke out in 1939, that Switzerland could be dragged into the conflict, and he decided to emigrate to the United States. The president of the New School of Social Research, Alvin Johnson, offered Kelsen a position, which made it possible for him and his wife to enter the United States. Once in the United States, he was offered in 1940 the one-year Oliver Wendell

[18] H. Kelsen, *Society and Nature. A Sociological Inquiry* (Chicago: The University of Chicago Press, 1943).

[19] N. B. Ladavac, "Hans Kelsens Genfer Jahre" in R. Walter, C. Jabloner, and K. Zeleny (eds.), *Hans Kelsen und das Völkerrecht* [Schriftenreihe des Hans Kelsen Instituts, vol. 26] (Vienna: Manz, 2004), 172.

[20] H. Kelsen, Autobiography in M. Jestaedt (ed.), *Hans Kelsen Werke*, 85–86.

Holmes Lectureship at Harvard University, which he preferred over the job offer at the New School. After that, he became a visiting fellow at Wellesley College, a position that the president of the university did not renew after its second year. During that time, he taught a seminar on legal sociology and gave lectures on international law, in which he dealt with the legal reorganization of international relations after the Second World War. The latter were published in 1942 as the Oliver Wendell Holmes Lectures under the title *Law and Peace in International Relations*.

In 1942, Kelsen went as a visiting professor to the University of California in Berkeley, where in 1945 he was appointed full professor for international law, jurisprudence, and the origin of legal institutions. Kelsen wrote about his years of teaching in Berkeley:[21] "My teaching is quite satisfactory. To be sure, with my pure theory of law I would be a better fit with a legal faculty. But American Law Schools are not especially interested in a scientific theory of law. They are legal-professional schools; their function is preparation for the practical profession as a lawyer." In spite of the "relatively minor" scholarly interest of his students in the political science department, Kelsen had enough time for scholarly work in addition to his teaching. In 1952, Kelsen published his comprehensive commentary on the UN Charter, *The Law of the United Nations*, which became an important legal point of reference in the political daily business of the United Nations, which was shaped by the Cold War. His Berkeley years also saw the publication of the second edition of the *Pure Theory of Law* and his textbook on international law, *Principles of International Law*. In the 1960s, Kelsen was working on a new edition of his legal theory, which radically questioned many axioms of the Pure Theory of Law, but he did not have it published.[22]

In 1973, only three-and-a-half months after the death of his wife Margarete, Kelsen died in Orinda, a town east of Berkeley.

Alfred Verdross (1890–1980)

Alfred Verdross was the oldest of Hans Kelsen's students[23] and an early member of the so-called Vienna School of Legal Theory. Through his early specialization on questions of international law, he provided crucial

[21] Ibid., 90. [22] *Allgemeine Theorie der Normen*.

[23] This is how Kelsen described him in his autobiography: M. Jestaedt (ed.), *Hans Kelsen Werke* (Tübingen: Mohr Siebeck, 2007), 45.

impulses, especially to Kelsen's theory of international law, but as early as the mid-1920s he turned away from the Neo-Kantian and value-relative foundation of the law in the Pure Theory. The committed Catholic's embrace of Christian natural law, together with the general principles interpreted through natural law, as the foundation of international law, as well as the idea of *ius cogens* norms he propagated, turned him into probably the most influential international lawyer from within Hans Kelsen's inner circle.[24]

Alfred Verdross was born on February 22, 1890 in Innsbruck, the son of a professional officer of noble background in the Habsburg army. He was a member of the Catholic Austrian upper class. In 1960, Stephan Verosta described the social milieu in which Verdross's parents moved as follows: "As a member of the professional military, Verdross' father belonged to an estate that was, alongside the dynasty and the civil service, one of the sustaining pillars of the Habsburg monarchy, committed in his life and thought to the multi-national Austria."[25] In the final years before the First World War, Verdross studied law at the University of Vienna, and like Kelsen a decade earlier, he attended Leo Strisower's seminar on legal philosophy. It was during this time that he came into contact with the young lecturer Kelsen. He finished his studies in 1913 with his doctorate. During the First World War, Verdross served on the Supreme Military Court, and he was part of the close circle of students in Kelsen's private seminar. During the final phase of the war, he was transferred as a legal expert to the Austro-Hungarian Foreign Office, where he was active as a legal advisor also after the First World War.

In 1921, Verdross successfully defended his *Habilitation* at the faculty of law and political science in Vienna. He became an associate professor in this department in 1924 and a full professor in 1925, a post he occupied for thirty-six years.

In 1927, Verdross delivered his first Hague Lectures, followed by his general course in 1929, and two specialized courses in 1931 and 1935. In 1928, he was also appointed an *associé* at the Institut de Droit international. When the democratic constitution in Austria was suspended in 1933, the new authoritarian Dollfuß government offered him the post of Minister of Justice, which Verdross turned down. In 1937, he became a member of the Austrian Academy of Sciences. That same year also saw

[24] On his theoretical contributions to the international legal debate Simma, "The Contribution of Alfred Verdross to the Theory of International Law," 33–54.

[25] S. Verosta, *Alfred Verdross – Leben und Werk* (Vienna: Springer Verlag, 1960), 1.

the first edition of his textbook on international law, which contained traces of the increasingly nationalistic and volkishly charged articulation of legal concepts in German and Austrian legal scholarship.[26] In 1938, following Germany's entry into Austria and the country's annexation to the German Reich, Verdross, like other professors in Vienna, was subjected to an examination by the new rulers. While this examination was in progress, his teaching duties were suspended. He was allowed to resume teaching positive international law from the middle of 1939, though he was stripped of his permission to teach legal philosophy until the end of the war, probably because of his well-known Christian natural-law orientation. In 1942, he became a judge at the German Prize Court of Appeals.

Immediately after the war, he was once again given full teaching permission in Vienna. In 1946, he was made dean of the law faculty for the second time, and in 1951 he became rector of the University of Vienna. From 1958 to 1976 he was a judge at the European Court of Human Rights, and from 1957 to 1966 he was a member of the UN International Law Commission. Between 1959 and 1961 he was also president of the Institut de Droit International. Verdross died in Innsbruck on April 27, 1980.

Josef Laurenz Kunz (1890–1970)

Josef Laurenz Kunz was the one student of Kelsen's who, more than any other international lawyer of his generation, transferred insights from the Pure Theory of Law into many subfields of international law.[27] His main areas of research, which he wrote about in his nine monographs and more than 140 essays, were general international law and international legal theory, the law of war and neutrality, the international law of minorities, the law of international organizations, the law of recognition, and questions of collective security.

[26] On the 1937 textbook see Simma, "The Contribution of Alfred Verdross to the Theory of International Law," 36; Carty, "Alfred Verdross and Othmar Spann," 78–97.

[27] E. H. Finch, "Josef L. Kunz (1890–1970)," *American Journal of International Law*, 65 (1971), 129–130; "In memoriam Prof. L. Kunz. A collection of essays on international law, legal history and legal theory in his memory," *University of Toledo Law Review*, 3 (1971); H. Kelsen, "Josef L. Kunz zu seinem siebzigsten Geburtstag am 7. April 1960," *Österreichische Zeitschrift für Öffentliches Recht*, 10 (1959–1960), 324–333; J. Kammerhofer, "Josef Laurenz Kunz" in R. Walter, C. Jabloner, and K. Zeleny (eds.), *Der Kreis um Hans Kelsen. Die Anfangsjahre der Reinen Rechtslehre* (Vienna: Manz, 2008), 243–259.

With Kelsen he shared an identification with the vanishing Austrian monarchy before and during the First World War, and basic cosmopolitan-pacifist convictions, which were reinforced by the World War. In contrast to Kelsen, he came from a fairly upper-class background, was fluent in five languages, published extensively in English, and established scholarly contacts in England and the United States early in his career. Moreover, it was his numerous writings on legal theory in English and Spanish that made the Pure Theory of Law truly known in Latin America and the United States. He can be regarded as Kelsen's closest student on international law, even if, as I have shown in this book, he did not shy from engaging in scholarly controversy with Kelsen on some theoretical issues of international law, and was also willing to chart his own path.

Josef Laurenz Kunz was born on April 1, 1890 in Vienna, the son of a respected and wealthy doctor. As a student, given his musical talent and the successful completion of his training as a concert pianist, he faced the question of whether to become a professional musician. Following his *Abitur*, he did a year of voluntary service in the Royal Austrian Cavalry (1908–1909). Between 1909 and 1913, he decided against the life of a professional musician and enrolled in the department of law and political sciences at the University of Vienna. His time at the university in Vienna was interrupted by a year at the Sorbonne, where he attended lectures by Louis Renault and Henri Bergson. From 1913 he lived in London and attended lectures on international law at University College. Shortly after obtaining his Dr. jur. in Vienna in 1914, he was conscripted into the Austrian army in the First World War and served until the end of the war in 1918.

Deeply shaken by the collapse of the Habsburg Empire, to which he was strongly attached, he enrolled once again at the University of Vienna after the war to work toward a doctorate in political science. During this time he attended lectures by Hans Kelsen and enthusiastically embraced his Pure Theory of Law.[28] Shaped by his experiences during the war, he devoted himself especially to the laws of war and neutrality. His doctoral dissertation, which earned him a Dr. rer. pol. in 1920, was entitled "The Problem of the Violation of Belgian Neutrality." Between 1920 and 1932, Kunz was also active as a legal advisor to the Austrian League of Nations Association.

[28] On this and the following see J. L. Kunz, "Einige Bemerkungen zu meinem Leben und meinen Arbeiten" (unpublished, handwritten autobiography, 1957 – papers, Hans Kelsen-Institut Vienna).

Between 1920 and 1927, his *Habilitation* process in the department of law and political sciences at the University of Vienna was repeatedly stymied by the conservative professor Hold-Ferneck. The latter charged, among other things, that Kunz, in his doctoral dissertation, had been too critical of the German invasion of Belgium in 1914. An additional problem was a sharp scholarly controversy between Kelsen and Hold-Ferneck at this time, which evidently prompted Hold-Ferneck to further obstruct the *Habilitation* process for Kelsen's student Kunz. As was the case with other younger German international lawyers, Kunz's openly expressed cosmopolitan attitude, his enthusiasm for the League of Nations, and his aversion to nationalistic distortions of international law proved an impediment to his career at most German-language universities. Deeply disturbed by the defeat in the war and by the Treaty of Versailles, the conservative mainstream among German and Austrian academia often regarded criticism of the "national cause" as treason against their own nation, "abused" by the Allies.

In 1927, Kunz was finally awarded his *Habilitation* by a majority vote of the faculty of the department of law and political sciences at the University of Vienna, in the face of the continuing opposition of Hold-Ferneck. Still without a chair of his own, Kunz, as a private lecturer, was twice honoured with the invitation to deliver the famous Hague Lectures, in 1930 and 1932.[29] This was a testimony to his early international reputation in the discipline of international law. From 1932 to 1934 he was a Rockefeller Research Fellow in the United States, where, through the offices of the American international lawyer Manley O. Hudson, he was given a chair in international law in Toledo, Ohio. He held that chair until 1960, when he was made a professor emeritus. He took US citizenship in 1940, and in 1944 he became a member of the editorial committee of the American Journal of International Law.

In addition to extensive travels and lecturing in Latin America, Kunz successfully carved out a place for himself in the American discipline of international law during the Second World War. In 1955 he delivered his third series of Hague Lectures.[30] In 1957, at the suggestion of the American members, he was made an associated member of the Institut de Droit International, and in 1969 a full member. He died in Toledo on August 5, 1970, at the age of 80.

[29] J. L. Kunz, "L'option de nationalité," *RCADI* 31 (1930), 111–171; J. L. Kunz, "L'article XI du Pacte de la Société des Nations," *RCADI* 39 (1932), 683–787.

[30] J. L. Kunz, "La crise et les transformations du droit des gens," *RCADI* 88 (1956), 9–104.

BIBLIOGRAPHY

Abbreviations

AJCL	The American Journal of Comparative Law
AJIL	The American Journal of International Law
AöR	Archiv des öffentliches Rechts
ARSP	Archiv für Rechts- und Sozialphilosophie
ARWP	Archiv für Rechts- und Wirtschaftsphilosophie
ASWSP	Archiv für Sozialwissenschaft und Sozialpolitik
BYIL	British Yearbook of International Law
Calif. L. R.	California Law Review
Cardozo L. R.	Cardozo Law Review
Col. L. R.	Columbia Law Review
DÖV	Die öffentliche Verwaltung
EJIL	European Journal of International Law
Harv. ILJ	Harvard International Law Journal
Harvard L. R.	Harvard Law Review
IZTR	Internationale Zeitschrift für die Theorie des Rechts
NJIL	Nordic Journal of International Law
ÖZöR	Österreichische Zeitschrift für öffentliches Recht
RCADI	Recueil des Cours de l'Académie de Droit International
RDI	Revue de droit international
RDILC	Revue de droit international et de législation comparée
RGDIP	Revue générale de droit international public
WRS	*Die Wiener Rechtstheoretische Schule. Ausgewählte Schriften von Hans Kelsen, Adolf Julius Merkl und Alfred Verdross*, ed. H. Klecatsky, R. Marcic, H. Schambeck (Munich: Pustel, 1968), vols. I and II.
Yale L. R.	Yale Law Review

ZaöRV	Zeitschrift für ausländisches öffentliches Recht und Völkerrecht
ZfV	Zeitschrift für Völkerrecht
ZöR	Zeitschrift für öffentliches Recht (continued as ÖzöR)
ZStW	Zeitschrift für die gesamte Staatswissenschaft

Part I Hans Kelsen's writings (in chronological order)

Die Staatslehre des Dante Alighieri. Wiener Staatswissenschaftliche Studien, ed. E. Bernatzik and E. von Phillippovich (Vienna and Leipzig: F. Deuticke, 1905)

"Zur Soziologie des Rechts. Kritische Betrachtungen," *ASWSP*, 34 (1912), 601–614

"Eine Grundlegung der Rechtssoziologie," *ASWSP*, 39 (1915), 839–876

"Book Review of: Rudolf Laun, *Zur Nationalitätenfrage Haag 1916*," *ZöR*, 3 (1917), 585–586

"Zur Theorie der Juristischen Fiktionen. Mit besonderer Berücksichtigung von Vaihingers Philosophie des Als-ob" [1919], *WRS*, I, 1215–1241 ["Theorie der Juristischen Fiktionen"]

"Der völkerrechtliche Strafanspruch wegen völkerrechtswidriger Kriegshandlungen," *Neue Freie Presse Wien* (September 8, 1920), 3–4

"Der Begriff des Staates und der Sozialpsychologie. Mit besonderer Berücksichtigung von Freuds Theorie der Masse" in Sigmund Freud (ed.), *Imago*, VIII/2 (1922)

"Rechtswissenschaft und Recht. Erledigung eines Versuches zur Überwindung der 'Rechtsdogmatik'," *ZöR*, 3 (1922), 98 *et seq.*

Über den juristischen und den soziologischen Staatsbegriff. Kritische Untersuchung des Verhältnisses von Staat und Recht (Tübingen: Mohr, 1922; reprint of the 2nd edn. of 1928, Aalen: Scientia, 1962) [*Staatsbegriff*]

Hauptprobleme der Staatsrechtslehre, entwickelt aus der Lehre vom Rechtssatz, 2nd edn. with an added preface (Tübingen: J. B. Mohr, 1923) [*Hauptprobleme*]

Allgemeine Staatslehre (Berlin: J. Springer, 1925) [*Staatslehre*]

"Souveränität," in Karl Strupp (ed.), *Wörterbuch des Völkerrechts und der Diplomatie* (Berlin and Leipzig: W. de Gruyter, 1925), vol. 2, 554 *et seq.* ["Souveränität"]

"Les rapports de système entre le droit interne et le droit international public," *RCADI*, 14/IV (1926), 231 *et seq.*

"Die Idee des Naturrechts," *ZöR*, 7 (1928), 221–250; reprint in *WRS* I, 251

Die philosophischen Grundlagen der Naturrechtslehre und des Rechtspositivismus (Charlottenburg: R. Heise, 1928), also printed in *WRS* I, 281 *et seq.* [*Grundlagen*]

Das Problem der Souveränität und die Theorie des Völkerrechts. Beitrag zu einer Reinen Rechtslehre [1920], 2nd edn. (Tübingen: J. C. B. Mohr, 1928) [*Problem der Souveränität*]

Rechtsgeschichte gegen Rechtsphilosophie? Eine Erwiederung (Vienna: J. Springer, 1928) [*Rechtsgeschichte*]

"Juristischer Formalismus und Reine Rechtslehre," *Juristische Wochenschrift*, 58 (1929), 1723–1726

"Wesen und Entwicklung der Staatsgerichtsbarkeit. Überprüfung von Verwaltungsakten durch die öffentlichen Gerichte" in H. Triepel, H. Kelsen, and M. Layer (eds.), *Veröffentlichungen der Vereinigung der Deutschen Staatsrechtslehrer, Heft 5, Tagung vom 23. und 24. April 1928 in Wien* (Berlin and Leipzig: W. de Gruyter, 1929), 30 *et seq.*

Vom Wesen und Wert der Demokratie, 2nd revised edn. (Tübingen: Mohr, 1929; 1st edn., Tübingen: Mohr, 1920; reprint of the 2nd edn., Aalen: Scientia Verlag, 1981) [*Wesen und Wert der Demokratie*]

"Wer soll Hüter der Verfassung sein?" [1931] reprint in *WRS* II, 1873 *et seq.*

"Théorie générale du droit international public," *RCADI*, 42/IV (1932), 148 *et seq.*

Unrecht und Unrechtsfolge im Völkerrecht (Vienna and Berlin: J. Springer, 1932)

The Legal Process and International Order. The New Commonwealth Research Bureau Publications (London: Constable & Co., 1934)

Reine Rechtslehre. Einleitung in die rechtswissenschaftliche Problematic (Leipzig and Vienna: F. Deuticke, 1934) [*Reine Rechtslehre*]

"Die Technik des Völkerrechts und die Organisation des Friedens," *ZöR*, 14 (1934), 240 *et seq.*

"Contribution à la théorie du traité internationale," *Revue internationale de la théorie du droit*, 10 (1936), 253 *et seq.*

Centralization and Decentralization. A Paper delivered at the Harvard Tercentenary Conference of Arts and Sciences (Cambridge, MA: Harvard University Press, 1936)

"Sanktionen sind Sache des Gerichts," *Geneva Press Service* (10 July 1936), 1–3

"La transformation du droit international public en droit interne," *RGDIP*, 43 (1936), 5 *et seq.*

"Zur rechtstechnischen Revision des Völkerbundstatuts," *ZöR*, 17 (1937), 401 *et seq.*, 590 *et seq.*

Legal Technique in International Law. A textual critique of the League Covenant (Geneva Research Center, 1939)

"Les résolutions de la SDN concernant la séparation du Pacte et des Traités de Paix," *RDILC*, 1 (1939), 101 *et seq.*

"Revision des Völkerbundstatuts" in *Legal Technique in International Law. A textual critique of the League Covenant* (Geneva Research Center, 1939) ["Revision des Völkerbundstatuts"]

"Théorie du droit international coutumier" in *Festschrift für Franz Weyer*, vol. 2 (Prague, 1939)

"International Peace – by Court or by Government?" *American Journal of Sociology*, XLVI (1941), 571 *et seq.*

"The Essential Conditions of International Justice" in *Proceedings of the Thirty-fifth Annual Meeting of the American Society of International Law*, April 24–26, 1941, 70 *et seq.*

"The Law as a specific Social Technique," *University of Chicago Law Review*, 9 (1941), 75 *et seq.*

Law and Peace in International Relations. The Oliver Wendell Holmes Lectures, 1940–1941 (Cambridge, MA: Harvard University Press, 1942)

"Collective and Individual Responsibility in International Law with Particular Regard to Punishment of War Criminals," *Calif. L. R.*, 31 (1943), 530–571

"Compulsory Adjudication of International Disputes," *AJIL*, 37 (1943), 397 *et seq.*

Peace through Law (Chapel Hill: University of North Carolina Press, 1944)

"The Principle of Sovereign Equality of States as a Basis for International Organization," *Yale L. R.*, 53 (1944), 207 *et seq.*

"The Strategy for Peace," *American Journal of Sociology*, XLIX (1944), 381 *et seq.*

"The Old and the New League: The Covenant and the Dumbarton Oaks Proposals," *AJIL*, 39 (1945), 45–83

"The Rule against Ex Post Facto Laws and the Prosecution of Axis War Criminals" in *Judge Advocate Journal*, 2 (1945), 8–12, 27, 46

"Zur Grundlegung der Völkerrechtslehre. Eine Auseinandersetzung mit Heinrich Drost," *ÖZöR*, 1 (1946/1948), 20 *et seq.*

"Will the Judgment in the Nuremberg Trial constitute a Precedent in International Law?" *International Law Quarterly*, 1 (1947), 153–171

General Theory of Law and State (Cambridge, MA: Harvard University Press, 1949) [*General Theory*]

The Law of the United Nations. A Critical Analysis of its Fundamental Problems, 2nd Impression (New York: F. A. Praeger, 1951; first edn. New York, 1950)

"Science and Politics," *American Political Science Review*, XLV (1951), 641 *et seq.*

Principles of International Law (New York: Rinehart, 1952)

"Reine Rechtslehre und egologische Theorie," *ÖZöR*, 5 (1953), 449 *et seq.*

"Was ist die Reine Rechtslehre?" [1953] *WRS*, I, 611 *et seq.*

"Law, State, and Justice in the Pure Theory of Law," *Yale Law Journal* 57 (1958)

"Josef L. Kunz zu seinem siebzigsten Geburtstag am 7. April 1960," *Österreichische Zeitschrift für Öffentiches Recht*, 10 (1959–1960), 324–333

Reine Rechtslehre. Mit einem Anhang: Das Problem der Gerechtigkeit, 2nd completely revised and expanded edn. (Vienna: Deuticke, 1960)

"Allgemeine Rechtslehre im Lichte materialistischer Geschichtsauffassung" in N. Leser (ed.), *Demokratie und Sozialismus* (Vienna: Wissenschaftliche Buchgesellschaft, 1967), 69 *et seq.*

Principles of International Law, 2nd edn., revised and ed. R. W. Tucker (New York: Holt, Rinehart and Winston, 1967)

Auseinandersetzungen zur reinen Rechtslehre: Kritische Bemerkungen zu Georges Scelle and Michael Virally, ed. Kurt Ringhofer and Robert Walter (Vienna and New York: Springer, 1987) [*Georges Scelle*]

Introduction to the Problems of Legal Theory, a translation of the 1st edn. of *Reine Rechtslehre* or *Pure Theory of Law*, trans. B. Litschewski Paulson and S. L. Paulson with an introduction by S. L. Paulson (Oxford University Press, 1992) [*Problems of Legal Theory*]

Werke, ed. M. Jestaedt (Tübingen: Mohr-Siebeck, 2007)

Part II

Abi-Saab G., "Cours général de droit international public," *RCADI*, 207/VII (1987)

Achterberg N., "Hans Kelsens Bedeutung in der gegenwärtigen deutschen Rechtslehre," *DÖV*, 27 (1974), 445 *et seq.*

"Kelsen und Marx. Zur Verwendbarkeit der reinen Rechtslehre in relativistischen und dogmatischen Rechtssystemen," *Politik und Kultur*, 2 (1975), 40 *et seq.*

Acker D., *Walter Schücking (1875–1935)* (Münster in Westfalen: Aschendorf, 1970)

Actes de la première Assemblée, Séances des Commissions, vol. 1. Geneva, 1921

Adorno Th. and M. Horkheimer, *Dialektik der Aufklärung Philosophische Fragmente* [1947] (Reprint, Frankfurt am Main: Suhrkamp, 1998)

Anghie A., "On Critique and the Other" in A. Orford (ed.), *International Law and its Others* (Cambridge University Press, 2006)

Anzilotti D., *Corso di diritto internazionale*, 2nd edn. (Rome: Athenaeum, 1912)

Lehrbuch des Völkerrechts (Berlin and Leipzig: W. de Gruyter, 1929)

Arendt H., *The Human Condition* (Chicago University Press, 1958)

Aron R., *Frieden und Krieg. Eine Theorie der Staatenwelt* (Frankfurt am Main: Fischer, 1986)

Peace and War. A Theory of International Relations, trans R. Howard and A. Baker Fox (Garden City, N.Y: Doubleday, 1966)

Baker P. J., *The Geneva Protocol* (London: P. S. King & Son Ltd., 1925)

"The Obligatory Jurisdiction of the Permanent Court of International Justice," *BYIL*, IV (1925), 68 *et seq.*

Baldus M., *Die Einheit der Rechtsordnung* (Berlin: Duncker & Humblot, 1995)

"Habsburgian Multiethnicity and the 'Unity of the State' – On the Structural Setting of Kelsen's Legal Thought" in D. Diner and M. Stolleis (eds.), *Hans Kelsen and Carl Schmitt: A Juxtaposition* (Gerlingen: Bleicher, 1999)

Baratta A., "Rechtspositivismus und Gesetzespositivismus: Gedanken zu einer 'naturrechtlichen' Apologie des Rechtspositivismus," *ARSP*, 54 (1968), 325 *et seq.*

Barthélemy J., "Le problème de la Souveraineté des États et la coopération européenne," *RDI*, 5 (1930), 420 *et seq.*
Bast J., "Das Demokratiedefizit fragmentierter Institutionalisierung," in H. Brunkhorst (ed.), *Demokratie in der Weltgesellschaft*, Soziale Welt Sonderband Nr. 18 (Baden-Baden: Nomos, 2009)
Becker L., "Schritte auf einer abschüssigen Bahn," *Das Archiv des öffentlichen Rechts (AöR) und die deutsche Staatsrechtswissenschaft im Dritten Reich* (Tübingen: Mohr Siebeck, 1999)
Behrend J., *Untersuchungen zur Stufenbaulehre Adolf Merkls und Hans Kelsens* (Berlin: Duncker & Humblot, 1977)
Beller S., *Vienna and the Jews, 1867–1938* (Cambridge, MA: Harvard University Press, 1989)
Benvenisti E. and G. W. Downs, "The Empire's New Clothes: Political Economy and the Fragmentation of International Law," *Stanford Law Review*, 60 (2007)
Berber F. J., *Sicherheit und Gerechtigkeit* (Berlin: C. Heymann, 1934)
Bergbohm C., *Staatsverträge und Gesetze als Quellen des Völkerrechts* (Dorpat: C. Mattiesen, 1877)
Jurisprudenz und Rechtsphilosophie (Leipzig: Duncker & Humblot, 1892)
Berman N., "A Perilous Ambivalence: Nationalist Desire, Legal Autonomy, and the Limits of the Interwar Framework," *Harv. ILJ*, 33 (1992), 353 *et seq.*
"But the Alternative is Despair: European Nationalism and the Modernist Renewal of International Law," *Harvard L. R.*, 106 (1993), 1792 *et seq.*
"Beyond Colonialism and Nationalism? Ethiopia, Czechoslovakia, and 'Peaceful Change'," *NJIL*, 65 (1996), 421 *et seq.*
Bernhardt R., "Ungeschriebenes Völkerrecht," *ZaöRV*, 36 (1976), 50 *et seq.*
von Bernstorff J., "Georg Jellinek – Völkerrecht als modernes öffentliches Recht im fin de siècle" in S. L. Paulson and M. Schulte (eds.), *Georg Jellinek. Beiträge zu Leben und Werk* (Tübingen: Mohr Siebeck, 2000)
Der Glaube an das universale Recht. Zur Völkerrechtstheorie Hans Kelsens und seiner Schüler (Baden-Baden: Nomos, 2001)
"Kelsen und das Völkerrecht. Rekonstruktion einer völkerrechtlichen Berufsethik" in R. Walter, C. Jabloner, and K. Zeleny (eds.), *Kelsen und das Völkerrecht, Schriftenreihe des Hans Kelsen Instituts Band 26* (Vienna: Manz, 2004)
"The Structural Limits of Network Governance. ICANN as a Case in Point" in Chr. Joerges, I.-J. Sand, and G. Teubner (eds.), *Transnational Governance and Constitutionalism* (Oxford: Hart, 2004)
"Sisyphus was an International Lawyer. On Martti Koskenniemi's *From Apology to Utopia* and *The Place of Law in International Politics*," *German Law Journal*, 7/12 (2006), 1015–1035

"The Changing Fortunes of the Universal Declaration of Human Rights: Genesis and Symbolic Dimensions of the Turn to Rights in International Law," *EJIL*, 19 (2008), 903–924

"Zivilgesellschaftliche Partizipation in Internationalen Organisationen: Form globaler Demokratie oder Baustein westlicher Expertenherrschaft?" in H. Brunkhorst (ed.), *Demokratie in der Weltgesellschaft, Soziale Welt Sonderband Nr. 18* (Baden-Baden: Nomos, 2009), 277–302

von Bernstorff J. and I. Venzke, "Ethos, Ethics and Morality in International Relations" in R. Wolfrum (ed.), *The Max Planck Encyclopedia of Public International Law* (Oxford University Press, 2010) -online edition [www.mpepil.com] - forthcoming

Beyleveld D. and R. Brownsword, "Methodological Syncretism in Kelsen's Pure Theory of Law" in S. L. Paulson and B. Litschewski Paulson (eds.), *Normativity and Norms. Critical Perspectives on Kelsenian Themes* (Oxford University Press, 1998), 47 *et seq.*

Bianchi A., "Human Rights and the Magic of Jus Cogens," *EJIL*, 19 (2008), 491–508

Bilfinger C., "Betrachtungen über politisches Recht," *ZaöRV*, 1 (1929), 57 *et seq.*

"Zum Problem der Staatengleichheit im Völkerrecht," *ZaöRV*, 4 (1934), 481–497

"Les bases fondamentales de la Communauté des États," *RCADI*, 63 (1938), 129 *et seq.*

Binder J., "Der Wissenschaftscharakter der Rechtswissenschaft," *Kantstudien*, 25 (1920), 321 *et seq.*

Philosophie des Rechts (Berlin: G. Stilke, 1925)

Binding K., "Die Gründung des norddeutschen Bundes" in O. Müller, B. Windscheid, and J. E. Kuntze (eds.), *Festgabe der Leipziger Juristenfakultät für Windscheid* (Leipzig: Veit, 1889)

Bleckmann A., "Die Handlungsfähigkeit der Staaten. System und Struktur der Völkerrechtsordnung," *ÖZöR*, 29 (1978), 173 *et seq.*

Die Funktionen der Lehre im Völkerrecht (Cologne: Heymann, 1981)

Grundprobleme und Methoden des Völkerrechts (Freiburg: Alber, 1982)

Bluntschli J. C., "Book Review of: G. Jellinek, *Die rechtliche Natur der Staatenverträge*," *Kritische Vierteljahresschrift für Gesetzgebung und Rechtswissenschaft*, 3 (1880), 579–583

Das moderne Völkerrecht der civilisierten Staaten, als Rechtsbuch dargestellt, 3rd edn. (Nördlingen: C. H. Beck'sche Buchhandlung, 1878)

Bobbio N., "Kelsen and Legal Power" in S. L. Paulson and B. Litschewski Paulson (eds.), *Normativity and Norms. Critical Perspectives on Kelsenian Themes* (Oxford University Press, 1998)

"Campagnolo alievo e critico di Hans Kelsen" in M. G. Losano (ed.), *Hans Kelsen – Umberto Campagnolo. Diritto internazionale e Stato sovrano* (Milan: A. Giuffrè, 1999), 81 *et seq.*

von Bogdandy A., "The European Union as a Supranational Federation," *Columbia Journal of European Law*, 6 (2000), 27–54

"Demokratisierung, Globalisierung, Zukunft des Völkerrechts – eine Bestandsaufnahme," *ZaöRV*, 63 (2003), 853–877

"Constitutionalism in International Law. Comment on a Proposal from Germany," *Harv. ILJ*, 47 (2006), 223–242

von Bogdandy A. and I. Venzke, *In Nome di Chi? Giurisdizione Internazionale e Teoria del Discorso* (Turin: Trauben, 2010)

Borradori G. (ed.), *Philosophy in times of Terror, Dialogues with Jürgen Habermas, and Jacques Derrida* (Chicago University Press, 2003)

Bourdieu P., "The Force of Law: Toward a Sociology of the Legal Field," *Hastings Law Journal*, 38 (1987), 805–853

Boyle J., "Ideals and Things: International Legal Scholarship and the Prison House of Language," *Harv. ILJ*, 26 (1985), 327 *et seq.*

Brierly J. L., "The Shortcomings of International Law," *BYIL*, III (1924), 4 *et seq.*

Law of Nations (Oxford: Clarendon Press, 1928)

"Le fondement du caractère obligatoire du droit international public," *RCADI*, 23/III (1928), 463 *et seq.*

"Règles générales de droit de la paix," *RCADI* 58 (1936), 5 *et seq.*

The Basis of Obligation and Other Papers (Oxford: Clarendon Press, 1958)

"The General Act of Geneva 1928," *BYIL*, XI (1930), 119 *et seq.*

"The Judicial Settlement of International Disputes" [1925] in his *The Basis of Obligation and Other Papers* (Oxford: Clarendon Press, 1958), 93 *et seq.*

Brunkhorst H., (ed.), "Verfallsgeschichten," *Deutsche Zeitschrift für Philosophie* (2004), 35–44

"Das freie Recht zum Kriege. Hegemonialer Großraum oder bürgerschaftlicher Konstitutionalismus? – Zwei Begriffe des Rechts" in H. Brunkhorst et al. (eds.), *Jenseits von Zentrum und Peripherie* (Munich: Hampp, 2005), 5–21

(ed.), *Einmischung unerwünscht? Menschenrechte und bewaffnete Intervention* (Frankfurt am Main: Fischer Verlag, 1998)

"Kritik am Dualismus des Internationalen Rechts" in R. Kreide and A. Niederberger (eds.), *Transnationale Verrechtlichung* (Frankfurt: Campus Verlag, 2008)

Brunner E., *Gerechtigkeit. Eine Lehre von den Grundgesetzen der Gesellschaftsordung* (Zurich: Zwingli-Verlag, 1943)

Bruns V., "Völkerrecht als Rechtsordnung I," *ZaöRV*, 1 (1929), 1 *et seq.*

"Bund oder Bündnis," *ZaöRV*, 7 (1937), 295 *et seq.*

Bülck H., "Zur Dogmengeschichte des europäischen Verwaltungsrechts" in *Recht im Dienste der Menschenwürde. Festschrift für Herbert Kraus* (Würzburg: Holzner Verlag, 1964), 29 *et seq.*

von Bulmerincq A. M., "Book Review of: G. Jellink, *Die rechtliche Natur der Staatenverträge*," *Jahrbuch für Gesetzgebung, Verwaltung und Volkswirthschaft*, 4 (1880), 254–257

"Völkerrecht und internationales Recht" in H. Marquarden (ed.), *Handbuch des öffentlichen Rechts*. (Freiburg: J. C. B. Mohr, 1887), vol. 1

von Bülow B. W., *Der Versailler Völkerbund* (Stuttgart: Kohlhammer, 1924)

Bulterman M., "Fundamental rights and the United Nations Financial Sanction Regime. The Kadi and Yusuf judgments of the Court of First Instance of the European Communities," *Leiden Journal of International Law*, 19 (2006), 753–772

Burckhardt W., *Über die Unvollkommenheit des Völkerrechts* (Bern: P. Haupt, 1923)

Butler Sir G., "Sovereignty and the League of Nations," *BYIL*, 1 (1920)

Carr E. H., *The Twenty Years' Crisis 1919–1939* (London: Macmillan and Co., 1939)

Carré de Malberg R., *Contribution à la théorie générale de l'état, spécialement d'après les donnés fournis par le droit constitutionnel français* (Paris: L. Tenin, 1920)

Carty A., "Alfred Verdross and Othmar Spann: German Romantic Nationalism, National Socialism and International Law," *EJIL*, 6 (1995), 78 *et seq.*

"Interwar German Theories of International Law: The Psychoanalytical and Phenomenological Perspectives of Hans Kelsen and Carl Schmitt," *Cardozo Law Review*, 16 (1995), 1235 *et seq.*

The Decay of International Law? (Manchester University Press, 1986)

"The Continuing Influence of Kelsen on the General Perception of the Discipline of International Law," *EJIL*, 9 (1998), 344 *et seq.*

Cathrein V., *Die Grundlage des Völkerrechts* (Freiburg i. Br: Herder, 1918)

Cohen J. L., "Sovereign Equality vs. Imperial Right: The Battle over the 'New World Order'" in W. Breckman et al. (eds.), *The Modernist Imagination. Intellectual History and Critical Theory: Essays in Honour of Martin Jay* (New York, Oxford: Berghahn Books, 2008), 346–367

Corbett P. E., "What is the League of Nations?" *BYIL*, III (1924), 119–148

Cossio C., "Egologische Theorie und Reine Rechtslehre," *ÖZöR*, 5 (1952), 16 *et seq.*

Crawford J., "International Law as an open System" in J. Crawford (ed.), *International Law as an Open System* (London: Cameron May, 2002)

"Negotiating Global Security Threats in a World of Nation States: Issues and Problems of Nation States" in J. Crawford (ed.), *International Law as an Open System* (London: Cameron May, 2002)

Crawford J. and S. Marks, "The Global Democracy Deficit: An Essay in International Law and its Limits" in J. Crawford(ed.), *International Law as an Open System* (London: Cameron May, 2002)

Dahm G., *Völkerrecht* (Stuttgart: Kohlhammer, 1961), vol. II

Degenhardt F., *Zwischen Machtstaat und Völkerbund. Erich Kaufmann (1880–1972)* (Baden-Baden: Nomos, 2008)

Derrida J., *Gesetzeskraft. Der mystische Grund der Autorität* (Frankfurt am Main: Suhrkamp, 1991)

Dicke K., *Effizienz und Effektivität internationaler Organisationen. Darstellung und kritische Analyse eines Topos im Reformprozeß der Vereinten Nationen* (Berlin: Duncker & Humblot, 1994)

Dilcher G., "Der rechtswissenschaftliche Positivismus," *ARSP*, 61 (1975), 497 *et seq.*

Diner D. and M. Stolleis (eds.), *Hans Kelsen and Carl Schmitt: A Juxtaposition.* Schriftenreihe des Instituts für Deutsche Geschichte, Universität Tel-Aviv, 20 (Gerlingen: Bleicher, 1999)

Dreier H., *Rechtslehre. Staatssoziologie und Demokratietheorie bei Hans Kelsen* (Baden-Baden: Nomos, 1986)

Dubischar R., *Einführung in die Rechtstheorie* (Darmstadt: Wissenschaftliche Buchgesellschaft, 1983)

Duguit L., *Souveraineté et liberté. Leçons faites à l'Université Columbia (New York) 1920–1921* (Paris: Alcan, 1922)

Traité du droit constitutionnel, 2nd edn. (Paris: E. de Boccard, 1921–1925)

Dupuis V., *Le droit des gens et les rapports des grandes puissances avec les autres états* (Paris: Plon-Nourrit et cie, 1924)

Dworkin R., *Law's Empire* (London: Fontana Press, 1986)

Dyzenhaus D., *Legality and Legitimacy. Carl Schmitt, Hans Kelsen and Hermann Heller in Weimar* (Oxford University Press, 1997)

Ebenstein W., *Die rechtsphilosophische Schule der Reinen Rechtslehre* (Prague: Taussig & Taussig, 1938; reprint Frankfurt am Main: Sauer & Auvermann, 1969)

"The Pure Theory of Law: Demythologizing Legal Thought," *Calif. L. R.*, 59 (1971), 617 *et seq.*

Ebers G. J., *Die Lehre vom Staatenbunde* (Breslau: M. & H. Marcus, 1910)

Ehrlich L., "The development of International Law as a science," *RCADI*, 105/I (1962), 178–263

von Elbe J., "The Evolution of the Concept of Just War in International Law," *AJIL*, 33 (1939), 665–688

Engisch K., "Der Begriff der Rechtslücke. Eine analytische Studie zu Wilhelm Sauers Methodenlehre" in *Festschrift für Wilhelm Sauer* (Berlin: W. de Gruyter, 1949), 94 *et seq.*

"Form und Stoff in der Jurisprudenz" [1967] in his *Beiträge zur Rechtstheorie* (Frankfurt am Main: V. Klostermann, 1984), 251 *et seq.*

"Vom Sinn des hypothetischen juristischen Urteils" in his *Beiträge zur Rechtstheorie* (Frankfurt am Main: V. Klostermann, 1984), 196 *et seq.*

Englard Y., "Nazi Criticism Against the Normativist Theory of Hans Kelsen – Its Intellectual Basis and Post-Modern Tendencies" in D. Diner and M. Stolleis (eds.), *Hans Kelsen and Carl Schmitt: A Juxtaposition* (Gerlingen: Bleicher, 1999), 133 *et seq.*

Esser J., "Richterrecht, Gerichtsgebrauch und Gewohnheitsrecht" in *Festschrift für Fritz von Hippel* (Tübingen: Mohr, 1967), 95 *et seq.*

Falk R., *The Status of Law in International Society* (Princeton University Press, 1970)

Fassbender B., "The United Nations Charter as Constitution of the International Community," *Columbia Journal of Transnational Law*, 36 (1998), 529–619

"Die Friedens-Warte," *Journal of International Peace and Organization*, 78 (2003), 297–302

Fastenrath U., *Lücken im Völkerrecht* (Berlin: Duncker & Humblot, 1991)

Feller A. H., "Book Review of: H. Kelsen, *The Law of the United Nations*," *Columbia Law Review*, LI (1951), 537 *et seq.*

Fikentscher W., *Methoden des Rechts in vergleichender Darstellung. Band IV: Dogmatischer Teil* (Tübingen: Mohr, 1977)

Finch, E. H., "Josef L. Kunz (1890–1970)," *AJIL*, 65 (1971), 129–130

"In memoriam Prof. L. Kunz A collection of essays on international law, legal history and legal theory in his memory," *University of Toledo Law Review*, 3 (1971)

Fischer-Lescano A. and G. Teubner, "Regime Collisions: The Vain Search for Legal Unity in the Fragmentation of Global Law," *Michigan Journal of International Law*, 25 (2004), 999–1046

Forst R., *Das Recht auf Rechtfertigung: Elemente einer konstruktivistischen Theorie der Gerechtigkeit* (Frankfurt am Main: Suhrkamp, 2007)

Fraenkel E., "Idee und Realität des Völkerbundes im deutschen politischen Denken," *Vierteljahreshefte für Zeitgeschichte*, 16 (1968), 1 *et seq.*

Franck Th., "The Emerging Right to Democratic Governance," *AJIL*, 86 (1992), 46–91

Fricker K. V., "Noch einmal das Problem des Völkerrechts," *Zeitschrift für die gesamte Staatswissenschaft*, 34 (1878), 368–405

Friedmann W. G., *The Changing Structure of International Law* (London: Stevens, 1964)

Friedrich M., "Erich Kaufmann (1880–1972). Jurist in der Zeit und jenseits der Zeiten" in H. Heinrichs et al. (eds.), *Deutsche Juristen jüdischer Herkunft* (Munich: C. H. Beck, 1993), 693 *et seq.*

Frowein J. A., "Der Beitrag der internationalen Organisationen zur Entwicklung des Völkerrechts," *ZaöRV*, 36 (1976), 147 *et seq.*

"Konstitutionalisierung des Völkerrechts," *Berichte der Deutschen Gesellschaft für Völkerrecht*, 39 (2000), 427–447

Le Fur L., "Guerre juste et juste paix," *RGDIP*, 26 (1919), 9–75, 268–309, 349–405

"La théorie du droit naturel depuis le XVIIème siècle et la doctrine moderne," *RCADI*, 18/III (1927), 259 *et seq.*

"Règles générales du droit de la paix," *RCADI*, 54/IV (1935), 5 *et seq.*

von Gagern H., *Critik des Völkerrechts. Mit praktischer Anwendung auf unsere Zeit* (Leipzig: F. A. Brockhaus, 1840)

Garner J. W., "Des limitations à la souveraineté nationale dans les relations extérieures," *RDILC*, 52 (1925), 36–58

"Le développement et les tendances récentes du droit international," *RCADI*, 35/I (1931), 605 *et seq.*

Gidel G., "Droits et devoirs des nations. Théorie classique des droits fondamentaux des États," *RCADI*, 10/V (1925), 541 *et seq.*

Goller P., *Naturrecht, Rechtsphilosophie oder Rechtstheorie. Zur Geschichte der Rechtstheorie an Österreichs Universitäten (1848–1945)* (Frankfurt am Main: P. Lang, 1997)

Grassi M., *Die Rechtsstellung des Individuums im Völkerrecht* (Winterthur: P. G. Keller, 1955)

Grewe W. G., "Vom europäischen zum universalen Völkerrecht," *ZaöRV*, 42 (1982), 449 *et seq.*

(ed.), *Fontes Historiae Iuris Gentium. Quellen zur Geschichte des Völkerrechts* (Berlin and New York: W. de Gruyter, 1992), vol. 3/2, 1815–1945

Gross R., "'Jewish Law and Christian Grace' – Carl Schmitt's Critique of Hans Kelsen" in D. Diner and M. Stolleis (eds.), *Hans Kelsen and Carl Schmitt: A Juxtaposition* (Gerlingen: Bleicher, 1999)

Guggenheim P., "Zum Verhältnis von Völkerrecht und Landesrecht," *IZTR*, 9 (1935), 90–100

"Contribution à l'histoire des sources du droit des gens," *RCADI*, 94 (1958), 52 *et seq.*

Günther K., "Hans Kelsen (1881–1973). Das nüchterne Pathos der Demokratie" in Th. Blanke et al. (eds.), *Streitbare Juristen: eine andere Tradition* (Baden-Baden: Nomos, 1988) 368–371

Habermas J., *Faktizität und Geltung* (Frankfurt am Main: Suhrkamp, 1992)

Der gespaltene Westen. Kleine politische Schriften X (Frankfurt am Main: Suhrkamp, 2004)

Haenel A., *Die vertragsmäßigen Elemente der Deutschen Reichsverfassung. Studien zum Deutschen Staatsrechte* (Leipzig: H. Haessel, 1873), vol. 1

Haesert J. P., "Book Review of: H. Kelsen, *Principles of International Law*," *AJCL*, 2 (1953), 576 *et seq.*

Hälschner P. E., "Zur wissenschaftlichen Begründung des Völkerrechts," *Zeitschrift für volkstümliches Recht und nationale Gesetzgebung*, 1 (1844), 26 *et seq.*

Hammer S., "Kelsens Grundnormkonzeption als neukantianische Erkenntnistheorie des Rechts?" in S. L. Paulson and R. Walter (eds.), *Untersuchungen zur Reinen Rechtslehre* (Vienna: Manz, 1986)

Hart H. L. A., *The Concept of Law* (Oxford: Clarendon Press, 1961)

Essays in Jurisprudence and Philosophy (Oxford: Clarendon Press, 1983)

"Kelsen's Doctrine of the Unity of Law" in H. L. A. Hart (ed.), *Essays in Jurisprudence and Philosophy* (Oxford: Clarendon Press, 1983), 309 *et seq.*

Hassel K., *Kriegsverbrechen vor Gericht. Die Kriegsverbrecherprozesse vor Militärgerichten in der britischen Besatzungszone unter dem Royal Warrant vom 18. Juni 1945 (1945–1949)* (Baden-Baden: Nomos, 2009)

Hatschek J., *Völkerrecht als System rechtlich bedeutsamer Staatsakte* (Leipzig and Erlangen: Deichert, 1923)

Hauser R., *Norm, Recht und Staat. Überlegungen zu Hans Kelsens Theorie der Reinen Rechtslehre* (Vienna and New York: Springer, 1968)

Hebeisen M., *Souveränität in Frage gestellt* (Baden-Baden: Nomos, 1995)

Heffter A. G., *Le droit international de l'Europe*, French trans. (Berlin and Paris: E. H. Schroeder, 1873)

Hegel G. W. F., *Die Philosophie des Rechts, die Mitschriften Wannemann (Heidelberg 1817/18) und Homeyer (Berlin, 1818/19)*, ed. and annotated by K.-H. Ilting (Stuttgart: Klett-Cotta, 1983)

Grundlinien der Philosophie des Rechts oder Naturrechts und Staatswissenschaft im Grundrisse. Auf Grundlage der Werke von 1832–1845. Mit Hegels eigenhändigen Notizen und den mündlichen Zusätzen, 4th edn., (Frankfurt am Main: Suhrkamp, 1995)

Heidemann C., *Die Norm als Tatsache. Zur Normentheorie Hans Kelsens* (Baden-Baden: Nomos, 1997)

Heilborn P., "Grundbegriffe des Völkerrechts" in F. Stier-Somlò (ed.), *Handbuch des Völkerrechts* (Stuttgart: Kohlhammer, 1912), vol. 1, part 1

Heller H., *Die Souveränität. Ein Beitrag zur Theorie des Staats- und Völkerrechts* (Berlin and Leipzig: W. de Gruyter, 1927)

Staatslehre (Leiden: A. W. Sijthoff, 1934)

Herrmann F., *Das Standardwerk. Franz von Liszt und das Völkerrecht* (Baden-Baden: Nomos, 2001)

Herz J. H., "Einige Bemerkungen zur Grundlegung des Völkerrechts," *Revue internationale de la théorie du droit*, 13 (1939), 275 *et seq.*

"Kelsen's Doctrine in the Nuclear Age" in S. Engel and R. A. Métall (eds.), *Law, State and International Legal Order. Essays in Honor of Hans Kelsen* (Knoxville: University of Tennessee Press, 1964), 107 *et seq.*

Hobbes Th., *Leviathan* [1651] (Harmondworth: Penguin, 1968)

Hofmann H., *Legitimität gegen Legalität. Der Weg der politischen Philosophie Carl Schmitts* (Berlin: Duncker & Humblot, 1964)

von Hold-Ferneck A., "Anerkennung und Selbstbindung. Ein Beitrag zur Lehre vom Wesen des Völkerrechts," *Zeitschrift für Rechtsphilosophie*, 4 (1929), 161 *et seq.*

Lehrbuch des Völkerrechts (Leipzig: Meiner, 1930)

Holzhey H., "Kelsens Rechts- und Staatslehre in ihrem Verhältnis zum Neukantianismus" in S. L. Paulson and R. Walter (eds.), *Untersuchungen zur Reinen Rechtslehre* (Vienna: Manz, 1986), 167–192

Horvarth B., "Comment on Kelsen," *Social Research*, 18 (1951), 313 *et seq.*

Huber M., "Beiträge zur Kenntnis der soziologischen Grundlagen des Völkerrechts und der Staatengesellschaft," *Jahrbuch des öffentlichen Rechts der Gegenwart*, 4 (1910), 95 *et seq.*

"Book Review of: Erich Kaufmann, *Das Wesen des Völkerrechts und die Clausula rebus sic stantibus*," *AöR*, 28 (1912), 551–553

Hueck I., "Die deutsche Völkerrechtswissenschaft im Nationalsozialismus" in D. Kaufmann (ed.), *Geschichte der Kaiser-Wilhelm-Gesellschaft im Nationalsozialismus. Bestandsaufnahme und Perspektiven der Forschung* (Göttingen: Wallstein, 2000), 490 *et seq.*

Hurrell A., *On Global Order. Power, Values, and the Constitution of International Society* (Oxford University Press, 2007)

Ipsen K., *Völkerrecht*, 3rd edn., (Munich: C. H. Beck, 1990)

Isak H., "Bemerkungen zu einigen völkerrechtlichen Lehren Hans Kelsens" in O. Weinberger et al. (eds.), *Reine Rechtslehre im Spiegel ihrer Fortsetzer und Kritiker* (Vienna and New York: Springer, 1988), 255 *et seq.*

Jabloner C., "Menschenbild und Friedenssicherung" in R. Walter and C. Jabloner (eds.), *Hans Kelsens Wege sozialphilosophischer Forschung* (Vienna: Manz, 1997), 59 *et seq.*

"Kelsen and his Circle: The Viennese Years," *EJIL*, 9 (1998), 368 *et seq.*

"Verrechtlichung und Rechtsdynamik," *ZöR*, 54 (1999), 261 *et seq.*

Jakab A., "Kelsen's doctrine of international law between epistemology and politics," *Austrian Review of International and European Law*, 9 (2006), 49–62

Jellinek G., *Die rechtliche Natur der Staatenverträge* (Vienna: A. Hölder, 1880)

Die Lehre von den Staatenverbindungen (Vienna: A. Hölder, 1882)

Allgemeine Staatslehre, Second, revised and expanded edition (Berlin: O. Häring, 1905)

Ausgewählte Schriften und Reden von Georg Jellinek (Berlin: O. Häring, 1911), vol. 1

"Moralstatistik und Todestrafe" [1874] in his *Ausgewählte Schriften und Reden von Georg Jellinek* (Berlin: O. Häring, 1911), vol. 1

"Die Zukunft des Krieges" in his *Ausgewählte Schriften und Reden* (Berlin: O. Häring, 1911), vol. 1

System der subjektiven öffentlichen Rechte, 2nd edn. (Tübingen: Mohr, 1919)

Allgemeine Staatslehre, revised 3rd edn. by Walter Jellinek, incorporating handwritten notes. Reprint of the 1914 edn. (Berlin: Springer, 1922)

Jöckel W., *Hans Kelsens rechtstheoretische Methode. Darstellung und Kritik ihrer Grundlagen und hauptsächlichsten Ergebnisse* (Tübingen: Mohr, 1930. Reprint, Aalen: Scientia, 1977)

Joerges C. (ed.), *Transnational Governance and Constitutionalism* (Oxford: Hart, 2004)

Kadelbach S. and T. Kleinlein, "International Law – A Constitution for Mankind? An attempt at a Re-appraisal with an analysis of Constitutional Principles," *German Yearbook of International Law*, 50 (2007), 303–348

Kaltenborn von Stachau C., *Kritik des Völkerechts* (Leipzig: G. Mayer, 1847)

"Zur Revision der Lehre von den internationalen Rechtsmitteln," *ZStW*, 17 (1861), 69 *et seq.*

Kammerhofer, J., "Josep Laurenz Kunz" in R. Walter, C. Jabloner, and K. Zeleny (eds.), *Der Kreis um Hans Kelsen. Die Anfangsjahre der Reinen Rechtslehre* (Vienna: Manz, 2008)

Kant I., *The Metaphysics of Morals*, trans. and ed. by Mary Gregor (Cambridge University Press, 1996)

Karenfort J., *Die Hilfsorganisationen im bewaffneten Konflikt. Rolle und Status unparteiischer humanitärer Organisationen im humanitären Völkerrecht* (Frankfurt am Main: P. Lang, 1998)

Kaufmann E., "Kritik der neukantischen Rechtsphilosophie" [1921] in E. Kaufmann, *Gesammelte Schriften, III, Rechtsidee und Recht* (Göttingen: O. Schwartz, 1960), 176 *et seq.*

Gesammelte Schriften, III, Rechtsidee und Recht (Göttingen: O. Schwartz, 1960)

Das Wesen des Völkerrechts und die Clausula rebus sic stantibus (Tübingen: Mohr, 1911. Reprint, Aalen: Scientia, 1964)

Kemmerer A., "The Turning Aside. On International Law and its History" in R. A. Miller and R. M. Bratspies (eds.), *Progress in International Law* (Leiden: Martinus Nijhoff, 2008), 71–94

Kennedy D., "Theses about International Law Discourse," *German Yearbook of International Law*, (1980), 353–391

International Legal Structures (Baden-Baden: Nomos, 1987)

"The Move to Institutions," *Cardozo L. R.*, 8 (1987), 841 *et seq.*

"International Law and the Nineteenth Century: History of an Illusion," *NJIL*, 65 (1996), 385–420

A Critique of Adjudication, fin de siècle (Cambridge, MA: Harvard University Press, 1997)

Kingsbury B., "Sovereignty and Inequality," *EJIL*, 9 (1998), 599–625

Klabbers J., "The Changing Image of International Organizations" in J.-M. Coicaud and V. Heiskanen (eds.), *The Legitimacy of International Organizations* (Tokyo: United Nations University Press, 2001), 221–255

"Book Review of: A. Aust, *Modern Treaty Law and Practice*," *NJIL*, 71 (2002), 203–205

"Book Review of: J. von Bernstorff, *Der Glaube an das universale Recht. Zur Völkerrechtstheorie Hans Kelsens und seiner Schüler*," *EJIL*, 14 (2003)

Klüber J. L., *Droit des gens moderne de l'Europe* (Stuttgart: J. G. Cotta, 1819)

Kohler J., *Grundlagen des Völkerrechts* (Stuttgart: Enke, 1918)

Koskenniemi M., *From Apology to Utopia. The Structure of International Legal Argument* (Helsinki: Finnish Lawyers' Pub. Co., 1989)

"The Wonderful Artificiality of States," *American Society of International Law Proceedings*, 88 (1994), 22 *et seq.*

"Lauterpacht: The Victorian Tradition in International Law," *EJIL*, 2 (1997), 215 *et seq.*

"Carl Schmitt, Hans Morgenthau, and the Image of Law in International Relations" in M. Byers (ed.), *The Role of Law in International Politics. Essays in International Relations and International Law* (Oxford University Press, 2000)

The Gentle Civilizer of Nations. The Rise and Fall of European International Law 1870–1960 (Cambridge University Press, 2001)

"The Lady Doth Protest Too Much. Kosovo and the Turn to Ethics in International Law," *Modern Law Review*, 65 (2002), 159–175

From Apology to Utopia. The Structure of International Legal Argument, reissue with new Epilogue (Cambridge University Press, 2005)

Fragmentation of International Law. Difficulties Arising from the Diversification and Expansion of International Law. Report of the Study Group of the International Law Commission (University of Helsinki, 2007)

Krabbe H., *Die Lehre der Rechtssouveränität* (Groningen: J. B. Wolters, 1906)

Kraft J., "Paradoxien des positiven Rechts," *Internationale Zeitschrift für Theorie des Rechts*, 9 (1935), 270 *et seq.*

Kraft-Fuchs M., "Kelsens Staatstheorie und die Soziologie des Staates," *ZöR*, 11 (1931), 402–415

Kraus H., *Vom Wesen des Völkerbundes* (Berlin: Deutsche Verlagsgesellschaft für Politik und Geschichte, 1920)

Krawietz W., "Reinheit der Rechtslehre als Ideologie?" in W. Krawietz, E. Topisch, and P. Koller (eds.), *Ideologiekritik und Demokratietheorie bei Hans Kelsen* (Berlin: Duncker & Humblot, 1982), 345 *et seq.*

"Sind Zwang und Anerkennung Strukturelemente der Rechtsnorm?" in O. Weinberger et al. (eds.), *Reine Rechtslehre im Spiegel ihrer Fortsetzer und Kritiker* (New York: Springer, 1988), 315 *et seq.*

Krisch N., "Legality, Morality and the Dilemma of Humanitarian Intervention after Kosovo," *EJIL*, 13 (2002), 323–335

"More Equal than the Rest? Hierarchy, Equality and US Predominance in International Law" in M. Byers and G. Nolte (eds.), *United States Hegemony and the Foundations of International Law* (Cambridge University Press, 2003), 133–175

Kuehl W. F., *Seeking World Order. The United States and International Organization to 1920* (Nashville: Vanderbilt University Press, 1969)

Kunz J. L., *Völkerrechtswissenschaft und Reine Rechtslehre* (Leipzig: F. Deuticke, 1923)

"Handlungsfähigkeit" in K. Strupp, *Wörterbuch des Völkerrechts und der Diplomatie*, (Berlin and Leipzig: W. de Gruyter, 1924), vol. 1, 520 *et seq.*

"Völkerrecht und Landesrecht" in K. Strupp (ed.), *Wörterbuch des Völkerrechts und der Diplomatie* (Berlin and Leipzig: W. de Gruyter, 1924), vol. 1, 787 *et seq.*

"Book Review of: Léon Bourgeois, Pour *la Société des Nations*," *ZöR*, 4 (1925), 199 *et seq.*

"Book Review of: Karl Heyland, *Die Rechtsstellung der besetzten Gebiete*," *ZöR*, 4 (1925), 194 *et seq.*

"Die Entstehungsgeschichte des Völkerbundpakts," *ZöR*, 4 (1925), 223 *et seq.*

"On the theoretical basis of the Law of Nations," *Transactions of the Grotius Society*, 10 (1925), 115–142

"Option" in K. Strupp (ed.), *Wörterbuch des Völkerrechts und der Diplomatie* (Berlin and Leipzig: W. de Gruyter, 1925), vol. 2, 177 *et seq.*

"La primauté de droit des gens," *RDILC*, VI (1925), 556 *et seq.*

Die völkerrechtliche Option, Handbücher des Ausschusses für Minderheitenrecht. (Breslau: F. Hirt, 1925), vol. 1.

"Die Rechts- und Staatslehre Léon Duguits," *Revue internationale de la théorie du droit*, I (1926/27), 204 *et seq.*

Die Anerkennung der Staaten und Regierungen im Völkerrecht (Stuttgart: Kohlhammer, 1928)

"Der Kellogg-Pakt," *Mitteilungen der deutschen Gesellschaft für Völkerrecht*, 9 (1929), 75 *et seq.*

Die Staatenverbindungen (Stuttgart: W. Kohlhammer, 1929)

"Völkerrechtsreform" in K. Strupp (ed.), *Wörterbuch des Völkerrechts und der Diplomatie* (Berlin and Leipzig: W. de Gruyter, 1929), vol. 3, 294 *et seq.*

"Die intrasystematische Stellung des Art. XI des Völkerbundpaktes," *Frankfurter Abhandlungen zum modernen Völkerrecht*, 21 (1931)

"L'option de nationalité," *RCADI*, 31 (1930), 111–172

"L'article XI du Pacte de la Société des Nations," *RCADI*, 39 (1932), 683–787

"Prolegomena zu einer allgemeinen Theorie des internationalen Rechtes nationaler Minderheiten," *Zeitschrift für öffentliches Recht*, 12 (1932), 221–272

"The Problem of Revision in International Law," *AJIL*, 33 (1939), 33 *et seq.*

"The Swing of the Pendulum: From Overestimation to Underestimation of International Law," *AJIL*, 44 (1950), 135–140

"The Nature of International Customary Law," *AJIL*, 47 (1953), 662–669

"La crise et les transformations du droit des gens," *RCADI*, 88 (1955), 9–104

"Die definitive Formulierung der Reinen Rechtslehre," *ÖZöR*, 11 (1961), 375 *et seq.*

"Bellum Justum and Bellum Legale" [1951] in J. L. Kunz, *The Changing Law of Nations. Essays on International Law* (Ohio State University Press, 1968), 575 *et seq.*

The Changing Law of Nations. Essays on International Law (Ohio State University Press, 1968)

"Experience and Techniques in International Administration," first published in *Iowa Law Review*, 31 (1945), in J. L. Kunz, *The Changing Law of Nations: Essays on International Law* (Ohio State University Press, 1968), 467 *et seq.*

"The 'Vienna School' and International Law" [1934] in J. L. Kunz, *The Changing Law of Nations: Essays on International Law* (Ohio State University Press, 1968), 59 *et seq.*

Ladavac, N. B., "Hans Kelsens Genfer Jahre" in R. Walter, C. Jabloner, and K. Zeleny (eds.), *Hans Kelsen und das Völkerrecht* [Schriftenreihe des Hans Kelsen Instituts, vol. 26] (Vienna: Manz, 2004), 172

Lador-Lederer J. J., "Some Observations on the 'Vienna School'," *Netherlands International Law Review* (1970), 126 *et seq.*

Lammasch H., *Das Völkerrecht nach dem Kriege* (Kristiana: H. Aschehoug, 1917)

Der Friedensverband der Staaten (Leipzig: Der Neue Geist Verlag, 1918)

Landauer C., "J. L. Brierly and the Modernization of Transnational Law," *Vanderbilt Journal of Transnational Law*, 25 (1993), 881–918

Lasson A., *Princip und Zukunft des Völkerrechts* (Berlin: W. Hertz, 1871)

Lauterpacht H., *Private Law Sources and Analogies of International Law* (London: Longmans, Green, 1927)

The Function of Law in the International Community (Oxford: Clarendon Press, 1933; reprints New York: Garland, 1973, and Union, NJ: The Lawbook Exchange, 2000)

International Law and Human Rights (London: F. A. Praeger, 1950)

"Some Observations on the Prohibition of 'Non Liquet' and the Completeness of the Law" in *Symbolae Verzijl* (The Hague: Nijhoff, 1958), 196 *et seq.*

"Kelsen's Pure Science of Law" in E. Lauterpacht (ed.), *International Law. Being the Collected Papers of Hersch Lauterpacht, systematically arranged and edited by E. Lauterpacht* (Cambridge University Press, 1977), vol. 3, 404 *et seq.*

Leben Ch., "Hans Kelsen and the Advancement of International Law," *EJIL*, 9 (1998), 287 *et seq.*

Lepsius O., *Die gegensatzaufhebende Begriffsbildung. Methodenentwicklungen der Weimarer Zeit und ihr Verhältnis zur Ideologisierung der Rechtswissenschaft im Nationalsozialismus* (Munich: C. H. Beck, 1994)

"Georg Jellineks Methodenlehre im Spiegel der zeitgenössischen Erkenntnistheorie" in S. L. Paulson and M. Schulte (eds.), *Georg Jellinek. Beiträge zu Leben und Werk* (Tübingen: Mohr Siebeck, 2000), 309–343

von Liszt F., *Völkerrecht*, 11th edn. (Berlin: Springer, 1918)

Loos F., *Zur Wert- und Rechtslehre Max Webers* (Tübingen: Mohr, 1960)

Luckau A., *The German Delegation at the Paris Peace Conference* (New York: Columbia University Press, 1941)

Lüderssen K., "Anerkennungsprobleme im Völkerrecht" in his *Genesis und Geltung in der Jurisprudenz* (Frankfurt: Suhrkamp, 1996), 223 *et seq.*

Luhmann N., "Positivität des Rechts als Voraussetzung einer modernen Gesellschaft" [1970] in his *Ausdifferenzierung des Rechts. Beiträge zur Rechtssoziologie und Rechtstheorie* (Frankfurt am Main: Suhrkamp, 1981), 113 *et seq.*

Das Recht der Gesellschaft (Frankfurt am Main: Suhrkamp, 1993)
Lundstedt A. V., *Superstition or Rationality in Action for Peace? Arguments against Founding a World Peace on the Common Sense of Justice. A Criticism of Jurisprudence* (London: Longmans, Green, 1925)
MacCormick N., "Persons as Institutional Facts" in O. Weinberger et al. (eds.), *Reine Rechtslehre im Spiegel ihrer Fortsetzer und Kritiker* (Vienna: Springer, 1988), 371–393
Man G., *L'école de Vienne et le développement du droit des gens* (Paris: Librairie technique et économique, 1938)
von Martens F., *Das internationale Recht der civilisierten Nationen*. German edn. C. Bergbohm (Berlin: Weidmann, 1883), vol. 1
Mausbach J., *Naturrecht und Völkerrecht* (Freiburg i. Br: Herder, 1918)
Mayer-Maly Th., "Die Natur der Sache und die österreichische Rechtspraxis" in W. Krawietz, Th. Mayer-Maly, and O. Weinberger (eds.), *Objektivierung des Rechtsdenkens. Gedächtnisschrift für Ilmar Tammelo* (Berlin: Duncker & Humblot, 1984), 273 *et seq.*
McDougal M. S., "International Law, Power and Policy: A Contemporary Conception," *RCADI*, 82 (1953), 133 *et seq.*
Merkl A., "Ueber das Verhältnis der Rechtsphilosophie zur 'positiven' Rechtswissenschaft und zum allgemeinen Teil derselben," *Grünhuts Zeitschrift für das Privat- und Öffentliche Recht der Gegenwart*, 1 (1874), 1–10, 402 *et seq.*
"Das doppelte Rechtsantlitz," *WRS*, I (1918), 1091 *et seq.*
"Das Recht im Lichte der Anwendung," *WRS*, I (1918), 1167 *et seq.*
"Die Rechtseinheit des österreichischen Staates," *WRS*, I (1918), 1115 *et seq.*
Allgemeines Verwaltungsrecht (Vienna: Springer, 1927)
"Prolegomena einer Theorie des rechtlichen Stufenbaus" in *Gesellschaft, Staat und Recht. Festschrift für Kelsen* (Vienna: Julius Springer, 1931), 252–294; reprinted in *WRS*, II, 1311 *et seq.*
Métall R. A., "Skizzen zu einer Systematik der völkerrechtlichen Quellenlehre," *ZöR*, XI (1931), 416 *et seq.*
Hans Kelsen. Leben und Werk (Vienna: Deutike, 1969)
Miliouch B., *Le Fondement du Droit International* (Paris: A. Pedone, 1928)
Miller D. H., *The Drafting of the Covenant* (New York: G. P. Putnam's Sons, 1928), vols. I–II
von Mohl R., *Das Staatsrecht des Königreiches Württemberg*, 2nd edn. (Tübingen: Laupp, 1846)
Die Geschichte und Literatur der Staatswissenschaften (Erlangen: Enke, 1855), vol. 1
"Die Pflege der internationalen Gemeinschaft als Aufgabe des Völkerrechts" in his *Staatsrecht, Völkerrecht und Politik* (Tübingen: Mohr, 1860; reprint Graz: Akad. Druck- und Verl. Anstalt, 1962), vol. 1: Staatsrecht und Völkerrecht

Möllers Ch., *Gewaltengliederung. Legitimation und Dogmatik im nationalen und internationalen Rechtsvergleich* (Tübingen: Mohr, 2005)

Moos R., *Der Verbrechensbegriff in Österreich im 18. und 19. Jahrhundert. Sinn und Strukturwandel* (Bonn: L. Röhrscheid, 1968)

Morgenthau H. J., *Politics Among Nations. The Struggle for Power and Peace*, revised by K. W. Thompson and W. D. Clinton (7th edn. New York: McGraw-Hill, 2006; 1st edn. New York: Knopf, 1949)

Mosler H., "Völkerrecht als Rechtsordnung," *ZaöRV*, 36 (1976), 6 *et seq.*

Mouffe C., *On the Political* (London, New York: Routledge, 2005)

Münch F., "Das Institut de droit international und die obligatorische Gerichtsbarkeit" in W. Wengler (ed.), *Justitia et Pace. Festschrift zum 100jährigen Bestehen des Institut de droit international* (Berlin: Duncker & Humblot, 1974), 101 *et seq.*

Nawiaski H., "Staatenbund und Bundesstaat" in K. Strupp (ed.), *Wörterbuch des Völkerrechts und der Diplomatie* (Berlin and Leipzig: W. de Gruyter, 1925), vol. 2

Nelson L., *Rechtswissenschaft ohne Recht* (Leipzig: Veit, 1917; 2nd edn. Göttingen: Verlag Öffentliches Leben, 1949)

Neumann U., "Juristische Logik" in A. Kaufmann and W. Hassemer (eds.), *Einführung in die Rechtsphilosophie und Rechtstheorie der Gegenwart* (Heidelberg: C. F. Müller, 1985), 4th edn., 237 *et seq.*

Neumeyer K., "Internationales Verwaltungsrecht" in K. Stengel and M. Fleischmann (eds.), *Wörterbuch des deutschen Staats- und Verwaltungsrechtes* (Tübingen: Mohr, 1911–1914)

"Vom Recht der Auswärtigen Verwaltung und von verwandten Rechtsbegriffen," *AöR*, 31 (1913), 99–130

Niemeyer Th., *Völkerrecht* (Berlin: W. de Gruyter, 1923)

Nippold O., *Die Fortbildung des Verfahrens in völkerrechtlichen Streitigkeiten* (Leipzig: Duncker & Humblot, 1907)

Die Gestaltung des Völkerrechts nach dem Kriege (Zurich: O. Füssli, 1917)

Der Völkerbundsvertrag und die Frage des Beitritts der Schweiz (Bern: K. J. Wyss Erben, 1919)

Nolte G., "Die USA und das Völkerrecht" in *Journal of International Peace and Organization* 78 (2003)

Oberkofler G. and E. Rabofsky, *Hans Kelsen im Kriegseinsatz der k.u.k. Wehrmacht. Eine kritische Würdigung seiner militärtheoretischen Angebote* (Frankfurt am Main and New York: P. Lang, 1988)

Oellers-Frahm K. and N. Wühler, *Dispute Settlement in Public International Law* (New York: Springer, 1984)

Öhlinger Th., *Der Stufenbau der Rechtsordnung* (Vienna: Manz, 1975)

von Ompteda D. H. L., *Literatur des gesamten natürlichen und positiven Völkerrechts*, Regensburg, 1785, vol. 1; reprint (Aalen: Scientia, 1963)

Oppenheim H. B., *System des Völkerrechts*, 2nd edn. (Stuttgart: A. Kröner, 1866)

Oppenheim L. F., *International Law. A Treatise* (London: Longmans, Green, 1905), vol. 1

"Zur Lehre des internationalen Gewohnheitsrecht," *Niemeyers Zeitschrift für internationales Recht*, 25 (1915), 1 *et seq.*

Paulson S. L., "Stellt die 'Allgemeine Theorie der Normen' einen Bruch in Kelsens Lehre dar?" in *Die Reine Rechtslehre in wissenschafttlicher Diskussion. Referate und Disussionen auf dem zu Ehren des 100. Geburtstages von Hans Kelsen vom 22. bis 27. September 1981 abgehaltenen Symposium* (Vienna: Manz, 1982)

"Zur Neukantianischen Dimension der Reinen Rechtslehre. Vorwort zur Kelsen-Sander-Auseinandersetzung" in S. L. Paulson (ed.), *Die Rolle des Neukantianismus in der Reinen Rechtslehre. Eine Debatte zwischen Sander und Kelsen* (Aalen: Scientia Verlag, 1988), 7 *et seq.*

"Läßt sich die Reine Rechtslehre transzendental begründen" in *Rechtstheorie*, 21 (1990), 155–179

"Methodological Dualism in Kelsen's *Das Problem der Souveränität*" in A. Carrino (ed.), *Kelsen e il problema della sovranità* (Naples: Edizioni scientifiche italiane, 1990), 83 *et seq.*

"Die unterschiedlichen Formulierungen der Grundnorm" in A. Aarnio et al. (eds.), *Rechtsnorm und Rechtswirklichkeit. Festschrift für Werner Krawietz zum 60. Geburtstag* (Berlin: Duncker & Humblot, 1993)

"On the Early Development of the Grundnorm" in F. Fleerackers (ed.), *Law, Life and the Images of Man. Festschrift for Jan M. Broekman* (Berlin: Duncker & Humblot, 1996), 217–230

"On the Kelsen–Kant Problematic" in E. Garzón Valdéz (ed.), *Normative Systems in Legal and Moral Theory. Festschrift for Carlos E. Alchourrón and Eugenio Bulgyin* (Berlin: Duncker & Humblot, 1997), 209–213

"Four Phases in Hans Kelsen's Legal Theory? Reflections on a Periodization," *Oxford Journal of Legal Studies*, 18 (1998), 157 *et seq.*

"Kelsen's Earliest Legal Theory: Critical Constructivism" in S. L. Paulson and B. Litschewski Paulson (eds.), *Normativity and Norms. Critical Perspectives on Kelsenian Themes* (Oxford University Press), 1998, 23 *et seq.*

Paulson S. L. and B. Litschewski Paulson (eds.), *Normativity and Norms. Critical Perspectives on Kelsenian Themes* (Oxford University Press, 1998)

Paulus A. L., *Die internationale Gemeinschaft im Völkerrecht. Eine Untersuchung zur Entwicklung des Völkerrechts im Zeitalter der Globalisierung.* With English summary. (Munich: Beck, 2001)

Pauly W., "Concepts of Universality. Hans Kelsen on Sovereignty and International Order" in D. Diner and M. Stolleis (eds.), *Hans Kelsen and Carl Schmitt: A Juxtaposition* (Gerlingen: Bleicher, 1999), 45 *et seq.*

Pawlik M., *Die Reine Rechtslehre und die Rechtstheorie H. L. A. Harts. Ein kritischer Vergleich* (Berlin: Duncker & Humblot, 1993)

Peters A., "Global constitutionalism revisited," *International Legal Theory*, 11 (2005), 39–67

Pfersman O., "De la justice constitutionnelle à la justice internationale: Hans Kelsen et la seconde guerre mondiale," *Revue française de droit constitutionnel*, 16 (1993), 761 *et seq.*

Sir W. G. F. Phillimore, "Droits et devoirs fondamentaux des États," *RCADI*, 8 (1923), 29 *et seq.*

Pitamic L., "Denkökonomische Voraussetzungen der Rechtswissenschaft," *ZöR*, 3 (1918), 339 *et seq.*

"Die Frage der rechtlichen Grundnorm" in F. A. von Heydte (ed.), *Völkerrecht und rechtliches Weltbild. Festschrift für Alfred Verdross* (Vienna: Springer, 1960)

Politis N., "Le problème des limitations de la souveraineté et la théorie de l'abus des droits dans les rapports internationaux," *RCADI*, 6 (1925), 5 *et seq.*

Posner E. A. and J. L. Goldsmith, *The Limits of International Law* (Oxford University Press, 2005)

Post H. H. G., "Classification of the rules of International Law according to spheres of validity," *Netherlands Yearbook of International Law*, 7 (1976), 157 *et seq.*

Potter P. A., "Le développement de l'organisation internationale1815–1914," *RCADI*, 64/II (1938), 71 *et seq.*

"The Origin of the Term International Organisation," *AJIL*, 39 (1945), 803 *et seq.*

Pufendorf S., *De jure naturae et gentium libri octo*. Reprint of the 1688 edn, ed. W. Simons (Oxford: Clarendon Press, 1934)

Pütter K. Th., "Die Staatslehre oder – Souveränität als Prinzip des praktischen europäischen Völkerrechts," *ZStW*, 6 (1850), 304 *et seq.*

Radbruch G., *Rechtsphilosophie*, ed. E. Wolf and H. P. Schneider, 8th edn. (Stuttgart: K. F. Koehler, 1973)

Raz J., *The Authority of the Law: Essays on Law and Morality* (Oxford: Clarendon Press, 1979)

"Kelsen's Theory of the Basic Norm" in S. L. Paulson and B. Litschewski Paulson (eds.), *Normativity and Norms. Critical Perspectives on Kelsenian Themes* (Oxford University Press, 1998), 47 *et seq.*

"The Purity of Pure Theory" in S. L. Paulson and B. Litschewski Paulson (eds.), *Normativity and Norms. Critical Perspectives on Kelsenian Themes* (Oxford University Press, 1998), 237 *et seq.*

Reckhard M., *Die rechtlichen Rahmenbedingungen der Sanktionierung von Beitragsverweigerung im System der Vereinten Nationen* (Frankfurt am Main: P. Lang, 1999)

Redslob R., *Das Problem des Völkerrechts* (Leipzig: Veit und Comp., 1917)

Théorie de la Société des Nations (Paris: Rousseau & Co., 1927)

Reinicke W. H., *global Public Policy. Governing Without Government?* (Washington, D.C: Brookings Institution Press, 1998)

Reinicke W. H. and F. Deng, *Critical Choices: The United Nations Networks and the Future of global Governance* (Ottawa: Internat. Development Research Centre, 2000)

Richter B., *Völkerrecht, Außenpolitik und Internationale Verwaltung bei Lorenz von Stein* (Hamburg: Hansischer Gildenverlag Heitmann, 1973)

Riedel E. H., *Theorie der Menschenrechtsstandards* (Berlin: Duncker & Humblot, 1986)

"Menschenrechte der Dritten Dimension," *Europäische Grundrechtezeitschrift*, 16 (1989), 9 *et seq.*

"The Progressive Development of International Law at the Universal and Regional Level" in R. Wolfrum (ed.), *Strengthening the World Order: Universalism v. Regionalism* (Berlin: Duncker & Humblot, 1990)

"Standards and Sources. Farewell to the Exclusivity of the Sources Triad in International Law," *EJIL*, 2 (1991), 58 *et seq.*

"International Environmental Law – A Law to Serve the Public Interest? An analysis of the Scope of the Binding Effect of Basic Principles (Public Interest Norms)" in J. Delbrück (ed.), *New Trends in International Law Making – International "Legislation" in the Public Interest* (Berlin: Duncker & Humblot, 1997), 61 *et seq.*

Rill H. P., "Zur Methodenlehre der Rechtswissenschaft von Karl Larenz," *ÖZöR*, 13 (1964), 281 *et seq.*

Rittberger V., *Regime Theory and International Relations*, ed. V. Rittberger with the assistance of P. Mayer (Oxford University Press, 1993)

Roehrsen C., "Die Kelsensche Auffassung vom Recht als ein Ausdruck der modernen sozio-politischen Kultur," *Der Staat*, 21 (1982), 211 *et seq.*

Roscher B., *Der Briand–Kellogg-Pakt von 1928. Der "Verzicht auf den Krieg als Mittel nationaler Politik" im völkerrechtlichen Denken der Zwischenkriegszeit* (Baden-Baden: Nomos, 2004)

Rosin H., *Souveränität, Staat, Gemeinde, Selbstverwaltung* (Munich: Hirth, 1883)

Ross A., "Völkerbund und Staatssouveränität," *ZöR*, 11 (1931), 441 *et seq.*

"Validity and the Conflict between Legal Positivism and Natural Law" in S. L. Paulson and B. Litschewski Paulson (eds.), *Normativity and Norms. Critical Perspectives on Kelsenian Themes* (Oxford University Press, 1998), 147 *et seq.*

Rub A., *Hans Kelsens Völkerrechtslehre. Versuch einer Würdigung* (Zurich: Schulthess, 1995)

Rudolf W., *Völkerrecht und deutsches Recht* (Tübingen: Mohr, 1967)

Rüthers B., "On the Brink of Dictatorship. Hans Kelsen and Carl Schmitt in Cologne 1933" in D. Diner and M. Stolleis (eds.), *Hans Kelsen and Carl Schmitt: A Juxtaposition* (Gerlingen: Bleicher, 1999)

Sander F., *Rechtsdogmatik oder Theorie der Rechtserfahrung. Kritische Studie zur Rechtslehre Hans Kelsens* (Vienna and Leipzig: Deuticke, 1921)

Scelle G., "La SDN est-elle un super état?" in *La vie des peuples*, 4 (1924), 410–435

Précis de droit des gens. Principes et systématique, 2 vols. (Paris: Librairie du Recueil Sirey, 1932–1934)

"Règles générales du droit de la paix," *RCADI*, 46/IV (1933), 327 *et seq.*

Théorie juridique de la révision des traités (Paris: Librairie du Recueil Sirey, 1936)

Schachter O., "Book Review of: H. Kelsen, *The Law of the United Nations*," *Yale L. R.*, 60 (1951), 189 *et seq.*

Schattkowsky R., *Deutschland und Polen von 1918/19 bis 1925: deutsch-polnische Beziehungen zwischen Versailles und Locarno* (Berlin and Vienna: Lang, 1994)

Schieder S., "Pragmatism as a Path toward a Discursive and Open Theory of International Law," *EJIL*, 11 (2000), 691–698

Schiffer W., *The Legal Community of Mankind* (New York: Columbia University Press, 1954)

Schilling O., *Das Völkerrecht nach Thomas von Aquin* (Freiburg i. Br: Herder, 1918)

Schluchter W., *Rationalismus der Weltbeherrschung. Studien zu Max Weber* (Frankfurt am Main: Suhrkamp, 1983)

Schmitt C., *Der Begriff des Politischen* (Hamburg: Hanseatische Verlagsanstalt, 1933; reprint Berlin: Duncker & Humblot, 1963) English translation: *The Concept of the Political*, trans. and with an introduction by G. Schwab (New Brunswick: Rutgers University Press, 1976)

Die Kernfrage des Völkerbundes (Berlin: F. Dümmler, 1926)

Politische Theologie. Vier Kapitel zur Lehre von der Souveränität, 2nd edn. (Munich and Leipzig: Duncker & Humblot, 1934)

Völkerrechtliche Grossraumordnung mit Interventionsverbot für Raumfremde Mächte (Berlin: Dt. Rechtsverlag, 1939)

Schmoeckel M., *Die Grossraumtheorie. Ein Beitrag zur Geschichte der Völkerrechtswissenschaft im Dritten Reich, insbesondere der Kriegszeit* (Berlin: Duncker & Humblot, 1994)

Schönberger C., *Das Parlament im Anstaltstaat. Zur Theorie parlamentarischer Repräsentation in der Staatsrechtslehre des Kaiserreichs (1871–1918)* (Frankfurt am Main: Suhrkamp, 1997)

"Ein Liberaler zwischen Staatswille und Volkswille. Georg Jellinek und die Krise des staatsrechtlichen Positivismus um die Jahrhundertwende" in S. L. Paulson and M. Schulte (eds.), *Georg Jellinek. Beiträge zu Leben und Werk* (Tübingen: Mohr Siebeck, 2000), 3 *et seq.*

"Introductory Note" in H. Kelsen, *Werke*, ed. M. Jestaedt (Tübingen: Mohr-Siebeck, 2008), vol. 2

Schorske C. E., *Fin-de-Siècle Vienna: Politics and Culture* (New York: Knopf, 1980)

Schot B., *Nation oder Staat? Deutschland und der Minderheitenschutz* (Marburg/ Lahn: J. G. Herder-Institut, 1988)

Schücking W., *Der Staatenverband der Haager Konferenzen* (Munich and Leipzig: Duncker & Humblot, 1912)

Der Weltfriedensbund und die Wiedergeburt des Völkerrechts (Leipzig: Verlag Naturwissenschaften, 1917)

Die völkerrechtliche Lehre des Weltkrieges (Leipzig: Veit, 1918)

Schücking W. and H. Wehberg, *Die Satzung des Völkerbundes*, 2nd, revised edn. (Berlin: Vahlen, 1924)

Die Satzung des Völkerbundes, 3rd, revised and extended edn. (Berlin: Vahlen, 1931)

Schwarzenberger G., *The Inductive Approach to International Law* (London: Stevens, 1965)

Schwarzenberger G. and E. D. Brown, *A Manual of International Law*, 6th edn. (Milton: Professional Books, 1976)

Schwind E., *Grundlagen und Grundfragen des Rechts* (Munich: M. Hueber, 1928)

Scobbie I. G. M., "The Theorist as a Judge: Hersch Lauterpacht's Conception of the International Judicial Function," *EJIL*, 2 (1997), 264 *et seq.*

Simma B., *Das Reziprozitätselement in der Entstehung des Völkergewohnheitsrechts* (Munich: W. Fink, 1970)

"From Bilateralism to Community Interests in International Law," *RCADI*, 250/IV (1994), 217–384

"The Contribution of Alfred Verdross to the Theory of International Law," *EJIL*, 5 (1994), 33 *et seq.*

"NATO, the UN and the Use of Force: Legal Aspects," *EJIL*, 10 (1999), 1–22

Slaughter A. M., "International Law in a World of Liberal States," *EJIL*, 6 (1995), 503–538

"The New World Order," *Foreign Affairs*, 76 (1997)

"Global Government Networks, Global Information Agencies, and Disaggregated Democracy," *Michigan Journal of International Law*, 24 (2003), 1041–1075

Sohn L. B., "Book Review of: H. Kelsen, *The Law of the United Nations*," *Harvard L. R.*, 64 (1950–51), 517 *et seq.*

Somek A., "Kelsen lives," *EJIL*, 18 (2007), 409–451

Somló F., *Juristische Grundlehre* (Leipzig: F. Meiner, 1917; 2nd edn., Leipzig: F. Meiner, 1927)

Sontheimer K., *Politische Wissenschaft und Staatsrechtslehre* (Freiburg: Rombach, 1963)

Spiliopoulou Åkermark A. and O. Mårsäter, "Treaties and the Limits of Flexibility," *NJIL*, 71 (2005), 509–540

Spiropolous J., *Théorie générale du droit international* (Paris: Librairie générale de droit & de jurisprudence, 1930)

Stammler R., *Die Lehre vom richtigen Rechte* (Berlin: J. Guttentag, 1902)

Theorie der Rechtswissenschaft (Halle: Buchhandlung des Waisenhauses, 1911)

Steck P. K., *Zwischen Volk und Staat. Das Völkerrechtssubjekt in der deutschen Völkerrechtslehre (1933–1941)* (Baden-Baden: Nomos, 2003)

Steiger H., "Völkerrecht" in O. Brunner, W. Kunze, and R. Koselleck (eds.), *Geschichtliche Grundbegriffe. Historisches Lexikon zur politisch-sozialen Sprache in Deutschland* (Stuttgart: E. Klett, 1992), vol. 7

"Völkerrecht und Naturrecht zwischen Christian Wolff und Adolf Lasson" in D. Klippel (ed.), *Naturrecht im 19. Jahrhundert* (Goldbach: Keip, 1997)

von Stein L., "Einige Bemerkungen über das internationale Verwaltungsrecht," *Schmollers Jahrbuch für Gesetzgebung, Verwaltung, Volkswirtschaft*, 6 (1882), 1 *et seq.*, 396 *et seq.*

Steinle S., *Völkerrecht und Machtpolitik. Georg Schwarzenberger (1908–1991)* (Baden-Baden: Nomos, 2002)

Stolleis M., *"Junges Deutschland," jüdische Emanzipation und liberale Staatsrechtslehre in Deutschland.* Sitzungsberichte der Wissenschaftlichen Gesellschaft an der Johann Wolfgang Goethe-Universität, Frankfurt am Main (Stuttgart: F. Steiner, 1994)

"Die Idee des souveränen Staates" in *Entstehung und Wandel verfassungsrechtlichen Denkens, Der Staat*, Beiheft 11 (Berlin: Duncker & Humblot, 1996), 63 *et seq.*

Der lange Abschied vom 19. Jahrhundert. Vortrag gehalten vor der Juristischen Gesellschaft zu Berlin am 22. Januar 1997 (Berlin and New York: W. de Gruyter, 1997)

Rechtsgeschichte als Kunstprodukt: Zur Entbehrlichkeit von "Begriff" und "Tatsache" (Baden-Baden: Nomos, 1997)

"In the Belly of the Beast" in his *The Law under the Swastika: Studies on Legal History in Nazi Germany*, trans. Thomas Dunlap (Chicago University Press, 1998), 87 *et seq.*

"A critique from the '*Wiener Kreis.*' Margit Kraft-Fuchs (1902–1994) on Carl Schmidt" in D. Diner and M. Stolleis (eds.), *Hans Kelsen and Carl Schmitt: A Juxtaposition* (Gerlingen: Bleicher, 1999), 123 *et seq.*

Public Law in Germany, 1800–1914 (New York: Berghahn Books, 2001)

A History of Public Law in Germany 1914–1945, trans. Thomas Dunlap (Oxford University Press, 2004)

Stone J., *International Guarantees of Minority Rights* (Oxford University Press, 1932)

Legal Controls of International Conflict (London: Stevens, 1954)

"Non Liquet and the Function of Law in the International Community," *BYIL*, 25 (1959), 124 *et seq.*

Strupp K., *Élements du droit international public universel, européen et américain* (Paris: Rousseau & Co., 1924)

Wörterbuch des Völkerrechts und der Diplomatie (Berlin and Leipzig: W. de Gruyter, 1924–1929)

Grundzüge des positiven Völkerrechts, 5th edn. (Bonn and Cologne: L. Röhrscheid, 1932)

"Les règles générales du droit de la paix," *RCADI*, 47/I (1934), 257 *et seq.*

Legal Machinery for Peaceful Change (London: Constable & Co., 1937)

Sukiennicki W., *Essai sur la souveraineté des états en droit international moderne* (Paris: A. Pedone, 1926)

Tammelo I., "On the Logical Openness of Legal Orders," *AJCL*, 8 (1959), 187 *et seq.*

"The Logical Structure of the Law Field," *ARSP*, XLV (1959), 95 *et seq.*

"Beziehungen zwischen der Völkerrechtsordnung und den staatlichen Rechtsordnungen in 'perspektivischer' Sicht" in *Rechtslogik und materiale Gerechtigkeit. Beiträge zur Rechtsphilosophie und zur Theorie des Völkerrechts von Ilmar Tammelo* (Frankfurt am Main: Athenaeum, 1971), 84 *et seq.*

Teubner G. (ed.), *Global Law Without a State. Studies in modern law and policy* (Brookfield: Dartmouth, 1997)

Thévénaz H., " À propos de la coutume" in S. Engel and R. A. Métall (eds.), *Law, State, and International Legal Order. Essays in Honor of Hans Kelsen* (Knoxville: University of Tennessee Press, 1964), 317 *et seq.*

"Kelsen et le droit international" in B. Dutoit and E. Grisel (eds.), *Mélanges Georges Perrin* (Lausanne: Diffusion Payot, 1984), 313 *et seq.*

Tietje C., "The changing legal structure of international treaties as an aspect of an emerging global governance architecture," *German Yearbook of International Law*, 42 (1999), 26–55

Tomuschat C., "International Law: Ensuring the survival of mankind on the eve of a new century," *RCADI*, 281 (1999), 9–438

Trendelenburg F. A., *Lücken im Völkerrecht. Betrachtungen und Vorschläge aus dem Jahre 1870* (Leipzig: S. Hirzel, 1870)

Triepel H., *Völkerrecht und Landesrecht* (Leipzig: C. L. Hirschfeld, 1899)

"Les rapports entre le droit interne et le droit internationale," *RCADI*, 1 (1923), 77 *et seq.*

Troper M., "Kelsen und die Kontrolle der Verfassungsmäßigkeit" in A. Carrino and G. Winkler (eds.), *Rechtserfahrung und Reine Rechtslehre* (Vienna and New York: Springer, 1995), 15 *et seq.*

"'The Guardian of the Constitution' – Hans Kelsen's Evaluation of a Legal Concept" in D. Diner and M. Stolleis (eds.), *Hans Kelsen and Carl Schmitt: A Juxtaposition* (Gerlingen: Bleicher, 1999), 81 *et seq.*

von Trott zu Stolz A., *Hegels Staatsphilosophie und das internationale Recht* (Göttingen: Vandenhoeck & Ruprecht, 1932)

Truyos y Serra A., "Verdross et la théorie du droit," *EJIL*, 6 (1995), 55 *et seq.*
von Ullmann E. R., *Völkerrecht* (Tübingen: Mohr, 1908)
Völkerrecht (Berlin: Springer, 1937)
Vagts D. F., "International Law in the Third Reich," *AJIL*, 84 (1990), 661 *et seq.*
de Vattel E., *Le droit des gens ou principes de la loi naturelle* [1758], ed. W. von Euler, P. Guggenheim, and W. Schätzel (Tübingen: Mohr, 1959)
Venzke I., "International Bureaucracies from a Political Science Perspective – Agency, Authority and International Institutional Law," *German Law Journal*, 9 (2008), 1401–1428
Verdross A. "Zur Konstruktion des Völkerrechts" [1914], reprinted in *WRS* II, 1995 *et seq.*
"Das Verhältnis der verfassungsmäßigen Staatsverträge zum österreichischen Gesetzesrecht, insbesondere zum Strafrecht. Ein Beitrag zur Anwendung der Haager Konvention von 1899 bzw. 1907 durch die Gerichte," *Juristische Blätter*, 46 (1917), 541 *et seq.*
"Reichsrecht und internationales Recht. Eine Lanze für Art. 3 des Regierungsentwurfs der deutschen Verfassung," *Deutsche Juristenzeitung*, 24 (1919), 291 *et seq.*
"Staatliches Recht und Völkerrecht. Die Stellung der neuen deutschen und österreichischen Verfassung zum Völkerrecht," *Schweizerische Juristenzeitung*, 17 (1920), 246 *et seq.*
Die völkerrechtswidrige Kriegshandlung und der Strafanspruch der Staaten (Berlin: H. R. Engelmann, 1920)
"Grundlagen und Grundlegungen des Völkerrechts," *Niemeyers Zeitschrift für Internationales Recht*, XXIX (1921), 65 *et seq.*
Die Einheit des rechtlichen Weltbildes auf Grundlage der Völkerrechtsverfassung (Tübingen: J. C. B. Mohr, 1923)
"Völkerrecht und einheitliches Rechtssystem," *ZfV*, XII (1923), reprinted in *WRS*, II, 2023 *et seq.*
"Die gesellschaftswissenschaftlichen Grundlagen der Völkerrechtstheorie," *ARWP*, XVIII (1924/1925), 413–431.
"Zur neuesten Lehre von den Staatenverbindungen," *Niemeyers Zeitschrift für internationales Recht*, XXXV (1926), 257 *et seq.*
Die Verfassung der Völkerrechtsgemeinschaft (Vienna: J. Springer, 1926)
"Le fondement du droit international," *RCADI*, 16 (1927), 247 *et seq.*
"Rechtstheorie Hans Kelsens" [1930], *WRS*, II, 1301 *et seq.*
"Die allgemeinen Rechtsgrundsätze des Völkerrechts" in *Gesellschaft, Staat, und Recht. Untersuchungen zur Reinen Rechtslehre. Festschrift für Hans Kelsen* (Vienna: J. Springer, 1931)
"Les principes généraux de droit comme source du droit des gens," *Annuaire de l'Institut de droit international*, 40 (1937), 183 *et seq.*
Völkerrecht (Berlin: Springer, 1937)

"Grundlagen und Grundsätze des Völkerrechts in christlicher Schau," *Schönere Zukunft*, XIII (1938), 385 *et seq.*

Völkerrecht, 3rd edn. (Vienna: Springer, 1955)

"Zum Problem der völkerrechtlichen Grundnorm" [1956] *WRS* II, 2203 *et seq.*

Statisches und dynamisches Naturrecht (Freiburg: Rombach, 1971)

Verosta S., *Alfred Verdross-Leben und Werk* (Vienna: Springer Verlag, 1960)

Vinx L., *Hans Kelsen's Pure Theory of Law* (Oxford University Press, 2007)

de Visscher Ch., *Théories et réalités en droit international public* (Paris: A. Pedone, 1953)

"Positivisme et 'jus cogens'," *RGDIP*, 75 (1971), 5–11

Wagner H., "Monismus und Dualismus: Eine methodenkritische Betrachtung zum Theorienstreit," *AöR*, 89 (1964), 212 *et seq.*

Waldock C. H. M., "The Plea of Domestic Jurisdiction before International Law," *BYIL*, XXXI (1954), 143 *et seq.*

Walter R., *Der Aufbau der Rechtsordnung* (Graz: Leykam, 1964; 2nd edn., Vienna: Manz, 1974)

"Das Problem des verhältnisses von Recht und Logik der Reinen Rechtslehre," *Rechtstheorie* 11 (1980), 299 *et seq.*

"Das Auslegungsproblem im Lichte der Reinen Rechtslehre" in G. Kohlmann (ed.), *Festschrift für Ulrich Klug zum 70. Geburtstag* (Cologne: P. Deubner, 1983), 187 *et seq.*

Walz G. A., "Zum Problem der 'monistischen' oder 'dualistischen' Konstruktion des Völkerrechts," *ZöR*, 10 (1930), 538 *et seq.*

Völkerrecht und Staatliches Recht. Untersuchungen über die Einwirkungen des Völkerrechts auf das innerstaatliche Recht (Stuttgart: W. Kohlhammer, 1933)

Wehberg H., "Der Weltschiedsvertrag der Generalakte," *Völkerbund. Monatsschrift der Deutschen Liga für Völkerbund*, 2 (1929), 39 *et seq.*

Weil P., "Towards Relative Normativity in International Law?" *AJIL*, 77 (1983), 413–442

Weiler J. H. H., "The Geology of International Law – Governance, Democracy and Legitimacy," *ZaöRV*, 64 (2004), 547–562

Weinberger Chr. and O. Weinberger, *Logik, Semantik, Hermeneutik* (Munich: C. H. Beck, 1979)

Weinberger O., "Der Begriff der Sanktion und seine Rolle in der Normenlogik und Rechtstheorie" in H. Lenk (ed.), *Normenlogik* (Pullach: Verlag Dokumentation, 1974), 89 *et seq.*

Normentheorie als Grundlage der Jurisprudenz und Ethik (Berlin: Duncker & Humblot, 1981)

"Kelsens These von der Unanwendbarkeit logischer Regeln auf Normen" in *Die Reine Rechtslehre in wissenschaftlicher Diskussion*. Schriftenreihe des Hans-Kelsen-Instituts (Vienna: Manz, 1982), vol. 7

"Reine oder funktionalistische Rechtsbetrachtung?" in O. Weinberger et al. (eds.), *Reine Rechtslehre im Spiegel ihrer Fortsetzer und Kritiker* (Vienna and New York: Springer, 1988)

Wenzel M., *Juristische Grundprobleme* (Berlin: F. Dümmlers Verlagsbuchhandlung, 1920)

Wiggenhorn H., *Verliererjustiz. Die Leipziger Kriegsverbrecherprozesse nach dem Ersten Weltkrieg* (Baden-Baden: Nomos, 2005)

Winkler G., *Glanz und Elend der Reinen Rechtslehre* (Saarbrücken: Europa-Institut, 1988)

von Wolff Ch. Freiherr, *Jus gentium*, reprint of the 1749 edn. (New York: Olms, 1972)

Wolfrum R., "The Attack of September 11, 2001, the Wars Against The Taliban and Iraq: Is There A Need To Reconsider International Law on the Recourse to Force and the Rules of Armed Conflict?" in *Max Planck United Nations Yearbook* 7 (2003)

von Wright G. H., "Is and Ought" in S. L. Paulson and B. Litschewski Paulson (eds.), *Normativity and Norms. Critical Perspectives on Kelsenian Themes* (Oxford University Press, 1998)

Wright Q., "The Outlawry of War," *AJIL*, 19 (1925), 76 *et seq.*

The Study of International Relations (New York: Appleton-Century-Crofts, 1955)

Wüst A., *Das völkerrechtliche Werk von Georges Scelle im Frankreich der Zwischenkriegszeit* (Baden-Baden: Nomos, 2007)

Zanten V., "Le problème de la souveraineté des états et le droit international," *RDILC*, XI (1930), 494 *et seq.*

Zimmern A., *The League of Nations and the Rule of Law 1918–1935* (1st edn., London: Macmillan, 1936; 2nd, revised edn., London: Macmillan, 1939; reprint New York: Russel & Russel, 1969)

Zolo D., "Hans Kelsen: International Peace through International Law," *EJIL*, 9 (1998), 306 *et seq.*

Zorn A., *Grundzüge des Völkerrechts*, 2nd edn. (Leipzig: J. J. Weber, 1903)

Zorn Ph., *Das Staatsrecht des Deutschen Reiches* (Berlin: J. Guttentag, 1880–1883)

Der Völkerbund (Berlin: Engelmann, 1919)

INDEX

CAMBRIDGE STUDIES IN INTERNATIONAL AND COMPARATIVE LAW

Books in the series

The Public International Law Theory of Hans Kelsen: Believing in Universal Law
Jochen von Bernstorff

The Concept of Non-International Armed Conflict in International Humanitarian Law
Anthony Cullen

The Challenge of Child Labour in International Law
Franziska Humbert

Shipping Interdiction and the Law of the Sea
Douglas Guilfoyle

International Courts and Environmental Protection
Tim Stephens

Legal Principles in WTO Dispute
Andrew D. Mitchell

War Crimes in Internal Armed Conflicts
Eve La Haye

Humanitarian Occupation
Gregory H. Fox

The International Law of Environmental Impact Assessment: Process, Substance and Integration
Neil Craik

The Law and Practice of International Territorial Administration: Versailles, Iraq and Beyond
Carsten Stahn

Cultural Products and the World Trade Organization
Tania Voon

United Nations Sanctions and the Rule of Law
Jeremy Farrall

National Law in WTO Law: Effectiveness and Good Governance in the World Trading System
Sharif Bhuiyan

The Threat of Force in International Law
Nikolas Stürchler

Indigenous Rights and United Nations Standards
Alexandra Xanthaki

International Refugee Law and Socio-Economic Rights
Michelle Foster

The Protection of Cultural Property in Armed Conflict
Roger O'Keefe

Interpretation and Revision of International Boundary Decisions
Kaiyan Homi Kaikobad

Multinationals and Corporate Social Responsibility: Limitations and Opportunities in International Law
Jennifer A. Zerk

Judiciaries within Europe: A Comparative Review
John Bell

Law in Times of Crisis: Emergency Powers in Theory and Practice
Oren Gross and Fionnuala Ní Aoláin

Vessel-Source Marine Pollution: The Law and Politics of International Regulation
Alan Tan

Enforcing Obligations Erga Omnes in International Law
Christian J. Tams

Non-Governmental Organisations in International Law
Anna-Karin Lindblom

Democracy, Minorities and International Law
Steven Wheatley

Prosecuting International Crimes: Selectivity and the International Law Regime
Robert Cryer

Compensation for Personal Injury in English, German and Italian Law: A Comparative Outline
Basil Markesinis, Michael Coester, Guido Alpa, Augustus Ullstein

Dispute Settlement in the UN Convention on the Law of the Sea
Natalie Klein

The International Protection of Internally Displaced Persons
Catherine Phuong

Imperialism, Sovereignty and the Making of International Law
Antony Anghie

Necessity, Proportionality and the Use of Force by States
Judith Gardam

International Legal Argument in the Permanent Court of International Justice: The Rise of the International Judiciary
Ole Spiermann

Great Powers and Outlaw States: Unequal Sovereigns in the International Legal Order
Gerry Simpson

Local Remedies in International Law
C. F. Amerasinghe

Reading Humanitarian Intervention: Human Rights and the Use of Force in International Law
Anne Orford

Conflict of Norms in Public International Law: How WTO Law Relates to Other Rules of Law
Joost Pauwelyn

Transboundary Damage in International Law
Hanqin Xue

European Criminal Procedures
Edited by Mireille Delmas-Marty and John Spencer

The Accountability of Armed Opposition Groups in International Law
Liesbeth Zegveld

Sharing Transboundary Resources: International Law and Optimal Resource Use
Eyal Benvenisti

International Human Rights and Humanitarian Law
René Provost

Remedies Against International Organisations
Karel Wellens

Diversity and Self-Determination in International Law
Karen Knop

The Law of Internal Armed Conflict
Lindsay Moir

International Commercial Arbitration and African States: Practice, Participation and Institutional Development
Amazu A. Asouzu

The Enforceability of Promises in European Contract Law
James Gordley

International Law in Antiquity
David J. Bederman

Money Laundering: A New International Law Enforcement Model
Guy Stessens

Good Faith in European Contract Law
Reinhard Zimmermann and Simon Whittaker

On Civil Procedure
J. A. Jolowicz

Trusts: A Comparative Study
Maurizio Lupoi

The Right to Property in Commonwealth Constitutions
Tom Allen

International Organizations Before National Courts
August Reinisch

The Changing International Law of High Seas Fisheries
Francisco Orrego Vicuña

Trade and the Environment: A Comparative Study of EC and US Law
Damien Geradin

Unjust Enrichment: A Study of Private Law and Public Values
Hanoch Dagan

Religious Liberty and International Law in Europe
Malcolm D. Evans

Ethics and Authority in International Law
Alfred P. Rubin

Sovereignty Over Natural Resources: Balancing Rights and Duties
Nico Schrijver

The Polar Regions and the Development of International Law
Donald R. Rothwell

Fragmentation and the International Relations of Micro-States: Self-determination and Statehood
Jorri Duursma

Principles of the Institutional Law of International Organizations
C. F. Amerasinghe